General Guide Series

Government Archives Division

Compiled by

Cynthia Lovering

With an Introduction by

Terry Cook

National Archives
of Canada

Archives nationales
du Canada

Canadian Cataloguing in Publication Data
National Archives of Canada.

    Government Archives Division

    (General guide series)
    Text in English and French with French text on inverted pages.
    Title on added t.p. : Division des archives gouvernementales.
    2nd ed. --cf. Foreword.
    Previously publ. separately under titles: Federal Archives Division. Public Archives Canada, 1983 ; and, Machine Readable Archives Division. Public Archives Canada, 1984.
    DSS cat. no. SA41-4/1-1-1991
    ISBN 0-662-58186-5 : free

1. National Archives of Canada. Government Archives Division. 2. Public records--Canada. 3. Archives--Canada. I. Lovering, Cynthia. II. Public Archives Canada. Federal Archives Division. III. Public Archives Canada. Machine Readable Archives Division. IV. Title. V. Title: Division des archives gouvernementales. VI. Series: National Archives of Canada. General guide series.

CD3623.N37 1991   354.710071'46   C91-099203-7E

Cover: Parliament Buildings, c. 1880, showing the original Centre Block completed in 1878 and destroyed by fire in 1916. Photograph by Samuel McLaughlin, photographer for the Department of Public Works (detail). (C-3760)

This publication is printed on alkaline paper.

National Archives of Canada
395 Wellington Street
Ottawa, Ontario
K1A 0N3
(613) 995-5138

Table
of Contents ─────────

Foreword ————

Since 1872, the National Archives of Canada has been acquiring a vast collection of archival records. Recently, the quantity of documents has been doubling every decade, while the diversity of material has become more and more pronounced, especially with the introduction of new technologies and new media for recording information.

Almost 40 years ago, the National Archives of Canada began a comprehensive program of preparing inventories and finding aids in order to inform researchers and other interested people of the documentation available and to make access to it easier. In some cases, the National Archives has sought to involve other Canadian institutions in this endeavour so that union catalogues covering almost all significant archival records could be produced.

Although this program has succeeded in describing a substantial portion of the National Archives' documentary resources, and although microfiche and published guides to more important records and series are available, the general public, researchers, and even Canadian archivists have difficulty obtaining a relatively accurate and complete overview of the enormous quantity of documents held by the National Archives of Canada.

It thus seemed useful, in fact necessary, to publish a brief description of the resources and services available to users of the Archives as a first step to using its holdings. Issued collectively under the title *General Guide Series* in 1983, convenient volumes containing descriptions of both private and public records at the National Archives were prepared by each division of the Historical Resources Branch. This is the second edition of the *Series*. It combines and updates earlier separate volumes on the Federal Archives and Machine Readable Archives Divisions to reflect the 1986 reorganization at the National Archives, which effected the amalgamation of these two divisions, and the tremendous growth of archival government records in the eight intervening years.

I wish to thank Eldon Frost, Director of the Government Archives Division, and his staff, and the Communications Division of the Public Programs Branch for contributing to the preparation and publication of this new *Guide*.

> *Jean-Pierre Wallot*
> *National Archivist of Canada*

Preface ————————————

The Government Archives Division permanently preserves those textual and electronic records of the federal government which have long-term value. The holdings of the Division form the collective memory of the national government and are essential to its continued effective operation. The functions of the Division are to select, preserve, describe, and make available to the public these historically significant records, in accordance with the appropriate legislation.

Earlier versions of this *Guide* were published as part of *Historical Records of the Government of Canada* in 1978 and 1981, and as the *General Guide Series 1983 — Federal Archives Division* and for the *Machine Readable Archives Division*. This new *Guide* has been revised and updated. It will serve to familiarize researchers, government officials, and the general public with the nature of the Division's activities and to provide a brief description of the textual and electronic government records in its custody. The first two parts outline the Division's activities and organization, and the concepts which have been developed to arrange original documentary material, as well as the services and reference aids offered by the Division. The third part explains the nature of the entries in the main body of the text and how to use this *Guide* to prepare for research in the Division's holdings. The main text consists of entries for each record group. Each entry includes a description of the records and a short paragraph explaining the principal functions and administrative historical background of the department or agency. This information should enable the reader to understand better the nature of the records and the administrative relationships between the various agencies represented by record groups.

This publication would not have been possible without the efforts of present and previous staff members who have collected and described the archives of the federal government. Unlike previous ones, this edition's record group entries have been written by the archivists in the Division, many of whom also edited and provided comments on the text. Cynthia Lovering coordinated the publication. Terry Cook wrote all the introductory sections. The administrative histories often follow closely or build upon those prepared by Glenn T. Wright and Terry Cook for previous editions, and also reflect earlier work by Katharine Gavrel and Walter Meyer zu Erpen on machine-readable records.

Eldon Frost, Director,
Government Archives Division

1 Profile of the Government Archives Division ___

The Government Archives Division is responsible for the appraisal, selection, custody, preservation, and specialized reference of the unpublished historical records of the Government of Canada. Its mandate includes all textual (paper), micrographic, and electronic records created by the federal government judged to have archival or historical value. Special collections of government architectural, cartographic, pictorial, photographic, and moving image and sound records are not included. In meeting its principal responsibility, the Division ensures that all departmental files and electronic records are examined, identifies those records with actual or potential research value, and arranges for their transfer to the Historical Resources Branch on a regular and continuing basis. To do this, the Government Archives Division works closely with the staff of the Government Records Branch of the National Archives of Canada as well as with officers of the various departments and agencies of the federal government. Records that have enduring legal, financial, evidential, or proprietary value to the government itself are retained permanently by the Division. Records are also selected for permanent retention if they document significantly the creation and implementation of acts, policies, and programs of a department (including their development and their impact on the public), or the internal operations and organizational structure of a department (including sources of ideas and methods of decision implementation). Finally, records are kept if their informational value is judged significant for research purposes; this is especially true for electronic records. Using these criteria, the Division attempts to identify and preserve records essential to both government officials and private researchers and to our collective memory as a nation.

Once the records have been selected for permanent archival retention, the Division conducts research and prepares suitable inventories, finding aids, and electronic records documentation packages in order to provide in-person public service and specialized reference, and to answer telephone and written inquiries concerning the records in its custody. The National Archives also attempts to ensure the conservation of its often fragile Divisional holdings through protective microfilming and physical restoration, as well as by timely rewinding and copying of magnetic tapes.

In addition to government institutions subject to the *National Archives of Canada Act*, the Division acquires and makes available records of the federal judiciary, Parliament, Commissions of Inquiry, and other selected federal institutions. With the accelerating pace of government decentralization, the Division is also assessing the historical value of regional and field office records of the federal government all across the country.

Holdings

The holdings of the Government Archives Division comprise over 50 kilometres of textual records, 19,000 master negative microfilm reels, and more than 2,000 data files. They document all aspects of Canadian history from the eighteenth century to the present. Ranging from centuries-old priceless Indian treaties to yesterday's computer file documenting the condition of the environment, from records created in the central Cabinet room of the government to those in its remotest field offices, from the highest level policy document to the lowest level micro-data on individual Canadians, from documents crucial to protecting the rights of citizens against official wrong-doing to information essential to every field of academic and heritage research, the Division's acquisition activities have resulted in a rich collection which attracts thousands of researchers every year.

The Division's holdings include dockets, files, letterbooks, reports, surveys, databases, registers, indexes, and similar types of written, typewritten, and electronic documentation. Individual photographs, posters, maps, plans, and printed items, if on the original file, are also normally retained in the Division's custody. Separate and easily identifiable blocks of other forms of government records, however, are transferred to or collected directly by other divisions of the Historical Resources Branch responsible for such records: photographs, paintings, drawings, and posters by the Documentary Art and Photography Division; maps, plans, and engineering and architectural drawings by the Cartographic and Architectural Archives Division; and oral history, film, and radio and television broadcast items by the Moving Image and Sound Archives Division. The careers of government officials are documented in the private papers of prime ministers, cabinet ministers, and senior public servants in the Manuscript Division, which also acquires "ministerial records" as defined in the *National Archives of Canada Act*.

The records of a few pre-Confederation government agencies, such as those represented by the records in Record Group (RG) 1, 4, 5, and 8, and parts of RG 7 and 14, are also the custodial responsibility of the Manuscript Division.

Origins

When the Canadian government appointed an Archivist in 1872, he had no responsibility for the records of the federal government, which would normally have been the major function of a national archives. For a long time, the Archives Branch (as his unit within the Department of Agriculture soon became known) for many years confined its activities to private papers and records of the governments of France and Great Britain relating to Canada. Yet the preservation of federal government archival records was not entirely ignored. In 1873, a Keeper of Records was appointed in the Department of the Secretary of State to arrange the official and historical records of the Government of Canada. For many years this official devoted his time to indexing the records of Canada East and Canada West.

Growing concern over the lack of a uniform system of records keeping, coupled with losses of older records in several disastrous fires, prompted the federal government to form a Departmental Commission on Public Records. As a result of its investigations, the Commission recommended in 1898 that the activities of the Archives Branch of the Department of Agriculture, the Records Branch of the Department of the Secretary of State, and sundry other records offices, be centralized in one agency. This was done in 1903 when an Order-in-Council made the Archives Branch responsible for public records as well as private manuscripts. The national archives would collect not only the official and historical records of the national government, but also documents of private individuals and institutions having national historical significance, as well as select records of foreign governments relating to Canadian history. This concept was enshrined in the *Public Archives Act* of 1912 which established the Public Archives of Canada as an independent agency responsible for "public records, documents and other historical material of every kind, nature and description...."

Perhaps because of the emphasis on private records in the old Archives Branch before 1903, "public records" remained a low priority in the new institution for many years. A Royal Commission on Public Records, appointed in 1912, recommended two years later that no government record be destroyed without the approval of the Treasury Board, and that all historical government records must be transferred to the Public Archives of Canada. Despite this hopeful sign, however, restraints imposed by two world wars and the Depression postponed the realization of such an orderly, efficient system of records management until the 1950s. For example, bills brought before Parliament in 1927 and 1936 seeking to extend the role of the Archives in the field of government records, even to the point of the possible creation of a separate Public Records Office, failed to win approval.

With World War II came the rapid proliferation of government programs and an accompanying growth in the volume of paperwork. This set the stage for important changes in the management of public records. An interdepartmental Public Records Committee was established in 1945, a forerunner of the Advisory Council on Public Records set up in 1966. Both bodies offered advice on the storage, microfilming, general management, and orderly disposal of federal government records. The cornerstone of this process was records scheduling. This increasing emphasis on the proper management of public records helps to explain the government's negative response to the recommendation of the Royal Commission on National Development in the Arts, Letters, and Sciences (Massey Commission), part of whose work was the examination of the Canadian archival scene. Ignoring the Commission's recommendation that a separate Public Records Office be established to deal with the past neglect of public records, the federal government opted instead for the creation of the Public Archives Records Centre in 1956 (later the Records Management, and now the Government Records Branch) which was to be located within the Archives.

This Branch was to be a "half-way house" between the records management work of the Public Records Committee and government departments on the one hand, and the archival programs of the Public Archives on the other. Its key roles were to coordinate departmental records schedules identifying the period of administrative and operational value of each record, to store dormant records in records centres, to arrange for the orderly destruction of routine records having no historical value, and to transfer to the Historical Resources Branch those records having potential archival or historical significance. The increase in government paperwork — the equivalent of 50 box-cars of paper generated annually — soon led to the creation of Regional Records Centres at Toronto, Montreal, Vancouver, Halifax, Winnipeg, and Edmonton. In the 1950s, the government's Central Microfilm Unit was also transferred to the Public Archives of Canada, thus ensuring the close relationship between micrographic creation, records management, and archival preservation.

Despite these improvements, the relentless growth of paper records generated by the modern welfare state, especially as it was decentralized during the 1960s, raised serious concerns (as reflected, for example, by the Glassco Commission of 1962) over the general efficiency of government administration, and about its paper burden in particular. These developments led to the passing of the *Public Records Order* in 1966. This was a crucial step, for it effectively and formally linked the Archives' traditional mandate to acquire historical records with one for improved management (including now-mandatory scheduling and orderly disposal) of current records still controlled by and located in departments. This linkage continued to be enhanced and strengthened in the 1970s and 1980s by new policies, directives, and legislation in records management and in access and privacy.

These postwar changes in the broader world of government information management proved to be a significant turning point in the acquisition of archival textual government records — more such records were acquired during the 1960s, than in the previous nine decades combined of the Archives' existence. These external developments were also reflected in the organizational structure of the Public Archives. In 1965, the Public Records Section was established within the Manuscript Division, the first time in the then 93-year history of the Public Archives that a specific unit became exclusively responsible for the archival records of the federal government. This unit grew to become the separate Public Records Division in 1973, which in 1979 was renamed the Federal Archives Division.

While their history is obviously a shorter one, electronic records have suffered from the same neglect as textual records in earlier times, and it has also been costly. Electronic records are extremely fragile and transient, and, unlike most other media, they cannot survive even relatively short periods of uncontrolled environmental conditions or failure to convert older data to keep pace with technological change. As a result, a few leading archives around the world began to respond to the changing nature of information signalled by the widespread introduction of computers into government and business. The Public Archives was one of the first to do so. The Machine Readable Archives Division was established in 1973 to address this new situation. Early on, the Division acquired electronic records of national significance from government institutions as well as from the private sector, although the primary focus remained government records (a seven-to-one ratio). The inexperience of the paper-based records management community concerning electronic records, however, combined with the absence within departments of a distinct group with a concern for the retention and disposal of electronic data, lead to early difficulties. Departments made little progress towards the orderly scheduling and disposal of their electronic records. Thus, significant acquisitions of electronic records resulted mainly from direct contacts between archivists and departments.

By the 1980s, as central agencies and departments began to concentrate on information as content and resource rather than as medium, the National Archives similarly moved towards information integration for the two key media found in all government institutions. Accordingly, the two divisions most concerned with government records — the Federal Archives Division and the Machine Readable Archives Division — were merged in December 1986 to form the new Government Archives Division. Its acquisition mandate reflected those of its two predecessors, with the exception that private electronic data would now fall within the mandate of the Manuscript Division.

Finally, with the promulgation of the *National Archives of Canada Act* in June 1987, government institutions must receive the permission of the National Archivist before destroying records. In addition, the *Act* provides for the transfer of records having historical or archival value to the National Archives in accordance with agreements. The *Act* also significantly expands the number of institutions with which such formal arrangements are required. Thus, the *Act* strengthens the role of the National Archives considerably and expands the scope of the Division's responsibilities.

Organization

The Government Archives Division is divided into four large sections and one administrative unit. Two sections deal directly with archival records and two provide related services.

The *State, Military, and Transportation Records Section* is composed of three units responsible for the records of those government agencies concerned with matters of state; military and international affairs; and economics and transportation.

The *Social Affairs and Natural Resources Records Section*'s three units are responsible for the records of government agencies dealing with social and cultural affairs; science and natural resources; and native, northern, and land issues.

The *Custodial Services Section* is responsible for many related services including the retrieval and circulation of textual records for staff and researchers; development and operation of information systems; application of descriptive standards; certain technical and operational functions required for the acquisition, custodial care, and storage of records; and coordination of the Division's activities relating to exhibitions and publications.

The *Access Section* ensures that archival records held by the Division are released for research in accordance with the *Access to Information Act* and the *Privacy Act* both by responding to individual researchers' requests for records that are not yet open and available for research and by undertaking the systematic declassification of archival records.

The Record Group Concept

In arranging records, archivists in the Government Archives Division divide records into record groups, and within record groups into series and sub-series of records. Given the centrality of the record group to the Division's operations and indeed to the organization of this *Guide*, some understanding of the record group concept is necessary for users of the Division's holdings.

Archivists follow two principles when organizing records. First, the principle of provenance states that the records of a given records creator must not be intermingled with those of other records creators. Second, the principle of original order states that the original filing or classification system of records in their office of origin (which may not be the order in which they are first received at the Archives) must as far as possible be respected and/or recreated. To do otherwise, to arrange and organize records by research-oriented subject areas, geographical location, or chronological period, for example, would destroy the evidential value represented by the records themselves; it would, in effect, remove them from the context in which they were created and thus destroy a significant part of the information they contain. Accordingly, the holdings of the Government Archives Division are organized into separate record groups as the means of following these two principles.

The archival record group (RG) is generally a body of records of a government department, agency, or branch that exhibited administrative continuity over a period of time. The records are related functionally and organizationally through common information systems. As can be seen from the following pages, most record groups are confined to single government departments or major branches within them. Series within record groups generally follow the same principle, being the records of administrative sub-units of the parent department or agency which defines the record group as a whole. Within series and sub-series, the

7

original order of records and systems is maintained. For example, three files on the same subject (perhaps even with identical titles) which come from three separate filing systems in the creating department would not be brought together, but rather placed in three separate series in the record group to reflect the three original filing systems to which they once belonged.

The record group concept has also been applied in several other ways, depending on the complexity of the agency and the volume of records involved. Often, for example, more than one record group relates to a specific organizational structure. The Department of Indian and Northern Affairs (INA) from 1966 to 1979 had three major responsibilities: native people, national parks and historic sites, and the administration of the Yukon and Northwest Territories. Major, autonomous units of INA administered these three areas, and each maintained distinct file registry systems to do so. Indeed, they had been doing so long before INA came into existence, as these units shifted since the late nineteenth century through four or five of INA's predecessors. These three units are therefore organized in the Government Archives Division into three record groups: Indian Affairs (RG 10), Canadian Parks Service (RG 84), and Northern Affairs (RG 85). In addition, however, certain functions of INA as a whole (Deputy Minister's Office, Legal Division, Information Services, Engineering and Construction Service, etc.) are related to all three programs. These common, department-wide concerns are organized into a fourth record group: Indian and Northern Affairs (RG 22). Similar situations exist for the Departments of Energy, Mines and Resources (RG 21), Environment (RG 108), Citizenship and Immigration (RG 26), and Employment and Immigration (RG 118).

Other record groups bring together for convenience small bodies of records of a similar nature that have no administrative relationship or continuity. Examples are the records of the 147 separate Royal Commissions in RG 33 and the 37 Boards, Offices, and Commissions in RG 36. Only Boards and Commissions of short duration or relatively minor importance are grouped in RG 36; more important and lasting bodies have been assigned separate record group status, for example, the Canadian Grain Commission (RG 80), National Battlefields Commission (RG 90), National Harbours Board (RG 66), and National Energy Board (RG 99).

The evolution of government organization has revealed two trends. On the one hand, as a department expanded with new branches and divisions, its records acquired a growing complexity. That is often reflected, when these records arrive in the Government Archives Division, by the creation of numerous record groups. The records of the

8

Department of the Interior (RG 15) are the best example. Although the records of the core Dominion Lands Branch remain in RG 15, the records documenting Interior's other functions are widely scattered: Indian Affairs (RG 10), Forestry (RG 39), Geological Survey of Canada (RG 45), Dominion Observatories (RG 48), Immigration (RG 76), Canadian Parks Service (RG 84), Northern Affairs (RG 85), Mines (RG 86), Surveys and Mapping (RG 88), and Water Resources (RG 89), to name only the most prominent. On the other hand, separate, independent government agencies are sometimes reorganized or merged together. In these cases, the records will be grouped into a single record group when they arrive at the Archives. The records of the Board of Transport Commissioners, Marine Transport Commission, and Air Transport Board are all series of RG 46, the Canadian Transport Commission, the body which combined and replaced the other three.

Electronic records also present new challenges to the application of traditional archival principles in the organization of record groups. For example, complex databases may serve two or more branches of a large department, or indeed be interdepartmental. The division of the resulting single data file, to which both branches may have had equal proprietary claim in creating and using, into two or more record groups must be addressed.

In short, the record group concept is in constant evolution because government organizations and their methods of creating records are also constantly changing. When using this publication, therefore, researchers should bear in mind that sources on their particular topic may well be located in numerous record groups, and in numerous series or data files within them. Any one issue has usually been examined or controlled or monitored by more than one agency or department, or parts of a department. An understanding of these historical administrative interconnections, changes, and organizational structures is necessary to utilize most profitably such government records for research purposes. Researchers should, therefore, constantly check for cross-references and organic links among the various record groups.

2 Services of the Government Archives Division ___

In addition to this *Guide*, there are three other levels of reference aids produced by the Government Archives Division to help researchers use its holdings:

Inventories

The inventory for each record group contains, for each series, a short administrative history of the sub-unit or individual involved and a brief general description of the type and nature of the textual and electronic records in the series, as well as the dates and extent of the records. Inventories also contain a more extensive administrative history of the agency as a whole, information on available finding aids, and a general note on access restrictions. Inventories also include brief descriptions of all unprocessed accessions, including those retained in the Division's holdings in Vancouver, Edmonton, Winnipeg, and Halifax. Several inventories have been published (RG 2, 10, 11, 18, 20, 27, 31, 33, 39, 43, 46, 55, 64, 65, 69, 81, 84, 85, 88, 115, and 126) and may be obtained free of charge from the Communications Division of the National Archives. This *Guide* attempts to summarize the most pertinent information in each of the Division's inventories.

Finding Aids

The Division controls through indexes or lists its textual records down to the single file as the basic unit. Finding aids take such forms as contemporary registers of correspondence and indexes to these registers, shelf lists, file lists, card indexes, and (for larger, more heavily used record groups) computer-generated subject indexes. For electronic records, a documentation package is prepared for each processed data file. Each package usually contains record layouts, data element descriptions, system descriptions and data flow charts, and related publications, printouts, etc. There is also an automated descriptive database which can be searched by title, principal investigator, and subject.

Thematic Guides

The Division also prepares special thematic guides which draw together references on a given topic from all (or many of) the record groups. These are aimed at areas of high research demand. While most of these are typescripts available for consultation at the National Archives, some have been published and are available free of charge: *Sources for the Study of Canada's National Parks*; *Sources for the Study of the Second World War*; *Sources for the Study of the Canadian North*; *Health Promotion Data Files*; *Alcohol, Drug and Tobacco Use Data Files*; and *Recreation and Leisure Data Files*. In addition, the Division's holdings are frequently profiled in articles written by archivists and published in the *Machine Readable Records Bulletin* and *The Archivist*.

Research Facilities

It is advisable for researchers to contact the National Archives before visiting the institution. There are several reasons for doing this. In the first instance, archivists can give a general indication of whether sufficient records on the subject exist to justify a trip. In certain cases, some or all of the desired records are on microfilm. Microfilm reels may be borrowed on behalf of the researcher by a local library or any institution which possesses a microfilm reader and participates in the interlibrary loan arrangement. Secondly, records that are not yet open and available for research because of restrictions imposed by the *Access to Information Act* or the *Privacy Act* will require review by the Access Section. Some lead time is needed to complete this review. Thirdly, direct access to electronic records is not permitted. Contact with the Archives will allow appropriate data files to be identified and copied where feasible.

Researchers contacting the National Archives for the first time, whether in person, by mail, or by telephone, should initially direct their inquiries to the Reference and Researcher Services Division, Public Programs Branch (c/o National Archives of Canada, Ottawa, Ontario, K1A 0N3, telephone 1-613-995-8094). That Division orients researchers, registers them, and issues research passes, introduces them to all inventories and finding aids in its reference area for all relevant divisions, and conducts research to answer general and all genealogical inquiries. It also ensures that researchers are referred to the appropriate archivist(s) of the relevant division(s) for specialized and more detailed inquiries. For researchers who are referred to the Government Archives Division for specialized consultation, archivists and access staff are available in the Division between 8:30 and 16:45. Researchers may consult the reference tools described above during these same hours, Monday to Friday, in the Division itself or in the Reference and Researcher Services Division.

Textual and microfilmed archival records which researchers thereby identify as being of interest may be ordered between 8:30 and 16:15 at the Circulation Desk in the Main Research Room. To consult holdings which are located in regional records centres, it is necessary to first contact the Government Archives Division in Ottawa in order to obtain correct references and a guide to possible services.

Because most records are stored off-site, it is advisable for researchers to consult the records location guide at the Circulation Desk when completing their requests in order to anticipate possible delays. The Main Research Room is open twenty-four hours a day, seven days a week, including statutory holidays. The Circulation Desk staff issues lockers in the adjacent Locker Room to hold archival records which researchers wish to consult outside of the normal office hours. Such material must be ordered and placed in the lockers during regular office hours. Besides the Circulation Desk personnel, there is a full-time staff member in the Microfilm Research Room to assist researchers in locating and using microfilm. Researchers must obtain a valid research pass issued by the National Archives to gain access to these facilities. Secure lockers on the ground floor are provided for personal belongings and coats which are not permitted in the Research Rooms.

To be fair to other researchers and to ensure that records are protected from harm or loss, no original documents may be borrowed for use outside the Archives building. However, the Division is committed to extensive microfilming of its holdings in order to preserve fragile original records while making information available to a wider audience. A significant number of its most frequently used series of records have been filmed. The existence of microfilm in a record group is indicated in a general way in this *Guide*; it is also identified specifically by series in the inventory of each record group. Further information on microfilm holdings is available through the Reference and Researcher Services Division, at the address given on the previous page.

In addition, the Division offers a limited copying service. Cash orders for small quantities of photocopies and reader-printer copies are filled on a daily basis in the Research Rooms described above, while larger requests are completed, invoiced, and subsequently mailed to researchers at a later date. Microfilm duplicates and photographic copies may also be ordered. It should be noted that copying limits are enforced and that the completion time for requests for copies may vary with demand levels.

The Division at present does not allow researchers direct access to its holdings of electronic records. It will, however, provide a copy of the data file to researchers on magnetic tape, or diskette for which the cost is billed to the researcher, as well as copies of the documentation packages described above, which are needed to interpret the data. Data extracts, including anonymization to mask personal information that would otherwise restrict the release of a data file, and the creation of data sub-sets from larger data files are other services offered by the Division.

Specific inquiries about the Division's holdings, its services, and its activities should be addressed to the Government Archives Division, National Archives of Canada, Ottawa, Ontario, Canada, K1A 0N3 (telephone 1-613-996-8507).

Access to Federal Government Records

Access to the records of most government institutions, including those at the National Archives of Canada, is governed by the *Access to Information Act* and the *Privacy Act*. The National Archives responds to requests under the *Acts* for records which have been transferred to the control of the National Archives for archival or historical purposes. Briefly, the *Access to Information Act* created a public right of access to government information except where specific exemptions prevent public disclosure, while the *Privacy Act* extends the individual's right of access to and ensures appropriate protection of personal information concerning himself or herself found in government records.

Records that have not already been reviewed and opened for research must be examined prior to their release to the public to ensure that information contained therein does not fall into one of the exempt categories of the *Access to Information Act* or infringe on an individual's rights to personal privacy guaranteed in the *Privacy Act*.

The Division has developed an informal access request process, complementary to the formal procedures for requesting government records under the *Acts*. It is recommended that researchers use this informal route in requesting access to its archival holdings. Such informal requests, in which records are reviewed consistent with the provisions of the *Acts*, account for some 90 per cent of the review work undertaken by the Access Section at the National Archives. Researchers can initiate this informal process by completing the normal request slip at the Circulation Desk. If the requested records have not yet been opened for research, staff of the Circulation Desk will so inform the researcher. An Access Control List is available for consultation in the reference areas. This list indicates the access status of government records under the control of the National Archives, at the container level.

As noted earlier, the length of time required to undertake an access review varies according to the size of the request and the backlog of other requests. Researchers should therefore submit requests well in advance of any deadlines they may have, and, if possible, before their visit to Ottawa. It is recommended that researchers contact the Access Section at the address cited on page 14 for further information.

A few agencies of the federal government are not subject to the *Access to Information Act* and the *Privacy Act*. In such cases, agreements exist between the creating agency and the National Archives of Canada which govern access to the archival holdings of such agencies. Reference staff will be pleased to explain to researchers the terms of such agreements.

3 Holdings of the Government Archives Division ___

The text of this *Guide* consists of descriptions of each record group arranged in numerical order, followed by a subject index and then an alphabetical index of record group titles. The entries are current to 30 June 1989.

In developing the new format for this edition of the *Guide*, the Division has attempted to anticipate the movement in the Canadian archival community towards fonds-level descriptive standards. It is hoped that these entries will be forerunners of full fonds-level descriptions for each record group that will be established in the future.

Each record group entry in the main text has four elements.

1. The **title statement** contains the name of the department or agency whose records are being described, the record group number, and the outside or inclusive dates of the records involved.

2. The **extent** lists, if there are relevant holdings, the metres of textual records and the number of data files and of microfilm reels and fiche. The absence of any entry for one or more of these media means that the record group does not yet contain that type of archival record.

3. The **administrative history** note gives the context in which the records were created. Included is a brief outline of the principal functions and administrative background of the department, branch, or agency. As far as space permitted, particular care has been taken to demonstrate the crucial links, for research purposes, between various units and their predecessor, successor, and parent organizations (often with RG cross-reference numbers being given). Where records of a similar nature but with no administrative relationship have been brought together in one RG, the administrative history provides general information about the type of creating organization (Commissions, Boards).

4. The **arrangement and content** note is not a listing of all the series titles and data files of the record group, as in the previous edition of the *Guide*, but a more global description of the central subjects and themes covered by the records. The intention is to provide the general flavour, rather than a less informative listing, of the archival holdings of the agency involved. Where formal series headings are given in the text, they appear in **bold print**. The words **electronic records** or **electronic form** have also been bolded to bring attention to their description. Researchers are cautioned that, with very few exceptions, unprocessed electronic records are not included in these descriptions, and unprocessed textual records are included only where archivists have been able to ascertain their contents. Also omitted, again with rare exceptions, are records held by the Division in Vancouver, Edmonton, Winnipeg, and Halifax.

For the actual record group entries, several explanatory notes might be helpful. Inclusive dates refer in all cases to the actual records, not the administrative unit. For example, the Mining Lands and Yukon Branch of RG 85 existed from 1909 to 1922, but its records date from 1898 to 1950. The Branch, therefore, incorporated some files of predecessor agencies while some of its own files were in turn continued by successor agencies.

The term "Central Registry Files" is used in many of the **arrangement and content** notes in the record group entries and therefore requires some explanation. A Central Registry Office in a government agency maintains the file system for the whole department — although in larger departments there may be several branch- and program-level central registries in addition to a department-wide one. Thus, the files from a central registry office generally constitute the most comprehensive series of a record group, for they document most, if not all, departmental functions and responsibilities: in effect, they offer one of the most important sources of information in any record group. In order to comprehend the scope of Central Registry Files, researchers need a knowledge of the creating agency's history, legislative mandates, and major responsibilities, as these indicate the nature of the subjects that will be reflected in such files. While the **administrative history** note in each record group entry supplies the highlights of such information, more detail may be found in the fuller administrative histories in each record group inventory (see Inventories on page 11), as well as in the *Canada Year Book 1976-77: Special Edition* (Ottawa, 1977), *Organization of the Government of Canada 1978-79* (Ottawa, 1979), and departmental annual reports, as well as in the records themselves.

The subject index of record group titles which follows the main text is naturally only a rough categorization in order to aid researchers. The various groupings used are by no means mutually exclusive. It does indicate, however, the interrelationship of the various agencies represented by record groups and the need for researchers to understand the administrative (and therefore archival) links between such agencies, as described above. For researchers already able to focus their investigations on particular departments, the alphabetical index which follows will provide them with the relevant record group number(s).

Record Group Entries in Numerical Order

Records of the Executive Council: RG 1
1764-1867

This record group is the custodial responsibility of the Manuscript Division, National Archives of Canada.

Records of the Privy Council Office: RG 2
1867-1986

682.8 metres
417 microfilm reels

Administrative history: The Privy Council Office (PCO) under the direction of the Clerk of the Privy Council was created to provide a secretariat to support the administrative activities of the Privy Council and to assist the President in council business. In 1940, the operation of the Office was modernized by instituting more business-like procedures such as pre-established agendas for Cabinet meetings, records of Cabinet decisions taken, notification of departments concerning required action and the creation of a central filing system. In 1968, further changes to the structure of PCO were introduced. These included an Operations Division to provide expanded secretarial services to the Cabinet and Cabinet committees, a Plans Division to provide services to the Planning committees and a Federal-Provincial Relations Division to provide liaison services between government departments and the provinces.

Arrangement and content: The records are arranged in four principle series: the records of the **Office of the Clerk of the Privy Council and Secretary to the Cabinet** (1867-1986), the **Administrative Records** (1867-1955), the records of **Special Administrative and Investigative Bodies** (1912-1984), and **Other Records** (1867-1943). Several important sub-series are located within the general series and include Orders-in-Council, annexes, records, and dormants (1867-1986); despatches (1867-1911); Cabinet records (1867-1958); oaths of office (1946-1966); reference files (1867-1907), including files on the Fishery Question, the Alaska Boundary, and the Abdication Crisis; the main **Central Registry Files** (1940-1958), including such subjects as Northwest Defence Projects, post-war reconstruction, social policies, and Cabinet business; records of the Board of Railway Commissioners (1912-1936); the Censorship Branch (1939-1963); the Office of the Special Commissioner for Constitutional Development in the Northwest Territories (1977-1984); various task forces (1966-1984) and commissions (1974-1985).

Records of the Post Office: RG 3
1799-1987

141.53 metres
512 microfilm reels

Administrative history: The Post Office was created as a federal department in 1867. Although postal operations in Canada date from 1755, postal services were under the control of British authorities until 1851. In 1981, the Post Office ceased to be a government department and became a Crown corporation. The mandate of the Post Office is to establish, operate, and maintain a full range of postal services in Canada. To achieve this objective, the corporation's functional activities are divided into corporate affairs, operational services, marketing, finance, personnel and administration, as well as systems and engineering.

Arrangement and content: The records are divided into several series consisting of administrative and operational files covering all aspects of the activities of the Post Office such as the establishment and closing of offices, air mail, censorship, rural mail delivery, Eastern Arctic patrol, equipment, international communications, contracts, railway mail, ocean mail, personnel, and various enquiries. Included are records from the **Office of the Postmaster General** (1862-1917) and the **Office of the Deputy Postmaster General** (1851-1920); **Registry Files** (1851-1976); **Postal Inspectors** (1838-1961); **Mail Services/Transportation Branch** (1799-1970); **Administrative Services** (1830-1960); **Financial Services** (1841-1952); **Regional and Local Records** (1807-1953), and **Commissions, Committees and Study Teams of Enquiry** (1980-1985).

Records of the Provincial and Civil Secretaries' Offices; Quebec, Lower Canada, and Canada East: RG 4
1760-1867

This record group is the custodial responsibility of the Manuscript Division, National Archives of Canada.

Records of the Provincial and Civil Secretaries' Offices; Upper Canada and Canada West: RG 5
1791-1867

This record group is the custodial responsibility of the Manuscript Division, National Archives of Canada.

Records of the Department of the Secretary of State: RG 6
1848-1978

135.7 metres
117 microfilm reels

Administrative history: When this Department was established at Confederation its functions included the responsibility for communications between the people and their government and between the government of Canada and that of Great Britain. The Department was also responsible for the management of Indian and Crown Lands, and the duties of the Registrar General. At various times it has been responsible for the RCMP, the Public Service Commission, State Protocol, Patents, Copyrights, Trade Marks and Industrial Designs, Elections, Government Printing and Stationery, the Custodian of Enemy Property, and Arts and Culture. The Secretary of State remains responsible for citizenship and naturalization, multiculturalism, education support, translation services to other government departments and agencies, and the application of the *Official Languages Act.*

Arrangement and content: This record group includes a **General Correspondence** series (1867-1952) containing the Arms of Canada and covering a cross section of records concerning most of the functions of government. Records of the **Clerk of the Crown in Chancery** (1866-1917) include general correspondence and writs of election. Records of the **Secretary of State for the Provinces** (1867-1873) consist of correspondence regarding practical and constitutional matters following Confederation, the creation of the province of Manitoba, and the Riel Rebellion. Records of **State Protocol and Special Events** (1868-1973) pertain to medals, official installations, royal visits and the National Flag Committee, and records of the **Chief Press Censor** (1915-

1920), to World War I. There are several other series of records: **Citizenship** records concerning both the Registration Branch and Multicultural Directorate, **Interdepartmental Coordination Records** (1857-1972); **Wartime Records** (1914-1951), related to First World War Custodian of Enemy Property, Internment Operations, War Charities, and a few World War II subject files and records of the **Cultural Affairs Branch** (1950-1978), including both registry and subject files.

Records of the Office of the Governor General: RG 7
1774-1984

278.77 metres
316 microfilm reels

Administrative history: The Office of Governor General is the product of a long evolution. Both the English and French Regimes in North America had a representative of their respective sovereigns at the seat of the colonial governments. The *British North America Act* of 1867 created the position of Governor General for the Dominion of Canada, and described some of the powers of the Office. At that time the Governor General was the head of state, but he governed on the advice of the King's Privy Councillors of Canada. The Governor General remains the head of state, but some of the powers that were vested in the Office at Confederation have been altered by subsequent events and legislation. The Imperial Conference of 1926 cut the remaining links between the Office of Governor General and the Imperial Government, leaving the Governor General as the representative of the Crown. The Letters Patent of 1947 delegated to the Office certain responsibilities that had previously vested with the Crown. The Office holder is appointed by the Queen on the advice of the Privy Councillors of Canada.

Arrangement and content: Custody of this record group is shared with the Manuscript Division, which holds pre-Confederation material. The post-Confederation records under the control of the Government Archives Division are divided into 19 series according to the type of record. Six of these series are composed of despatches to and from the Colonial Office in London (1856-1913) and the British Minister in Washington (1804-1914). There is also one series of letterbooks of despatches to the Colonial Office (1867-1902). There are two series of registry files (1818-1941 and 1859-1966) and four other series dealing with a range of correspondence covering such subjects as external affairs, militia and defence, and appointments. The records of the **Military Secretary** (1813-1907) and the **Civil Secretary** (1867-1909), two of the officials attached to the Office of the Governor General, are also the subjects of series in this group. There are four other series covering such subjects as administration, honours, royal tours, and Rideau Hall.

British Military and Naval Records: RG 8
1757-1903

This record group is the custodial responsibility of the Manuscript Division, National Archives of Canada.

Records of the Department of Militia and Defence: RG 9
1776-1960

1,515.9 metres
337 microfilm reels

Administrative history: Legislation governing militia affairs dates back to 1777 when the *Militia Act* for Lower Canada was passed and to 1793 when the first *Militia Act* for Upper Canada was enacted. Although the militia had been organized in the Canadas by the late eighteenth century, a full-fledged department was not established until 1868. In 1916, an Overseas Ministry was created "to relieve the Department of Militia and Defence of the administration of the forces overseas and to establish a ministry in London, immediately in touch with His Majesty's Government and conveniently situated with relation to the theatre of effective operations." In 1922, Militia and Defence amalgamated with the Department of the Naval Service and the Air Board to form the Department of National Defence (RG 24).

Arrangement and content: The records in this group are arranged in three general series. The **Pre-Confederation** (1776-1869) series contains records from the offices of the Adjutants General of Upper and Lower Canada and includes correspondence (1777-1869), returns (1793-1869), orders (1805-1868), paylists (1812-1868), and registers of officers (1808-1869). The **Post-Confederation** (1847-1960) records are organized in the following manner. From 1867 until 1 July 1903, the headquarters correspondence of the Department of Militia and Defence was registered in the appropriate branch of the Department. Consequently, there were often several files in the Department dealing with the same subject. A central registry system was put into operation on 1 July 1903 and was continued as the headquarters central registry system for the Department of National Defence until 1946. Thus headquarters files created since 1903 and subsequently transferred to the National Archives will be found in Record Group 24. The Post-Confederation series con-

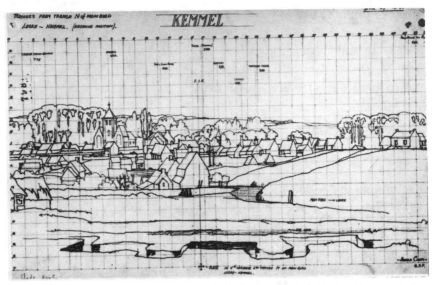

Sketch of the town of Kemmel, Belgium showing artillery ranges from the trench line north of the main Locre-Kemmel Road. (RG 9, III, C-3, Volume 4119, File 15) (C-96604)

tain records from the Deputy Minister's Office (1847-1960), Adjutant General's Office (1867-1922), Military Intelligence (1895-1913), Contracts Branch (1896-1912), Engineer Branch (1880-1903), Accounts and Pay Branch (1855-1915), Stores Branch (1864-1903), Quartermaster General (1893-1898), Chief Inspector of Arms and Ammunition (1906-1922), Royal Canadian Artillery (1871-1922), and Schools of Military Instruction (1864-1932). Medal registers are included in the records of the Deputy Minister's Office (1847-1960). They give limited information on medal recipients for the Fenian Raids of 1866, the Red River Expedition, the North West Rebellion and the South African War. In the final series, the records of the **Overseas Military Forces of Canada and the Canadian Expeditionary Force (CEF)** (1914-1922) include records of the Overseas Minister (1914-1919), Canadian Sections at General Headquarters (1915-1919), CEF Siberia Files (1918-1919), Administrative Offices Records (1914-1920), Canadian Corps and Unit Files (1914-1922), as well as files of the Canadian War Records Office (CWRO) (1914-1920). War diaries are included in the CWRO records.

Records Relating to Indian Affairs: RG 10
1677-1987

2,155.13 metres
257 microfilm reels
898 microfiches
46 data files

Administrative history: Throughout the eighteenth century and the first half of the nineteenth century, it was the British Imperial Government that, mainly through the actions of its military commanders, governors general, and lieutenant governors, regulated relations between European colonists and the original peoples of North America. In the Maritimes, the colonial legislatures of Nova Scotia, New Brunswick and Prince Edward Island dealt with Indian matters by appointing commissioners and passing legislation as specific needs arose. In the united Canadas, the Department of Crown Lands assumed responsibility for Indian administration in Canada East and Canada West in 1860. On the Prairies and in British Columbia, the operations of the Hudson's Bay Company constituted Britain's initial dealings with the Indian nations. At Confederation, the federal Department of Secretary of State (RG 6) undertook the management of the Canadian government's role with respect to Indians in Canada, then shifting to the Department of the Interior (RG 15) in 1873. In 1880, a separate Department of Indian Affairs was created, which gave full departmental status to Indian Affairs. This arrangement lasted for 56 years, after which Indian Affairs reverted to branch status within the following departments: Mines and Resources (see RG 21 and 22) from 1936 to 1949, Citizenship and Immigration (RG 26) from 1949 to 1965, Northern Affairs and National Resources (RG 22) from 1965 to 1966, and Indian Affairs and Northern Development (RG 22) from 1966 to the present. Inuit programs were handled by the Northern Affairs Program and its predecessors (RG 85) until 1971. At that time, the Indian and Eskimo (later Inuit) Affairs Program (RG 10) came into existence. It remains responsible for native self-government and a wide variety of aboriginal claims, for the registration of Indian lands and membership, and for funding of education, economic development, and social assistance. Finally, under the current Indian Affairs' policy of devolution, a greater degree of responsibility for the administration of many important services is being transferred to individual Indian bands.

Arrangement and content: The **Administrative Records of the Imperial Government** (1677-1864) contains pre-Confederation records dating mostly from about 1750 to 1864. This series consists largely of records created or collected by the British Indian Department in its

Northern Department (responsible for the colonies in northeastern North America), in Upper and Lower Canada (1791-1840), and in the Province of Canada (1841-1867). As records of the military, governors, and Indian Affairs superintendents, this series covers many aspects of Britain's early relations with North American Indians. While these files usually pertain to general concerns within the area of present day southern Ontario and southern Quebec, there are also some specific local records that were created by Indian Affairs' field officers working in British Columbia. Included are many records on land and financial matters, some census records, and some minutes of Indian councils. The **Ministerial Administration Records** (1680-1980) consists of mainly post-Confederation headquarters files. Having been created or held in Ottawa, these records reflect the federal government's management of and fiduciary responsibility for Indian lands and monies throughout Canada as well as its administration of various programs, most of which were for status Indians. A wide variety of subjects is covered in the Central Registry System sub-series; moreover, there are other sub-series for records on specific topics such as schools, financial matters, and certain commissions. Other types of records in this series are individual case files, census returns, and the early records of Deputy Superintendents General of Indian Affairs (Deputy Ministers). There is also a small amount of material on matters relating to the Inuit, the Métis, and non-status Indians. The **Field Office Records** (1809-1987) are records created or held by Indian Affairs personnel working outside headquarters at various agencies and in regional offices, inspectorates, and superintendencies across Canada. The records generally pertain to the affairs of specific Indian bands, agencies, or localities. RG 10 has some records from almost every agency; however, a few of the agency records are held by other repositories. Land records are scattered throughout this record group; however, those that deal exclusively with land transactions and management have been brought together in the series **Indian Land Records** (1680-1978). They include surrender, sale, and lease records for all regions. **Electronic records** in this record group come from various programs undertaken by the Department and include data on Indian membership, off-reserve housing, and education.

Records of the Department of Public Works: RG 11
1827-1980

1,443.52 metres
533 microfilm reels
2 data files

Administrative history: The Board of Works was established in 1839 for Lower Canada and its jurisdiction extended to the United Provinces of Canada in 1841. After a substantial reorganization in 1846 it was replaced by the Department of Public Works in 1859. This body was responsible for canals, works in navigable waters, harbours, lighthouses, beacons and buoys, slides and booms, roads, bridges, and public buildings. In 1867, its functions were assumed by the federal Department of Public Works which also became responsible for similar public works in New Brunswick and Nova Scotia. Control of most roads and bridges and certain public buildings were relinquished to the provinces at Confederation while the operation and administration of marine works, though not their construction, was transferred to the Marine Branch of the new Department of Marine and Fisheries in 1868 (RG 42). The management of all railways and canals and their related works was assumed by the Department of Railways and Canals (RG 43) in 1879. The Government Telegraph and Telephone Service, a Public Works operation since 1876, went to the Department of Transport (RG 12) in 1968. Currently, Public Works responsibilities include the management of real property; the construction and maintenance of public buildings, wharves, piers, roads, and bridges; improvement to harbours and navigable waters; and the acquisition of land and accommodation for government use.

Arrangement and content: The records of the Department of Public Works, including those of the **Board of Works** (1827-1866), consist of six Central Registry systems covering the years 1839-1980 including correspondence, subject files, and the registers and indexes created to locate information within the systems. These systems were in use during the years 1839-1979 respectively. Also included are records from the registry systems used by the Railway Branch (1867-1879), and the Government Telegraph Service (1910-1948); they contain various committees and commissions, reports, and estimates. Other series of records include the **Arbitrator's Office** (1821-1887), containing minute books, correspondence claims, and cases; the **Chief Engineer's Office** (1867-1946), including correspondence, records of the proposed Georgian Bay Ship Canal, and Pacific Region records; and records from the **Chief Architect's Office** (1873-1920), consisting of correspondence, specifications, and drawings. Records in **electronic form** consist of the Central Property Inventory for 1976 and 1977.

Records of the Department of Transport: RG 12
1825-1984

1,496.3 metres
1,287 microfilm reels
28,500 microfiche
27,555 micro-jackets
42 data files

Administrative history: The Department of Transport was established in November 1936 with the amalgamation of the former Departments of Marine (RG 42) and Railways and Canals (RG 43), and the Civil Aviation Branch of the Department of National Defence (RG 24). The Department's fundamental role is to attend to the development and operation of a safe and efficient national transportation system through capital assistance and administrative programs in air, marine, and surface transportation, the development of policy, and the regulation of the statutory requirements of federal legislation related to transportation. Over the years, the Department has also been responsible for several other interrelated administrative areas, including travel and tourism (RG 20, 25, and 124), telephone and telegraphy, radiophone and radio, television, private and commercial broadcasting, telecommunications (RG 41, 97, and 100), and meteorology (RG 93). The Department is a corporate structure that includes Crown corporations with varying degrees of autonomy and agencies and boards which report to Parliament through the Minister of Transport: Air Canada (RG 70), Canadian National Railways (RG 30), the Canada Ports Corporation (formerly the National Harbours Board, RG 66), the St. Lawrence Seaway Authority (RG 52), the Canadian Aviation Safety Board (records in RG 12), the National Transportation Agency (formerly the CTC, RG 46), the Pacific Pilotage Authority (RG 136), and VIA Rail, amongst others.

Arrangement and content: Approximately 90 per cent of the documents in this record group consist of subject files located in the **Registry Records** (1841-1984). The Registry may be divided into three main generic fields: Air, Marine, and Surface. Subject files classified under "Air" include aircraft registration and operation, aircraft types and specifications, airport establishment and operation, air traffic operations, aviation medicine, air traffic control, pilots, air engineers, and air traffic control officers. Under "Marine" are records covering agencies and depots, harbours and ports, lifesaving, aids to navigation, navigable waters protection, pilotage, seamen, Canadian government ships, measuring and surveying, ships' registration, steamship inspection, wrecks, casualties, and salvage. Under the classification "Surface," are motor vehicle safety, road safety countermeasures development, vehicle

Certificate of Airworthiness issued by the former Civil Aviation Branch of the Department of National Defence. (RG 12, Volume 58, File CF-AEF) (C-76361)

safety regulations, railway subsidies, railway lands, railway buildings, railway charters, railway track construction, highways, motor carriers, and ferries. There are additional subject file blocks arranged for purely administrative, executive, and classified (restricted) records. The remaining 10 per cent of the holdings in this record group were created and maintained by various administrative bodies within the Department, but were not incorporated into the registry systems. These records have been arranged into five series. The **Canadian Marine Transportation Administration** records (1825-1975) including registers of Canadian ships (1904-1965), wreck reports (1936-1974), registers of marine certificates (1872-1971), marine casualty investigation records (1936-1960), wreck registers (1870-1975), Canal Division records (1825-1976), records of the Central Registry of Seamen (1900-1983) and records of the Marine Historian's Office (c.1885-1975). The **Canadian Air Transportation Administration** records (1939-1980) includes airport registers (1939-1941), International Civil Aviation records (1945-1977) and records of the Commission of Inquiry on Aviation Safety (1979-1980). The **Canadian Surface Transportation Administration** records (1866-1951), cover the Railway Index (1866-1936) and letterbooks of the Superintending Engineer of the Ontario-St. Lawrence Canals Office. **Executive Records** (1936-1972), include the contracts, deeds and leases entered into by the Department in all aspects of its work. Records of the **Office of the Minister** (1975-1979), include the office files of the Honourable Otto Lang. Records held in **electronic form** include data files related to take-offs and landings of aircraft at airports in Canada (1971-1975), national roadside surveys of blood alcohol concentration of nighttime Canadian drivers (1974), and the Canada travel surveys (1978-1981), undertaken to promote greater understanding of passenger travel characteristics and associated modal transportation choices as well as to study traveller and tourist behaviour.

Records of the Department of Justice: RG 13
1597-1976

443.6 metres
365 microfilm reels
28 data files

Administrative history: The creation of the Justice Department was sanctioned on 22 May 1868, during the first session of the Parliament of the Dominion of Canada. The Department is now governed by the *Department of Justice Act*. The responsibilities of the Department have remained basically unchanged since the adoption of the *Act* in 1868. The Department serves as the official legal adviser to the government and the Queen's Privy Council for Canada. It is responsible for supervising all matters related to the administration of justice in Canada (excluding the jurisdiction of provincial governments), drafting legislation, contracts, and other legal documents, and advising on legislation and proceedings in the provincial legislatures. The Minister of Justice is automatically the Attorney General and, as such, advises federal government departments and is responsible for all litigation for or against the Crown or any government department. The Department's legal functions are carried out by headquarters in Ottawa and nine regional offices.

Arrangement and content: This record group, which closely reflects the various activities of the Department, consists of **Central Registry Files** (1859-1934), including a series of alphabetical indexes and numerical registers used to identify correspondence received or sent by the Department. This series also contains files on appointments and salaries of judges (1848-1958), extradition procedures (1848-1951), correspondence on seigneurial cases, requests for amendments to the Criminal Code, and Canada-U.S. relations, among others. A second series, the **Legal Services Files**, consists of capital case files (1867-1976), and files dealing with restriction and retention orders (1939-1941), the arbitration of unsettled accounts between the Dominion, Quebec, and Ontario (1867-1901), civil litigation involving the government (1863-1934), and files on the legislative section responsible for drafting territorial bills (1948-1949). In addition to the remission registers and individual files contained in the **Remissions Branch** series (1888-1962), the record group also includes the **Penitentiary Branch** series (1834-1962), which contains records on the reform of the criminal justice system. One of the series in the **Subject Files** consists of information on matters under the jurisdiction of the Attorney General, Canada West (1832-1866). It also contains files pertaining to historical controversies such as the Labrador Border Controversy (1926), the Hague Tribunal Arbitration for North Atlantic Fisheries (1910), the American Annexationists (1893-1894), and the preparation by James White, Technical Adviser of the Dominion defense regarding the Canada-Newfoundland border (1597-1926). Of particular interest in this series are the records on Louis Riel and the North-West Uprising (1873-1886). This record group also includes documents from the **Bankruptcy Branch** (1932-1955) and portions of **Civil and Property Disputes** (1884-1897, 1904-1950), and **electronic records** on procedure and the disposition of cases heard by the Exchequer Court, the Federal Court, and the Supreme Court (1920-1979), as well as copies of the Constitutional Acts.

Records of Parliament: RG 14
1828-1984

562 metres
666 microfilm reels
153 data files

Administrative history: Canada's Parliament was established in 1867 under provisions of the *British North America Act* and consists of an appointed upper house, the Senate, and the House of Commons elected by universal sufferage. Under the constitution, the Parliament of Canada is vested with legislative power. Most of the records of the House of Commons date after the 1916 fire which destroyed the Centre Block of the Parliament Buildings.

Arrangement and content: In general, these records cover the post-Confederation period. Most of the pre-Confederation parliamentary records are in the custody of the Manuscript Division, National Archives. The records are arranged according to sessions of Parliament and include the following material of the **House of Commons** (1866-1983), Sessional Papers (1916-1983), Appendices to the Journals (1919-1965), bills and statutes (1869-1960), committee records (1874-1945), electoral records (1867-1950), debates (1867-1974), records of the Clerk, records of the Speaker, Test Rolls (1867-1974), Scrolls (1903-1968), administrative records (1828-1945), Votes and Proceedings (1926-1961), Unfinished Business (1896-1965), Supply Resolutions (1909-1963), and records on the Mace (1917). Records of the **Senate** (1867-1974) include those of the Gentleman Usher of the Black Rod (1903-1974), sessional records, a letterbook of the Legislative Council (1854-1870), and Senate and committee records (1895-1971). Other parliamentary records include those of the **Library of Parliament** (1858-1956), and records of the **Inter-Parliamentary Union** (1926, 1933-1937). **Electronic records** include House of Commons Debates 1973-1986; and some House of Commons Committee proceedings from 1979-1986.

Records of the Department of the Interior: RG 15
1821-1916

654.3 metres
169 microfilm reels
258 aperture card books

Administrative history: The Department of the Interior was formed in 1873 to administer all federal lands and natural resources on the Canadian prairies, the Railway Belt of British Columbia, and the Far North. Inheriting functions from the Departments of the Secretary of State (RG 6) and Public Works (RG 11), Interior was charged with incorporating the largely unsettled areas of Canada into John A. Macdonald's National Policy, which envisioned an integrated nation from sea to sea. As population began to flow to the West, Interior also received responsibility for immigration from the Department of Agriculture (RG 17) in 1892. The rapid expansion of the West and the North from the mid-1890s until World War I forced the Department to widen its horizons and structures, with various branches sub-dividing again and again to cope with their enlarged responsibilities.

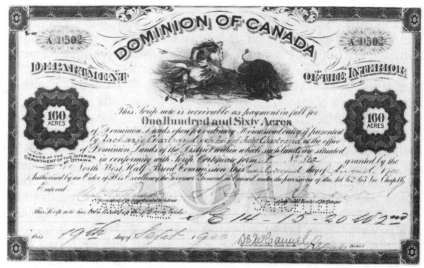

An example of script issued by the Department of the Interior. The note could be surrendered by the holder for cash, or exchanged for 160 acres of homestead lands. At various times script was issued to the Métis, original white settlers of the Red River area, and members of the militia. (RG 15, Volume 1407, 22 August 1900) (C-89332)

In 1930, with the settlement process largely completed, control of public lands and natural resources in the prairie provinces was handed over to the provincial governments and Interior lost most of its *raison d'être*. On its abolishment in 1936, a large portion of the Department's active records were transferred to the three prairie provinces, especially those concerning surveys, lands, timber, water, and minerals. Others were transferred to the new Department of Mines and Resources (and its many successors, see RG 21 and 22).

The many branches of the Department of the Interior maintained separate record systems and these continued after 1936 in other departments. Accordingly, these records have been assigned to separate record groups, including Indian Affairs (RG 10), Royal Canadian Mounted Police (RG 18), Forestry (RG 39), Geological Survey of Canada (RG 45), Dominion Observatories (RG 48), Immigration (RG 76), Canadian Parks Service (RG 45), Northern Affairs (RG 85), Mines (RG 86), Mineral Resources (RG 87), Surveys and Mapping (RG 88), Water Resources (RG 89), National Battlefields Commission (RG 90), Yukon Territorial Government (RG 91), and Chief Geographer (RG 92). Throughout its existence, however, Interior's principal function concerned land Administration and Settlement, as represented by the Dominion Lands Branch and related units, the records of which form the core of RG 15. Nevertheless, the records in RG 15 reflect to some degree the activities of all the branches that at one time or another were part of the Department.

Arrangement and content: Administrative and operational records of the Department may be found under the series **Office of the Deputy Minister** (1873-1958); financial records under **Accounts Branch** (1876-1959); and legal records under **Solicitor's Branch** (1898-1928). The series **Dominion Lands Administration** (1821-1959) contains administrative records and subject files on western lands administration and settlement, including settlements established by ethnic groups and colonization companies. Records specially related to ordnance lands are included under **Ordnance and Admiralty Lands Branch** (1821-1947) and to school lands under **Schools Lands Branch** (1904-1934). Homestead grant registers and letters of patent are found under the series **Lands Patent Branch** (1835-1916). The series **Timber and Grazing Branch** (1873-1953) includes records concerning natural resource development by the private sector, in particular grazing leases, and timber, irrigation, and mining permits. Three much smaller series include the **North Territories Branch** (1873-1883), which primarily contains letters addressed to the Minister of the Interior and correspondence of Lieutenant-Governor of the Northwest Territories; the **British Columbia Lands Branch** (1885-1957), which contains correspondence regarding the railway belt through British Columbia; and the **Ordnance, Admiralty and Railway Lands Branch** (1922-1932), which consists of field survey notes.

Records of the Department of National Revenue: RG 16
1787-1981

215 metres
61 microfilm reels

Administrative history: The Department of National Revenue — or Revenue Canada, as it is known today — was created shortly after Confederation. In 1868, two separate departments were established: Customs, which was responsible for collecting customs duties and canal tolls, and Inland Revenue, which was responsible for collecting all excise duties, indirect taxes, and stamp duties.

In 1887, the ministers of these departments were reduced to controllers and responsibility for them was placed under the Department of Trade and Commerce from 1892 to 1897, when once again they were elevated to full departmental status. The two departments were merged as Customs and Inland Revenue in 1918. From 1921 to 1927, the Department was known as Customs and Excise. The collection of income tax, which had been the responsibility of the Department of

Finance since 1917, was transferred to the Department of Customs and Excise in 1924. In 1927, its name was changed to the Department of National Revenue.

The current Department is divided into two functional components: *Customs and Excise* and *Taxation*.

Arrangement and content: This record group is divided into three series. The first contains documents pertaining to customs, excise, and inland revenue, and consists primarily of the **Correspondence and Port Records** of customs collectors, and correspondence sent to the Commissioner of Customs (1790-1882). This correspondence is arranged chronologically, by port name. The Port Records (1795-1965) consist of vessel control registers, import and export information, and accounting records. Legislation, proclamations, Orders-in-Council, circulars and directives dealing with the administration of the Department are contained in the Special Records (1928-1970). A number of Tariff Files (1920-1965) have been kept as samples. The records of the Commissioner of Customs (1893-1963) deal with the legislation governing distilleries and tobacco producers. The second series consists of **Customs and Excise** records created by the Office of the Deputy Minister (1925-1961) which contain the replies of the Minister to the House of Commons, and documents regarding certain fraudulent practices within the Department. The third series, **Taxation**, contains sample income tax return forms (1917-1965), minutes of the Royal Commission on Government Organization (Glassco) (1962-1968), a selection of the pension plans submitted by pension plan companies, some Business Profits War Tax files (1915-1921), and a selection of case studies on succession duties.

Records of the Department of Agriculture: RG 17
1845-1987

1,632.4 metres
435 microfilm reels
1 data file

Administrative history: Many of the federal Department of Agriculture's initial responsibilities after Confederation were outside the realm of agriculture per se, namely immigration (RG 76, 26, and 15), census and statistics (RG 31), marine and emigrant hospitals (RG 29), international exhibitions (RG 72), patents, copyrights, and industrial designs (RG 105), archives (RG 37), and quarantine and public health (RG 29). Research in agricultural science and practice through the Experimental Farms System significantly broadened the Department's early work in agriculture by the turn of the century. The responsibilities of the Department expanded in the twentieth century to include all aspects of agricultural research, production, marketing, trade, and economic assistance. The non-agricultural functions of the Department were gradually transferred to other federal departments between 1867 and 1919. Thus the Department of Agriculture's mandate increasingly came to reflect purely agricultural concerns.

Arrangement and content: RG 17 is divided into several records series. The Department's first major central registry system, **Records of the Minister, Deputy Minister, and Secretary** (1852-1920), documents Departmental activity in agriculture, immigration, quarantine and public health, census and statistics, patents, copyrights, timbermarks, international exhibitions, and archives. (Smaller series comprised of letterbooks and other corespondence also deal with the functions listed above).

The second Departmental central registry system, **Central Registry Files and Indexes** (1918-1953), and several individual branch registries, richly document Departmental affairs from 1920 to the early 1950s. Records deal with the Experimental Farms System, all facets of animal, plant, and plant product research, forest biology, wartime administration, racetrack betting, agricultural marketing, food certification and inspection, international trade, assistance programs, and Departmental administration. The third central registry system, **Central Registry Files** (1959-1974), established in 1960, contains subject files created up to the mid-1980s which reflect the activities of the operational branches of Agriculture Canada: Research, Food Production and Inspection, Communications, Marketing and Economics, Finance and Administration, and Farm Income Services Branch.

Other records series document related Departmental matters such as the work of the Alachlor Review Board (1987). Material in **electronic form** consists of a data file containing information on the Canadian Dairy Commission producer records for 1975.

Records of the Royal Canadian Mounted Police: RG 18
1863-1982

473 metres
416 microfilm reels

Administrative history: In 1873, the North West Mounted Police (NWMP) was established to administer justice in the Northwest Territories, in particular, to pacify the Indians, to suppress the liquor traffic, and to collect customs dues. The NWMP was originally organized with two responsibility centres — the Comptroller, located in Ottawa who reported through the responsible department to Parliament, and the Commissioner, located in the West, who was responsible to the Comptroller for the day to day operations of the Force.

In the 1920 reorganization, the name of the Force changed to the Royal Canadian Mounted Police (RCMP), the Office of the Comptroller was abolished and the Commissioner's Office was relocated to headquarters in Ottawa. At the same time, the Force absorbed the responsibilies and staff of the Dominion Police in the area of domestic security.

The RCMP now administers the enforcement of all federal laws in Canada and by agreement enforces criminal and provincial laws in all provinces except Quebec and Ontario. The Force has been under the jurisdiction of numerous departments since 1873 but now reports to Parliament through the Solicitor General.

Arrangement and content: The records are arranged according to the lines of administrative responsibility starting with the **Comptroller's Office** (1874-1919), and the **Commissioner's Office** (1876-1920). These two series of records are subject files with similar filing systems and represent the incoming correspondence covering all operations of the Force. Very often a copy of the outgoing correspondence has also been added to the file. There are letterbooks to complement both series. These series also contain records related to Finance, Supply, Quarantine Services, Northern Patrols, and early Criminal Investigation. Other series of records represent **Division and Detachment Records** (1874-1980), a sampling of the journals, telegrams, local orders, and letterbooks of some of the divisions and detachments (more complete records of the daily operations of the divisions and detachments will be found in the records of the Commissioner's Office); **Dominion Police Records** (1872-1919), a few letterbooks of the Commissioner of Police and personnel registers; **Yukon Records** (1898-1951), consisting of letterbooks, daily journals, general orders, and a few subject files (the records of both the **Comptroller's Office** and the **Commissioner's Office** also contain patrol reports, investigative reports, and administrative files related to the Yukon); records of the **Royal Canadian Mounted Police** (1902-1982), records from the post-1920 Headquarters Registry Files; Criminal Investigation Branch files; Security Records and **Personnel Records** (1873-1954). The personnel files cover the NWMP, RNWMP, and the RCMP.

Records of the Department of Finance: RG 19
1775-1981

835 metres
835 microfilm reels

Administrative history: The Department was officially created in 1869, although its origins can be traced to the functions administered by the Office of the Receiver General established in the eighteenth century. At various times in its history, the Department of Finance has been responsible for the Treasury Board (RG 55), the Royal Canadian Mint (RG 120), tax collection (RG 16), old age pensions, the superannuation fund, and the Tariff Board (RG 79). Some of these activities were transferred to other departments and agencies in the 1930s, so that Finance could concentrate on central analytical and policy work. Today, the Department is principally responsible for assisting the government in developing and implementing financial and economic policies and measures to best accomplish its major fiscal objectives. To accomplish these duties, the Department is divided into the following branches: tax policy and legislation, federal-provincial relations and social policy, economic programs and government finance, fiscal policy and economic analysis, and international trade and finance. Lastly, the Finance Minister is responsible for the application of more than 60 acts of Parliament.

Arrangement and content: The records of the Finance Department are divided into six main series. The records on the **Abolition of Seigneurial Tenure** (1853-1929) contain general correspondence, and supporting documents for indexes and registers. The **Office of the Receiver General** (1775-1879) records consist of accounting records, payment authorities, and correspondence received and sent. The series entitled **Agencies and Acts Administered by the Department of Finance** contains records pertaining to the acts and agencies for which the Department is responsible. The **Financial Records** series (1810-1966) complements the Office of the Receiver General series described above. It contains different types of accounting records, such as general ledgers, payment authorities, and the pay list. The **Ministerial Correspondence** documents include ministerial correspondence for the period 1840-1957. This series, like the one described below, is frequently consulted by researchers. Its chief characteristic is that it contains information on the ministers, deputy ministers, and senior officials who worked in the Department during this period. This series also includes records pertaining to various committees. The **Central Registry Files** contain documents created by various Departmental branches and divisions, except for records created by the Office of Finance Minister Donald M. Fleming. These files cover such topics as international programs, international economic relations, tariffs, international finance, legislation, the special council on taxation, and the committee on tax structure. Files dealing with federal-provincial relations, social policy, resource programs, economic development, and federal finances are also included. A "special subjects" heading consisting of the files of the Central Mortgage and Housing Corporation, a collection of press releases, and records of the Canada Deposit Insurance Corporation and Municipal Development and Loan Board is also included in this series.

Records of the Department of Industry, Trade and Commerce: RG 20
1880-1983

1,339.9 metres
161 microfilm reels
29 data files

Administrative history: The Department of Trade and Commerce was established in 1892, and assumed jurisdiction over trade and commerce matters formerly administered by the Finance Department (RG 19). At various times in its history the Department has been responsible for steamship subsidies and mail subventions, Chinese immigration (RG 76), census and statistics (RG 31), the grain trade, the exhibition commission (RG 72), and a host of operational activities now performed by other departments.

The Department of Industry was established in 1963 with the responsibility of fostering the efficient development of the Canadian manufacturing industry; improving the balance of payments; encouraging research and development; and promoting efficiency in industry. In addition, the Department's Area Development Agency was responsible for formulating and implementing activities to encourage economic development in designated areas.

In 1969, Trade and Commerce amalgamated with the Department of Industry to form the Department of Industry, Trade and Commerce (ITC). The main objective of ITC was to further the growth, productivity, employment opportunities, and prosperity of the Canadian economy through the efficient development of Canada's manufacturing and processing industries and the expansion of trade and tourism. In 1982, responsibility for domestic industrial development was transferred to a new department, Regional Industrial Expansion, and the international trade function of ITC was assumed by External Affairs (RG 25).

Arrangement and content: A large part of the material in RG 20 is found in the central registry systems of the three departments involved which cover all aspects of the departments' activities. The Department

A display of Canadian-made products in a Glasgow store window representing the Canada calling promotion. (RG 20, Volume 203, File 28804, Part 3) (C-98901)

of Trade and Commerce had four systems; a correspondence registry and three subject file registries used for the periods 1893-1905, 1906-1961, 1961-1966, and 1966-1969 respectively. The Department of Industry and the Department of Industry, Trade and Commerce each had a single registry system throughout their existence. In addition to the central systems, the record group contains records produced by specific components of the departments. These include: administrative and reference files of the **Economic Research and Development Branch** (1926-1955); records of the **Commodities Branch** (1946-1959); records of the

National Design Branch — later Design Canada — including correspondence, officers' files, and award records (1947-1985); records of the **International Trade Relations Branch** which cover such subjects as international tariffs and GATT (1912-1969); material relating to Expo'67 from the **Fairs and Missions Branch** (1963-1971); records of the **Trade Commissioners Service** consisting mainly of commissioners' reports (1921-1960) and records of the **Agriculture and Fisheries Branch** covering primarily grain production and export. Office and subject files of various ministers and deputy ministers of these departments (1892-1977) are also held in RG 20. The latter includes files of the **Historical Records Section** (1892-1977) compiled by the Departmental Historian. The records held in **electronic form** relate to tourism surveys, 1971-1974, consumer surveys 1977, industrial and investment surveys, 1975-1978, employment and labour force history surveys, 1977-1979, and vacation surveys, 1967-1983.

Records of the Department of Energy, Mines and Resources: RG 21
1883-1985

97.2 metres
7 data files

Administrative history: When the Department of the Interior (RG 15) was abolished in 1936, federal responsibility for mapping and surveys, mines, energy, and a number of other resource functions was placed in three departments in direct succession: Mines and Resources (1936-1949), Mines and Technical Surveys (1949-1966), and Energy, Mines and Resources (1966-1979). (For information on other direct successors to the Department of Interior, see the entry for RG 22.) RG 21 primarily contains general policy development records maintained in the central registries of these departments. Operational records, which document the implementation of these policies, including records which date from the time when the functions were administered by the Department of the Interior, are now maintained in the following record groups: Geological Survey of Canada (RG 45), Dominion Observatories (RG 48), Dominion Coal Board (RG 81), Mines Branch (RG 86), Mineral Resources Branch (RG 87), Surveys and Mapping Branch (RG 88), Water Resources Branch (RG 89), and Geographical Branch (RG 92). Unlike the particular subject focus of each of these records groups, RG 21 contains information on all the functions they document. The records of RG 21 also document the activities of a number of agencies that reported through the Minister of Energy, Mines and Resources. These include Atomic Energy of Canada Limited, Eldorado Nuclear Limited and its subsidiaries (RG 134), Atomic Energy Control Board (RG 60), the National Energy Board (RG 99), Uranium Canada Limited, and the Interprovincial Boundary Commission.

Arrangement and content: The records are arranged in a number of series. The registry files of the **Deputy Minister's Office** (1931-1969, 1983-1984) document the wide range of activities undertaken by the Department and its predecessors; information on committees, boards, advisory groups, and specific resource and energy issues are contained in this series of records. The **Central Registry Series** (1930-1981) contains both administrative and operational records relating to the functions and activities of the Department and its various branches. Administration, finance, general services, property, personnel, materiel management, information services, and a wide range of operational subjects are the general categories contained in this series. In addition, there are series of records relating to the **Special Projects Branch** (1939-1949), the **Canadian Permanent Committee on Geographical Names** (1883-1973), and files documenting the Canadian Institute of Mining and Metallurgy (1965-1975), the Royal Commission on Energy (Borden Commission, 1958-1959), and the ENERSAVE/HOMEPLAN Program (1966-1985). **Electronic records** contain data on the distribution and concentration of trace metals in lake sediments.

Records of the Department of Indian and Northern Affairs: RG 22
1867-1988

219.7 metres
2 data files

Administrative history: After the Department of the Interior (RG 15) was dissolved in 1936, many of its responsibilities for resource development in the West and North and also for native affairs were taken up by four federal departments in succession: the Departments of Mines and Resources (1936-1949), Resources and Development (1949-1953), Northern Affairs and National Resources (1953-1966), and Indian Affairs and Northern Development (1966), which is now Indian and Northern Affairs. (See the entry for RG 21 for additional successors to the Department of the Interior.) The various responsibilities of Interior were thus scattered across the many, and frequently changing, administrative components of these departments during these years. At the same time, many new responsibilities were undertaken by these departments.

Records which were created by the Department of the Interior's four successor departments (as noted above), and which document the development of policy across or above these various programs, were maintained by these departments separately from the records which document the actual implementation of policy in particular program areas. The registry systems for the former records are contained in RG 22. The operational or implementation records of various programs which were administered by one or more of these departments, including the Department of the Interior, are now maintained in separate record groups: Indian Affairs (RG 10), Forestry (RG 39), Canadian Parks Service (RG 84), Northern Affairs Program (RG 85), Mines (RG 86), Mineral Resources (RG 87), Surveys and Mapping (RG 88), Water Resources (RG 89), National Battlefields Commission (RG 90), Yukon Territorial Records (RG 91), and Canadian Wildlife Service (RG 109).

RG 22 also contains records created by a number of commissions and committees created after 1936 (such as the Alaska Highway Pipeline Inquiry) which also deal with policy concerns across the various program areas handled by Interior's administrative successors. Other records include those of the many agencies that reported to Parliament through the various ministers responsible for these departments. Records of this kind in RG 22 include those of the Commissioner of the Yukon Territory, the Commissioner of the Northwest Territories and the Northern Canada Power Commission (RG 96).

Arrangement and content: The records are grouped into series that reflect the departments they represent. They are the **Department of Resources and Development** (1867-1957), the **Department of Northern Affairs and National Resources** (1944-1966), the **Department of Indian Affairs** (1937-1975), the **Office of the Deputy Minister** (1953-1967), **Indian Affairs and Northern Development** (1922-1977), and **Indian and Northern Affairs** (1967-1988). Of particular interest in this record group are the records created by the Deputy Minister's Office (1922-1983), the Information Division and its Predecessors (1920-1972), the Engineering and Architecture Branch and its predecessors (1913-1976), and the Administration Program (1937-1977). Also included are records that relate specifically to the Advisory Commission on the Development of Government in the Northwest Territories (1965-1966), the Alaska Highway Pipeline Inquiry (1974-1977), the Coordinator of the Advisory Committee on Northern Development (1953-1967), the Senior Science Advisor (1968-1977), the Office of Native Claims (1976-1987), and the Office of the Task Force to Review Comprehensive Claims Policy (1973-1986). **Electronic records** in this record group consist of canal use surveys for 1977-1978 and document traffic flow through federally managed canals.

Records of the Department of Fisheries and Oceans: RG 23
1883-1984

544.8 metres
372 microfilm reels
1 data file

Administrative history: In 1868, the new Dominion established its own Department of Marine and Fisheries which became responsible for promoting and protecting Canada's seacoast and inland fisheries. After being placed under the Department of Naval Service in 1914, Marine and Fisheries was reinstated as a distinct department in 1920. In 1930, a separate Department of Fisheries was created, an arrangement which endured until 1969 when the federal government's fisheries and forestry programs were joined to form the Department of Fisheries and Forestry (see RG 39). This latter Department was soon dissolved, and in 1972 its programs became the principal components of the new Department of the Environment. Following the demise of the short-lived Department of Fisheries and Environment in the mid-1970s, the government's fisheries activities were moved to the newly-created Department of Fisheries and Oceans in 1979.

Various agencies of the Canadian government have been involved in oceanographic research since the late nineteenth century (see RG 42 and 139). Following an earlier period of effort to organize oceanographic research during the 1930s and 1940s, growing Canadian and international attention to Law of the Sea issues during the 1950s and 1960s, influenced the federal government to develop and organize on a more formal and coordinated basis its oceanographic activities in waters contiguous to Canada for scientific, defensive, and economic purposes. By the early 1960s, the Department of Mines and Technical Surveys had become heavily involved in the surveying and investigation of Canada's coastal waters, and in 1961 a separate Division of Oceanographic Research of its Surveys and Mapping Branch (RG 88) was created, which was followed a year later by the establishment of a Marine Sciences Branch. This Branch inherited the Department's Canadian Hydrographic Service (RG 139), the Division of Oceanographic Research, and the Ship Division. It was around this time, too, in 1962, that the Bedford Institute of Oceanography and the Institute of Ocean Sciences were created. The Marine Sciences Branch was subsequently transferred to the Department of Energy, Mines and Resources (RG 21) in 1966 and then to Environment (RG 108) in 1972. Finally, the oceanographic program was placed with Fisheries and Oceans in 1979 where the federal government's fisheries management and ocean science programs are now jointly located.

Arrangement and content: The records from Fisheries and Oceans fall principally into the following series: **Ministerial Administrative Records** (1908-1979), records on various commissions, councils, and committees from the offices of several departmental ministers and deputy ministers; **Central Registry Records** (1883-1915), records covering a wide array of subjects related to fisheries protection and fisheries conservation; **Central Registry Files** (1915-1960s) which, in addition to the subjects covered in the earlier file classification system, also includes files concerning legislation and regulations; conferences, conventions, and meetings; species investigations and fish breeding; fish vessel, storage and catch technologies, economic development programs, and international scientific and economic agreements and cooperation; and **Fisheries Research Board of Canada** (1953-1979), including central registry files and transcripts of interviews with leading government officials. Finally, there are also files from a more recent Fisheries and Oceans' registry system. These span the 1940s-1970s period and cover subjects similar to those found in the above central registry systems. Holdings in **electronic form** consist of a data file containing the data from the Foreign Fishing Vessel Licencing Information System for 1977.

Records of the Department of National Defence: RG 24
1870-1982

8,290.4 metres
6,506 microfilm reels
870 microfiches
19 data files

Administrative history: The Department of National Defence (DND) was established in 1922 by the amalgamation of the Department of Militia and Defence (RG 9), the Department of the Naval Service, and the Air Board. In 1968, the Royal Canadian Navy, the Canadian Army, and the Royal Canadian Air Force were unified into a single force. DND is responsible for the control and management of the Canadian Armed Forces, the former Defence Research Board, and all matters relating to national defence including the construction and maintenance of defence establishments and facilities.

Arrangement and content: The records are arranged into eight general series which include the **Minister's Office** (1917-1920, 1947-1957), the **Tri-Service Functions** (1942-1970), the **Joint Staff**, as well as the records of the **Army** (1870-1967), the **Navy** (1903-1970), the **Air Force** (1920-1965), the unified **Canadian Armed Forces** (1940-1982), and the **Defence Research Board** (1943-1974). Each arm of the Forces and the Defence Research Board, as well as the staff areas, had their own registry system which has been retained by the Archives within the individual series. For the three arms of the Forces and the Armed Forces after unification, there are Headquarters Registry Files or Central Registry Files consisting of administrative, policy, and operational records. There are also records on a wide variety of subjects including recruiting and training, pay and benefits, orders, committees, and records on arms, equipment, research, and the like; also included are records created by the Directorate of History. The Army files contain corps records, unit records, war diaries, military district records, as well as claims and internment files and the records of the Canadian Military Headquarters, London, England in World War II. The Navy files include ships' logs, ships' books, and ships' files, intelligence records, the records of the Atlantic, Pacific, and Newfoundland Commands, naval divisions, and naval liason records. The Air Force records include operations record books and diaries, air station site plans, and the Air Board minutes. For the unified Armed Forces there are files on the more ceremonial functions of the Forces and files on the unification. The Defence Research Board records contain administrative and operational files, some Chairman's Records, public relations files, and newspaper clippings. The record group also contains the records of the War Purchasing Commission, Parliamentary Returns, records of the Dependents Board of Trustees, and files on signals. Subjects held in **electronic form** include a file on the personal information of all traceable Canadian Airmen in World War I, as well as files on the evaluation of recruits, work attitudes, quality of life, officer motivation, personnel assessments, relocation, and release.

Records of the Department of External Affairs: RG 25
1803-1984

1,052 metres
154 microfilm reels

Administrative history: The Department of External Affairs was formed in 1909 to be responsible for the conduct of Canadian relations with other countries, within the context of the British Empire. In 1931, the scope of this responsibility was constitutionally broadened by the Statute of Westminster to include all aspects of Canadian international relations. The Department is now responsible for the coordination and formulation of all Canadian international activity relating to diplomatic posts, representation at international organizations, and the negotiation of international treaties and agreements.

Arrangement and content: These records are arranged according to the office which created them and the operational function they served, including series for Headquarters, Foreign Posts, International Conferences and Commissions, and International Negotiations. The records within the **Headquarters** series (1887-1974) are arranged according to the Departmental heirarchy beginning with the Records of the Secretary of External Affairs and the Minister of External Relations (1973-1984), then, the Records of the Under-Secretary of External Affairs (1908-1952), followed by the Central Registries (1909-1976), Briefing Books (1887-1976), and the Divisional Records (1891-1963). The **Foreign Posts** series (1880-1984) is arranged by the post where the records were created. The Canadian High Commission in London (1880-1976) and the Washington Embassy (1927-1970) comprise the largest part of this series. Thirteen other Canadian foreign posts are covered in the remainder of this series. The **International Conferences and Commissions** series (1911-1984) is composed of records from conferences or meetings which are of indefinite duration. Included in this series are Imperial Conferences (1897-1933), the League of Nations (1922-1938), Commonwealth Conferences (1944-1973), the United Nations (1945-1958), La Francophonie (1960-1985), and a number of other conferences and meetings (1922-1984). The records in the **International Negotiations** series (1883-1965) are divided into two sub-series. The first contains actual treaties, agreements, statutes, and protocols signed by Canada (1910-1985). The other sub-series consists of correspondence and prints in support of these and other negotiations (1883-1985). There is also a series of **Miscellaneous** records (1803-1976) within this record group which are largely comprised of documents created by foreign or international bodies in which Canada had an interest. Included among these are Foreign Office Prints (1803-1949), United Kingdom Intelligence Documents (1915-1919), and War Crimes Documents (1944-1948).

Records of the Department of Citizenship and Immigration: RG 26
1880-1979

23.6 metres

Administrative history: Until 1917, immigration was first the responsibility of the Department of Agriculture (RG 17) and then the Department of the Interior (RG 15). In 1917, the Department of Immigration and Colonization was established, and since then Immigration has existed as a separate department, except for the period from 1936 to 1949, when it was the responsibility of the Department of Mines and Resources. The Department of Citizenship and Immigration existed from 1949 to 1966, when the Department of Manpower and Immigration was established, (called since 1977 the Department of Employment and Immigration). In addition to immigration, the Department of Citizenship and Immigration was responsible for such diverse programs as Citizenship (RG 6), Indian Affairs (RG 10 and 22), the National Gallery of Canada, and the Public Archives of Canada (RG 37). The operational records of the Immigration Branch remained a distinct series from 1893 to the present and have been preseved as such in RG 76.

Arrangement and content: The main series in RG 26 is the **Deputy Minister's Records** (1923-1972). These records include subject files from the Deputy Minister's Registry, legal files, committee agendas, meeting minutes, correspondence, reports, statistical tabulations, and miscellaneous briefing books. The bulk of the records document three of the Department's programs: Immigration, Manpower, and Indian Affairs, although some relate to Citizenship, the National Gallery, the Public Archives, and the Dominion Carillonneur. The Deputy Minister's files contain subject files on immigration policy, legislation and regulations, Departmental organization, and various parliamentary, Departmental and interdepartmental committees on immigration. There are also files on the administration of the Immigration program, showing occupational selection, processing and documentation, medical and security examinations, settlement, employment and welfare services for immigrants, assisted passage, and non-governmental services. The legal files contain reference material on issues such as Indian Affairs, federal lands and resources, immigration, citizenship, manpower, and radio censorship. There are also two detailed statistical compilations relating to immigration to Canada from 1880 to 1964. Within the records of the **Citizenship Branch** (1941-1961) are those of the Editorial Section, which was responsible for the research, translation, and correspondence necessary to report on the political complexion of the ethnic press in Canada during World War II.

Records of the Department of Labour: RG 27
1882-1988

1,750 metres
305 microfilm reels

Administrative history: The Department of Labour was created pursuant to the *Conciliation Act* of 1900. The principal objectives of the Department were the preparation and publication of the *Labour Gazette*; settlement of industrial disputes under the terms of the *Conciliation Act*; promotion of fair wage payment and proper conditions; for those employed on public work; and administration of the *Alien Labour Acts*.

Responsibility for administering the Department was initially placed with the Postmaster General. (The Office of Minister of Labour as a separate Cabinet portfolio was not to be established until 1909.)

The Department was given important additional responsibilities over the years. It participated in the creation of a system of national employment offices after 1918, and implemented Canada's first old age pension scheme after 1926. During the Depression, it was responsible for federal unemployment relief and, with the Department of National Defence, administered camps for the single unemployed. In 1940, the Department began to administer unemployment insurance in Canada. During World War II, the Department of Labour was responsible for the manpower policy of the federal government, through the National Selective Service. After 1945, the Department became increasingly involved in the creation, planning, and administration of the Canada Labour Code.

Legislation administered by Labour Canada in 1989 includes responsibility (for workers under federal jurisdiction) for working conditions such as hours of work, minimum wages, annual vacations, holidays with pay, equal wages, unjust dismissal, group and individual terminations of employment, severance pay, the regulation of fair wages and hours of labour contracts made with the federal government for construction, remodelling, repair or demolition of any work; federal mediation and conciliation services; government employee and merchant seamen compensation; occupational safety and health; and labour adjustment assistance benefits for workers affected by redundancies and layoffs.

Arrangement and content: Sixty-nine records series make up the records of Labour Canada. Almost all the records in the group are central registry files. RG 27 holds over 10 metres of **Minister's Office** records and close to 90 metres of **Deputy Minister's** records. The records are more complete for the years after 1930, and Deputy Minister's records for the period 1900-1914 are rare. In the **Lacelle Files** there are over 20 metres of records covering all major activities of the Deputy Minister's Office between 1902 and 1945. "Administration" and "General Services" series contain the main subject and correspondence files of the Deputy Minister's Office for the years 1930 to 1974 while another series, "Committees, Conferences, Meetings," illustrates the Department of Labour's participation in a number of important boards and dominion-provincial conferences between 1920 and 1966. An important part of the Department of Labour's original mandate was to collect industrial relations information and to make it available to employers and unions in Canada as well as to retain it for Departmental purposes. Three series of records in RG 27 document this function. The **Strikes and Lockouts**

Files provide information on every strike and lockout occurring in Canada between 1907 and 1977. Consisting mainly of newspaper clippings, the files have been microfilmed. Companions to the Strikes and Lockouts Files in the record group are the **Collective Agreements** series (1910-1986), and the **Conciliation and Arbitration** files (1944-1981). For many years the Department maintained a **Press Clipping Division** which clipped Canadian newspapers on a wide variety of topics of interest to Departmental officials, covering the years 1900-1971. Also available is the **Vertical Files** series created by the Department of Labour Library which contains early pamphlets, leaflets, and bulletins on labour subjects not usually found in other collections. (The Departmental library at Labour Canada retains a copy of these files on microfiche as well as an index to them.) Other series in this record group document important activities undertaken by the Department of Labour. In 1930, the Department became responsible for Ottawa's program of unemployment relief payments to Canada's provinces and municipalities. The Department's key responsibility for Canadian manpower policy during World War II is documented in the **National Selective Service** records. (The activities of the Department's **Japanese Division** are represented in a section of the central registry files.) As World War II came to an end, the Department of Labour became responsible, along with the Department of Immigration, for the government's policy of expanded immigration to Canada after 1945. The Department also supervised an extensive farm labour program in Canada during these years. More and more in the past 20 years, Labour Canada has been involved in the development and implementation of the Canada Labour Code for industries under federal jurisdiction. Key series include the **Labour Standards Branch** (1949-1979), the **Employment Relations and Conditions of Work Branch** (1944-1983), and the **Occupational Safety and Health Branch** (1919-1981). Included are policy and administrative records as well as company compliance files and some complaint files.

Records of the Department of Munitions and Supply: RG 28
1939-1953

153.2 metres
1 microfilm reel

Administrative history: In September 1939, the Department of Munitions and Supply was established with responsibility for the allocation and control of raw materials and services, the conversion of industry to wartime production, establishment of new industries, and ensuring fair prices to meet the demands of war. The Department of Reconstruction was created in 1944 to formulate and coordinate plans and projects for post-war reconstruction. These two departments were merged in December 1945 as the Department of Reconstruction and Supply and continued in existence until 1951. The procurement function was transferred to the Canadian Commercial Corporation (RG 65) in 1947, and the Department ceased to exist with the creation of the Department of Defence Production (RG 49) in 1951.

Arrangement and content: The records are arranged in two series covering **Munitions and Supply** (1939-1953) and **Reconstruction and Supply** (1942-1949). Under Munitions and Supply are the records of the wartime functions including a series of history files; the central registry covering such topics as the development of the Canadian Wartime Atomic Energy Project; the Economics and Statistics Branch covering labour and industrial capabilities; Kotlarsky Files regarding personnel; the Wartime Industries Control Board; War Supplies Limited; and miscellaneous related records. The records of Reconstruction and Supply pertain to planning for the post-war period and include a series of reference files for the minister's office central registry system, financial records, studies prepared by the Directorate of Air Development Economic Research Branch, Wartime Shipbuilding Limited, and related records.

Records of the Department of National Health and Welfare: RG 29
1815-1986

1,973.5 metres
4 microfilm reels
56 data files

Administrative history: Responsibility for public health and quarantine, was initially vested in the Department of Agriculture (RG 17) from 1867 to 1919. An independent Department of Public Health was created in 1919, primarily as a result of the swine flu epidemic of that year. In 1928, the Department of Health amalgamated with the Department of Soldiers' Civil Re-Establishment (1918-1928) to create the Department of Pensions and National Health. In 1944, this Department was split into the Department of National Health and Welfare (RG 29) and the Department of Veterans Affairs (RG 38). National Health and Welfare provides health and social welfare services to a wide variety of Canadians. Health programs include services to Indians, Inuit and other northern residents, the public service, immigrants, and civil aviation personnel, quarantine, food and drug investigation, inspection of medical devices, environmental health, hospital and medical care insurance (in conjunction with the provinces), poison control, aid to the blind, and medical research. The Department also administers a variety of income security programs such as Old Age Security, Canada Pension Plan, Guaranteed Income Supplements, Family Allowance, Youth Allowance, and the Canada Assistance Plan. It is also responsible for Fitness and Amateur Sport, which reports to Parliament through a separate Minister of State.

Arrangement and content: This record group contains a wide range of records which include central registry files of an administrative and operational nature, subject files, personal case files, policy files, research grant files, minute books, ledgers (mainly for hospital attendance), medical files, briefing books, publications and pamphlets, correspondence files, working papers, and various reports. Subjects covered in these records relate to most of the programs for which Health and Welfare is responsible, such as administration of quarantine regulations; the development of medical and hospital insurance; inspection of food, drugs, and medical devices, either as a prelude to marketing in Canada, or as a result of a consumer complaint; administration and operation of a variety of income security programs such as Family Allowance, Youth Allowance, Old Age Security, Guaranteed Income Supplement, and the Canada Pension Plan; improvement of the nutritional standards and habits of all Canadians; the treatment of mental health problems; encouragement of physical fitness and the funding of amateur sport; and the provision of medical services to natives, Northern residents, the civil service, and immigrants. There is also a large amount of research and statistical material on health and welfare. The majority of the records date from after World War II, predominantly the late 1950s to the early 1980s. Information held in **electronic form** is largely survey data from studies commissioned by Health and Welfare, mainly in the 1970s, on such subjects as the use of dangerous drugs, the effects of retirement, the use of recreational facilities, the nature and amount of alcohol consumption, nutrition in Canada, the smoking habits of Canadians, and health attitudes and behaviour.

Records of the Canadian National Railways: RG 30
1836-1975

1,540.4 metres
1,208 microfilm reels

Administrative history: The Canadian National Railway Company (CNR) was incorporated in 1919 for the purpose of consolidating the railways, works and undertakings comprising the Canadian Northern Railway, and operating them together with the Canadian Government Railways as a national railway system. In 1923, the Grand Trunk Railway Company of Canada was amalgamated with the CNR, and there have subsequently been many other railway companies merged with the federal company. Some of these include the Canadian Northern Railway, the Canadian Government Railways, and the Grand Trunk Railway, themselves the products of numerous amalgamations and purchases. Canadian National (CN) is the historical by-product of over 500 corporate components. CN is a proprietary corporation established to operate and manage a national system of railways and other transportation and related enterprises, which over the years have included trucking and bus lines, telecommunications, hotels, radio broadcasting, real estate, and marine services. In recent years, the corporation has divested itself of many of its subsidiary interests and concentrated almost exclusively on rail freight.

Arrangement and content: The records are generally organized into five "system" series — the **Grand Trunk Railway System**, the **Central Vermont Railway System**, the **Canadian Northern System**, the **Canadian Government Railways System**, and the **Canadian National Railways System**. The records are further sub-divided by component railway "groups" which made up the larger systems. These include the Grand Trunk Pacific Railway System, the Great Western Railway System, the Northern Railway Group, the Midland Railway Group, the Canada Atlantic System, and the Intercolonial Railway. There are also a number of artificial groupings which were created to rationalize some of the record holdings within the series such as **Grand Trunk Properties in Quebec and New England, Grand Trunk Properties in Ontario, Grand Trunk Properties in the United States, Canadian Northern Railways on the Prairies, Canadian Northern Railways in Ontario, Canadian Northern Railways in Quebec, Canadian Northern Land and Real Estate Companies,** government acquired railways in New Brunswick, Nova Scotia and in Quebec, the **Newfoundland Railway,** the **Northern Alberta Railways,** the **London and Port Stanley Railway,** and others. Under the Canadian National Railways System, in addition to the subsidiaries, the company has been sub-divided by departments, including the **Bureau of Economics and Department of Research and Development,** the **Operations and Maintenance Department,** the **Office of the Chief Engineer,** the **Colonization and Agricultural Department, Canadian National Land Settlement Association,** and the **Legal Department.** Ultimately, there is a unique document series for every corporate predecessor and subsidiary of Canadian National of which the National Archives has records. These series are identified under the relevant corporate name. The records consist primarily of corporate-business documents such as journals, cash books, ledgers, stock and bond books, minute books, traffic and equipment registers, registers and files of correspondence, subject files of operating departments and senior administrators, annual reports, deeds, leases and contracts, balance sheets and statements, personnel registers, traffic rates and accounts, tariffs, engineering and operational records related to construction, and property records. There is also a fairly large collection of railway systems generated memorabilia and ephemera (posters, menus, schedules, tickets, photographs, passes, correspondence, etc.), many of these items being gathered together in the Museum Train series.

Legal restrictions on access: Access to the records described herein is governed by conditions agreed upon between the transferring institution and the National Archives. These are explained in the inventory. Some records contain information to which access is restricted.

Records of Statistics Canada: RG 31
1825-1983

201.09 metres
1,255 microfilm reels
53 data files

Administrative history: Statistics Canada's roots can be traced back to the establishment in 1847 of the Board of Registration and Statistics which became part of the Bureau of Agriculture in 1855. At Confederation, responsibility for census and statistics was placed under the Department of Agriculture (RG 17) where it remained until 1918. In that year, the Dominion Bureau of Statistics (Statistics Canada since 1971) was created as a central statistical gathering agency. The main functions of Statistics Canada include the compilation, analysis, and publication of statistical data relative to the commercial, industrial, financial, social, and general condition of the people, and the regular undertaking of a census of population and agriculture in Canada.

Arrangement and content: The records consist of administrative and operational files primarily from the **Office of the Chief Statistician**, (1900-1975), and the **Office of the Assistant Chief Statistician**, (1941-1973). Also included are census returns from the **Census Field**, (1825-1901), and in **electronic form**, the **1871 Census Index Project** undertaken by the Ontario Genealogical Society.

Records of the Public Service Commission: RG 32
1868-1984

490.6 metres
13 microfilm reels

Administrative history: In 1908, the Civil Service Commission (CSC) was created under the *Civil Service Act*. This legislation introduced the merit principle, which resulted in the holding of competitions for employees posted in Ottawa. The *Civil Service Act* of 1918 gave the CSC complete authority over the Public Service, making it responsible for its control and organization, including recruitment, selection, appointment, classification, and pay. The *Civil Service Act* of 1962 reaffirmed the independence of the Commission and the 1967 *Public Service Employment Act* redefined its powers and changed its name to the Public Service Commission. At that time, the Commission became a central staffing agency that could delegate its powers to the departments. Although responsibility for pay, classification, and conditions of employment was transferred to the Treasury Board, the Commission retained responsibility for the administration of the appeals system. The Commission reports directly to Parliament, with the Secretary of State submitting its report to the House of Commons.

Arrangement and content: This record group consists of **Competition Files** (1921-1979) containing correspondence, lists or registers of examinations administered to candidates, Public Service competitions, and decisions regarding the appeal of appointments. One series consists of the **Organizational Charts of Government Departments** (1935-1960) and salary data. A collection of **Personnel Files** (1885-1972) contains historical information on former senior Public Service managers. The **Subject Files** (1882-1960) deal with issues such as demobilization during the period 1940-1946, strikes, policies, and procedures, as well as information on the Commission's history. **Central Registry Files** (1918-1960) containing correspondence, surveys, reports, minutes, and statistics on the organization and various programs of the Commission. **Operational Analyses** of various departments (1946-1967) comprise another series; other series contain documents created by the **Special Committee on Personnel Management and the Merit Principle** (1977-1979) and documents on the operations of the **Office of the Chairman of the Commission** (1963-1976). This record group also contains documentation on the reassignment of senior managers under the **Bicultural Development Program** (1966-1977), appointments from under-represented groups, appointments to the Management Category, as well as information on the official languages program and the Commission's regional operations.

Records of Royal Commissions: RG 33
1873-1987

916.3 metres
176 microfilm reels
88 data files

Administrative history: A royal commission results from a memorandum of a minister of a department, or the Prime Minister, to the Governor-General-in-Council (Cabinet) stating the need for a public inquiry on a specified subject. When approved, this memorandum forms the basis of an Order-in-Council which sets out the terms of reference for the proposed inquiry. It also names the commissioner(s) and usually the statutory authority under which the commission is to operate. In the case of a royal commission, the statutory authority cited in the Order-in-Council is Part I of the *Inquiries Act* which regulates "Public Inquiries." (The first statute in British North America relating to public inquiries was enacted in 1846.)

After the Order-in-Council is passed, a commission appointing the commissioner(s) is issued by letters patent under the Great Seal of Canada. The commission is the formal authority for the commissioner(s) to conduct the inquiry. Similar to the Order-in-Council, the commission sets out the terms of reference and the statutory authority for the inquiry. Commissions granted under the Great Seal of Canada are considered "royal" because they originate with the Crown. In practice, commissions are issued by the Governor General, acting in the name of the Crown, and on the recommendation of the Governor-General-in-Council (the Cabinet).

Most of the records in this group are from royal commissions. The remainder are either "Departmental Investigations" appointed under Part II of the *Inquiries Act*; inquiries appointed under the *Inquiries Act*, but with the part of the *Act* under which they were appointed remaining unknown; or inquiries for which the authorizing statute appointing them is unknown.

Arrangement and content: The records consist of exhibits, submissions, transcripts of hearings, correspondence, working papers, reports, minutes of meetings, research material, and research studies. The records are organized by series. Each series represents the records of one commission (i.e., RG 33/1, RG 33/2, etc.). The list of 147 separate commissions below indicates the series, subject, the name of the Chief Commissioner(s), and the outside dates of the records. Some series contain **electronic records.**

1. Canadian Pacific Railway, 1873, Commissioner, J.C. Day.

2. Stony Mountain Penitentiary, Manitoba, 1897, Commissioner, F.C. Wade.

3. Transportation of Canadian Products through Canadian Ports, 1903-1905, Commissioner, John Bertram.

4. Life Insurance, 1891-1907, Commissioner, D.B. MacTavish.

5. Grain Trade, 1906-1908, Commissioner, John Miller.

6. Quebec Bridge, 1897-1910, Commissioner, H. Holgate.

7. Baie Verte Canada, 1875, Commissioner, J. Young.

8. Drill Sheds, Province of Ontario, 1915, Commissioner, R.A. Pringle.

9. Department of Manpower and Immigration, Montreal, 1959-1976, Commissioner, Mme C. l'Heureux-Dubé.

10. Air Canada, 1968-1975, Commissioner, W.Z. Estey.

11. Records of Public Departments, 1912-1914, Commissioner, Jos. Pope.

12. Railways and Transportation, 1905-1920, Commissioner, A.H. Smith.

13. Pulpwood, 1923-1925, Commissioner, Jos. Picard.

14. Radio Broadcasting, 1923-1939, Commissioner, John Aird.

15. Technical and Professional Services, 1928-1931, Commissioner, E.W. Beatty.

16. Transportation, 1917-1932, Commissioner, L.P. Duff.

17. Banking and Currency, 1928-1934, Commissioner, H.P. Macmillan.

18. Price Spreads, 1921-1935, Commissioner, H.H. Stevens.

19. Financial Arrangements between the Dominion and the Maritime Provinces, 1863-1935, Commissioner, T. White.

20. Textile Industry, 1871-1938, Commissioner, W.F.A. Turgeon.

21. Anthracite Coal, 1936-1937, Commissioner, H.M. Tory.

22. Grain, 1907-1938, Commissioner, W.F.A. Turgeon.

23. Dominion-Provincial Relations, 1936-1940, Commissioners, N.W. Rowell and Jos. Sirois.

24. Taxation of Annuities and Family Corporations, 1943-1945, Commissioner, W.C. Ives.

25. Co-operatives, 1937-1945, Commissioner, E.M.W. McDougall.

26. Administrative Classifications, 1940-1946, Commissioner, Walter L. Gordon.

27. Transportation, 1877-1951, Commissioner, W.F.A. Turgeon.

28. National Development in the Arts, Letters, and Sciences, 1946-1951, Commissioner, Vincent Massey.

29. Lot Rentals in Banff and Jasper National Parks, 1950, Commissioner, H.O. Patriquin.

30. Staking of Crown Land in the Northwest Territories, 1951, Commissioner, K.J. Christie.

31. Quartz and Placer Mining in the Yukon Territory, 1954, Commissioner, G.E. Cole.

32. Patents, Copyright, Trade Marks and Industrial Design, 1954-1955, Commissioner, J.L. Ilsley.

33. Hurricane Damage, Humber River Valley, Province of Ontario, 1954, Commissioner, J.B. Carswell.

34. Coasting Trade, 1931, 1945-1958, Commissioner, W.F. Spence.

35. Canada's Economic Prospects, 1951-1960, Commissioner, Walter L. Gordon.

36. Broadcasting, 1950-1957, Commissioner, R.M. Fowler.

37. Employment of Firemen on Diesel Locomotives, 1903-1958, Commissioner, R.L. Kellock.

38. Newfoundland Finances, 1947-1958, Commissioner, J.B. McNair.

39. Energy, 1950-1960, Commissioner, Henry Borden.

40. Price Spreads of Food Products, 1948-1960, Commissioner, Andrew Stewart.

41. Great Slave Lake Railway, 1954-1961, Commissioner, Marshall E. Manning.

42. Coal, 1954-1960, Commissioner, I.C. Rand.

43. Political Partisanship of Edmund Louis Paradis, 1960, Commissioner, J.V. Tremblay.

44. Station CHEK-TV, Victoria, Province of British Columbia, 1960, Commissioner, Andrew Stewart.

45. Automotive Industry, 1950-1961, Commissioner, V.W. Bladen.

46. Government Organization, 1951-1963, Commissioner, J. Grant Glassco.

47. Publications, 1949-1963, Commissioner, M. Grattan O'Leary.

48. *Unemployment Insurance Act*, 1961-1963, Commissioner, E.C. Gill.

49. Transportation, 1899-1963, Commissioner, M.A. MacPherson.

50. Natural Resources of Saskatchewan, 1900-1935, Commissioner, A.K. Dysart.

51. Natural Resources of Alberta, 1870-1935, Commissioner, A.K. Dysart.

52. Natural Resources of Manitoba, 1868-1929, Commissioner, W.F.A. Turgeon.

53. Cost of News Print Paper, 1916-1921, Commissioner, R.A. Pringle.

54. Toronto Harbour Commissioners, 1926-1927, Commissioner, J.H. Denton.

55. Horse Race Meets and Betting, 1919-1920, Commissioner, J.G. Rutherford.

56. Disturbances at Arvida in July 1941, Commissioners, Sévéren Létourneau and W.L. Bond.

57. Halifax Disorders, 7 and 8 May 1945, 1939-1945, Commissioner, R.L. Kellock.

58. Prices, 1948-1949, Commissioner, C.A. Curtis.

59. The S.S. *Northland* Incident, 1919, Commissioner, F.E. Hodgins.

60. Japanese Black Dragon Society, Province of British Columbia, 1939-1942, Commissioner, J.C.A. Cameron.

61. Shell Committee Contracts, 1915-1916, Commissioners, W. Meredith and L.P. Duff.

62. Espionage in Government Service ("Gouzenko Affair"), 1942-1946, Commissioners, R. Taschereau and R.L. Kellock.

63. Coal, 1930-1947, Commissioner, W.F. Carroll.

64. Banking and Finance, 1945-1964, Commissioner, D.H. Porter.

65. Taxation, 1950-1967, Commissioner, K.L. Carter.

66. Bren Machine Gun Contract, 1929-1938, Commissioner, H.H. Davis.

67. Purchase of the Oliver Property, Township of Sandwich West, Province of Ontario, under the *Veterans' Land Act*, 1945, Commissioner, D.M. Brodie.

68. Veterans' Qualifications, 1939-1946, Commissioner, H. Bovey.

69. Disposal of Property of Japanese-Canadians, 1935-1950, Commissioner, H.I. Bird.

70. Distribution of Railway Box Cars, 1951-1958, Commissioner, John Bracken.

71. Public Complaints, Internal Discipline and Grievance Procedures within the RCMP, 1974-1975, Commissioner, R.J. Marin.

72. Marketing of Beef and Veal, 1974-1976, Commissioner, M.H. Mackenzie.

73. Maritimes Claims, 1926, Commissioner, Andrew R. Duncan.

74. Administration of the *Pension Act*, 1932-1933, Commissioner, T. Rinfret.

75. Dismissal of George Walker from Prairie Farm Assistance Administration, 1960-1964, Commissioner, H.W. Pope.

76. Charges of Misconduct Against Officials of the Yukon Territory, 1898, Commissioner, Wm. Ogilvie.

77. Operation of the *Civil Service Act* and Kindred Legislation, 1907, Commissioner, J.M. Courtney.

78. Health Services, 1961-1965, Commissioner, E.M. Hall.

79. Marketing Problems of Freshwater Fish Industry, 1965-1967, Commissioner, George H. McIvor.

80. Bilingualism and Biculturalism, 1963-1971, Commissioners, A. Davidson Dunton and André Laurendeau.

81. Atlantic Salt Fish Industry, 1964-1965, Commissioner, D.B. Finn.

82. Martineau Defalcation and other matters, 1903, Commissioner, J.M. Courtney.

83. The Public Service, 1911, Commissioner, A.B. Morine.

84. Crash of Trans Canada Airlines DC8F Aircraft at Ste. Thérèse de Blainville, Province of Quebec, 1963-1965, Commissioner, George Challies.

85. Complaints by Walter H. Kirchner regarding Veterans' Pension Treatment Services, 1948, Commissioner, J.J. McCann.

86. Political Partisanship in the Department of Soldiers' Civil Re-establishment, 1927, Commissioner, A.T. Hunter.

87. Future of Trans-Canada Air Lines Overhaul Base at Winnipeg International Airport, 1965, Commissioner, D.A. Thompson.

88. Customs and Excise Department, 1926-1927, Commissioners, Francis Lemieux and J.I. Brown.

89. Status of Women in Canada, 1969-1971, Commissioner, Florence B. Bird.

90. Working Conditions in the Post Office Department, 1965, Commissioner, André Montpetit.

91. Farm Machinery, 1966, Commissioner, C.L. Barber.

92. Dealings of the Hon. Mr. Justice Leo A. Landreville with Northern Ontario Gas Limited, 1958-1966, Commissioner, I.C. Rand.

93. Allegations against Counsel acting upon an application for the Extradition of Lucien Rivard, 1965, Commissioner, F. Dorion.

94. Pilotage, 1962, Commissioner, Y. Bernier.

95. Industrial Relations, 1919, Commissioner, T.G. Mathers.

96. Inquiry into the case involving Gerda Munsinger, 1966, Commissioner, W.F. Spence.

97. Wage Rates in Coal Mines of British Columbia and Alberta, 1943-1944, Commissioner, G.B. O'Connor.

98. Government Printing and Stationary Office, 1920, Commissioner, G.C. Snyder.

99. Immigration of Italian Labourers to Montreal, 1903-1905, Commissioner, J. Winchester.

100. Naturalization, 1931, Commissioner, J.G. Wallace.

101. Non-Medical Use of Drugs, 1969-1974, Commissioner, G. LeDain.

102. Steel Profits, 1974, Commissioner, W.Z. Estey.

103. Airport Inquiry, 1973-1974, Commissioner, H.F. Gibson.

104. Indian Lands and Indian Affairs in the Province of British Columbia, (McKenna-McBride), 1913, Commissioner, Nathaniel W. White.

105. Potentialities of Reindeer and Musk-ox Industries in the Arctic, 1919, Commissioner, J.G. Rutherford.

106. Crash of a Panarctic Electra Aircraft at Rea Point, Northwest Territories, 30 October 1974, 1974-1976, Commissioner, W.A. Stevenson.

107. Claims of Certain Canadian Pelagic Sealers, 1913-1915, Commissioner, L.A. Audette.

108. Indian Elders' Testimony, 1977, Commissioner, L. Barber.

109. Reconveyance of Land to British Columbia, 1927, Commissioner, W.M. Martin.

110. The Treadgold and other Concessions in the Yukon Territory, 1903-1904, Commissioners, B.M. Britton and J.E. Hardman.

111. Grain Handling and Transportation, 1975-1977, Commissioner, Emmett Hall.

112. Parliamentary Accommodation, 1974-1976, Commissioner, D.C. Abbott.

113. Corporate Concentration, 1975, Commissioner, R.B. Bryce.

114. Working of the Law Branch of the House of Commons, 1912, Commissioners, W.D. Hogg and A. Shortt.

115. Indian Claims, 1966-1977, Commissioner, Lloyd Barber.

116. West Coast Oil Ports, 1977-1978, Commissioner, Andrew R. Thompson.

117. Canadian Automotive Industry, 1973-1978, Commissioner, S.S. Reisman.

118. Task Force on Canadian Unity, 1976-1979, Commissioners, J.-L. Pépin and J.P. Robarts.

119. Newfoundland Transportation, 1949-1979, Commissioner, A. M. Sullivan.

138. Seals and Sealing in Canada, 1984-1986, Commissioner, Albert Malouf.

139. Unemployment Insurance, 1985-1987, Commissioner, Claude Forget.

140. Certain Banking Operations (collapse of the Canadian Commercial Bank and the Northland Bank), 1985-1986, Commissioner, Willard Z. Estey.

141. Foreign Claims, 1945-1987, Commissioner, T.D. MacDonald.

142. Sentencing, 1984-1987, Commissioner, J.R. Omer Archambault.

143. Hinton Train Collison, 1986-1987, Commissioner, René P. Foisy.

144. War Criminals, 1986, Commissioner, Jules Deschênes.

145. Chinese and Japanese Immigration to British Columbia, 1900-1902, Commissioner, R.C. Clute.

146. Chinese Frauds and Opium on the Pacific Coast, 1910-1911, Commissioner, Dennis Murphy.

147. Westbank Indian Band, 1986-1987, Commissioner, John E. Hall.

Records of the National Capital Commission: RG 34
1883-1985

188.15 metres
23 microfilm reels

Administrative history: As the successor of the Ottawa Improvement Commission (OIC) (1899-1927) and the Federal District Commission (FDC) (1927-1959), the National Capital Commission (NCC) is responsible for developing the National Capital Region in accordance with its national significance as the seat of the Canadian government. The Commission acquires, develops, and maintains federal land in the National Capital Region; undertakes urban planning; provides financial support to local municipalities; and advises the Department of Public Works on the location and appearance of all federal buildings in the Region.

Arrangement and content: The records are arranged into 10 general series, of which only two deal exclusively with the former agencies of the NCC. These include the letterbooks of the **Secretary** (1899-1911) and **Engineer** (1900-1905) of the OIC. Other records of the OIC and FDC are located in three series continued by the NCC: **Central Registry Files** (1883-1958), **Minute Books of the Executive Committee** (1899-

1985), and **Annual Reports** (1901-1981). These three series cover all aspects of the Commission's functions and responsibilities since its inception and include administrative and operational records. Publicity and personnel records of commissioners of the FDC and NCC are contained in the files of the **Information Division** (1948-1966). Records regarding property transactions are found in the files of the **Property Division** (1929-1981). The series on **Contracts and Agreements** (1958-1975) contains contracts and technical specifications on a number of NCC projects while the series **Heritage Register, Case Files** (1930-1976) provides information on properties of heritage value in the National Capital Region. The records of the **Office of the Chairman** (1978-1984) contain correspondence and transcripts of public addresses by C.M. Drury.

Records of Interdepartmental Committees: RG 35
1897-1966

10.2 metres

Administrative history: This record group consists of the records of eight interdepartmental committees. Additional committees' records may be located with the records of the creating departments.

Arrangement and content: The records contain minutes, correspondence, memoranda, studies and reports.

1.   Departmental Commission on Public Records, 1897.

2.   Committee of Enquiry on Printing and Stationery, 1933.

3.   Commission on Statistics, 1912.

4.   Interdepartmental Housing Committee, 1942-1946.

5.   Interdepartmental Committee on the Book of Remembrance, 1931-1942.

6.   Interdepartmental Committee on Veterans Affairs, 1945-1946.

7.   Public Records Committee, 1909-1966 (est. 1945).

Records of Boards, Offices, and Commissions: RG 36
1896-1972

189.3 metres

Administrative history: This collection consists of records created by a wide variety of non-continuing boards, offices, and commissions, some of which were departmental investigations established under Part II of the *Inquiries Act*. (There are also departmental commissions located in the records of Royal Commissions, RG 33). This record group is closed and the records of subsequent departmental commissions may be located in the records of the responsible department or the department through whom the commission's report is filed.

Arrangement and content: The records include agenda, correspondence, proceedings, evidence, working papers, studies, reports, and newspaper clippings. There are 37 commissions in this record group.

1.   Commissioners of the Transcontinental Railway, 1904-1921.

2.   St. John River Commission, 1909-1916.

3.   Canadian Shipping Board, 1939-1946.

4.   National War Labour Board, 1941-1947.

5.   Historical Manuscript Commission, 1907-1915.

6.   Board of Commerce, 1918-1921.

7.   Office of the Special Commissioner for Defence Projects in Northwest Canada, 1943-1947.

8.   Tariff Commissions, 1896-1897, 1920.

9.   Eastern Rockies Forest Conservation Board, 1947-1955.

10.   Department of Labour, Conciliation Boards (Railway), 1949-1962.

11.   Advisory Board on Tariff and Taxation, 1926-1930.

12.   Dominion Trade and Industry Commission, 1935-1949.

13.   Advisory Commission on Development of Government in the Northwest Territories, 1965-1966.

14.   Forest Insect Control Board, 1945-1953.

15.   Canada Food Board, 1917-1919.

16.   Special Products Board, 1941-1949.

17.   Fielding Tariff Inquiry Commission, 1898-1906.

18. Dependents Allowance Board, 1942-1955.

19. Industrial Defence Board, 1948-1951.

20. Commissioner General for Visits of State, 1966-1967.

21. Mutual Aid Board, 1940-1947.

22. Committee on Election Expenses, 1965-1966.

23. Advisory Committee on Broadcasting, 1964-1965.

24. Canadian Committee on Corrections, 1965-1969.

25. St. Lawrence River, Joint Board of Engineers, 1952-1963.

26. Atlantic Tidal Power Programming Board, 1966-1970.

27. British Columbia Security Commission, 1942-1948.

28. Preparatory Committee on Collective Bargaining in the Public Service, 1960-1967.

29. Industrial Inquiry Commission on Shipping on the Great Lakes and St. Lawrence River, 1962-1963.

30. Prices and Incomes Commission, 1969-1972.

31. Wartime Information Board, 1939-1946.

32. Committee to Survey the Organization and Work of the Canadian Pension Commission, 1965-1968.

33. Committee on Juvenile Delinquency, 1961-1963.

34. Correctional Planning Committee, 1958-1960.

35. Board of Arbitration on the Grand Trunk Railway, 1920.

36. Board of Arbitration, Intercolonial Railway and Grand Trunk Railway, 1904-1905.

37. Board of Arbitration on the Canadian Northern Railway, 1917.

Records of the National Archives of Canada: RG 37
1871-1985

111.41 metres
2 data files

Administrative history: The National Archives (its name was changed in 1987 from the Public Archives of Canada) was established in 1872 to collect, preserve, and make available for research documentation relating to the historical development of Canada. In addition to federal government records and private papers, the Archives acquires maps, paintings, photographs, sound recordings, film, and electronic records that are worthy of permanent preservation. The Archives is also responsible for promoting efficiency and economy in the management of federal government records. Until 1903, the Archives was a branch of the Department of Agriculture (RG 17), but since then has reported through the Secretary of State (RG 6) and, from 1981, the Department of Communications (RG 97).

Arrangement and content: Different types of records such as correspondence, surveys, and registry files of an administrative and operational nature on acquisition, accommodation, policy, departments, and exhibitions are contained in this record group. Of particular interest are early subject files and correspondence files of the various Dominion Archivists. Other subjects include special projects such as the war archives survey, war trophies, and a draft of the *Canadian Directory of Parliament*. Agendas and minutes of the Canadian Board on Geographical Place Names and the Historic Sites and Monuments Board (for which related records exist in RG 84) are in this record group. Also included are records on the operations of the National Archives' branch office in London. **Electronic records** include an electronic version of the *Guide to Canadian Photographic Archives* which is a union list of photographic collections in Canadian archives.

Records of Veterans Affairs Canada: RG 38
1896-1985

67.7 metres
51 microfilm reels
21 data files

Administrative history: Veterans Affairs can trace its origins to the creation of the Military Hospitals Commission (MHC) in 1915. In February 1918, the MHC was disbanded and the Department of Soldiers' Civil Re-establishment (SCR) was created in its place. In 1928, SCR was merged with the Department of Health to form Pensions and National Health. A separate Department of Veterans Affairs was created in 1944. The Pension Review Board, the Canadian Pension Commission, the War Veterans Allowance Board and the Bureau of Pensions Advocates report to Parliament through the Minister for Veterans Affairs.

Arrangement and content: The records include service files, land grant claims, and some pension files for Canadians who served in the South Africa War (1899-1902) and minutes, circulars, and subject files of the Military Hospitals Commission (1915-1918). Pensions and National

Health records include files relating to the Westminster Hospital inquiry (1933-1944), neuropsychiatric services in the Department and some subject files. Veterans Affairs' records include Departmental instructions and procedures, medical research records, some pension claims, newspaper clippings and press releases, and some subject files. Veterans Land Administrations' records include a small sample of case files (both headquarters and Toronto District Office) veterans claim cards, platt books, accounts, and a series of historical research reports on various aspects of land settlement. This record group also includes some records of the Canadian agency of the Imperial War Graves Commission, replica copies of the Books of Remembrance and service records of the Royal Newfoundland Regiment (1914-1919). **Electronic records** in this group relate to the overall responsibility of the Department for the management of special programs for veterans.

Records of the Canadian Forestry Service: RG 39
1874-1979

246 metres

Administrative history: In 1884, the Forestry Commission was created within the Department of the Interior (RG 15) to survey forest conditions. In 1898, this work became the responsibility of the Timber and Forestry Branch and involved the active development and conservation of forests. A fire protection service was inaugurated in 1900; a forestry nursery station was established in 1904; and in 1906 over 20 timber reserves in the four western provinces were placed under the management of the Superintendent of Forestry. From 1908 to 1911, the Branch also controlled national parks (RG 84), and from 1908 to 1912, irrigation (RG 89). With the abolition of the Department of the Interior in 1936, Forestry was from 1936 to 1960 a distinct unit of three parent organizations (see RG 22). In 1960, a new Department of Forestry was formed from the old Forestry Branch of the Department of Northern Affairs and Natural Resources and the Forest Biology Division of the Research Branch of the Department of Agriculture (RG 17). In 1966, this became the Department of Forestry and Rural Development (RG 124), and in 1969 the Department of Fisheries and Forestry (RG 23). The name "Canadian Forestry Service" was adopted as the official title of the forestry component of the new Department. This Department in turn became the core of the new Department of the Environment established in 1971 (RG 108). In 1985, the Service became a ministry of state under Agriculture Canada, and in 1988 it was elevated to departmental status and named Forestry Canada.

Arrangement and content: The records are grouped in series according to administrative units within the Service as follows: **Headquarters Records** (1894-1973), **Eastern Forest Products Laboratory** (1911-1974), **Field Office Records** (1919), **Office of the Chief Forester of the Commission of Conservation** (1909-1922), and **Forest Management Institute** (1963-1973). Within these units, records are maintained according to registry systems and in some cases, by individual record type, such as land registries, surveys, or project files. The records document the Service's activities as the principal agency through which the contribution of the federal government to forestry and forest products is made. The early administration of timber inspection and logging, the development of silviculture and forest resource management and protection, forest survey reports, and economic studies of the Canadian forest industry are reflected in the records. This record group also contains transcripts of oral history interviews with early Service employees and documents the administration and operation of the Eastern and Western Forest Product Laboratories prior to their privatization as Forintek in 1979.

Records of the Office of the Superintendent of Financial Institutions: RG 40
1839-1982

9.9 metres

Administrative history: Formerly known under the name "Insurance," this record group is now known as the Office of the Superintendent of Financial Institutions and has, since 1987, assumed the responsibilities that were once carried out by the Department of Insurance (created in 1875) and the Inspector General of Banks. The Superintendent is responsible for protecting the public against financial loss from the operations of federally registered or licensed insurance companies and financial institutions, ensuring the solvency of pension plans and providing actuarial services for government departments and agencies.

Arrangement and content: The first series includes all documents dealing with the former **Insurance Branch**. It contains the Annual Statements of Canadian, British, and Other Insurance Companies (1872-1934), the Central Registry Files (1930-1961), records pertaining to the drafting of the *Unemployment Insurance Act* (1934-1955), and Liquidation Records for insurance companies (1839-1904). The second series consists of records pertaining to the former **Office of the Inspector General of Banks**. It contains Central Registry Files (1921-1982), including the inspection reports of various banks and files created by the Office of the Inspector General (1870-1964).

Records of the Canadian Broadcasting Corporation: RG 41
1923-1982

283.3 metres
11 microfilm reels

Administrative history: The CBC is a crown corporation which was established in 1936 to replace an earlier public broadcasting agency, the Canadian Radio Broadcasting Corporation, created in 1932. It is designed to provide a national broadcasting service. It also provides a regular television and radio broadcasting service in English and French and operates Radio Canada International and a northern service. The CBC reports to Parliament through the Minister of Communications (RG 97).

Arrangement and content: The core of the holdings is the **Records of the CBC Headquarters** (1923-1982). This series includes minutes, agenda, reports, briefs, press clippings, subject files, and chronological correspondence coming from the office of the president, the offices of senior executives, the Canadian Radio Broadcasting Corporation, and the Corporate Affairs Department. Of particular interest are the records of the **CBC's Historical Archives Section** (1923-1979) pertaining to all aspects of the agency at its headquarters in Ottawa, the English Services Division in Toronto, and the French Services Division in Montreal. The subject files and program files of the **Central Registry Office** (1933-1967) are also worthy of note. This record group also contains **Records of the CBC's English Services Division** (1948-1976) and includes records of the managerial officers and transcripts of special programs as well as **Records of the Regional Broadcasting Division** (1948-1967) created by the Northern Service and the Armed Forces Service of the English Services Division.

Records of the Marine Branch: RG 42
1762-1967

178.6 metres
119 microfilm reels

Administrative history: A branch of the Department of Marine and Fisheries was established in 1868 to administer Canada's national marine services and all matters related to navigation within territorial waters: aids to navigation; pilots and pilotage; harbours and ports; classification and registration of vessels; examination and certification of masters and mates; steamship inspection; inquiries into the causes of shipwrecks; shipping masters and shipping officers; marine and seamen's hospitals; lifesaving and the lifeboat service; and the management of Canadian government vessels. During its operational life, the Branch was twice rated as a department in its own right (1884-1892, 1930-1936), and was eventually merged together with the Department of Railways and Canals (RG 43) and the Civil Aviation Branch of the Department of National Defence (RG 24) to form the Department of Transport (RG 12) in 1936. Aside from purely navigational and marine matters, the functions of the Branch involved a variety of activities with some related medical, scientific, and technological interest, including wireless telegraphy and radio (RG 12, 41, and 97), hydrography (RG 139), and northern exploration (RG 85).

Arrangement and content: The records are arranged into five general series, each of them sub-divided by subject, organizational function, or type of document. The **Records of Predecessor Agencies** (1762-1866) comprise records from offices which eventually became part of the Marine Branch portfolio following Confederation, and include St. Lawrence River pilots' certificates issued in Quebec City (1762-1840), pilots' certificates from the Trinity House of Montreal (1832, 1866), and records related to the quarantine station on Grosse Isle (1833-1839). There are two separate series of Departmental headquarters records, the parameters of which correspond roughly to the replacement of one central registry system with another about the year 1923. The **Headquarters Records** for the years 1868-1923 consist of a large collection of central registry files (1887-1923) covering subjects related to all aspects of Marine Branch activity, records related to the **Canadian Arctic Expedition** (1913-1918), the *Empress of Ireland* **Inquiry** (1914), and the *Princess Sophia* **Inquiry** (1918-1919). Also included are letterpress copies of reports to Privy Council from Marine Branch (1868-1910), records of pilotage (1913-1918) and the **Canadian Government Radiotelegraphic Service** (1912-1923), and various document series such as ships' logs (1909-1914) and examinations for marine engineers (1871-1909). The **Headquarters Records** to 1936 are similarly composed of central registry files, the records of various offices, and miscellaneous documents: **Records of the Dominion Wreck Commissioner** (1901-1936), **Records of the Hudson Straits Expedition** (1927-1928), **Log books of the Radio Branch** (1927-1936), and **Marine Certificates** (1872-1936). The fourth general series consists of **Local Records**, principally records created or collected by the registrars of shipping at the ports of Quebec (1850-1945), Toronto (1886-1958), Parrsboro (1916-1951), Picton (1872-1907), Port Rowan (1882-1925), and Ottawa (1881-1965), but including a collection of miscellaneous ships' logs and articles of agreement (1895-1938), and shipping engagement records (1887). The records in the final series consist of shipping registers compiled in various ports throughout Canada, including first registers, and registers of subsequent transactions (1787-1966).

Records of the Department of Railways and Canals: RG 43
1791-1964

336.25 metres
267 microfilm reels

Administrative history: The Department of Railways and Canals was created in 1879 by extracting from the Department of Public Works (RG 11), its Railway Branch and the operational responsibilities for canals administered by the Office of the Chief Engineer, and combining them to form a new ministry composed of two branches (Railway Branch and Canal Branch). The Railway Branch was responsible for the construction, operation, and maintenance of government-owned railways, and administered a program of financial assistance (land grants, cash subsidies, etc.) designed to encourage railway companies to construct new lines. The Canal Branch supervised the operation, maintenance, and enlargement of the Canadian canal system and undertook the construction of new canals when required. In 1936, the Department of Railways and Canals was amalgamated with the Department of Marine (RG 42) and the Civil Aviation Branch of the Department of National Defence (RG 24) to form the Department of Transport (RG 12). The administration of the Welland, Cornwall, Lachine, and Sault Ste. Marie canals was transferred from the Department of Transport to the St. Lawrence Seaway Authority in 1959 (RG 52); Parks Canada (RG 84) assumed responsibility for the Trent, Rideau, Ste. Anne de Bellevue, Murray, Carillon, St. Ours, Chambly, Beauharnois, St. Peter's, Chignecto, and Grenville canals in 1972.

Arrangement and content: The documents are arranged into four basic series, including **Railway Branch Records** (1867-1936), **Canal Branch Records** (1838-1955), **Canal Records** (1819-1964), and **Legal Records** (1791-1957). Each of these general groupings has been further divided into a number of sub-series. Both the **Railway Branch** and the **Canal Branch** had their own registries, initially correspondence registers (1879-1901), but after 1901, numeric subject file systems (to 1936) covering all aspects of their respective operational mandates. In addition to the central registry system, operational documents, files of correspondence, agreements, estimates, contracts, reports, registers, and indices, were also maintained by various administrative offices. Within the Railway Branch, the **Office of the Chief Engineer** kept records on railways directly the responsibility of the federal government, including for a time portions of the **Canadian Pacific Railway** (1875-1892), the **Cape Breton Railway** (1886-1892), the **Oxford and New Glasgow Railway** (1187-1897), the **Annapolis and Digby Railway** (1889-1892), and the **Intercolonial and Prince Edward Island Railways** (1877-1906), as well as general records related to the construction of various railways in Canada. Similarly, the **Office of the Chief Engineer, Canal Branch**, maintained a series of correspondence and subject files (1868-1907, 1912-1936) and letterbooks (1873-1896), although the records following 1892 document the period when the Railway Branch and the Canal Branch had actually been merged under one Chief Engineer. Since all canals fell under federal control, the Department developed separate offices to deal with the local day-to-day operation, maintenance, and administration of each canal, reporting through a superintending engineer to the Chief Engineer in Ottawa. The records of these offices, including letterbooks and registers of correspondence, subject files, inspection reports, lockmasters' journals, paymasters' records, account books, ledgers, etc. are available principally for the Rideau (1834-1942) and Welland (1824-1959) canals, but include the Trent (1837-1959), Lachine (1819-1842), St. Peter's (1885-1929), and St. Lawrence Canals (1833-1950, Beauharnois, Cornwall, Farran's Point, Rapide Plat and Galops). The Legal Records series (1791-1957) comprises contracts, deeds, leases and correspondence related to canals and railways, but also includes records of various public works (roads, prisons, court houses, wharves, lighthouses, etc.) up to the year 1879.

Records of the Department of National War Services: RG 44
1939-1949

17.43 metres

Administrative history: The Department of National War Services was created in 1940 to coordinate the activities of the voluntary war organizations in Canada to avoid wasteful duplication of services. In 1941, a National Salvage Division was established and the Department began to give increased attention to the organization of women's voluntary services on a community basis. In 1942, as the federal government undertook to finance the auxiliary services of all national organizations, the Department's responsibilities increased. Responsibility for administration of the *War Charities Act* was assigned to it and a Division of Government Offices Economies Control was also created. In 1947, the Department was abolished, and its principal remaining functions were transferred to the Department of National Health and Welfare.

Arrangement and content: These records consist of subject and correspondence files on the major responsibilities of the Department. Only a small portion of the files were part of the original central registry system of the Department. The major series include files from the Minister's and Deputy Minister's Offices, from the Division of Government Offices Economies Control, and from the divisions which dealt with war charities and voluntary war relief.

Records of the Geological Survey of Canada: RG 45
1842-1966

53.3 metres
42 microfilm reels

Administrative history: The Geological Survey of Canada (GSC) was established in 1842 to conduct scientific investigations and field surveys to determine the extent of Canada's natural resources, with special emphasis on non-renewable energy and mineral resources. Its purpose is achieved by means of geological investigations in the field, supplemented by office and laboratory studies. The GSC has remained an integral scientific organization which was reported to Parliament through numerous departments, most notably the Provincial and Civil Secretaries' Offices, 1842-1867 (RG 4 and 5); Secretary of State, 1867-1873 (RG 6); Interior, 1873-1890 (RG 15); Mines, 1907-1936 (RG 86);

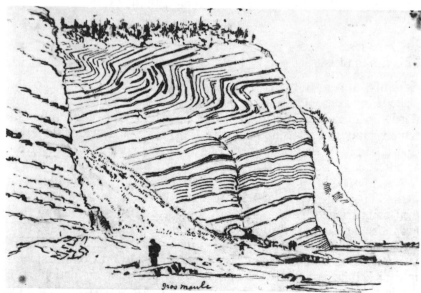

Sketch from the notebook of William Logan, first Director of the Geological Survey of Canada, 1844-1845. (RG 45, Volume 158) (C-102974)

Mines and Resources, 1936-1949 (RG 21); Mines and Technical Surveys, 1949-1966 (RG 21); and Energy, Mines and Resources, 1966-1980 (RG 21). From 1890 to 1907, the GSC was an independent department. It also controlled the national museums (RG 132) for many years and collected mineral statistics (RG 87).

Arrangement and content: Correspondence of the GSC and its research staff can be found in several different series: **Register of Letters Received** (1869-1881, 1869-1919 and 1914-1921); **Letterbook of R.W. Ells** (1884-1910); **Director's Letterbooks** (1865-1908); **Central Registry Files** (1863-1966); and **Miscellaneous Correspondence** (1866-1897). Records documenting field work by GSC scientific staff are contained in **Field Notebooks — Robert Bell** (1860-1907), **George Mercer Dawson Field Notebooks** (1875-1900), **Field Notebooks** (1842-1925), and **Register of Instruments in Use** (1872-1876). The series **Division of Mineral Statistics and Mines** (1858-1887) includes Eugene Coste's drafts of statistical reports on mineral production in Canada. **Office of the Chief Geologist** (1934-1956) includes a wide range of material on a variety of subjects, such as employment of individuals, publications, field work, and dealings with professional associations. Reports by GSC staff concerning ground water quality are found in **Well Water Records** (1943-1947) and **Ground Water Resource Reports, Prairie Provinces** (1936-1954).

Records of the Canadian Transport Commission: RG 46
1857-1979

298.7 metres
7 microfilm reels

Administrative history: The Board of Railway Commissioners of the United Provinces of Canada was created in 1857 to establish and enforce standards for railway construction and operation. At Confederation its responsibilities were assumed by the Railway Committee of the Privy Council. In 1888, the Committee's powers were expanded to include the adjudication of railway disputes. A Board of Railway Commissioners was established in 1904 to undertake the duties of the Committee with the addition of the responsibility for approving rates. In 1908 and 1910, the Commissioners were granted authority to regulate the telegraph and telephone industry and the marine cable industry respectively. In 1933, the Board became responsible for approving any railway line abandonment. The Board was renamed the Board of Transport Commissioners in 1938 and its responsibilities enlarged to include the regulation of air services and shipping on inland waterways. Air services became the responsibility of the Air Transport Board in 1944 while, in 1948, the

Canadian Maritime Commission was created to control and develop the Canadian shipping industry. In 1967, the Canadian Transport Commission was established, absorbing the Board of Transport Commissioners, the Air Transport Board, and the Canadian Maritime Commission. Under the *National Transportation Act* of 1967 the Canadian Transport Commission has been superseded by the National Transportation Agency.

Arrangement and content: The records in RG 46 largely consist of the formal proceedings of each of the component agencies and the correspondence and subject files from their central registry systems. The proceedings include the minutes of the **Provincial Board of Railway Commissioners** (1857-1864) and of the **Railway Committee of the Privy Council** (1868-1904); the **Board of Railway Commissioners and the Board of Transport Commissioners** (1918-1956); the **Air Transport Board** (1944-1960), and the **Canadian Maritime Commission** (1948-1967). Another form of proceeding includes the transcripts of hearings before the Commissioners (1904-1955, 1959-1979) with accompanying exhibits and indexes as well as the orders resulting from the hearings. Central Registry correspondence with accompanying journals and registers are held from the Railway Committee of the Privy Council (1867-1903). Central Registry subject files exist for the Boards of Railway and Transport Commissioners (1904-1967), the Air Transport Board (1945-1967), and the Canadian Maritime Commission (1918-1967). Other holdings in this record group include the **Annual Reports of Railway and Express Companies** (1878-1949); the records of the **Subsidies Branch of the Canadian Maritime Commission** (1892-1973), including material originally from the Department of Trade and Commerce (1892-1967); and records of the **Park Steamship Company** (1942-1966).

Records of the Federal-Provincial Conferences: RG 47
1927-1971

10.2 metres

Administrative history: The Office of Federal-Provincial Conferences was created recently (1975); the functions it carries out were once the responsibility of a division of the Privy Council Office.

Arrangement and content: The documents contained in this record group come from the Federal-Provincial Conference Secretariat. They generally consist of copies of briefs, presentations made by the first ministers, proposals and policy statements. Listed below are the conferences from which the National Archives has documentation, albeit incomplete:

1. Resources for Tomorrow Conference (23-28 October 1961), 1959-1962.

2. Dominion-Provincial Conference (3-10 November 1927), 1927.

3. Dominion-Provincial Conference (10-13 December 1935), 1935-1937.

4. Dominion-Provincial Conference on Road Transport, 1933.

5. Dominion-Provincial Conference (January 1934), 1933-1934.

6. Dominion-Provincial Conference on Reconstruction, 1946.

7. National Finance Committee (a body established by the Dominion-Provincial Conference of 1935), 1936.

8. Dominion-Provincial Conference, 1941.

9. Dominion-Provincial Conference on Outstanding Debt (31 March 1944), 1944.

10. Dominion-Provincial Conference, 1945.

11. Dominion-Provincial Conference on Correctional Reform, 1968.

12. Federal-Provincial Secretariat, Constitutional Conference (Ottawa, February and December 1969, and September 1970; and Victoria, June 1971), 1968-1971.

Records of the Dominion Observatories: RG 48
1842-1980

39 metres

Administrative history: Magnetism and positional astronomy were the basis of nineteenth-century surveying. Thus, when Canada's first Chief Astronomer was appointed in 1890, he was placed with the Topographical Surveys Branch (RG 88) of the Department of the Interior (RG 15). The construction of the new Dominion Observatory at Ottawa in 1905, was anticipated by the establishment of a separate Astronomical Branch of the Department — the first of several branch names — in 1903. In 1917, the Dominion Astrophysical Observatory at Victoria was completed, thus considerably expanding the work of the Branch. When the Department of the Interior was abolished in 1936, the Branch continued to exist as a distinct unit of several successive departments (see RG 21).

In 1970, the astronomical functions of the Observatories Branch were transferred to the National Research Council (RG 77), while its geophysical activities were grouped in the Earth Physics Branch of Energy, Mines and Resources (RG 21).

Arrangement and content: Included are the following series of records: **Dominion Astrophysical Observatory** (1842-1930), including records from the Royal Observatory at Greenwich, England concerning the International Boundary Surveys (1842-1848), and the records of Boundary Commissioner, Captain D.R. Cameron (1872-1876); records from the **Office of the Chief Astronomer** (1945-1947), records from the **Division of Geomagnetism** (1948-1969), and records concerning the proposed construction of the **Queen Elizabeth II Telescope** (1959-1972). The records also include numerous registry files, director's correspondence, technical reports and research data from the **Dominion Astrophysical Observatory, Victoria, B.C.** (1909-1980).

Records of the Department of Defence Production: RG 49
1942-1968

172.5 metres

Administrative history: Established in April 1951 under the *Defence Production Act*, Defence Production replaced the wartime Departments of Munitions and Supply and Reconstruction and Supply (RG 28). It was responsible for the acquisition of defence supplies and for the mobilization, conservation, and coordination of economic and industrial facilities in wartime. Beginning in 1966, Defence Production also assumed responsibility for the central purchasing and supply function in the federal government. The Department was reorganized as the Department of Supply and Services (RG 98) in 1969.

Arrangement and content: The largest single series of records in this record group consists of the **Central Registry Files** (1942-1968) on all aspects of Defence Production's administrative and operational activities, both domestic and foreign. Also included are small quantities of files created in the **Office of the Minister** (1963-1968), the **Office of the Deputy Minister** (1951-1966) and the **International Program Branch** (1961-1969).

Records of the Unemployment Insurance Commission: RG 50
1900-1982

498.26 metres

Administrative history: The Unemployment Insurance Commission was created in 1940 to administer the provisions of the *Unemployment Insurance Act*. The *Act* empowered the federal government to promote the economic and social security of Canadians by protecting workers against the uncertainties of employment through the payment of premiums or contributions for unemployment protection. The Unemployment Insurance Commission is a corporate body functioning through a network of Canada Employment Centres throughout the country. In 1977, the Unemployment Insurance Commission was merged with the Department of Manpower and Immigration to create Employment and Immigration Canada (see RG 118).

Arrangement and content: The records in this record group consist of operational and subject central registry files as well as numerous case file series created by the Unemployment Insurance Commission. The central registry files contain correspondence, senior management committee minutes, policy manuals, statistical reports, and press clippings documenting the evolution of the Commission's policies and activities over time. Most records date from the 1960s and 1970s although some volumes cover such topics as *British North America Act* amendments, the Commission's establishment and organization, unemployment insurance eligibility rulings, and legislative program changes. The record group also contains numerous accessions of unemployment insurance appeals (Umpire, Board of Referees, and Ministerial), benefit claims, annuities, and complaints and inquiries case files.

Records of the International Joint Commission: RG 51
1909-1978

3.2 metres

Administative history: The International Joint Commission (IJC) was established under a treaty signed by Great Britain and the United States in 1909, and ratified by the Canadian government in 1911. The Commission is composed of six members (three from each country) and has authority over the use, obstruction, and diversion of boundary waters (i.e., waters through which the international boundary passes). Problems arising from a common frontier are also referred to the Commission. The IJC coordinates activities under the Canada-United States Agreement on

Great Lakes Water Quality, and under the auspices of the Commission a number of international boards have been established to investigate common environmental problems.

Arrangement and content: When conducting its investigations, the Commission relies on experts and technicians in other government departments and agencies. As a result, many of the files of the Commission are housed in the records of other government departments. The files maintained by the National Archives under this record group consist of a manual summarizing issues on the navigation and development of waters common to the United States and Canada. The collection also includes 112 reports compiled by the Windsor Office of the IJC. These reports focus on different aspects of Great Lakes Basin Water Quality.

Records of the St. Lawrence Seaway Authority: RG 52
1868-1982

145.7 metres

Administrative history: The St. Lawrence Seaway Authority is a proprietary corporation established in 1954 to acquire land and to construct, maintain, and operate, in conjunction with the appropriate authority of the United States, all works that are necessary for the continued operation of the St. Lawrence Seaway. It reports to Parliament through the Minister of Transport.

Arrangement and content: The documents are divided into six main series, including the **Central Registry Files** (1868-1982), **Newspaper Clippings** (1955-1973), and information on **Water Levels** (1912-1959). Also included are numerous documents regarding the Welland Canal project (1964-1967). The Charts and Maps Division has about 50 maps covering the international portion of the St. Lawrence Seaway (1919-1936). These records also include biographies and photos of the directors of the St. Lawrence Seaway (1954-1970).

Records of the National Film Board: RG 53
1939-1969

1.5 metres
2 microfilm reels

Administrative history: The National Film Board (NFB) was established in 1939 to review government film acitivites. In 1941, it absorbed the Government Motion Picture Bureau which had been part of the Department of Trade and Commerce (RG 20) since 1921. The *National*

Film Act of 1950 repealed previous authorities and redefined the functions and aims of the Board. It is authorized to initiate and promote the production and distribution of films in English and French that interpret Canada to Canadians and to other nations.

Arrangement and content: The records of the National Film Board are composed of two series. The **Minutes and Estimates** (1939-1943) are copies of the minutes of meetings and estimates of the NFB. The records of the **McGill Study of Expo '67** (1967-1969) consist of draft reports and working papers of a research project McGill University undertook for the NFB to study and assess the audio-visual and multi-media aspects in selected national and theme buildings at Expo '67.

Records of the Office of the Comptroller of the Treasury: RG 54
1930-1969

31.2 metres

Administrative history: The Office of the Comptroller of the Treasury was established in 1931 as part of the Department of Finance. The Comptroller assumed responsibility for the control of issue and the pre-audit of government expenditures from the Auditor General (RG 58). Departmental Treasury Officers were attached to all departments to provide cheque issue and accounting services. In 1969, the duties of the Office of the Comptroller were absorbed by the Department of Supply and Services (RG 98).

Arrangement and content: The records include a series of **Central Registry Files** (1930-1969) as well as a seperate series of accounting files and Treasury Journals of the Comptroller. In addition, there are three series which reflect the activities of Treasury Officers in two government departments; that of Welfare (1946-1967) and National Defence (1946) as well as the Canadian Overseas Treasury Office (1939-1941). Also included are records from the Treasury Officers' Conference held in Ottawa in 1967.

Records of the Treasury Board: RG 55
1868-1988

599.65 metres
416 microfilm reels
20,823 fiche
1 data file

Administrative history: The Treasury Board was established on 2 July 1867 as a committee of the Privy Council to approve federal government expenditures. The administrative responsibility for this and Treasury Board's other functions rested with the Department of Finance until 1966, when a separate department was established under the *Organization of Government Act*, 1966. At this time, the ministerial position of President of Treasury Board was created. Before this, the Minister of Finance had been ex officio the minister responsible. In addition to responsibility for expenditure control, the Treasury Board is responsible for Official Language Policy, and the coordination of personnel and administrative policies in the federal public service.

Arrangement and content: The records in this group are arranged into 14 series, representing different functions and activities carried out by Treasury Board. The **Records of Decisions** and the documentation to support these decisions (1868-1984) are the main series in this group. An item taken to Treasury Board, the Privy Council Committee, for a decision is known as a "minute," and this series contains these minutes and the registers and indexes by which they are organized. **Registry Files** (1916-1967) make up the central filing system of the Treasury Board Secretariat, and include such subjects as pensions, job classifications, banking, and public works. The **Special Committees** series consists of records from committees which were struck to explore claims and advise the government on subjects under the Treasury Board mandate (1872-1963). The **Personnel Policy and Management** series (1886-1982) is material dealing with examinations, collective bargaining, benefits, and pay research. The **Budget and Estimates** series (1920-1967) contains information on federal budgets and estimates. The Records of the **Administrative Policy Branch** (1959-1980) deal with the development of administrative standards, contract review, realty policy, and information systems. The federal government's involvement in the planning of the 1976 Olympics is also contained in these records. The records of the **Office of the Secretary of the Treasury Board** (1968-1973) and the **Official Languages Branch** records (1962-1980) cover the development of language policy, reports, reviews, and related issues. The **Personnel Policy Branch** series (1954-1976) contains records covering personnel issues before the government, including pay scales, regulations, grievances, and terms of employment. Records of the **Planning Branch** (1962-1979) concern both planning and program analysis. There is also material in this series on the organization of government departments. The records of the **Office of the President** (1963-1988) are from the office of the Cabinet Minister responsible for Treasury Board. The records of **Program Branch** (1960-1980) relate to the review of departmental estimates and the overall control of government programs. The **Human Resources Branch** records (1955-1975) consist of material on training and development and the utilization of human resources within the public service. The **Miscellaneous Records** (1951-1972) deal with some specific subjects, including the Cape Breton Development Corporation and the Northumberland Strait Crossing, (1951-1972). This record group also holds **electronic records** concerning a travel pattern survey, 1975-1976.

Records of Canada Mortgage and Housing Corporation: RG 56
1935-1985

306 metres

Administrative history: The *Dominion Housing Act* of 1935 (replaced by the *National Housing Act* (NHA) of 1938) made available increased funds for home mortgages and was administered by the Department of Finance (RG 19). In 1945, the Central Mortgage and Housing Corporation (CMHC) was created to administer the NHA and other wartime housing measures, and to prepare for an anticipated post-war housing boom. Aside from insuring mortgage loans, CMHC has been involved with land assembly, low cost rental programs, and the testing of construction material in cooperation with the National Research Council (RG 77). CMHC has also been active in native, cooperative, public, and assisted ownership housing in Canada. Between 1971 and 1979, CMHC reported through the Minister of State for Urban Affairs (RG 127). In 1979, CMHC changed its name to Canada Mortgage and Housing Corporation, and since then it has reported through the Ministers for the Department of Regional and Economic Expansion (RG 124), Public Works (RG 11), Labour (RG 27), Public Works (RG 11) once again, and most recently, the Ministry of State (Housing).

Arrangement and content: The records are arranged in a number of series that include **Central Registry Files** (1950-1964), (operational and administrative) generated at headquarters and in branch offices, including the **Central Mortgage Bank, Originals** (1938-1945), the **Ajax Development Project** (1943-1967), **Joint Loan Mortgages, Originals** (1935-1969) and **Orders-in-Council** (1935-1968). Other series include **Administrative Files** (1942-1954) that relate to a conference on Com-

84

munity Planning and Home Extension Loans, and records pertaining to **Maritime Rural Housing, Emergency Shelter** (1944-1953), dealing with the activities of the Emergency Shelter Administration (1944-1946). The records also contain a series that relates to a CMHC research project that investigated alternative financial solutions to existing mortgage practices. In addition, the record group features material on the Vincent Massey Awards (1971-1975), loan files, and records from the Office of the President (including operational correspondence, and files reflecting federal-provincial relations in the field of housing).

Records of the Emergency Measures Organization: RG 57
1948-1976

52 metres

Administrative history: The Emergency Measures Organization (EMO) was established within the Privy Council Office on 1 June 1957 primarily to plan for the continuity of government authority, essential government services, and resource management in the event of nuclear war. In 1959, the Organization was given the responsibility for the coordination of civil defence planning by departments and agencies of the government as well as liaison with the various provincial organizations, NATO and other countries. In 1974-1975, the EMO was initially renamed the National Emergency Planning Establishment within the Department of National Defence and subsequently became Emergency Planning Canada with a greater responsibility for peacetime disaster planning.

Arrangement and content: The records of Emergency Planning Canada and its predecessors consist of a series of **Central Registry Files** (1952-1976), dealing with all aspects of government reestablishment, survival and disaster planning and liaison with various organizations (1949-1976), a series of central registry files of the Emergency Operations Coordination Division (1950-1970), the Governmental War Books established to identify appropriate responsibility areas for the reestablishment of government, the economic situation and routine operations in the event of a national emergency (1948-1958), the Economic Planning Division transcript sheets detailing a variety of Canadian economic conditions, as well as NATO Emergency Planning Committee files (1958-1967).

Records of the Office of the Auditor General: RG 58
1827-1982

714.6 metres

Administrative history: An independent Auditor General (AGO) was first appointed in 1878 to audit the public accounts of the government. Although some changes to the Office were effected in 1931 under amendments to the *Consolidated Revenue and Audit Act*, the AGO remained relatively unchanged until its mandate was redefined and broadened with the proclamation of the *Auditor General Act* (1976-1977). The Auditor General is required to audit government departments, agencies, Crown corporations and the Accounts of Canada, and to report the results of his examinations to the House of Commons. The auditors may conduct three types of audits, depending upon the function to be examined: Attest and Authority audits on a yearly basis, Comprehensive audits on a four-year cycle, or Special audits of specific functions as required.

Arrangement and content: The records include several series which reflect the activities of several predecessor agencies the functions for which the Auditor General eventually assumed partial or complete responsibility. These records include the **Auditor General of Public Accounts, Lower Canada** (1827-1840), the **Inspector General of Public Accounts, Upper Canada** (1832-1840), the **Board of Audit** (1855-1867), the **Audit Office** (1855-1882) and the **Registrar of Free Banks** (1854-1870). The records of the **Office of the Auditor General** (1899-1982), consist principally of audit subject files.

Records of the Office of the Representation Commissioner: RG 59
1964-1976

5.4 metres

Administrative history: In 1963, pursuant to the *Representation Commissioner Act*, responsibility for readjusting electoral boundaries was given to the Office of the Representation Commissioner. The Commissioner was therefore responsible for preparing population distribution maps following the decennial census and, in light of this information, recommending new electoral boundaries for each of the provinces and the Northwest Territories. The Commissioner had to provide suitable maps to each of the 11 electoral boundaries commissions established in these provinces and territories. He was also responsible for analysing the methods governing the registration of voters and reporting on the recommendations resulting from this analysis. Since the *Government Organization Act* eliminated the position of Commissioner in 1979, these duties have been carried out by the Chief Electoral Officer.

Arrangement and content: This record group contains the reports of the electoral boundaries commissions for 1964-1965 and 1972-1976. It also contains the minutes of the meetings of various boundaries commissions and the proceedings of public hearings held in various areas in the provinces. Also included are presentations made by individuals at public hearings, public notices of the hearings, and correspondence between commissioners or with the press or the general public.

Records of the Atomic Energy Control Board: RG 60
1947-1982

9.3 metres

Administrative history: The Atomic Energy Control Board (AECB), a departmental corporation, was created in 1946 to perform two related functions. In the interests of national security, the AECB worked with the federal Departments of Trade and Commerce (RG 20), and National Revenue, to establish a comprehensive licencing and permit system (RG 16) that controlled the movement of radioactive materials and equipment. In conjunction with federal and provincial health authorities, the AECB also regulated, inspected, and provided advice on the operation and construction of nuclear reactors, particle accelerators, and on the handling of radioactive materials. Closely associated with the records of the AECB, are the records of Eldorado Nuclear Limited (RG 134), which until 1958 was responsible for the sale of all uranium ores and concentrates produced in Canada.

Arrangement and content: This record group includes general **Atomic Energy Control Board** material (1947-1955, 1980-1981), records created by the task force to recover *Cosmos 954*, a Soviet satellite that crashed in the Northwest Territories in 1978 (1978-1982), minutes of meetings held by the **Advisory Mining Committee on Radio-active Minerals** (1948-1951), and information on AECB assistance to universities (1950-1977).

Records of Allied War Supplies Corporation: RG 61
1940-1946

1.5 metres

Administrative history: This wartime corporation, established in June 1940, was responsible for the supervision, administration, and direction of both the construction and operation of all government chemical, explosives, and ammunition plants. The Corporation was disbanded in 1948.

Arrangement and content: The records consist of a history of the Corporation prepared by John Leslie in 1945, summary files for all the projects administered between 1940 and 1946, and subject files dealing with the production of ammonia-ammonium nitrate.

Records of Loto Canada/Canadian Sports Pool Corporation: RG 62
1966-1985

140.62 metres

Administrative history: Established as a Crown corporation in June 1976, Loto Canada began operations following the termination of the Olympic Lottery in September 1976. It assisted in the financing of the 1978 Commonwealth Games at Edmonton. Following an agreement between Ottawa and the provinces in 1979 ceding the lottery field to the provinces, Loto Canada ceased the sale of tickets and closed its regional offices. Between 1980 and 1984, Loto Canada staff in Ottawa formulated a plan for betting pools involving professional sports contests. In 1983, the Canadian Sports Pool Corporation was formed as a result. Provincial authorities claimed the new scheme violated the 1979 agreement, and in 1985 both Loto Canada and the Canadian Sports Pool Corporation were dissolved by act of Parliament.

Arrangement and content: These records consist of central registry headquarters files and corporate records (executive minutes, by-laws, etc.) for both Loto Canada and the Canadian Sports Pool Corporation. Regional office records for London, Toronto, Ottawa, and Vancouver are included for the Canadian Sports Pool Corporation. The headquarters records cover all important activities of both organizations.

Records of the Canada Council: RG 63
1956-1989

595.69 metres

Administrative history: The Canada Council is a Crown corporation established in 1957 by the *Canada Council Act* to encourage the arts, humanities, and social sciences in Canada. This mandate was amended in April 1978 and responsibility for the humanities and social sciences was transferred to the Social Sciences and Humanities Research Council (RG 133). The Canada Council promotes the study, enjoyment, and production of works in the arts, shares responsiblility for Canada's cultural relations abroad, and administers a broad program of scholarships, awards, and grants.

Arrangement and content: The records are arranged into two general series: operational files and grant files. The **Operational Records** (1956-1975) include information on surveys conducted between 1958 and 1962 on ballet, symphonies, and orchestras in Canada. These files also contain material on Stanley House, donation files, the Canada Council's scholarship policy, and records detailing federal-provincial relations in the field of arts policy. The **Grant Files** (1958-1973) contain records of grant applications and awards approved by the Council. They are arranged in catagories in accordance with the division or program that created the records. Such catagories include the Arts Division, the Humanities and Social Sciences Division, Exploration Programs, and the Cultural Exchange Program.

Records of the Wartime Prices and Trade Board: RG 64
1939-1951

180 metres

Administrative history: The Wartime Prices and Trade Board (WPTB) was created in September 1939 to provide safeguards against unfair price increases in food, fuel, and other necessities of life. The Board was also responsible for ensuring an adequate supply and distribution of these goods during wartime. In addition, the Board had authority to investigate costs, prices, and profits. The WPTB maintained its headquarters in Ottawa and included a number of commodity and industry coordinators. A large number of regional and field organizations operated throughout the country. The work of the Board also required the creation of several companies: Commodity Prices Stabilization Corporation, Wartime Food Corporation, Canadian Wool Board, Wartime Salvage, and the Canadian Sugar Stabilization Corporation. The WPTB continued its work until 1951 when it was dissolved.

Arrangement and content: The records of the WPTB consist of central registry files covering all administrative and operational activities of the Board (1939-1951), including records created in the offices of the Chairman of the Board and the Secretary. The registry files are organized in such a way to reflect the activities of the following administrations: Foods; Dairy Products; Tea, Coffee, and Spices; Cocoa, Chocolate, and Confectionery; Oils and Fats; Wood and Metal Products; Consumer Credit; Enforcement; Distribution and Trade; Capital Equipment and Durable Goods; Ships' Stores; Research and Statistics; Pulp and Paper; Non-Ferrous Metals; Office Machinery and Hospital Equipment; and the Stove Advisory Committee. Other sub-series include the records of the Simplified Practice Division, Ottawa Prices Division, Emergency Import Control, Consumer Branch, and the Interdepartmental Committee on Industrial Studies. The records of the following wartime companies are also available as part of the same registry system: **Commodity Prices Stabilization Corporation** (1941-1951), **Wartime Food Corporation** (1941-1951), **Canadian Wool Board** (1942-1947), **Wartime Salvage Limited** (1942-1943), and the **Canadian Sugar Stabilization Corporation** (1940-1950).

Records of the Canadian Commercial Corporation: RG 65
1944-1972

9.6 metres

Administrative history: The Corporation was established in 1946 by the *Canadian Commercial Corporation Act* to assume the functions of the Canadian Export Board in the procurement of goods and services in Canada for foreign governments and the United Nations. In 1947, the Canadian Commercial Corporation (CCC) assumed responsibility for the procurement requirements of National Defence until the formation of the Department of Defence Production (RG 49) in 1951. The Corporation was integrated with this Department, now Supply and Services (RG 98), in 1963. In 1976, the CCC assumed more responsibility for facilitating export trade by closer cooperation with the private sector and, two years later, it established headquarters independent of Supply and Services and with majority representation from the private sector on its Board of Directors. The main functions of the Corporation are to assist in the development of export trade and to assist Canadians in procuring goods and services from abroad.

Arrangement and content: The records are subject files which include **Minutes of Meetings of the Board of Directors** (1946-1952) and the **Pricing Committee** (1944-1947), contractual arrangements with the Ming Sung Industrial Company for the export of goods and supplies to

China (1946-1950), general operational and administration records (1944-1952) and a special series on "Operation Pinetree," a joint air defence arrangement between Canada and the United States, primarily contracts for military supplies (1950-1951).

Records of the National Harbours Board: RG 66
1886-1981

59.3 metres

Administrative history: The National Harbours Board (NHB) was created in 1936 as an agency corporation with jurisdiction over various harbours and grain elevators, including the harbours at St. John's, Newfoundland; Halifax, Nova Scotia; Saint John and Belledune, New Brunswick; Chicoutimi, Ha Ha Bay, Quebec City, Sept-Îles, Trois-Rivières, and Montreal, Quebec; Churchill, Manitoba; and Prince Rupert and Vancouver, British Columbia; and the grain elevators at Prescott and Port Colborne, Ontario. Prior to the establishment of the NHB, these harbours were administered by a local board. The Board reports to Parliament through the Minister of Transport.

Arrangement and content: Most of the documents are part of the **Central Registry Files** (1886-1981). There are also **Procedures Manuals** (1954-1959) used in the Board offices, a reference file on the Port of Montreal inspection vessel (1910-1968), financial records (1962-1965), and information on the **Collective Bargaining Agreements** (1943-1967).

Records of the Export Development Corporation: RG 67
1944-1976

24.1 metres

Administrative history: In 1969, the Export Development Corporation succeeded the Export Credits Insurance Corporation, a Crown corporation established in 1944 to promote trade by insuring Canadian exporters against non-payment by foreign buyers. The Corporation received authorization in 1959 to provide financial assistance for the purchase of goods in Canada.

Arrangement and content: In addition to the **Central Registry Files** (1944-1970), this record group contains the **Berne Union Files** (1946-1976) and **Case Study Files** (1954-1974), including enquiry and policy files (1945-1974).

Records of the Registrar General of Canada: RG 68
1760-1988

93.07 metres
650 microfilm reels

Administrative history: The Registrar General registers all instruments including proclamations, commissions, letters patent, and other documents issued under the Great Seal and the Privy Seal of Canada. Prior to Confederation, the registration function was the responsibility of the Provincial Secretary for each province. In 1867, this responsibility was assumed by the Secretary of State (RG 6). It continued in that Department until 1966 when the Registrar General became a separate department. In 1967, the new Department of Consumer and Corporate Affairs (RG 103) took over all the duties and functions of the Registrar General.

Arrangement and content: The records consist mainly of registers, arranged in chronological order, which contain copies of documents registered under the various seals of Canada and include: proclamations, commissions, warrants and pardons, bonds, letters patents, charters of incorporation, land documents, licences, writs, exemplifications, etc. Also included are some original proclamations, letterbooks, receipts, correspondence, and warrants authorizing the use of the Great Seal.

Records of the Centennial Commission of Canada: RG 69
1960-1970

197.1 metres

Administrative history: Planning for Canada's centennial of Confederation was initiated in 1959. The Commission was created as a Crown corporation in 1963 to promote interest in, and to plan and implement programs and projects relating to, the historical significance of Canada's Confederation. To carry out these goals the Commission was organized into various committees whose directors were charged with planning, public relations, and information, as well as responsibility for regional offices. The Commission reported to Parliament through the Secretary of State.

Arrangement and content: The records are organized to reflect the administrative structure and committees system under which the Commission operated. The records of the **Office of the Commissioners and Secretariat** (1960-1970) executive of the Commission include the Minister's Office, the Commissioner and Chairman of the Board, the Associate Director, and the Office of the Assistant to the Commissoners and Secretary of the Centennial Commission. The **Planning Branch**

records (1963-1968) include the office of the Director of Planning, Train and Caravans Division, Cultural Division, Performing Arts Division, Athletic Division, Historical Division, and Voyageur Canoe Pageant and Ceremonial Division. The **Public Relations and Information Branch** (1963-1968) records include the offices of the Director and Assistant Director, the Coordinator of Promotion Abroad, Publicity Division, Information Division, Library and Information Centre, Speakers' Bureau, Promotion Division, and Publication Division. The **Regional Office** (1963-1968) records include the Directors Office and records from representatives in the provinces. There is also a series of Registry Files.

Records of Air Canada: RG 70
1936-1980

97.9 metres
8 microfilm reels

Administrative history: Trans-Canada Air Lines was incorporated in 1937. Its mandate was to provide publicly owned air transportation services, both domestic and international, for passengers, mail, and cargo. Since its incorporation, it has seen a great expansion of its routes and range of activities. Originally a wholly owned affiliate of Canadian National Railways, in 1978 ownership was assumed directly by the federal government. The corporation reports to Parliament through the Ministry of Transport. The name Air Canada was adopted in 1964. As a proprietary Crown corporation, shares in Air Canada have been available to the public since 1988.

Arrangement and content: Much of the material in RG 70 is arranged according to corporate organization. The records of the **President's Office** (1936-1968) cover the administration of the first two presidents, H.J. Symington and G.R. McGregor. The records of the **Secretary's Office** (1937-1978) deal with financial and property matters. **Operating Records** include records of the Operations Branch and the Operations Planning Division, Flight Operations Division, Engineering Division (1937-1970), and Passenger Service Divisions (1937-1971). Records of Purchases and Stores Branch (1937-1970) cover all aspects of the procurement of aircraft facilities and equipment while those of **Marketing Services** (1960-1975) deal with surveys, studies agreements, plans, and programs in the marketing area. Files are also held from Administrative and Corporate Services (1945-1979) primarily concerning internal matters. Other records cover the corporation's activities in the Congo and Guyana and at Expo '67, corporate publications and advertising material, annual and monthly reports and reviews, timetables, fare histories, and route studies.

Records of the Canadian Corporation for the 1967 World Exhibition (Expo'67): RG 71
1962-1969

469.2 metres

Administrative history: The Corporation was federally incorporated in 1962 and was responsible for the planning, organizing, and administration of the 1967 World Exhibition held in Montreal from 28 April to 27 October 1967.

Arrangement and content: The records cover all aspects of the activities of the Corporation and consist of administrative and operational files from the **Board of Directors and the Executive Committee** (1963-1969), the **Secretariat** (1963-1967), **Finance and Administration** (1963-1967), the **Department of Installations** (1963-1967), the **Department of Exhibitions** (1963-1967), the **Vistors' Branch** (1963-1967), and the **Department of Public Relations** (1963-1967).

Records of the Canadian Government Exhibition Commission: RG 72
1875-1978

91 metres

Administrative history: The Canadian Government Exhibition Commission is responsible for Canadian representation at international fairs and exhibitions. The Commission was administered by the Department of Agriculture (RG 17) until 1918, the Department of Immigration and Colonization until 1927, and from then until 1970 was the responsibility of the Department of Industry, Trade and Commerce (RG 20). In 1970, Information Canada (RG 94) assumed the function, but when it was disbanded in 1976 the Commission was transferred to the Department of Supply and Services (RG 98).

Arrangement and content: The records consist of numbered and unnumbered general correspondence, letterbooks, visitors' books, souvenir booklets, plans and designs, preliminary studies, promotional brochures, posters, press clippings, lists of awards, and participants. They are organized by exhibition.

Records of the Solicitor General of Canada: RG 73
1834-1986

428.07 meters
97 microfilm reels
1 data file

Administrative history: The position of Solicitor General was created by statute in 1887 (the act was not proclaimed until 1892) to serve as assistant to the Minister of Justice. In 1966, the Solicitor General became a separate department and was given several responsibilities formerly held by the Department of Justice (RG 13), including federal reformatories, prisons, and penitentiaries parole, and remissions and law enforcement which is handled by the Royal Canadian Mounted Police (RG 18).

Arrangement and content: The records are arranged into four series, namely **Minister's Office** (1960-1980), **Secretariat** (1962-1978), **Penitentiary Branch** (1874-1970), and the **National Parole Board** (1903-1970). The records contain correspondence of the Minister's Office (1967-1980) and the Secretariat (1962-1978); records of Task Forces on justice for victims of crime (1982-1986), the role of the private sector in criminal justice (1972-1979), and the role of the federal government in law enforcement (1973-1981); records of the Chairman, National Parole Board (1903-1970); inmate (1886-1972) and parole (1932-1973) case files; records of Stony Mountain Penitentiary (1871-1984), British Columbia Penitentiary (1878-1975), Dorchester Penitentiary (1932-1982), and Kingston Penitentiary (1934-1974); and operational records of headquarters (1874-1981) and regional offices (1960-1973) on activities in various penal institutions. Material in **electronic form** includes an inmate database for 1978.

Records of the Canadian International Development Agency: RG 74
1950-1977

317.4 metres

Administrative history: The Canadian International Development Agency (CIDA) grew out of the Economic and Technical Assistance Branch of the Department of Trade and Commerce (RG 20). The functions of this Branch were transferred to the External Aid Office, in 1960. In 1968, the office was designated as a department and the name changed to CIDA.

CIDA is responsible for advising the government of Canada on international assistance policies, the level of its contribution, the operation and administration of the program in Asia, francophone and anglophone Africa, the Commonwealth Caribbean, and Latin America. The operations of the Department are administered through several branches which deal with policy, administration, and financial control, specific aspects of the aid program, and its application in principal geographic regions.

Arrangement and content: The records in this group are those created by CIDA and its predecessors, the Economic and Technical Assistance Branch of the Department of Trade and Commerce and the External Aid Office. The records consist of the central registry files of the Economic and Technical Assistance Branch (1950-1968), program and country files (1965-1976) dealing with specific regional programs, bilateral food aid files including the world food aid program (1974-1977), project files pertaining to individual funded projects (1962-1976), Commonwealth Scholarship Fellowship Trainee files (1955-1971), Canadian Commercial Corporation (1974-1977), files relating to the provision of machinery and small equipment to assist in the application of the food aid programs, Warsak Project files (1955-1958) and records of the Development Assistance Committee (1959-1970).

Records of the Economic Council of Canada: RG 75
1960-1984

113 metres

Administrative history: Established in 1963 under the *Economic Council Act*, the Economic Council of Canada (ECC) is a departmental corporation with a mandate to study and recommend measures that will achieve high levels of employment and efficient production to ensure consistent economic growth in Canada. Membership is representative of private business, labour, agriculture, industry, commerce, and the general public. The Council prepares an annual report and various studies on Canada's economic prospects. It reports to Parliament through the Prime Minister.

Arrangement and content: Among the principal series are the **Central Registry Files** (1963-1984) and the files of the **National Productivity Council** (1960-1963). Many of the Central Registry documents are available in both official languages. The **Economic Council of Canada** series (1963-1973) provides information on the transformation of the National Productivity Council into the Economic Council of Canada and on other activities of the ECC.

Pères de famille.... A proof of a 1925 advertisement placed in a French language newspaper in New England to promote the repatriation of French Canadians to Canada. (RG 76, Volume 239, File 146011, Reel C-7388) (C-221058)

Records of the Immigration Branch: RG 76
1865-1988

944.37 metres
740 microfilm reels
16 card trays (index)
20 data files

Administrative history: From 1868 to 1892, the immigration and quarantine functions of the federal government were carried out by the Department of Agriculture (RG 17). In 1892, responsibility for immigration was transferred to the Department of the Interior (RG 15) in order to bring immigration together with land settlement. Records relating to the settlement of Western land itself are found in RG 15. A separate Immigration Branch was established in 1893. In 1917, an independent Department of Immigration and Colonization was created to take the immigration function from Interior. Reduced once again to branch status in 1936 — this time within the new Department of Mines and Resources (see RG 21 and 22) — Immigration has never recovered the departmental rank it enjoyed during this period. As a result of the post-war immigration boom, the Department of Citizenship and Immigration (RG 26) was formed in 1950 by uniting the Immigration Branch, the Indian Affairs Branch from Mines and Resources, and the Citizenship and Citizenship Registration Branches of Secretary of State (RG 6). The Department of Citizenship and Immigration was dissolved in 1966, and immigration became the responsibility of the new Department of Manpower and Immigration (RG 118). Manpower and Immigration was then merged with the former Unemployment Insurance Commission in 1977, forming the Canada Employment and Immigration Commission (CEIC), the principal operational component of the Ministry of Employment and Immigration. The Immigration Branch administers the recruitment, selection, and settlement of immigrants.

Arrangement and content: This record group contains a variety of record types, including central registry files, case files, ledgers, registers, letterbooks, subject files, briefing books, petitions, immigration manuals, circulars, instructions, and forms. The core of the record group consists of the four Headquarters central registry files series which date from 1892. Material in these series is generally of an administrative and policy nature, but also includes some subject files on unusual immigration cases, investigations, or background information on a specific topic. The records document many aspects of Canadian immigration, including the development and implementation of federal immigration policy, the activities of various emigration/immigration agents and organizations, and the opening of the Canadian West. There are also significant records on the immigration of various occupational and ethnic groups. Another significant series of records is the Ships' Passenger Lists (1865 to 1918), which document the arrival of immigrants at Canadian ports, including Halifax, Quebec, Montreal, Saint John, Vancouver, and Victoria. Border Entry Point Lists (1908 to 1918) are also available. The record group also contains case files relating to assisted passage and transportation loans from the 1960s and 1970s, records relating to the Canadian Immigration and Population Study (1969-1976), and files from Immigration Field Offices after the 1970s, including Department of External Affairs Overseas posts which carry out immigration screening functions. The records in **electronic form** in this record group include 60 data files from the Landed Immigrant Data System (LIDS) covering the years 1927-1986. LIDS holds annual vital statistics for each immigrant landed in Canada during a particular year.

Records of the National Research Council: RG 77
1919-1987

242.3 metres
5 microfilm reels

Administrative history: The main functions of the National Research Council (NRC) have been to conduct research and to promote and provide financial and technical support to Canadian scientific and industrial research. Created in 1916, the National Research Council was an outgrowth of the Sub-Committee of the Privy Council on Scientific and Industrial Research. Only in 1925 did the Council's own laboratory operations begin, and by 1929 the Council had established its first four scientific research divisions: Chemistry, Physics (which in 1935 split off into Physics and Mechanical Engineering), Biology, and Agriculture and Research and Information.

The NRC experienced dramatic expansion in response to the demands of World War II. With increasing involvement in radar, sound ranging, and other areas of communication, gunsights and ballistics, biological warfare and aerodynamics, and atomic research, its staff grew from 300 to 3,000 people. Canada's participation in the war also gave rise to new peacetime research responsibilities at the NRC. In the aftermath of the war, the NRC established several new and important scientific divisions: Atomic Energy (1946), the Division of Building Research (1947), the Prairie Regional Laboratory (1948), and the Division of Medical Research (1948). In 1946-1947, the NRC also became responsible for the administration of the recently-established Atomic Energy Control Board at Chalk River (RG 60). Later, the NRC established the Atlantic Regional Laboratory (1952), the National Aeronautical Establishment (1958), the Space Research Facilities Branch (1960s), and the Herzberg Institute of Astrophysics (1975).

Arrangement and content: Included are records from several of the above-named scientific divisions and other parts of the Council. Most of the records fall into one of five main series: **Departmental Correspondence** (1920-1973), consisting of several blocks of administrative and operational files of various divisions from a central registry system established by the NRC in the 1940s; **Laboratory Notebooks** (1933-1973), which pertain to miscellaneous experiments conducted at the NRC laboratories, including the Prairie Regional Laboratory; **Patents** (1924-1968), consisting of a single volume of files for inventions by NRC staff; **Executive Officers** (1939-1967), records from the office of A.G.L McNaughton, C.J. Mackenzie and F.T. Rossner; and **Herzberg Institute of Astrophysics** (1965-1988), chronologically arranged UFO sighting reports.

Records of the Northern Ontario Pipeline Corporation: RG 78
1954-1967

5.1 metres

Administrative history: Established in June 1956, the Northern Ontario Pipeline Corporation supervised the construction of the Northern Ontario section of the all-Canadian natural gas pipeline. The section was then leased, with an option to purchase, to Trans-Canada Pipe Line Limited. In 1963, the latter exercised its option and purchased the Northern Ontario section of the pipeline. The Corporation was dissolved four years later.

Arrangement and content: This record group consists of five series which collectively detail many aspects of the Corporation, from the design and planning stage to its transfer to the private sector. Among these records are those of **Defence Construction Limited** (1954-1967).

Records of the Tariff Board: RG 79
1933-1985

95.8 metres

Administrative history: Established in 1931, the Tariff Board derived its authority from the *Tariff Board Act*, the *Customs Act*, the *Excise Tax Act*, and the *Anti-Dumping Act*. It replaced the Board of Customs created in 1903. Under the *Tariff Board Act*, the Board inquired into and reported on matters relating to goods brought into Canada that were subject to or exempt from customs duties or excise taxes. Under the *Customs Act*, the *Excise Tax Act*, and the *Anti-Dumping Act*, the Board acted as a court to hear appeals of decisions by the Department of National Revenue, Customs and Excise, concerning excise taxes, tariff classification, value for duty, drawback of customs duties, and determination of normal value or export price in dumping matters. Reports of the Board were tabled in the House of Commons by the Minister of Finance (RG 19). In 1989, the Tariff Board was amalgamated with the Canadian Import Tribunal and the Textile and Clothing Board to form the Canadian International Trade Tribunal.

Arrangement and content: The records are arranged in four series which include inquiry reports and advice on matters relating to tariffs, trade, and commerce in **References** (Nos. 1-163), hearing transcripts in **Appeals** (Nos. 1-2540), general correspondence and reports on tariffs and their effect on Canada's trade relations with other countries in **Country Files** (1910-1959), as well as **Administration files** (1933-1977).

Records of the Canadian Grain Commission: RG 80
1912-1973

8.4 metres

Administrative history: Established in 1912, the Board of Grain Commissioners provides general supervision of the physical handling of prairie grain by licensing elevators, inspecting, grading, and weighing grain at terminals, and operating Canadian Government Elevators. The Commission, which operates out of Winnipeg, has reported to the Department of Trade and Commerce (RG 20) from 1912 to 1960, and since that date to Agriculture Canada (RG 17). In 1971, the Board's name was changed to the Canadian Grain Commission.

Arrangement and content: The records consist of central registry files, published reports, and maps. The most comprehensive series in the record group contains subject files (1912-1962), which document grain inspection, weighing, and storage, and the maintenance of elevators.

Records of the Dominion Coal Board: RG 81
1917-1971

30 metres

Administrative history: The establishment of the Dominion Coal Board (DCB) in 1947 marked the last in a long line of government institutions designed to oversee the nation's coal industry. The first of these, the Office of the Fuel Controller, was founded in 1917 to ease coal shortages during World War I. The Dominion Fuel Board, created in 1922, aimed to secure national fuel self-sufficiency. In 1941, most of the Board's functions were transferred to the Coal Administrator of the Wartime Prices and Trade Board (RG 64) to avoid duplication of responsibilities. Shortly after the end of World War II, the DCB was established and given a mandate which included not only the development and marketing of Canadian coal, but also the improvement of working conditions within the collieries. The Board was dissolved and its residual functions transferred to the Department of Energy, Mines and Resources in 1970. Over the course of its history, the DCB and its predecessors have reported to the Departments of Mines, 1922-1936 (RG 86), Mines and Resources, 1936-1941 (RG 21), Labour, 1941-1943 (RG 27), Munitions and Supply, 1943-1948 (RG 28), Trade and Commerce, 1948-1951 (RG 20), Mines and Technical Surveys, 1951-1966 (RG 21), and Energy, Mines and Resources, 1966-1970 (RG 21).

Arrangement and content: The records in this record group are in two series. The **Central Registry Files** (1917-1971) and the **Reference Files** (1927-1970) reflect the Board and it predecessors' involvement in the production, marketing, and use of coal in Canada.

Records of the Immigration Appeal Board: RG 82
1956-1988

265.7 metres

Administrative history: The Immigration Appeal Board (IAB), a successor to the General Board of Immigration Appeals of the Department of Citizenship and Immigration (RG 26), was established in 1967. Completely independent of any other department and reporting to Parliament through the Minister of Employment and Immigration, the Board provided an avenue of appeal to persons ordered deported from Canada or whose sponsored relatives were refused admission. Prior to 1967, deportation orders were carried out by the Immigration Branch (RG 76). The IAB was replaced by the Immigration and Refugee Board in January 1989.

Arrangement and content: Records in this record group consist of case files documenting appeals brought before and decided by the **Immigration Appeal Board** (1956-1967 and 1967-1988). Within the files are documents such as Deportation Orders, Notices of Appeal, Notices of Hearing, Minutes of the Inquiry, Inquiry Officer's Summary, Decisions of the Appeal Board, confidential reports from the Board Chairman to the Minister, and the Notification of the Appellant of the Board's decision. Some files also contain character assessments of the individuals as offered by family doctors or other social agencies, as well as correspondence on the individual's status and the eventual outcome of the case.

Records of Defence Construction Limited: RG 83
1941-1972

23.1 metres

Administrative history: In 1950, Defence Construction Limited was created as a Crown corporation to handle contracts for major military construction and maintenance projects for the Department of National Defence. In 1951, Defence Construction (1951) Limited was created under the authority of the *Defence Production Act* and assumed the responsibilities of the predecessor corporation. Initially, the company reported to Parliament through the Minister of Defence Production but from 1963 through 1965, it reported through the Minister of Industry. Since April 1965, it has reported to Parliament through the Minister of National Defence. The company is responsible for the construction of defence projects which may involve the awarding of construction contracts as well as the supervision of specific projects. In addition to having involvement in projects for National Defence in Canada, the corporation is also involved in construction projects in Europe for DND through NATO agreements and in offering advice and assistance to other government departments and agencies on construction matters.

Arrangement and content: The majority of the records are composed of a series of central registry files concerning the Mid-Canada early warning line and date from 1951 to 1969. Related records of the corporation include records on the acquisition of structural steel for contruction projects (1951-1952), the Pinetree warning line (1951-1959), and the Experimental Army Signal Establishment Project (1959-1960). The record group also includes agreements and general ledgers of income and expenditures (1950-1962). Some records of the Wartime Housing Limited (1941-1951), which was established to provide accommodation for individuals involved in the production of munitions of war and on defence projects, are also included in this record group.

Records of the Canadian Parks Service: RG 84
1873-1986

498.2 metres
45 microfilm reels
988 microfiches
113 data files

Administrative history: Since the initial reservation of the Hot Springs at Banff in 1885, the Canadian Parks Service has grown to encompass more than 30 national parks, more than 70 national historic parks and major sites, and 10 historically significant canal systems. The Canadian Parks Service plans, develops, and operates National Parks and National Historic Parks and Sites. First controlled by the Dominion Lands Branch of the Department of the Interior (RG 15) through its Superintendent of Rocky Mountains Park, Parks became, in 1908, a unit of the Forestry Branch (RG 39) and, in 1911, a separate entity known as the Dominion (later National) Parks Branch. From 1918 to 1966, the Canadian Wildlife Service (RG 109) was a unit within the National Parks Branch. In 1973, Parks acquired control of historic canals previously administered by the Department of Public Works, 1841-1879 (RG 11), Railways and Canals, 1879-1936 (RG 43), and Transport 1936-1973 (RG 12). The Conservation or Parks Canada Program and its predecessors have maintained their distinctiveness as units of several larger departments (for an explanation of these parent organizations, see RG 22). From 1922 to 1964, Wood Buffalo National Park was administered by the Northern Affairs Program and its predecessors (RG 85). In 1979, Parks Canada (as it was called) became part of the Department of the Environment (RG 108), and in 1988 it was renamed the Canadian Parks Service.

Arrangement and content: There are five general series of headquarters textual records which reflect the different file classification systems in use over the years, and one series of miscellaneous headquarters records. Records from the **Secretariat Branch** (1873-1928) cover the growth of national parks in Canada, most particularly Banff, Waterton, Yoho, and the other western parks, as well as Point Pelee. The most extensive series of central registry files in RG 84 are from the **Dominion Parks Branch** (c. 1886-1969); these records relate to all the activities of national and historic parks administration from 1911 to the mid-1960s, such as land leases, wildlife, tourism, wartime work camps, forest fire prevention, and interpretive services. Also included are files on the activities of the National Historic Sites and Monuments Board (see also RG 37). Central registry files from the **Conservation Program of the National and Historic Parks Branch** (1917-1985), which was reorganized in the mid-1960s, continue to cover all aspects of national and historic parks development except wildlife, because the Canadian Wildlife Service (RG 109) was separated from Parks and elevated to Branch status in 1966. Records of the **Parks Canada Program** (1963-1981) cover all traditional park activities, as well as more recent ones such as public hearings, wilderness zones, Federal-Provincial Parks Conferences, and so on. The role of the Canadian Parks Service in recent years has led to the creation of numerous socio-economic surveys, which are presently in **electronic form**. These surveys provide information on park use, outdoor recreation, and tourism.

Records of the Northern Affairs Program: RG 85
1867-1974

393.1 metres

Administrative history: Although the first federal government agency charged exclusively with the administration of the Canadian North was not created until 1921, federal involvement in the North dates from the late nineteenth century. The Klondike Gold Rush of 1898 forced the federal government, through various units within the Department of the Interior, to establish local government services in the Yukon and to expand lands and mining administration to include northern areas. By the end of World War I, wildlife conservation and Arctic sovereignty were added to the Department's responsibilities. This expanding mandate led in 1921 to the creation of the Northwest Territories Branch in Interior (renamed in 1922 the Northwest Territories and Yukon Branch).

By the early 1950s the federal government's approach to the administration of the North had become increasingly interventionist. This was the result of mineral discoveries in the Northwest Territories in the 1930s, the boom generated by wartime projects such as the Alaska Highway and the Canol Pipeline, the role of the North in Cold War diplomatic relations, and the growing need for social and other services in the North. The wide-ranging services provided by the Northern Administration Branch, which was established in 1950, reflect these developments in the post-World War II period. In 1973, the northern services of the federal government were brought together under the new Northern Affairs Program. Although the Department of the Interior was abolished in 1936, the Northern Affairs Program and its predecessors have maintained their distinctiveness as units within a variety of larger departments (for an explanation of these parent organizations, see RG 22).

Arrangement and content: The records of the Northern Affairs Program are arranged in series that reflect the registry or filing systems of the administrative entity that created them. The most important series are the following central registry series: the **Mining Lands and Yukon Branch** (1884-1968) records detail mining and resource development in the North, the records of the **Northwest Territories and Yukon Branch** (1894-1954) provide details on all aspects of federal government involvement in the North for the period from late 1910 to the early 1950s, and the records contained in the central registry series of the **Northern Administration Branch** (1892-1973) chronicle the increasingly active federal involvement in northern development in the 1950s and 1960s. Finally, the central registry series of the **Northern Affairs Program** (1947-1987) documents the work of the Department of Indian and Northern Affairs.

Records of the Mines Branch: RG 86
1911-1968

16.7 metres

Administrative history: The Mines Branch's progenitor, the Office of the Superintendent of Mines, was created in 1884 in response to increased levels of mining activities in the Canadian Rockies. This interest persuaded the Department of the Interior to appoint a field officer, whose responsibilities included the inspection of mining operations, the collection of mining statistics, and the promotion of mining activities on federal lands. This led to the establishment of a Mines Branch in the Department of the Interior (RG 15) in 1903. In 1907, the Mines Branch was coupled with the Geological Survey of Canada (RG 45) to form the new Department of Mines. The Branch continued to gather and verify mining statistics and to collect specimens for experimentation and exhibition. When the Department of Interior was abolished in 1936, Mines was reduced in status within the Mines and Geology Branch of the new Department of Mines and Resources. Over the next 40 years, Mines operated as a branch within several larger departments (for an explanation of these parent organizations, see RG 21). In 1974-1975, the Mines Branch was reorganized and became the Canada Centre for Mineral and Energy Technology (CANMET) within the Department of Energy, Mines and Resources, with research laboratories specializing in energy, mining, mineral sciences, and physical metallurgy.

Arrangement and content: The records are contained in five small series: the records of the **Office of the Director** (1911-1968); the **Mining Roads Division** (1936-1940); the **Fuels and Power Section** (1953-1966); the **Dominion Power Board** (1918-1922); and the **Bureau of Mines** (1920-1960).

Records of the Mineral Resources Branch: RG 87
1885-1961

37 metres

Administrative history: In 1886, the Division of Mineral Statistics and Mines was created within the Geological Survey and Museum Branch of the Department of the Interior (RG 15). The principal functions of this division included the collection of mining statistics, publication of information on mineral resources, analysis of factors affecting the mining industry, development of training programs, and administration of federal mining acts. In 1907, the Geological Survey of Canada was combined with the Mines Branch (RG 86) to form the new Department of Mines. The Mineral Resources and Statistics Division within the new department continued to collect and publish statistics related to mineral production and the metallurgical industries in Canada. In 1920, the statistics gathering responsibilities of the Division were transferred to the Dominion Bureau of Statistics (RG 31), although the Division continued to analyze and interpret such information for government and industry. After 1936, when the Department of the Interior was abolished, the Mineral Resources Division was integrated into a number of larger departments (see RG 21). In 1968, the Division was elevated to branch status within the Department of Energy, Mines and Resources, before being dissolved in a 1973 reorganization of EMR's Mineral Development Sector.

Arrangement and content: The records of the Mineral Resources Branch are contained in three series. The records of the **Mineral Resources and Statistics Division** (1885-1920) relate to the collection, compilation, and publication of mineral production and metallurgical statistics to 1920. The records of the **Mineral Resources Division** (1894-1961) deal with international mining affairs, mining regulations, field reports, and National Energy Board (RG 99) hearings. The records of the **Office of the Special Mineral Projects Officer** (1939-1947) deal primarily with assistance provided by the government to companies involved in exploration for strategic minerals during World War II.

Records of the Surveys and Mapping Branch: RG 88
1857-1971

65.6 metres

Administrative history: The Surveys and Mapping Branch was primarily responsible for developing an accurate, comprehensive, and coordinated survey system for all of Canada. The maps and charts it produced became the basis for the discovery, development, and administration of Canada's resources; as well, they were considered vital to Canada's defence requirements and were an important component in meeting recreational and educational needs. At times, the Branch and its predecessors have also been involved in astronomical and meterological work, irrigation, hydro development, international and interprovincial boundary surveys, and toponymy.

With the transfer of Rupert's Land to Canada in 1869, the Department of Public Works (RG 11) became responsible for surveying the newly acquired territory. In 1871, a Surveyor General of Dominion Lands was appointed in the Department of the Secretary of State (RG 6). The surveying function was transferred to the new Department of the Interior (RG 15) in 1873, where, under various names, it grew to play such an important part in western development that the Surveyor General sometimes attained the rank of Deputy Minister in the Department. After the abolition of the Department of the Interior in 1936, the Surveys and Mapping Branch maintained its distinctiveness as a unit under the Department of Mines and Resources and its successors. (For further explanation of these parent organizations see RG 21.)

Arrangement and content: The records of the Survey and Mapping Branch are arranged under the three major units that comprise the Branch. These include **Office of the Surveyor General** (1875-1969), **Topographical Surveys Branch** (1917-1932), and **Surveys and Mapping Branch** (1857-1971). Under the Office of the Surveyor General, Numbered Registry series (1880-1969) includes files on a wide variety of surveying subjects. The series Letterbooks (1881-1915) contain copies of the Surveyor General's outgoing correspondence. Miscellaneous Survey files (1883-1923) contain records on survey systems, Indian reserves, and boundary surveys. Surveyors' diaries and notebooks are included in the series Dominion Land Surveyors Diaries (1881-1930). The appointments of Surveyors General J.S. Dennis and E. Deville are contained in Commissions of Appointment (1875-1885). Reports on survey operations in British Columbia and the Yukon are included under the Administration series (1917-1931). Files on Survey instrument testing are contained in the series Physical Testing Laboratory (1917-1931). The series Board of Topographical Surveys and Maps (1920-1925) includes minutes of meetings and deliberations concerning map standardization. The series Interdepartmental Committee on Air Surveys (1924-1972) documents the activities of this committee. Under the Surveys and Mapping Branch, the Administration records include a central registry system and records pertaining to map standardization. The series Legal Surveys Division (1918-1959) contains survey notebooks on Indian reserves and files on the transfer of federal survey records to the provinces. Geodetic Survey of Canada (1921-1943) consists of records on the status of Geodetic work in Newfoundland in the 1940s and the reorganization of the Topographic Survey in the 1920s. Finally, records concerning the appointment of Dominion Land Surveyors are found under the series Board of Examiners for Dominion Land Surveyors (1857-1965).

Records of the Water Resources Branch: RG 89
1887-1982

190 metres
2 data files

Administrative history: The Water Resources Branch was established in 1955. Starting in the late-nineteenth and early-twentieth centuries, its predecessor federal agencies were responsible for several aspects of national water resource management: irrigation, reclamation, and water power development, as well as hydrometry and other research activities. The enactment of the *North-West Territories Act* in 1894 vested all water rights in Canada's Northwest Territories (Saskatchewan and Alberta) in the Crown while permitting leasing to private companies for irrigation projects. Over the next 30 years, both the irrigation and water power functions, and later reclamation service, of the federal government were moved through successively different, usually newly-created, branches of the Department of the Interior.

Following the abolition of the Department of the Interior in 1936, the water resource function moved to the new Department of Mines and Resources, where it remained until 1949, and then to several successor departments, including Resources and Development, 1949-1953; Northern Affairs and National Resources, 1953-1966 (see RG 31, 22, and 85). In 1966, the Water Resources Branch was amalgamated with the Marine Sciences Branch of the Department of Mines and Technical Surveys (see RG 21 and 88) to form the Water Group, or Water Sector, of the new Department of Energy, Mines and Resources. After the Department of Forestry and Fisheries was dissolved in the early 1970s, most of its programs, including the water-related functions, were taken over by the new Department of the Environment. Most of the water-related functions now reside in the Department of the Environment's Inland Waters Directorate.

Arrangement and content: The records are organized in five series: reports and various registry files from the **Dominion Water Power and Reclamation Service** (1894-1951), reference material from **Engineering and Water Resources Branch** (1950-1952), a file and engineering reports from the **Water Resources Branch** (1920-1968), files from the registry system of the **Inland Waters Branch** (1881-1948), and files from the **Policy and Planning Branch (Water Sector)** of the Department of Energy, Mines and Resources (1950-1971). Finally, the records also include additional registry files from the Inland Waters Directorate, Inland Waters Branch, and Water Resources Branch. The record group contains in **electronic form** sampling data from the Department of the Environment's NAQUADAT data base for the years 1960-1979.

Records of the National Battlefields Commission: RG 90
1907-1985

.91 metre
1 microfilm reel

Administrative history: The Quebec Landmark Commission was appointed by the mayor of Quebec City to advise on matters relating to the preservation of the city's historic buildings and landmarks. The Commission's 1907 report was the impetus to preserve the historic Plains of Abraham as a National Battlefields Park. Following the report, and on the occasion of the Tercentenary of Quebec in 1908, the National Battlefields Commission was created to acquire, restore, and maintain the historic site and, thereby, commemorate the tercentenary of Quebec in a permanent way. During its early years, the Commission's budget came from public subscriptions and private donations, which were collected to purchase the historic grounds needed for the proposed park. By 1939 the land had been acquired, buildings removed, the park landscaped, Martello towers and other structures restored, and several monuments and numerous historic plaques erected. Later the Commission began to operate on an annual grant from Parliament and reported through the Minister of Indian Affairs and Northern Development, who was responsible through Parks Canada for other national historic sites (see also RG 22). In 1979, the Department of Environment (RG 108) assumed control of Parks Canada (now the Canadian Parks Service).

Arrangement and content: Records consist of National Battlefields Commission reports, microfilmed minutes of proceedings (including highlights of discussions), records of the treasurer concerning the early subscriptions, a list of historical tablets and their locations in Quebec City, landscaping activities, and a list of commissioners and officers until 1969. Also included in RG 90 is a microfilmed copy of the 1907 report of the Quebec Landmark Commission.

Yukon Territorial Records: RG 91
1894-1951

214 microfilm reels

Administrative history: The *Yukon Territory Act* (1898), separated the Yukon District from the old North-West Territories and established it as a distinct political and administrative entity with its own executive, judicial, and legislative institutions. A commissioner administered the district with an appointed (later elected) council. The former reported to the Deputy Minister of the Department of the Interior. The commissioner had legislative powers similar to those of provincial governments, but did not control the development of natural resources and the management of Crown lands. Certain financial and other constraints were also imposed by Ottawa through the Department of Indian and Northern Affairs and its predecessors (RG 15, 22, and 85). Following World War II, more and more control was given to the territorial government over matters of local jurisdiction.

Arrangement and content: The Yukon Territorial records are organized into four series which reflect the methods of arrangement preferred by the agency: numbered files, subject files, letterbooks, and registers and indexes. Among these series, the record group contains Commissioner's Office Letterbooks (1899-1902), Gold Commissioner's Office Letterbooks (1899-1924), and Controller's Office Letterbooks (1899-1902). Together, these series reveal much about the history of the Yukon, including postal service, Indian affairs, Dawson City's water system, territorial road constructions, land sales, applications for town lots, and liquor and marriage licenses.

Records of the Geographic Branch: RG 92
1945-1968

11.6 metres

Administrative history: A Chief Geographer was appointed in 1890 in the Department of the Interior (RG 15) to be responsible for Canadian geographic nomenclature as well as the production of maps and general information on explorations and geography. A separate Chief Geographer's Branch emerged in 1909, which in 1923 merged with the Natural Resources Intelligence Bureau of the Department of the Interior. The collection of geographical data and the control of place names was subsumed in the Surveys and Mapping Branch (RG 88) from 1933 to 1947. In 1947, a Geographical Bureau (Branch in 1949) was reestablished. It reported through three successive departments (for an explanation of these parent organizations, see RG 21). In 1968, when geographical responsibilities were again given to the Surveys and Mapping Branch, the Geographical Branch was abolished.

Arrangement and content: The records in this group focus on the later period of the Branch and have been organized under a single series: **Central Registry Series** (1945-1968). The records cover a wide range of subjects: urban geography, land use studies, area economic surveys, hydrology, and projects falling under the scope of the *Agricultural Rehabilitation and Development Act*. Also included are general files on the administration of the Branch and various Branch publications.

Records of the Atmospheric Environment Service: RG 93
1870-1984

166.2 metres
5 microfilm reels

Administrative history: The first official meteorological observations in Canada took place in 1839 following the establishment of an observatory at Toronto by the Imperial government. The province of Canada took over the observatory in 1853. At the time of Confederation, the meteorological function was placed with the Department of Marine and Fisheries (RG 42). By 1874, the Department decided to create the Canadian Meteorological Office. This Office remained with Marine and Fisheries until 1936, when it moved to the newly-created Department of Transport (RG 12). Finally, in 1971, by which time the Office bore the name Canadian Meteorological Service, the Service was moved to the new Department of the Environment (RG 108) and renamed the Atmospheric Environment Service. The Service provides historical, current, and predictive meteorological data, and sea-state and ice information for all areas of Canada and adjacent waters to various departments of the government, primarily Transport and National Defence. It also provides weather forecasting information to the general public.

Arrangement and content: The records fall into the following series: **Correspondence Registers** (1874-1933), **Numbered Correspondence** (1884-1913), **Numbered Files** (1901-1933), **Quebec Observatory Correspondence** (1840-1947), **Director's Correspondence** (1880-1955), **Instrument Ledgers** (1900-1906), and **Registers of Accounts** (1885-1921). This record group also includes registers of daily weather observations for various locations in Ontario, Quebec, and the Maritimes for the period 1870-1914. Finally, there are numerous files from central registry systems of the Department of Transport and the Department of Environment dating from the 1900s to the 1980s. Correspondence files in the above series deal with departmental, interdepartmental, national, and international meetings, conferences, and symposia; the establishment, operation, and automation of weather stations across Canada; scientific research on various meteorological phenomena and environmental issues; and the development of meteorological monitoring, observation, and data-gathering technologies.

Information Canada Records: RG 94
1969-1976

78.3 metres

Administrative history: Information Canada was established on 1 April 1970 (PC 1970-559, 26 March 1970) on the recommendation of the Task Force on Government Information to act as a central source of public information on federal government policies, programs, and services. It also coordinated federal information programs involving more than one departmental portfolio and initiated special programs where the public need was clear but the responsibility did not fall under the jurisdiction of any one department. It also provided professional resource assistance to help other agencies improve the quality and effectiveness of their information work and marketed and distributed federal publications. Information Canada was disbanded as of 31 March 1976.

Arrangement and content: The records are divided into several series consisting of administrative and operational files, speeches, studies, and minutes of meetings. Included are records from the **Central Registry Files** (1969-1976), the **Office of the Director-General** (1972-1974), the **Communications Branch** (1971-1975), the **Regional Operations Branch** (1971-1975), the **Research and Evaluation Branch** (1971-1975), and the **Atlantic Region** (1973-1976).

Records of the Corporations Branch: RG 95
1967-1973

72 metres

Administrative history: This Branch of the Bureau of Corporate Affairs, Consumer and Corporate Affairs (RG 103), is responsible for the administration of the *Canada Business Corporations Act* and its predecessors. It deals with the incorporation of businesses, the filing of financial statements and annual summaries, and the maintenance of a register of mortgages. This function formerly belonged to the Secretary of State (RG 6), which was transferred to Consumer and Corporate Affairs in 1967. Under the authority of such legislation, the Corporations Branch develops federal commercial institutions through incorporation, and protects investors and creditors in the financial market.

Arrangement and content: The records in this group consist of files relating to companies that have voluntarily surrendered their charter in the process of winding up the company's affairs (1967-1972), and files on companies that have been dissolved (1968-1973).

Records of the Northern Canada Power Commission: RG 96
1898-1970

.9 metre

Administrative history: Established in 1948, the Northwest Territories Power Commission oversaw the construction and operation of power and utility plants in the territories. In 1950, the Commission's mandate was enlarged to include the Yukon Territory and, accordingly, the agency's name was changed to the Northern Canada Power Commission. By agreement with the territorial governments, the federal government transferred the responsibilities of the Commission to the Yukon and Northwest Territories in 1987 and 1988 respectively. The Commission is now defunct.

Arrangement and content: The series which comprise this small record group are for the most part the records of various companies taken over in 1966 by the **Northern Canada Power Commission** (1898-1970). These companies include Northern Light, Power and Coal Limited (1909-1912), Dawson Electric Light and Power Company Limited (1898-1966), Dawson City Water and Power Company Limited (1900-1966), and Yukon Telephone Syndicate Limited (1900-1966).

Records of the Department of Communications: RG 97
1902-1982

188.5 metres
48 data files

Administrative history: The Department was established in 1969 to promote the orderly operation and development of communications in Canada by recommending national policies and programs, encouraging growth and efficiency in current systems, and by assisting in the development of new communications facilities and resources. It is also responsible for managing the radio frequency spectrum in Canada, protecting Canadian interests in international matters, and coordinating telecommunications services for departments or agencies of the federal government. Prior to 1969, many of these duties were performed by the Marine Branch (RG 42), and the Department of Transport (RG 12). Finally, in 1981, responsibility for arts and culture was transferred from the Secretary of State (RG 6) to the Department of Communications.

Arrangement and content: The records are arranged into seven general series. The **Records of the 1969 Central Registry System** (1904-1982), consist of administrative, policy, and operational files, many of which were inherited from its predecessors. The **Records of the 1982 Functional Registry System** (1936-1982), also consist of administrative, policy, and operational files. This series is composed of records coming from the Cultural Policy and Program Branch, the Federal-Provincial Relations Branch, the International Relations Branch, and the Senior Assistant Deputy Minister's Office. The **Records of the Minister's Office** (1968-1975), as well as the **Records of the Deputy Minister's Office** (1968-1978), were comprised of policy files, subject files, and diaries. The **Records of the Communications Research Centre** (1962-1974) consist of printouts of data transmitted by satellites *Alouette I* and *II*. The **Records of Commissions and Committees** (1928-1982), includes briefs, chronological correspondence, hearing schedules, press clippings, and discussion papers. Of particular interest are the records of the Federal Cultural Policy Review Committee (1979-1982), otherwise known as the Applebaum-Hébert Committee. The last series consists of **Miscellaneous Records** (1902-1959), which were not part of any registry system and relate to various topics. **Electronic records** collected from the Department relate to data from the Communications Research Centre's satellite communications program.

Records of the Department of Supply and Services: RG 98
1935-1981

332.3 metres

Administrative history: The Department was created in April 1969 by merging the Departments of Defence Production (RG 49), and Public Printing and Stationery of the Secretary of State (RG 6), the Shipbuilding Branch of the Department of Transport (RG 12), the Office of the Comptroller of the Treasury (RG 55), and the Bureau of Management Consulting Services of the Public Service Commission (RG 32).

As supplier, contractor, printer, and government manager, the Department of Supply and Services provides important shared services in the areas of supply, storage, distribution and printing, accounting and payments, financial auditing, and management consulting. In 1985, in order to combine operations, the Department merged the administration of Supply with the administration of Services.

Arrangement and content: The records are divided into six series. The first contains records of the **Deputy Minister, Services Sector** (1960-1975); more specifically, it contains the documents of H.R. Balls, the former Comptroller of the Treasury, when he was Deputy Minister of Services. The second is composed of **Central Registry Files** (1951-1974) and includes files from many of the Department's branches: Shipbuilding (1965-1974), Industrial and Naval Products Centre (1951-1972), Administrative and Personnel Services Branch (1970-1973), Aerospace and Armament Branch (1957-1975), Purchasing Research Branch (1966-1970), Audit Services Bureau (1961-1969), and Accounting and Bank Management Branch, which contains the government's *Central Control Ledgers* (1961-1976). The third series is on the **Canadian Government Printing Services** (1965-1971) and contains Central Registry Files. The fourth series contains files on **Information Canada** (1961-1970). The fifth series is composed of documents from the **Canadian Commercial Corporation** (1965-1970). Finally, the sixth series contains documents on the **Polymer Corporation** (1942-1970)

Records of the National Energy Board: RG 99
1901-1983

99.2 metres

Administrative history: The National Energy Board (NEB) was established by the *National Energy Board Act* in 1959 to ensure the best use of energy resources in Canada. As a court of record, with the same powers as a superior court, the NEB regulates the construction and operation of all oil and gas pipelines, the export and import of oil and gas, and the export of electrical power. It performs this work through public hearings, investigations, and the issuance of orders and certificates. Following the passage of the *Petroleum Administration Act* in 1975, the Board was also empowered to administer the export charge on crude oil and the pricing of natural gas for interprovincial and international trade. The NEB reports through the Minister of Energy, Mines and Resources (RG 21).

Arrangement and content: The records of the NEB are arranged in a number of series. The **Office of the Chairman** (1901-1979) series contains oil company submissions to the Board, and energy policy reports, briefs, and memoranda. The **Central Registry Office** series (1930-1983) contains information on legislation; liaison between NEB and companies, departments, and governments; NEB involvement on various committees; and a variety of administrative records. Other records in this record group include cancelled gas contracts and agreements, records of Board hearings, submissions presented to the Royal Commission on Energy (the Borden Commission, 1957-1958), and exhibits presented to the NEB by resource development, power, and pipeline companies.

Records of the Canadian Radio-Television and Telecommunications Commission: RG 100
1910-1981

7.5 metres
232 microfilm reels
229 microfiches
8 data files

Administrative history: This Commission, established in 1968 under the provisions of the *Broadcasting Act*, regulates and supervises all aspects of the Canadian broadcasting system. It replaced the Board of Broadcast Governors created in 1958. In April 1976, the CRTC assumed authority over federally-regulated telecommunications carriers formerly exercised by the Canadian Transport Commission (RG 46). The Commission has the power to issue, review, and suspend broadcasting licences. The CRTC reports to Parliament through the Minister of Communications (RG 97).

Arrangement and content: The records are arranged in four general series. **Records of the Office of the Chairman** (1971-1973) consist mainly of reports on public hearings. **Records of the Office of the**

Secretary General (1947-1981) include circular letters, press releases, and the transcripts of the public hearings held by the Commission. **Records of the Office of the Senior Executive Director of Operations** (1970-1979) comprise office files relating to administrative and operational activities, as well as radio and television station program logs. **Reference Material** (1925-1974) consists of records pertinent to broadcasting in Canada gathered by T.J. Allard, a former Director General of the Canadian Association of Broadcasters. **Electronic records** relate to regulation of both public and private broadcasters. The records contain program logs and audience data.

Records of the Crown Assets Disposal Corporation: RG 101
1943-1980

71.6 metres

Administrative history: This agency was originally incorporated in 1943 as the War Assets Corporation Limited. In 1944, it was renamed the War Assets Corporation and its primary responsibility was to dispose of Crown assets that became surplus with the termination of the war. Five years later the corporation became known as the Crown Assets Disposal Corporation and was made responsible for the sale of federal government surplus assets through tenders, auction, or rentals. The Corporation derives its authority from the *Surplus Crown Assets Act* and reports to Parliament through the Minister of Supply and Services.

Arrangement and content: This record group contains central registry files dealing with the administrative and operational functions of the Corporation. Also included are special subject files such as head office papers and records of the United States Army facilities at Prince Rupert, Port Edward, and Watson Island, as well as records relating to contracts and sales.

Records of the Ministry of State for Science and Technology: RG 102
1959-1983

28.7 metres

Administrative history: The Ministry of State for Science and Technology was created in 1971. Its primary purpose has been to formulate and develop policies in relation to the activities of the Government of Canada that affect the development and application of science and technology. Since 1972, the Ministry has undergone numerous reorganizations and mandate changes. The latest of these changes (as of 1988) involves the Department's integration into the new Ministry of Industry, Science and Technology.

Arrangement and content: The records include a chronologically arranged series of copies of ministerial correspondence from the **Office of the Secretary of the Ministry** (1978-1983), agendas, minutes, letters, memoranda, and other items tabled before the Ministry's Executive Committee (1976-1980), and general correspondence from the **Office of the Minister** (1978-1983). Most other records in this record group fall within Science and Technology's central registry system (1964-1978). Among the subjects covered are affiliation with international scientific bodies, liaison with the national and international scientific community, Departmental organization and membership in associations, committees and societies.

Records of the Department of Consumer and Corporate Affairs: RG 103
1914-1980

78.9 metres
13 data files

Administrative history: Established in 1967 following the reorganization and expansion of the Department of the Registrar General, the Department of Consumer and Corporate Affairs is responsible for consumer affairs, corporations and corporate securities, combines, mergers, monopolies, restraint of trade (RG 110), bankruptcies, and insolvencies (RG 104); and patents, copyrights, trade marks, and industrial designs (RG 105). The Minister of Consumer and Corporate Affairs is also the Registrar General (RG 68).

Arrangement and content: The records are arranged in five series relating to the **Minister's Office** (1973-1974), the **Bureau of Intellectual Property** (1934-1972), the **Bureau of Consumer Affairs** (1968-1970), the **Consumer Standards Directorate** (1914-1971), and the **Prices Group** (1970-1975), and consist of correspondence, reports, and working papers on consumer interests and complaints, commodity standards, patents and copyright, and prices and incomes. This record group also contains **electronic records** concerning drug prices (1976), all incorporated companies in Canada (1971-1975), wages and labour force data (1935-1972), and wages and prices inflation (1947-1971).

Records of the Bankruptcy Branch: RG 104
1943-1976

63.8 metres

Administrative history: This agency is administered by the Department of Consumer and Corporate Affairs (RG 103) and is responsible for carrying out the provisions of the federal bankruptcy legislation. Until 1969, the *Bankruptcy Act* was administered by the Department of Justice (RG 13).

Arrangement and content: The records consist of a selection of case files indicating a variety of personal and commercial bankruptcies from all provinces and territories.

Records of Patents, Trade Marks, Copyright, and Industrial Design: RG 105
1861-1985

106.9 meters
140 microfilm reels

Administrative history: The administration of legislation relating to patents, trademarks, copyright, and industrial design is the responsibility of the Bureau of Intellectual Property, Department of Consumer and Corporate Affairs (RG 103). Patent legislation in Upper and Lower Canada was administered by the respective Provincial Secretary, but in 1852 the responsibility was assumed by the Minister of Agriculture. The registration of patents, trademarks, copyright, and industrial design remained with the Department of Agriculture (RG 17) until 1918. At that time, it was transferred to the Department of Trade and Commerce (RG 20), and in 1927 became the responsibility of the Secretary of State (RG 6). Finally, in 1967 Consumer and Corporate Affairs assumed control of the administration of intellectual property.

Arrangement and content: The records are arranged in chronological order and consist of the following types of documents: industrial design registrations; copyright registrations and indexes; trade mark applications and indexes to registrations; exemplifications of patents of inventions and copies of Canadian and American radio patents; and registers of correspondence and letterbooks on copyright, trade marks, and industrial designs.

Records of the Office of the Co-ordinator, Status of Women (Status of Women Canada): RG 106
1965-1976

6.1 metres

Administrative history: The Office of the Co-ordinator was established in 1971, as a result of the recommendations of the Royal Commission on the Status of Women (Bird Commission, 1967-1971, RG 33/89). Originally affiliated with the Privy Council Office (1971-1976), the Office became an independent department on 1 April 1976, and is now known as Status of Women Canada. Its chief responsibilities are to analyse and develop policies regarding women, to coordinate requests from women's groups and to disseminate information on federal government programs. Its mandate also involves ensuring that the federal government adheres to its commitment to promote equality between the sexes in every sector of Canadian society.

Arrangement and content: This record group includes working papers, minutes of meetings, reports, proceedings, and documentation on projects resulting from the various International Women's Year Programs (1975). Other documents include correspondence, articles, and studies on day care.

Records of the Office of the Administrator, *Anti-Inflation Act* : RG 107
1975-1984

41.7 metres

Administrative history: The Office of the Administrator, *Anti-Inflation Act*, was created in December 1975 as one of three components to administer the program of restraint on prices and incomes. The Office of the Administrator was responsible for enforcing the provisions of the *Anti-Inflation Act* and making binding decisions where contravention of the guidelines existed. The Office was empowered to investigate all aspects of disputes arising from the *Act* and to issue legally binding orders, which set a maximum limit on a price or wage increase. The Office of the Administrator ceased to exist after 1980.

Arrangement and content: The records consist of case files, compliance files, general files, copies of orders, and administrative correspondence.

Records of the Department of the Environment: RG 108
1899-1983

366.4 metres
113 data files

Administrative history: The Department of the Environment was established in 1971 to bring together the principal government activities relating to environmental quality in general and pollution in particular. Building on the basis of the Department of Fisheries and Forestry (RG 23 and 39), the Department incorporated the Canadian Wildlife Service (RG 109) from Indian Affairs and Northern Development (RG 22); the Water Sector (RG 89) from Energy, Mines and Resources (RG 21); Air Pollution Control and Public Health Engineering from National Health and Welfare (RG 29); Canadian Meteorological Service (RG 93) from Transport (RG 12); and the Canada Land Inventory from Regional Economic Expansion (RG 124). The Department has undergone numerous organizational changes since 1971. In 1974, the fisheries units began reporting through a separate Minister of State and became, in 1979, with some water resources units the Department of Fisheries and Oceans (the Inland Waters Directorate remained a part of Environment Canada). Parks Canada (RG 84) was transferred to Environment from Indian Affairs and Northern Development in 1979, and the Canadian Forestry Service was transferred to Agriculture Canada (RG 17) in 1985.

Arrangement and content: Holdings in this record group include central registry files of an administrative and operational nature covering pollution, various conservation acts and legislation such as the *Canada Water Act*, research activities, and task forces on environmental issues. As environmental concerns do not often respect legal boundaries, many of the records demonstrate the Department's involvement with international and provincial governments, private organizations, and international associations such as the World Meterological Organization. There is a significant volume of records from the Minister's and Deputy Minister's offices covering Departmental activities policy for the years 1965 to 1979. In addition to textual records, **electronic records** contain survey information from the 1960s and 1970s on water quality, municipal waterworks and waste water management systems, park forest resources, tree data (1918-1930), and forest weather data (1931-1966).

Records of the Canadian Wildlife Services: RG 109
1905-1978

126.37 metres

Administrative history: Following the Treaty for International Protection of Migratory Birds in 1916 between Canada and the United States and the subsequent *Migratory Bird Convention Act* of 1917, a Dominion Ornithologist was appointed in the Dominion Parks Branch in 1918 (RG 84 and 22). When responsibility for wildlife protection in the North (RG 85) and national parks was added in 1919, this official became the Supervisor of Wildlife Protection. The Supervisor's unit assumed more responsibility in 1930 when under the new *National Parks Act*, Canada's national parks became absolute game sanctuaries and all bird sanctuaries became federal preserves. By 1947, this unit of the National Parks Branch grew into the Dominion Wildlife Service (its name was changed to the Canadian Wildlife Service (CWS) in 1950) and, in 1966, the CWS formed an independent branch in the Department of Indian Affairs and Northern Development (RG 22). In 1971, the CWS joined the new Department of the Environment (RG 108). It is primarily responsible for migratory bird regulations, and also advises the provinces and national parks on wildlife management and endangered species.

Arrangement and content: Although the Canadian Wildlife Service has always been part of a larger branch or department and used its file classification system, CWS operational records have nevertheless remained separate and apart. By far the majority of records are **Central Registry Files** (1909-1970), covering CWS administrative and operational activities. These files reflect a wide range of responsibilities such as enforcement of wildlife legislation, ornithology in general, mammals, fish, reptiles, and wildlife management. Other records include field office records of the **Canadian Reindeer Project** (1929-1973), which document the day-to-day management of reindeer herds maintained in the Mackenzie Delta region. A small portion of records concerns bird banding throughout North America in the twentieth century, correspondence of the **Chief Migratory Bird Officer of the Prairie Provinces** (1920-1954), and a bibliography of unpublished CWS studies and reports (1978).

Records of the Combines Investigation Branch: RG 110
1910-1965

24 metres

Administrative history: The Combines Investigation Branch was established in 1910 as part of the Department of Labour. It was charged under the *Combines Investigation Act*, 1910, with the investigation and prosecution of alleged combines. The statutory power of the office was amended in 1923 with the passage of a wider *Combines Investigation Act*. In 1947, the Branch was transferred to the Department of Justice, and it remained there until it was replaced in 1967 by the Bureau of Competition Policy, part of the newly formed Department of Consumer and Corporate Affairs (RG 103).

Arrangement and content: The records of the Combines Investigation Branch are arranged into one series, **Investigations Records**, and mainly consist of material collected for different cases pursued under the *Combines Investigation Act*. There are also files of memoranda to the Minister of Justice (1945-1958).

Records of the Public Service Staff Relations Board: RG 111
1958-1986

33.7 metres
37 data files

Administrative history: The Public Service Staff Relations Board (PSSRB) was established in 1967 by the *Public Service Staff Relations Act*. It was set up to serve as a third party in disputes between the public service and the employer. The PSSRB also took over responsibility for the Pay Research Bureau, which is responsible for studying pay scales and benefits from both outside and inside the federal public service in order to assist the collective bargaining process.

Arrangement and content: This record group is arranged into six series, reflecting the administrative structure of the Board and its predecessor, the Pay Research Bureau. The records of the **Pay Research Bureau** series (1958-1973) consist of memoranda and studies on the pay of various occupational groups. The records of the **Preparatory Committee on Collective Bargaining** (1963-1967) consist of general administrative files, correspondence, and committee minutes on the subject of collective bargaining in the federal public service. The **Central Registry** records (1968-1986) are files on individual unions or staff associations and their presentations to the collective bargaining process. The **Legal Services** records (1970-1975) were created by the Bryden

Committee in its study of the *Public Service Staff Relations Act*. The records of the **Chairman's Office** (1962-1975) contain files of the first PSSRB Chairman, Mr. J. Finkelman, and include general material on collective bargaining in the public service. The **Mediation Service** series (1968-1980) consists of case files, each containing a request for a conciliator, an acknowledgement, the Treasury Board response, the notice of appointment, and the report of the conciliation. Material in **electronic form** (1973-1982), consists of pay research data including such vocational groups as Foreign Service Officers, Police, and Hospital Employees.

Records of the Bilingual Districts Advisory Board: RG 112
1970-1975

4.5 metres
1 data file

Administrative history: In order to ensure that services are provided to Anglophone and Francophone minorities by all the public authorities concerned, the Royal Commission on Bilingualism and Biculturalism (1963-1971) recommended the creation of bilingual federal districts. For this reason, the *Official Languages Act* of 1969 provided for the creation of a Bilingual Districts Advisory Board responsible for designating bilingual districts. Boards made up of five to ten commissioners were to be created to represent the residents of various provinces or major regions in Canada. Because the government felt that the recommendations of the First and Second Boards (created in 1970 and 1972 respectively) were not compatible with its official-languages policy, the project to create bilingual districts was abandoned.

Arrangement and content: This record group contains the minutes of the meetings of the First and Second Boards, reports, recommendations, briefs, and correspondence with various federal government departments. It also contains the proceedings of public hearings held in the various areas across the country, statistical data from the cooperation agreements with various federal departments, and briefs or presentations by individuals. Records in **electronic form** consist of a bilingual district survey of 1972.

Records of the Office of the Chief Electoral Officer (Elections Canada): RG 113
1867-1980

6 metres
994 microfilm reels
6 data files

Administrative history: The Office was established in 1920 under the provisions of the *Dominion Elections Act*. Before that time, elections were conducted pursuant to provincial legislation and, between 1867 and 1884, held at different times in different ridings. The right to vote or run for office was restricted to a minority comprised of male property owners. The *Dominion Elections Act* of 1874 established the secret ballot and the holding of a general election on the same day in every riding in the country. From 1920 on, the Office of the Chief Electoral Officer was responsible for the electoral process. The Office has been a department since 1952 and reports directly to Parliament through the President of the Privy Council. Known today as Elections Canada, the Office continues to provide direction and carries out the general administrative duties related to federal elections, including the election of members to the Councils of the Yukon and Northwest Territories.

Arrangement and content: This record group contains correspondence, reports (1867-1980), and documentation on the appointment of the Chief Electoral Officer and deputy returning officers and on the operational administration of the Office. In also contains microfilm series of **Notices of Grant of Poll** (1945-1979) describing the geographical boundaries of ridings in every province and listing of the candidates and the electors who nominated them. Other microfilm series contain documents such as **Preliminary Voters Lists** (1935-1979) for provincial general elections and by-elections and for elections to the **Councils of the Northwest Territories** (1951-1975), statistical and comparative data on **Election Returns** (1867-1980), and statutory reports of the Chief Electoral Officer. **Electronic records** consist of election results since 1972 and include data on individual ridings, candidates, number of votes received, and expenditures.

Records of the Food Prices Review Board: RG 115
1973-1976

21.5 metres
10 data files

Administrative history: Established in May 1973 (PC 1973-1239), the Board was created to conduct research and prepare publications on food price changes; the Board also conducted investigations, monitored prices, and recommended policies. The FPRB was disbanded in October 1975 to make way for the Anti-Inflation Board.

Arrangement and content: Most of the documents are contained in the Central Registry Files of the **Office of the Secretary** (1973-1975). All of these documents describe the administrative and operational activities of the Board and its role, responsibilities, and functions. This record group also contains a large number of newspaper articles (1973-1975) providing an idea of the view that the written media had of the Board's role, and **electronic records** which mostly consist of surveys carried out during the 1970s on food prices in a number of major Canadian cities.

Records of the Company of Young Canadians: RG 116
1965-1976

39.4 metres

Administrative history: The Company of Young Canadians was created in 1966 as a federal government corporation designed to harness the energies and talents of Canadian youth for useful social and economic development projects. The *Company of Young Canadians Act* empowered the corporation to encourage voluntary programs for social, economic, and community development in Canada or abroad. The Company reported through the Secretary of State (RG 6) and was permitted to liaise with federal, provincial, or other interested government authorities in furthering of its objectives. In early 1976, the Company was abolished.

Arrangement and content: The records in this record group consist primarily of operational and subject central registry files containing correspondence, internal studies, consultants' reports, day-books, project information sheets, and other miscellaneous records documenting the Company's activities, functions, projects, and ultimate dissolution. The bulk of records date from 1970-1976 and cover such topics as the Company's organization, staff relations, project program activities, community planning, and housing development.

Records of the Office of the Custodian of Enemy Property: RG 117
1903-1975

97.57 metres
183 microfilm reels

Administrative history: The Office of the Custodian of Enemy Property was established in 1916 under the authority of the *War Measures Act* of 1914. Its function was to take action under the Trading with the Enemy regulations, including the seizure and liquidation of enemy property. From 1919 to 1939, it served the function of administering war claims and reparations. With the outbreak of World War II, the Office once again was given responsibility for Trading with the Enemy regulations. In 1942, the role of the Custodian was expanded to include the administration of property taken from Japanese Canadians.

Arrangement and content: The records in this record group are arranged into four main series according to the offices of the Custodian and the functions these offices served. The **Headquarters Series** (1903-1975) consists of files covering the whole range of activities engaged in by the Office, but deal mostly with the war claims and reparations functions of the Office. The **Clearing Office Records** (1920-1939) come from the London Office of the Custodian, which was established to act with its British counterpart in dealing with war claims and reparations. The records in the **Vancouver Office Series** (1904-1958) consist of information on the seizure of property from individuals of enemy origin and the evacuation of Japanese Canadians from the coastal areas of British Columbia. The **War Claims Branch Series** (1950-1969) contains records concerning the claims of Canadians for compensation for deaths, loss of property, or personal injury as a result of World War II.

Records of the Department of Employment and Immigration: RG 118
1918-1985

1,084.26 metres
19 data files
86 microfilm reels

Administrative history: The Department of Manpower and Immigration was established in 1966 to maximize the development and utilization of Canada's human resources. The new department united under one umbrella the Immigration Branch of the former Department of Citizenship and Immigration (RG 26 and 76) and a number of components formerly part of the Department of Labour (RG 27). In 1977, under the authority of the *Employment and Immigration Reorganization Act*, the

Unemployment Insurance Commission (RG 50) was merged with the Department of Manpower and Immigration to create Employment and Immigration Canada. The newly created Employment and Immigration Canada, comprised of the Canada Employment and Immigration Commission and its allied Department of Employment and Immigration, would henceforth be responsible for all federal employment, unemployment, and immigration programs in Canada.

Arrangement and content: This record group is comprised of operational central registry files as well as numerous case file series created by Employment and Immigration Canada and its predecessor agencies. The central registry files contain policy records, research studies, planning and evaluation reports, administrative files, and project case files detailing Departmental programs and services. The policy and operational records document Employment and Immigration Canada's programs, services, and research activities in the employment, unemployment, and immigration areas. The record group also includes **electronic records** containing data on such employment creation programs as the Canada Manpower Training Program, Canada Works, Opportunities for Youth, and the Local Initiatives Program.

Records of the Canadian Habitat Secretariat: RG 119
1966-1979

58.2 metres

Administrative history: Habitat: the United Nations Conference on Human Settlements was held in Vancouver from 31 May to 11 June 1976. Canadian activity as host and participant was coordinated through the Canadian Habitat Secretariat, a separate agency responsible to the Minister of State for Urban Affairs (see RG 127). The development of Canada's policy positions on the matters facing the Conference also rested with the Secretariat.

Arrangement and content: The records consist of the administrative papers and speeches of the Secretary General for the Canadian Habitat delegation, and the records of the Commissioner General of Habitat, the senior government official responsible for the Conference. **Habitat History Files** (1975-1976) consist of such items as newspaper clippings, Habitat reports, and publications. **Central Registry Files** (1973-1976) of the Canadian Habitat Secretariat also exist, as well as files created on an individual basis by officers of the Secretariat. In addition, the record group includes the files of **An Association in Canada Serving Or-**

ganizations For Human Settlements (ACSOH) (1972-1979), which handled the hosting arrangements for Habitat Forum, the collective name for all non-governmental activities related to the Conference.

Records of the Royal Canadian Mint: RG 120
1899-1974

14 metres

Administrative history: The Royal Canadian Mint has been in operation since 1908, when it was established as the Ottawa Branch of the Royal Mint in London. It became a fully Canadian enterprise in 1931 and operated as a branch of the Finance Department (RG 19) until 1969, when it was reconstituted as a Crown corporation reporting to Parliament through the Minister of Supply and Services (RG 98). The Mint produces and arranges to produce coins for Canada and other countries; melts, assays, and refines gold and other metals; buys and sell such metals; fabricates and engraves dies for coinage, medals, and official seals; and administers various *Currency Act*, Mint, and Exchange Fund regulations.

Arrangement and content: This record group contains accounting records (1907-1973), including wage books (1908-1931) and bullion records (1907-1973). It also contains some of the documents of the first Deputy Master of the Mint, James Bonar (1899-1907), and records created by the Office of the Master of the Mint.

Records of Canadian Patents and Development Limited: RG 121
1919-1981

43 metres

Administrative history: Canadian Patents and Development Limited (CPDL) is a Crown corporation incorporated in 1947 as a wholly owned subsidiary of the National Research Council (NRC) (RG 77). It was originally created to handle patentable inventions of NRC and other government-financed research. By the passage of the *Public Servants Inventions Act* in 1954, CPDL became the prime patenting and licensing agency for inventions by public servants; these inventions belong to the federal government.

Arrangement and content: Most of the documentation consists of individual files (1926-1981) on inventions, as well as other documents dealing with the Committee on Patents (1949-1971) and the Inventions Board of the National Research Council (1939-1947).

Records of the Commissioner of Official Languages: RG 122
1970-1984

7.5 metres
1 data file

Administrative history: The Office of the Commissioner of Official Languages was created in 1968 on the recommendation of the Royal Commission on Bilingualism and Biculturalism (1963-1971). The first *Official Languages Act* (1969), which resulted from this Commission, made the Commissioner an indepentent officer who reports directly to Parliament. He is to act as the ombudsman who protects all Canadians' language rights, the auditor who ensures that federal departments and agencies comply with the requirements of the *Act*, and the promoter who encourages equal status for both official languages through his efforts.

Arrangement and content: This record group contains correspondence, reports, and opinions on the *Official Languages Act* submitted by students, public servants, or private citizens. It also contains comments sent by children who used the *Oh! Canada* kit. Other kinds of documents deal directly with the Commissioner's three responsibilities mentioned above. Therefore, this group contains complaint and follow-up files, Departmental policies and procedures, reports on meetings, conferences, workshops, and symposiums, and correspondence on language disputes and departmental audits. This group also brings together information on liaison policies and programs and promotional material used in protecting the rights of minority language groups. Records in **electronic form** consist of a survey of second official languages used by graduates in the public service, 1976.

Records of the Canadian Film Development Corporation (Telefilm Canada): RG 123
1961-1976

1.2 metres

Administrative history: Also known commercially since 1983 as Telefilm Canada, the Canadian Film Development Corporation was established in 1967. The objective of the Corporation is to promote the development of a feature film industry in Canada through investment in production, loans to producers, awards, and advice and assistance in distribution and administrative matters. The Canadian Film Development Corporation reports to Parliament through the Department of Communications (RG 97).

Arrangement and content: The records of the Canadian Film Development ment Corporation consist of **Central Registry Files** (1961-1976). The majority of these files are of an operational nature and are representative of the various activities for which the corporation is responsible.

Records of the Department of Regional Economic Expansion: RG 124
1949-1982

338.6 metres
3 data files

Administrative history: The Department of Regional Economic Expansion was established in 1969 to consolidate the federal government's efforts to alleviate regional disparities and to stimulate economic development and employment in disadvantaged areas of Canada. The Rural Development Branch of the Department of Forestry and Rural Development (RG 39) was the basis for the consolidation, for it administered the *Agricultural and Rural Development Act* (ARDA), the Fund for Rural Economic Development (FRED), and the *Maritime Marshland Rehabilitation Act*. To this core was added the Area Development Agency from the Department of Industry, the Atlantic Development Board, the Experimental Projects Branch (Canada NEWSTART Program) from Manpower and Immigration (RG 118 and 27), and the *Prairie Farm Rehabilitation Act* from Agriculture (RG 17). New programs initiated included Special ARDA in 1972, which was designed to provide aid to areas with high populations of native people, and General Development Agreements and Special Area Agreements with the provinces and territories. In 1983, the Department of Regional Economic Expansion was amalgamated with components of the Department of Industry, Trade and Commerce (RG 20) to form the Department of Regional Industrial Expansion.

Arrangement and content: Headquarters Records (1949-1979) created by the Department include files from the Office of the Deputy Minister (1968-1977), concerning the establishment and reorganization of the Department; committees and meetings; and relations with other departments, with provinces, and with the private sector. Other Headquarters records are Administrative files (1963-1972), and ARDA files created by the Department of Agriculture (1963-1972), covering ARDA activity both in general and individual cases. The records include additional ARDA material located in **Regional Records** (1975-1977) created in the **Western Region**. Records from the **Atlantic Development Board** include files created by the Planning Division (1962-1972), and others relating to the Conference on Poverty and Opportunity (1965). Files created by the **Canadian Council on Rural Development** (1965-

1979) cover administrative subjects as well as plans, activities of the Council, research, reports, and studies. **Electronic records** in this record group consist of the New Brunswick NEWSTART quality of life surveys for 1971-1973.

Records of the Supreme Court of Canada: RG 125
1875-1987

99.35 metres
492 microfiches

Administrative history: The Supreme Court of Canada, consisting of the Chief Justice and eight puisne judges, was established in 1875 by the *Supreme and Exchequer Court Act*. Since the abolition of appeals to the Judicial Committee of the Privy Council in 1949, the Supreme Court has been the highest court for legal issues within federal and provincial jurisdiction and the highest court of appeal for both civil and criminal cases in Canada. Questions of interpretation of the Constitution, the Charter of Rights and Freedoms, the *British North America Act*, as well as issues of federal and provincial jurisdiction may be referred to the Supreme Court.

Arrangement and content: The majority of these records are consecutively numbered case files for the appeals heard by the Supreme Court from 1876 to 1922 and can be found by using the docket books and indexes. There are also judges rolls, administrative records, and judgement books and reports on bills which are indexed alphabetically.

Records of the Mackenzie Valley Pipeline Inquiry: RG 126
1970-1977

15.8 metres

Administrative history: Under Commissioner Mr. Justice Thomas R. Berger, the Mackenzie Valley Pipeline Inquiry investigated the conditions under which a pipeline might be built down the Mackenzie Valley. The Inquiry paid particular attention to the social, economic, and environmental impact of such a project on the corridor and on native land claims. The Inquiry began in 1974 and reported in 1977.

Arrangement and content: The records of the Mackenzie Valley Pipeline Inquiry are arranged in several series of hearing transcripts, exhibits, and administrative files. Because of its many and widely scattered hearings, and the numerous exhibits it received, the Inquiry's records mirror every aspect of life in the North.

Records of the Ministry of State for Urban Affairs: RG 127
1969-1979

317.81 metres
1 data file

Administrative history: Created in 1971 as a policy development agency, the Ministry of State for Urban Affairs (MSUA) sought to develop federal policies to enhance the effects of growing urbanization, to integrate such urban policies with other federal programs and policies, and to coordinate urban development with the provinces and municipalities. One highlight of the Ministry's work was the 1976 United Nations Conference/Exposition on Human Settlements, held in Vancouver and widely referred to as Habitat (RG 119). The Ministry was abolished in 1979. Uncompleted projects were transferred to the Canada Mortgage and Housing Corporation (RG 56), Transport (RG 12), and Public Works (RG 11).

Arrangement and content: The records include subject files from the **Office of the Secretary** (1972-1978) as well as **Central Registry Records** (1969-1979). The latter are of an administrative and operational nature, and contain both subject and project files covering such areas as urban development, transportation, intergovernment liaison, MSUA projects, federal land management policy, minutes of the Executive Committee of Urban Affairs, and the Habitat Conference held in Vancouver. Three smaller series consist of MSUA studies and reports, issues of the bulletin *Urbanite*, and subject files dealing with various topics that fell within the Ministry's legislative mandate. Another series contains files related to MSUA's involvement in the United Nations Economic Commission for Europe (ECE) Seminar on the impact of energy on human settlements (held in Ottawa in 1977). Records in **electronic form** consist of data on neighbourhood perceptions in Montreal for 1973-1974.

Records of the Medical Research Council: RG 128
1954-1983

193.2 metres

Administrative history: The Medical Research Council was originally an autonomous subsidiary of the National Research Council (RG 77) from 1960 to 1969. At this time, it was designated as a departmental Crown corporation within the meaning and purpose of the *Financial Administration Act*. The Council's primary function is to promote and support research in the health sciences in Canada. To do this, the Council maintains a program of support to research trainees and investigators, to research programs in Canadian universities, hospitals and related institutions, and to promotional activities designed to stimulate new research efforts. It is also responsible for administering the Queen Elizabeth II Research Fund. The Council consists of 21 members appointed by the Governor-in-Council, and reports to Parliament through the Minister of National Health and Welfare (RG 29).

Arrangement and content: Records in this record group include central registry files relating mainly to liaison functions, grant files, administrative and subject files, committee minutes, research files, operational reports, and grant committee award files. There are many grant files on individual researchers, including applications, reports on finished research, evaluations, and requests for extensions. Another significant series consists of the correspondence, speeches, reports, and research material from the first fulltime President of the Council, Dr. G. Malcolm Brown (1965-1977). The Grant Committee files contain information on the activities of the five grant committees: Clinical Metabolism Endocrinology and Nephrology, Molecular Biology, Microbiology and Pathology, Metabolism and Endocrinology, and Psychology. There are also cooperation and liaison files relating to the Council's relations with agencies and departments such as National Defence, the World Health Organization, and the Ontario Ministry of Health.

Records of the Science Council of Canada: RG 129
1947-1978

70.1 metres
3 data files

Administrative history: The Science Council of Canada was established in 1966. The Council assesses the scientific and technological resources of the federal government as well as Canada's national scientific requirements and potentialities. The Council is also responsible for increasing public awareness of scientific and technological issues and opportunities and the interdependence between government, industry, universities, and citizens in the development and application of science and technology. To fulfil these responsibilities, the Council creates temporary study cells which conduct specialized studies and inquiries whose results are made available to the public.

Arrangement and content: The records consist of Council meeting files and documentation created and collected during the preparation of Council studies of the computing sciences, earth sciences, psychology, climate, and population; energy, mathematics, health sciences, policies and poisons, northern development, knowledge, power, and public policy; policy objectives for basic research, industrial research, and environmental impact. **Electronic records** in this record group pertain to the education-employment adjustment processes of Canadian graduates in the physical sciences during the late 1950s to 1960s and a survey of university graduates in the mathematical sciences in 1975.

Records of the Northern Pipeline Agency: RG 130
1977-1978

4 metres

Administrative history: Following the 1968 discovery of oil and gas at Prudhoe, Alaska, both Canada and the United States entered into negotiations to determine the best means of bringing those resources to southern markets. In 1977, the two countries signed an agreement to construct a pipeline through Canada. Subsequently, the Northern Pipeline Agency (NPA) was established to implement the agreement. Receiving federal powers previously invested in Indian and Northern Affairs (RG 22), Energy, Mines and Resources (RG 21), and the National Energy Board (RG 99), the NPA became the central regulatory body for controlling the social, economic, and environmental impact of the pipeline.

Arrangement and content: Arranged in a single series, the **Office of the Northern Pipeline Commissioner, Registry Records** (1977-1978), the records of the Northern Pipeline Agency and its predecessor, the Northern Pipeline Commission, document the role of the federal government in the construction of the pipeline for the years 1977-1978.

Records of the Ministry of State for Social Development: RG 131
1978-1982

10.2 metres

Administrative history: The Ministry of State for Social Development was created in June 1980 under the *Ministers of State Act*. Its specific mandate was to "formulate and develop new and comprehensive policies in relation to the activities of the government of Canada that affect the welfare of the individual and social development." This so-called "super ministry" supported the Minister of State for Social Development who through the Cabinet Committee on Social Development was responsible for planning and coordinating social policies and related priorities across all relevant federal government departments. In 1984, as part of federal government reorganization, the Ministry of State for Social Development was disbanded.

Arrangement and content: This record group contains operational and subject central registry files of the Consultative Group on Métis and Non-Status Indians as well as office files of the Special Assistant to the Minister. The former files concern joint provincial government and native associations' discussions on socio-economic development, while the latter files largely consist of reports and studies on various Canadian social development organizations such as the Native Council of Canada, Constitutional Review Commission, Acadia Student Union, and various Canadian universities.

Records of the National Museums of Canada: RG 132
1881-1983

18.6 metres
3 data files

Administrative history: The National Museums of Canada (NMC) was a Crown corporation established in 1968 by the *National Museums Act.* It incorporated within a single administration seven organizational elements: the National Gallery of Canada; the National Museum of Man, the Canadian War Museum; the National Museum of Natural Sciences; the National Museum of Science and Technology, the National Aviation Museum; the National Programmes Branch; the Corporate Management Branch; and the Corporate Services Branch. The NMC reported to Parliament through the Minister of Communications (RG 97), and was charged with the task of demonstrating the products of nature and the works of man, with special but not exclusive reference to Canada, so as to promote interest therein throughout Canada and to disseminate knowledge thereof. The NMC was declared defunct in 1987, and its responsibilities were transferred to the component museums and the Department of Communications.

Arrangement and content: At present, these records are from only one of the national museums, the National Museum of Natural Sciences. One series includes the field notebooks and correspondence of early botanists, while another consists of the field notebooks of noted vertebrate palaeontologists. The record group also contains operational files of the Museum (1964-1983); these files cover such topics as the Museum's relationship to provincial museums, federal government departments, various groups and associations, and its role in a number of committees (such as the International Committee on Museums). **Electronic records** consist of an inventory of North American Salix (1966-1977), and a valid species records file for 1968-1979.

Records of the Social Sciences and Humanities Research Council of Canada: RG 133
1978, 1981

2 data files

Administrative history: The Social Sciences and Humanities Research Council (SSHRC) was created in 1977. In 1978, it took over the programs previously administered by the Humanities and Social Sciences Division of the Canada Council (RG 63). The SSHRC administers federal funds for university-based research and other scholarly activity. It is primarily a grant-giving body, and its mandate is to promote and assist research and scholarship in the social sciences and humanities, and to advise the Minister on issues relevant to research directed to the Council's attention.

Arrangement and content: Holdings in this record group are in **electronic form** and consist of a survey of Canadian Archives for 1978 and a survey of Canadian law professors in 1981.

Records of Eldorado Nuclear Limited: RG 134
1932-1982

63 metres

Administrative history: Eldorado Gold Mines Limited staked its first mineral claims on Great Bear Lake in the Northwest Territories in 1930. By 1933, the company had begun to mine pitchblende ore at Port Radium which it transported to its radium refinery at Port Hope, Ontario. The company's mine, refinery, and transportation subsidiary, Northern Transportation Company Limited, were nationalized by the Canadian government in 1944.

The company's first mine shaft at Beaverlodge, Saskatchewan, was completed in 1952, one year before the company obtained its second wholly owned subsidiary, Eldorado Aviation Limited. During the 1950s the company reported to Parliament through the Minister of Munitions and Supply, Defence Production, and Trade and Commerce. When the Department of Energy, Mines and Resources was created in 1966, Eldorado reported through its minister. Eldorado was privatized in 1985. The records of Eldorado Nuclear Limited are closely related to the records of the Atomic Energy Control Board (RG 60); the AECB deals with national security and health and safety aspects of nuclear substances.

Arrangement and content: The records of Eldorado Nuclear Limited are primarily contained in three series. The corporate records (1932-1975), relate to all aspects of the company's activities. The records of various senior management personnel are contained in the administration series (1937-1981). Senior personnel maintained a separate filing system and these records augment the historical record of the activities of the company. In 1976, Eldorado created a historical project to locate and review sources relating to the history of the company. All aspects of the company's history are covered by the contents of the files. Of particular note are the files created in 1945 when J. Grant Glassco was appointed by the Minister of Munitions and Supply, to investigate all Eldorado activities. Other records provide detailed information on the company's uranium mining operation at Beaverlodge (1953-1982).

Records of the Canadian Wheat Board: RG 135
1948-1974

.9 metre
92 data files

Administrative history: The Board of Grain Supervisors (established in 1917) and the first Canadian Wheat Board (established in 1919) were the first federal marketing agencies for prairie wheat. These organizations were disbanded in 1920. During the depression of the 1930s, the federal government again intervened in prairie grain marketing by establishing the Canadian Wheat Board in 1935. In 1949, the Wheat Board's jurisdiction was expanded to include oats and barley.

Arrangement and content: The **electronic records** in this record group contain information which dates from 1952 to 1983 on the subjects of wheat acreage and yields, rail transportion of grain, grain storage, and individual grain producers. This record group contains a series of textual records produced by the Office of the Secretary between 1948 and 1974. The textual records are maintained in the Winnipeg Federal Records Centre. In order to use this material, the Government Archives Division in Ottawa must be contacted to obtain correct references and guidelines to possible services.

Records of the Pacific Pilotage Authority: RG 136
1904-1970

.3 metre

Administrative history: The New Westminster Pilotage Authority was formed in 1879. The chairman and commissioners were appointed by Order-in-Council on the recommendation of the Minister of Marine (later the Minister of Transport). It was responsible for providing pilot service for the port and surrounding coast of New Westminster, British Columbia. It became part of the British Columbia Pilotage Authority (now the Pacific Pilotage Authority), a Crown corporation, in 1970.

Arrangement and content: The records consist of three minute books and one folder giving the boundaries of the New Westminster pilotage district at the various stages of its development. These records are maintained in the Vancouver Federal Records Centre. The Government Archives Division in Ottawa must first be contacted to obtain correct references and guidelines to possible services.

Records of the Canadian Unity Information Office: RG 137
1977-1985

44.5 metres
41 data files

Administrative history: The Canadian Unity Information Office (CUIO) was established under the Secretary of State in 1977 (responsibility was transferred to the Minister of Justice in 1978) as an information centre to counteract the "subversive propaganda" generated by the Parti québecois government in the period leading up to the referendum in Quebec in 1980. CUIO's mandate was to gather, develop, and distribute information on Canadian federalism and federal programs and services, to guide and advise private groups and federal departments and agencies in coordinating components of their information programs relating to national unity. Shortly after the Conservative government came to power in the fall of 1984, it decided to terminate the mandate of CUIO as of 31 March 1985.

Arrangement and content: The records include correspondence, research material, public opinion polls and surveys, data, reports, and material on conferences, committees, and media coverage. They relate to a wide variety of topics including: constitutional issues, the Quebec referendum, Western Canadian attitudes, attitudes of francophones outside the province of Quebec, and related matters affecting national unity, as well as records on federal government programs and services, the use of national symbols, media surveys, exhibitions, special events, and the history of the CUIO. Much of the survey and opinion poll data exists in **electronic form.**

Records of the National Library of Canada: RG 138
1947-1981

42.9 metres

Administrative history: The National Library of Canada (NLC) originated with the Canadian Bibliographic Centre, established in May 1950. Following the recommendations of the Royal Commission on National Development in the Arts, Letters and Sciences, 1949-1951 (the Massey Commission), the NLC was formally created in June 1952. The NLC now operates under the provisions of the *National Library Act* of 1969 and reports to Parliament through the Minister of Communications (RG 97). The mandate of the National Library is to ensure that Canada's published heritage is preserved and made available to all Canadians. The Library collects and promotes the Canadian literary heritage by cataloguing the nation's publications to facilitate their retrieval, availability, and use; by providing reference, information, and referral services; and by coordinating and participating in national and inter-national library programs and activities.

Arrangement and content: The records contain registry and non-registry files created in the Public Services Branch of the National Library, and include registry files created in the Office of the Director and Assistant Director of the Branch. These records document the growth and expansion of public services in the Library since the 1950s, especially with the use of automated systems. The record group also contains operational files from the Office of the National Librarian (1966-1980), the Cataloguing Branch (1968), the Public Services Branch (1970-1978), the Collection Development Branch (1970-1979), the Director General (1962-1981), General Administration records (1973-1974), and Canadian Library Association material (1947-1970).

Records of the Canadian Hydrographic Service: RG 139
1948-1979

4 metres

Administrative history: The Canadian Hydrographic Service (CHS) was established in 1883 to conduct hydrographic surveys and to publish, maintain, and distribute navigational charts, sailing directions, and tide tables needed to permit safe and efficient navigation in all navigable

Canadian waters. Since its inception, the Service has come under the mandate of a number of different government departments but it has always maintained a separate identity. When first established, the CHS was under the authority of the Department of Marine and Fisheries (RG 23) where it remained until 1910 when it was transferred to the Department of Naval Service (RG 24). With the creation of the Department of Mines and Resources in 1936, the CHS was placed under its jurisdiction (and that of its many successors, see RG 21). In 1971, it was transferred to the newly created Department of the Environment (RG 108), and again in 1979 to the Department of Fisheries and Oceans (RG 23).

Arrangement and content: There are three series of records: the **Ships Logs** (1905-1967), **Fieldbooks** (1883-1909), and **Registry Files** (1938-1965), as well as two groups of records which were collected from separate units within the Service. The Arctic Data Section (1948-1962), includes mostly published materials (charts, reports, articles, etc.) on a broad spectrum of topics related to the North. The Marine Sciences Branch (1962-1979), consists of reports from the CHS manuscript series on descriptive, theoretical, and methodological issues in oceanography, hydrography, and limnology.

Records of the Canadian Livestock Feed Board: RG 140
1962-1973

3.3 metres

Administrative history: The Canadian Livestock Feed Board is a Crown corporation which reports to Parliament through the Minister of Agriculture (RG 17). The Board was created by the *Livestock Feed Assistance Act* of 1967. Its principal objectives are to ensure the availability of feed grain in eastern Canada and British Columbia, the availability of adequate grain storage space in eastern Canada, and the reasonable stability and fair equalization of feed grain prices in eastern Canada, British Columbia, the Yukon, and Northwest Territories. The Board allots subsidies to assist in the transportation of feed grain under the Feed Freight Equalization Program. It also studies feed grain requirements and advises the Minister on the availability of feed grain storage facilities and on all questions related to the price of feed grain. Data on domestic feed grain prices, shipments, and markets are published. The Board's functions were closely related to those of the Canadian Federation of Agriculture, the Canadian Grains Council, the Board of Grain Commissioners (RG 80), and the Canadian Wheat Board (RG 135).

Arrangement and content: Central registry files comprise the records of the Canadian Livestock Feed Board. Records dating from 1962 to 1966 deal with the Winnipeg Grain Exchange and the allocation of responsibility for feed grain administration in the federal government. Records created between 1967 and 1973 document meetings of the Board's Advisory Committee as well as labour disputes affecting grain handling.

Records of the Standards Council of Canada: RG 141
1970-1984

17.4 metres

Administrative history: The *Standards Council of Canada Act* was passed in 1970 to foster and promote voluntary standardization in fields relating to the construction, manufacture, quality, performance, and safety of buildings, structures, manufactured articles, products and other goods, not expressly provided by law as a means of advancing the national economy, benefiting the health, safety, and welfare of the public, assisting and protecting consumers, facilitating domestic and international trade, and furthering international cooperation in the field of standards. Between 1970 and 1984 the Standards Council of Canada, while not an agent of Her Majesty, was funded by government appropriations. In 1984, the Standards Council of Canada became a Crown corporation.

Arrangement and content: The records consist of central registry files which include minutes of the Executive Committee, advisory and sector committees, and general operational records.

Records of the Law Reform Commission of Canada: RG 143
1973-1975

2 data files

Administrative history: The Law Reform Commission of Canada was established to study and review Canadian legislation systematically and continuously. Under an act of Parliament which came into force by proclamation on 1 June 1971, this permanent body was given the mandate to improve, modernize, and reform the laws and regulations that make up Canada's legal system. The Commission seeks to eliminate anachronisms, anomalies, and obsolete regulations, and also to reconcile differences and conflicts between the formulation and application of the law. In formulating legal methods and concepts to ensure that the law reflects changes in society and the individuals composing it, the Commission seeks to reflect the distinctive concepts and institutions of the common law and civil law systems in Canada.

Arrangement and content: This record group consists of two **data files,** each containing a series of questionnaires sent to Crown attorneys and defence lawyers across the country. Among other things, these consultations led to recommendations promoting the abolition of preliminary hearings and the adoption of a formal system of rules and procedures for discovery.

Subject Index to Record Groups

Cultural and Communication Records
RG 3   Post Office
RG 37   National Archives of Canada
RG 41   Canadian Broadcasting Corporation
RG 53   National Film Board
RG 63   Canada Council
RG 69   Centennial Commission
RG 71   Expo' 67
RG 72   Canadian Government Exhibition Commission
RG 94   Information Canada
RG 97   Communications
RG 100 Canadian Radio-Television and Telecommunications Commission
RG 123 Canadian Film Development Corporation
RG 132 National Museums of Canada
RG 133 Social Sciences and Humanities Research Council
RG 137 Canadian Unity Information Office
RG 138 National Library of Canada

External Affairs Records
RG 7   Governor General's Office
RG 25   External Affairs
RG 51   International Joint Commission
RG 74   External Aid Office

Financial Records
RG 16   National Revenue — Taxation
RG 19   Finance

RG 54	Comptroller of the Treasury
RG 55	Treasury Board
RG 58	Auditor General
RG 75	Economic Council of Canada
RG 120	Royal Canadian Mint

Public Works and Economic Records
RG 11	Public Works
RG 20	Trade and Commerce
RG 31	Statistics Canada
RG 34	National Capital Commission
RG 40	Insurance
RG 62	Loto Canada/Sports Pool
RG 64	Wartime Prices and Trade Board
RG 65	Canadian Commercial Corporation
RG 67	Export Development Corporation
RG 79	Tariff Board
RG 95	Corporations Branch
RG 103	Consumer and Corporate Affairs
RG 104	Bankruptcy Branch
RG 105	Patents, Trademarks, Copyrights, and Industrial Designs
RG 107	Administrator, *Anti-Inflation Act*
RG 110	Combines Investigation Branch
RG 115	Food Prices Review Board
RG 121	Canadian Patents and Development Limited
RG 124	Regional Economic Expansion
RG 141	Standards Council of Canada
RG 144	Trade Negotiations Office

Administration of Justice
RG 13	Justice
RG 18	Royal Canadian Mounted Police
RG 73	Solicitor General
RG 125	Supreme Court of Canada
RG 143	Law Reform Commission of Canada

Military Records
RG 8	British Military and Naval Records
RG 9	Militia and Defence
RG 24	National Defence
RG 28	Munitions and Supply
RG 38	Veterans Affairs

RG 44   National War Services
RG 49   Defence Production
RG 57   Emergency Measures Organization
RG 61   Allied War Supplies Corporation
RG 83   Defence Construction Limited
RG 117   Office of the Custodian of Enemy Property

Mineral and Energy Resources Records
RG 21   Energy, Mines and Resources
RG 60   Atomic Energy Control Board
RG 81   Dominion Coal Board
RG 86   Mines Branch
RG 87   Mineral Resources Branch
RG 99   National Energy Board
RG 134   Eldorado Nuclear Limited

Natural Resources and Scientific Research Records
RG 15   Interior
RG 17   Agriculture
RG 23   Fisheries and Oceans
RG 39   Forestry
RG 77   National Research Council
RG 80   Canadian Grain Commission
RG 84   Parks Canada
RG 89   Water Resources Branch
RG 90   National Battlefields Commission
RG 92   Geographical Branch
RG 93   Atmospheric Environment Service
RG 102   Science and Technology
RG 108   Environment Canada
RG 109   Canadian Wildlife Service
RG 128   Medical Research Council
RG 129   Science Council of Canada
RG 135   Canadian Wheat Board
RG 140   Canadian Livestock Feed Board

Northern Records
RG 22   Indian Affairs and Northern Development
RG 78   Northern Ontario Pipeline Corporation
RG 85   Northern Affairs Program
RG 91   Yukon Territorial Records
RG 96   Northern Canada Power Corporation

RG 126   Mackenzie Valley Pipeline Inquiry
RG 130   Northern Pipeline Agency

Parliamentary and State Records
RG 1   Executive Council
RG 2   Privy Council Office
RG 4   Provincial and Civil Secretaries' Offices: Quebec, Lower
         Canada, and Canada East
RG 5   Provincial and Civil Secretaries' Offices: Upper Canada and
         Canada West
RG 6   Secretary of State
RG 14   Parliament
RG 32   Public Service Commission
RG 33   Royal Commissions
RG 35   Interdepartmental Committees
RG 36   Boards, Offices, and Commissions
RG 47   Federal-Provincial Conferences
RG 58   Auditor General
RG 59   Electoral Boundaries Commission
RG 68   Registrar General
RG 98   Supply and Services
RG 101   Crown Assets Disposal Corporation
RG 111   Public Service Staff Relations Board
RG 112   Bilingual Districts Advisory Board
RG 113   Chief Electoral Officer
RG 122   Commissioner of Official Languages

Social Development and Citizenship Records
RG 10   Indian Affairs
RG 22   Indian Affairs and Northern Development
RG 26   Citizenship and Immigration
RG 27   Labour
RG 29   National Health and Welfare
RG 50   Unemployment Insurance Commission
RG 56   Canada Mortgage and Housing Corporation
RG 76   Immigration Branch
RG 82   Immigration Appeal Board
RG 106   Office of the Co-ordinator, Status of Women
RG 116   Company of Young Canadians
RG 118   Employment and Immigration
RG 119   Canadian Habitat Secretariat
RG 127   Urban Affairs

RG 131 Ministry of State for Social Development
RG 145* Canada Labour Relations Board
        * This is a newly created record group for which no
        description is yet available.

Surveying Records
RG 45   Geological Survey of Canada
RG 48   Dominion Observatories
RG 88   Surveys and Mapping Branch
RG 89   Water Resources Branch
RG 139 Canadian Hydrographic Service

Transportation Records
RG 12   Transport
RG 30   Canadian National Railways
RG 42   Marine Branch
RG 43   Railways and Canals
RG 46   Canadian Transport Commission
RG 52   St. Lawrence Seaway Authority
RG 66   Canada Ports Corporation
RG 70   Air Canada
RG 136 Pacific Pilotage Authority

Alphabetical Index to Record Groups

151

Appendix _____

The following publications were produced by the Government Archives Division and its predecessors, the Public Records Division, the Federal Archives Division, and the Machine Readable Archives Division. They can be obtained free of charge, subject to availability, upon request from Marketing and Distribution, National Archives of Canada, 344 Wellington Street, Room 136, Ottawa, Ontario, Canada, K1A 0N3.

RG 10 *Records Relating to Indian Affairs.* Ottawa, 1975.
RG 20 *Records of the Department of Trade and Commerce.* Ottawa, 1977.
RG 27 *Records of the Department of Labour.* Ottawa, 1988.
RG 31 *Records of Statistics Canada.* Ottawa, 1977.
RG 33 *Records of Federal Royal Commissions, Volume 1: Series 33/1 to 33/75.* Ottawa, 1989.
RG 39 *Records of the Canadian Forestry Service.* Ottawa, 1982.
RG 43 *Records of the Department of Railways and Canals.* Ottawa, 1986.
RG 46 *Records of the Canadian Transport Commission.* Ottawa, 1984.
RG 55 *Records of the Treasury Board.* Ottawa, 1977.
RG 69 *Records of the Centennial Commission of Canada.* Ottawa, 1979.
RG 81 *Records of the Dominion Coal Board.* Ottawa, 1981.
RG 84 *Records of Parks Canada.* Ottawa, 1985.
RG 88 *Records of the Surveys and Mapping Branch.* Ottawa, 1979.
RG 115 *Records of the Food Prices Review Board.* Ottawa, 1979.
RG 126 *Records of the Mackenzie Valley Pipeline Inquiry.* Ottawa, 1980.

Major Accessions, 1974/75. Ottawa, 1975.
Major Accessions, 1975/76. Ottawa, 1977.
Major Accessions, 1976/77. Ottawa, 1977.
Major Accessions, 1977/78. Ottawa, 1978.
Accessions, 1978/79. Ottawa, 1979.
Accessions, 1979/80. Ottawa, 1980.
Accessions, 1980/81. Ottawa, 1981.
Accessions, 1981/82. Ottawa, 1982.

Accessions, 1982/83. Ottawa, 1983.
Accessions, 1983/84. Ottawa, 1984.
Accessions, 1984/85. Ottawa, 1985.
Accessions, 1985/86. Microfiche. Ottawa, 1986.
Accessions, 1986/87. Microfiche. Ottawa, 1987.

General Guide Series: Government Archives Division. Ottawa, 1991.

General Guide Series 1983: Machine Readable Archives Division. Ottawa, 1984.

Machine Readable Archives: Alcohol, Drug and Tobacco Use Data Files. Ottawa, 1982.

Machine Readable Archives Bulletin. Ottawa, began in 1983. (Now called *Machine Readable Records Bulletin*)

Machine Readable Archives: Catalogue of Holdings. Ottawa, 1981.

Machine Readable Archives: Recreation and Leisure Data Files, Ottawa, 1983.

Material Relevant to British Columbia Labour History in RG 27, Canada Department of Labour Records. Ottawa, 1975.

Sources for the Study of Canada's National Parks. Ottawa, 1979.

Sources for the Study of the Canadian North. Ottawa, 1980.

Sources for the Study of the Second World War. Ottawa, 1979.

The following publication may be obtained by writing to Canada Communication Group — Publishing, Supply and Services Canada, Ottawa, Ontario, Canada, K1A 0S9.

A Catalogue of Census Returns on Microfilm 1666-1881. Canada: $10.00; Other Countries: $12.00.

Collection de guides généraux ⸻

Division des archives gouvernementales

Guide compilé par

Cynthia Lovering

Introduction de

Terry Cook

 Archives nationales
du Canada

National Archives
of Canada

Données de catalogage avant publication (Canada)
Archives nationales du Canada.

Division des archives gouvernementales

(Collection de guides généraux)
Texte en français et en anglais disposé tête-bêche.
Titre de la p. de t. addit.: Government Archives Division.
2ᵉ éd. --cf. Av.-pr.
Publ. antérieurement sous les titres: Division des archives fédérales. Archives publiques Canada, 1983; et, Division des archives ordinolingues. Archives publiques Canada, 1984.
Cat. MAS no SA41-4/1-1-1991
ISBN 0-662-58186-5 : gratuit

1. Archives nationales du Canada. Division des archives gouvernementales. 2. Archives publiques--Canada. 3. Archives--Canada. I. Lovering, Cynthia. II. Archives publiques Canada. Division des archives fédérales. III. Archives publiques Canada. Division des archives ordinolingues. IV. Titre. V. Titre: Government Archives Division. VI. Collection: Archives nationales du Canada. Collection de guides généraux.

CD3623.N37 1991   354.710071'46   C91-099203-7F

Couverture : L'édifice du Parlement, v. 1880; on peut voir l'édifice central du premier parlement qui a été complété en 1878 et détruit par un incendie en 1916. Photographie par Samuel McLaughlin, photographe du ministère des Travaux publics (détail). (C-3760)

Le papier de cette publication est alcalin.

Archives nationales du Canada
395, rue Wellington
Ottawa (Ontario)
K1A 0N3
(613) 995-5138

©Ministre des Approvisionnements et Services Canada 1991
Nᵒ de cat. : SA41-4/1-1-1991
ISBN : 0-662-58186-5

Table des matières ⎯⎯⎯⎯

Avant-propos ———

Depuis 1872, les Archives nationales du Canada ont réuni une quantité impressionnante de fonds et de collections d'archives. Au cours des dernières années, le nombre de documents a doublé tous les dix ans, et l'avènement de nouvelles technologies et de nouveaux supports d'information en a accentué la diversité.

Voilà bientôt quarante ans, les Archives nationales du Canada ont mis sur pied un programme complet de préparation d'inventaires et d'instruments de recherche destinés à informer les chercheurs et les autres personnes intéressées sur le contenu des fonds et à leur en faciliter la consultation. Soucieuses d'établir des catalogues collectifs couvrant la presque totalité des documents d'archives importants, les Archives ont fait appel, dans certains cas, à d'autres établissements canadiens.

Bien que ce programme ait permis de décrire une part importante des ressources documentaires des Archives nationales et de publier sur papier et sur microfiches des guides des principaux documents et séries, le grand public, les chercheurs et même les archivistes canadiens ont de la difficulté à évaluer de façon précise et exacte l'énorme quantité de documents conservés aux Archives nationales du Canada.

Aussi a-t-il paru utile, voire nécessaire, de publier une brève description des ressources et des services mis à la disposition des usagers, comme première étape à l'utilisation des fonds d'archives. Chaque division de la Direction des ressources historiques a donc préparé des volumes commodes, publiés collectivement en 1983 sous le titre de *Collection de guides généraux* et renfermant les descriptions des documents publics ou privés déposés aux Archives nationales. Il s'agit ici de la deuxième édition, qui réunit et met à jour les précédents volumes sur la Division des archives fédérales et la Division des archives ordinolingues. Cette nouvelle édition reflète à la fois la réorganisation des Archives nationales, qui a amené la fusion de ces deux divisions en 1986, et l'augmentation spectaculaire des archives gouvernementales au cours des sept dernières années.

Je désire remercier Eldon Frost, directeur de la Division des archives gouvernementales, et son personnel, ainsi que la Division des communications de la Direction des programmes publics, pour leur participation à la préparation et à la publication de ce nouveau guide.

Jean-Pierre Wallot,
Archiviste national.

Préface ━━━━━━━━━

Les Archives gouvernementales assurent la conservation permanente des documents textuels et informatiques du gouvernement fédéral qui présentent une valeur durable. Ces fonds constituent la mémoire collective du gouvernement et sont tout aussi essentiels à la poursuite des activités gouvernementales qu'aux recherches historiques en général. La division sélectionne, conserve et met à la disposition du public les documents historiques importants, conformément aux lois applicables en la matière.

Les versions antérieures de ce guide ont été publiées en 1978 et 1981 dans les *Documents historiques du gouvernement du Canada*, puis sous les titres *Division des archives fédérales* (1983) et *Division des archives ordinolingues* (1984) dans la *Collection de guides généraux*. Révisé et mis à jour, le nouveau guide vise à faire connaître les activités de la division aux chercheurs, aux fonctionnaires et au public, et à donner une description concise des fonds de documents gouvernementaux textuels et informatiques dont elle a la garde. Les deux premières parties décrivent les activités et l'organisation de la division, les principes qui ont servi à classer les documents originaux, ainsi que les services et les outils de référence disponibles. La troisième partie explique la nature des notices et la façon d'utiliser le guide pour préparer des recherches dans les fonds de la division. Le corps du texte se compose de notices pour chaque groupe d'archives, qui comprennent un bref historique du ministère ou de l'organisme, un court paragraphe expliquant les fonctions et une description sommaire des documents. Ces renseignements permettront de mieux comprendre la nature des archives conservées et les rapports administratifs entre les divers organismes.

Cette publication n'aurait pu voir le jour sans les efforts conjugués des membres du personnel qui ont recueilli et décrit les archives du gouvernement fédéral. Les notices des groupes d'archives ont été rédigées par les archivistes de la division. Plusieurs d'entre eux ont révisé et commenté le texte. Cynthia Lovering a coordonné la publication. Terry Cook a rédigé tous les textes d'introduction. Les historiques suivent souvent de près ceux qui ont été rédigés par Glenn T. Wright et Terry Cook pour des éditions antérieures. Les travaux de Katharine Gavrel et de Walter Meyer zu Erpen sur les documents informatiques ont également été très utiles à cette fin.

Eldon Frost, Directeur de la
Division des archives gouvernementales.

1 Profil de la Division des archives gouvernementales —

La Division des archives gouvernementales (DAG) évalue, sélectionne, conserve et préserve des archives du gouvernement du Canada, en plus d'offrir un service spécialisé de consultation. Son mandat s'applique à tous les documents textuels (sur papier), micrographiques et informatiques du gouvernement fédéral ayant une valeur archivistique ou historique durable, à l'exception des collections spéciales de documents architecturaux, cartographiques, iconographiques, photographiques, cinématographiques et sonores. Conformément à sa mission, la division s'assure que tous les dossiers et documents informatiques des ministères sont examinés, détermine la valeur informative réelle ou éventuelle de ces documents, et veille à leur transfert régulier et continu à la Direction des ressources historiques. À cette fin, la division collabore étroitement avec le personnel de la Direction des documents gouvernementaux, ainsi qu'avec les représentants des divers ministères et organismes fédéraux. Elle conserve en permanence les documents qui ont une valeur juridique, financière, intrinsèque ou une valeur de témoignage durable pour le gouvernement. La division garde en permanence les documents qui fournissent des renseignements utiles sur la création et l'application des lois, politiques et programmes d'un ministère (y compris sur leur élaboration et leurs répercussions sur les citoyens), ou sur le fonctionnement et l'organisation d'un ministère (y compris sur les sources d'idées et les méthodes de mise en œuvre des décisions). Enfin, elle conserve les dossiers qui présentent un intérêt documentaire pour les chercheurs, comme c'est souvent le cas pour les documents informatiques. À l'aide de ces critères, la division essaie de sélectionner et de conserver les archives essentielles aux fonctionnaires du gouvernement, aux chercheurs du secteur privé et à la mémoire collective des Canadiens.

Après avoir choisi les documents qu'elle gardera en permanence, la division effectue des recherches et prépare des inventaires, des instruments de recherche et des dossiers documentaires sur les documents informatiques, afin d'offrir au public un service spécialisé de consul-

1

tation. Grâce au microfilmage et à la restauration, ainsi qu'à la duplication et au rebobinage des bandes magnétiques, les Archives nationales tentent de conserver les fonds souvent fragiles dont elles ont la garde.

En plus des documents des institutions fédérales soumises à la *Loi sur les Archives nationales du Canada,* la division acquiert et rend disponibles les archives des organismes juridiques, du Parlement, des commissions d'enquête et d'autres organismes du gouvernement fédéral. Enfin, depuis que le gouvernement a intensifié sa politique de décentralisation, la division évalue aussi la valeur historique des documents des bureaux régionaux et locaux de l'administration fédérale.

Fonds d'archives

Les fonds de la Division des archives gouvernementales comprennent plus de cinquante kilomètres de documents textuels, dix-neuf mille bobines de microfilm et plus de deux mille fichiers de données. Ils traitent de tous les aspects de l'histoire canadienne du dix-huitième siècle à nos jours. Les acquisitions ont permis de constituer un corpus documentaire qui attire chaque année des milliers de chercheurs et renferme des documents extrêmement divers : traités indiens d'une valeur inestimable remontant à plusieurs siècles, fichiers informatiques tout récents sur l'état de l'environnement, dossiers du Cabinet, documents des bureaux régionaux les plus éloignés, documents de politique établis aux paliers les plus élevés, données sur de simples particuliers, documents essentiels à la protection des droits des citoyens contre les erreurs administratives, renseignements indispensables à tous les domaines de la recherche universitaire et historique.

Les fonds se présentent sous des formes très variées : chemises, registres d'enregistrement du courrier, rapports, enquêtes, bases de données, registres, index et autres documents semblables manuscrits, dactylographiés et informatiques. Normalement, les photographies, les affiches, les cartes, les plans et les autres documents imprimés qui se trouvent dans le dossier d'origine y demeurent. Toutefois, les articles qui font partie d'une entité homogène facilement identifiable sont transmis aux autres divisions de la Direction des ressources historiques responsables de ces documents, ou recueillis directement par celles-ci. C'est le cas des photographies, peintures, dessins et affiches conservés par la Division de l'art documentaire et de la photographie; des cartes, plans, dessins architecturaux et industriels déposés à la Division des archives cartographiques et architecturales; des articles reliés à l'histoire orale, aux films, aux émissions de radio et de télévision recueillis par la Division des archives audio-visuelles. La Division des manuscrits con-

serve les papiers personnels de premiers ministres, de ministres et de hauts fonctionnaires. Elle a aussi la garde des documents ministériels tels que définis dans la *Loi sur les Archives nationales du Canada,* ainsi que les documents de quelques organismes antérieurs à la Confédération, placés notamment dans les groupes d'archives RG 1, 4, 5, 8 et dans certaines parties des RG 7 et 14.

Historique

Le gouvernement canadien nomme un archiviste en 1872, mais celui-ci n'est pas responsable des archives du gouvernement fédéral, ce qui aurait dû normalement constituer la principale activité d'un service national d'archives. Pendant de nombreuses années, la Direction des archives — alors intégrée au ministère de l'Agriculture — limite ses activités aux papiers personnels et aux documents des gouvernements de France et de Grande-Bretagne relatifs au Canada. Cependant, la conservation des archives fédérales n'est pas pour autant complètement négligée : en 1873, un conservateur des documents publics est nommé au Secrétariat d'État pour classer les documents officiels et historiques du gouvernement canadien. Il consacre de nombreuses années à répertorier les archives du Haut et du Bas-Canada.

De plus en plus préoccupé par l'absence d'un système uniforme de conservation des archives ainsi que par la perte de documents anciens au cours de plusieurs incendies désastreux, le gouvernement fédéral décide alors de créer une commission ministérielle des documents publics. À la suite de son enquête, la commission recommande en 1898 que soient centralisées au sein d'un seul organisme les activités de la Direction des archives du ministère de l'Agriculture, de la Direction des documents publics du Secrétariat d'État et de divers autres dépôts d'archives. En 1903, un décret rend la Direction des archives responsable des documents publics et des manuscrits privés. Les archives nationales doivent recueillir non seulement les documents officiels et historiques du gouvernement fédéral, mais aussi les documents de particuliers et d'organismes privés ayant une importance nationale et ceux de gouvernements étrangers relatifs au Canada. Ce mandat est enchâssé dans la *Loi de 1912 sur les archives publiques,* qui fait des Archives nationales du Canada, alors appelées Archives publiques, un organisme indépendant responsable « des actes et documents publics, ainsi que des pièces historiques de toute espèce, nature et description... »

Peut-être en raison de l'importance qu'accordait l'ancienne Direction des archives aux documents privés avant 1903, la nouvelle institution n'accordera longtemps qu'une importance secondaire aux docu-

ments publics. Puis une commission royale d'enquête mise sur pied en 1912 recommande, en 1914, qu'aucun document public ne soit éliminé sans l'approbation du Conseil du Trésor, et que tous les documents gouvernementaux présentant une valeur historique soient transférés aux Archives publiques du Canada. Malgré ces signes encourageants, les restrictions imposées par les deux guerres mondiales et la crise économique retardent la mise en œuvre du projet, et il faudra attendre les années 50 pour assister à la création d'un système efficace et ordonné de gestion des documents. Des projets de loi avaient bien été présentés au Parlement en 1927 et en 1936 dans le but d'étendre le rôle des Archives dans le domaine des documents publics, et même de créer un Bureau distinct des documents publics, mais les deux tentatives avaient échoué.

Avec la Seconde Guerre mondiale, on assiste à une rapide augmentation des programmes gouvernementaux et des documents connexes. Cette situation provoque des changements importants dans la gestion des documents publics. En 1945, on crée un comité interministériel des documents publics, qui deviendra en 1966 le Conseil consultatif des documents publics. Les deux organismes doivent faire des recommandations en matière d'entreposage, de microfilmage, de gestion générale et d'élimination ordonnée des documents fédéraux. L'établissement des calendriers de conservation et d'élimination constitue la pierre angulaire de ce processus. La priorité croissante accordée à la bonne gestion des documents publics explique la réponse négative du gouvernement à la recommandation formulée par la Commission royale d'enquête sur l'avancement des arts, des lettres et des sciences (Commission Massey), dont le mandat consistait en partie à étudier l'état des archives canadiennes. La recommandation favorisait la création d'un Bureau des documents publics distinct pour s'occuper des graves négligences maintenant reconnues dans le secteur des archives. Le gouvernement fédéral choisit plutôt de créer en 1956 le Centre de documents des Archives publiques, au sein même des Archives, appelé par la suite la Direction de la gestion des documents et, aujourd'hui, la Direction des documents gouvernementaux.

Cette direction devait jouer un rôle d'intermédiaire entre le travail de gestion des documents accompli par le Comité des documents publics et les ministères d'une part, et les Archives d'autre part. Ses fonctions essentielles consistaient à coordonner les calendriers de conservation des dossiers ministériels en précisant la valeur administrative et opérationnelle de chaque document, à entreposer les dossiers inactifs dans des centres de documents, à veiller à l'élimination des dossiers dépourvus de valeur historique et à transférer à la Direction des archives historiques les documents dotés d'une valeur archivistique ou historique réelle ou éventuelle. L'énorme quantité de papiers produits —

4

l'équivalent de cinquante wagons de marchandises couverts chaque année — allait bientôt entraîner la création de centres régionaux de documents à Toronto, Montréal, Vancouver, Halifax, Winnipeg et Edmonton. Enfin, dans les années 50, le transfert aux Archives du Service central du microfilm du gouvernement canadien assure la liaison voulue entre la microphotographie, la gestion des documents et la conservation des archives.

Malgré ces améliorations, l'augmentation constante du nombre de documents sur papier produits par l'État-providence moderne, surtout après la décentralisation des années 60, suscite de graves préoccupations, exprimées par exemple par la Commission Glassco de 1962, quant à l'efficacité générale de l'administration gouvernementale et à sa lourdeur bureaucratique en particulier. Ces éléments amènent en 1966 l'adoption du *Décret sur les documents publics*, qui constitue une étape cruciale. Celui-ci vient ajouter officiellement au mandat traditionnel des Archives — à savoir l'acquisition des documents historiques —, la responsabilité d'améliorer la gestion des documents actifs encore contrôlés et conservés par les ministères, notamment grâce à l'établissement, désormais obligatoire, de calendriers de conservation et d'élimination des documents. Ce lien entre acquisition et gestion est encore renforcé dans les années 70 et 80 par des politiques, des directives et des lois nouvelles relatives à la gestion des documents, à leur consultation et à la protection des renseignements personnels.

Les changements survenus après la guerre dans le domaine de la gestion de l'information gouvernementale ont constitué des étapes décisives dans l'acquisition des documents textuels gouvernementaux : au cours des années 60, les Archives ont acquis plus de documents publics que pendant les neuf décennies précédentes. Ces transformations extérieures vont se refléter également dans la structure organisationnelle des Archives. En 1965, la Section des documents publics est établie au sein de la Division des manuscrits; c'est la première fois dans les quatre-vingt-treize ans d'histoire des Archives nationales qu'une section distincte reçoit la responsabilité exclusive des archives du gouvernement fédéral. Cette section va prendre de l'ampleur et devenir en 1973 la Division des archives fédérales.

Bien que leur histoire soit évidemment plus récente, les documents informatiques ont souffert de la même coûteuse négligence que jadis les documents textuels. Les documents informatiques, il est vrai, sont très fragiles et éphémères et, à la différence des autres supports d'information, ils ne peuvent survivre à des séjours même relativement courts dans des conditions environnementales non contrôlées; la non conversion des données pour les adapter aux changements technologi-

ques les rend à toutes fins utiles peu pratiques. Devant cet état de choses, quelques services d'archives de par le monde ont commencé à s'adapter à l'évolution de l'information marquée par l'utilisation massive d'ordinateurs au gouvernement et dans le monde des affaires. Les Archives ont été parmi les premières institutions à réagir en créant, en 1973, la Division des archives ordinolingues. Dès sa création, cette division a acquis des documents informatiques importants sur le plan national, produits aussi bien par le gouvernement que par le secteur privé, mais elle a toujours mis l'accent sur les documents gouvernementaux, dans une proportion de sept contre un. Toutefois, le manque d'expérience en matière de documents informatiques d'une collectivité habituée à gérer des documents sur papier, allié à l'absence, au sein des ministères, de personnes expressément chargées de la conservation et de l'élimination des données informatiques, ont rapidement causé des problèmes. Les ministères ont accompli peu de progrès en matière de conservation et d'élimination ordonnées de leurs documents informatiques. Les acquisitions importantes se sont donc faites principalement grâce à des contacts directs entre les archivistes et les ministères.

Au cours des années 80, lorsque les organismes et les ministères ont commencé à concevoir l'information comme un contenu et une ressource, plutôt que comme un support, les Archives nationales se sont orientées vers une intégration des deux principaux supports documentaires utilisés par les organismes gouvernementaux. Dans la même foulée, les deux divisions les plus concernées par les documents publics — la Division des archives fédérales et la Division des archives ordinolingues — ont été fusionnées en décembre 1986 pour former la Division des archives gouvernementales. En matière d'acquisition, son mandat ressemble à ceux de ses devancières, à l'exception des documents informatiques privés qui relèveraient désormais de la Division des manuscrits.

Enfin, depuis l'adoption de la *Loi sur les Archives nationales du Canada*, promulguée en juin 1987, les organismes gouvernementaux doivent d'abord obtenir la permission de l'archiviste national avant de détruire des documents. De plus, la Loi prévoit, en vertu d'ententes, le transfert aux Archives nationales des documents présentant une valeur historique ou archivistique. Elle accroît aussi de façon substantielle le nombre d'institutions soumises à ces dispositions. Elle renforce donc considérablement le rôle des Archives nationales et élargit le champ des responsabilités de la division.

La Division des archives gouvernementales comprend quatre grandes sections et une unité administrative. Deux des sections s'occupent directement des documents d'archives, tandis que les deux autres fournissent des services connexes.

La *Section des archives militaires, d'État et de transport* compte trois sous-sections responsables des documents des organismes gouvernementaux chargés des affaires de l'État; des archives militaires et des affaires internationales; des archives économiques et de transport.

La *Section des sciences sociales et ressources naturelles*, qui compte également trois sous-sections, est responsable des documents des organismes gouvernementaux qui s'occupent des affaires sociales et culturelles; des sciences et ressources naturelles; des questions autochtones, du Nord et des terres.

La *Section du service de conservation* assure de nombreux services connexes, tels que l'extraction des documents et leur diffusion au personnel et aux chercheurs, l'élaboration et la mise en œuvre de systèmes d'information et l'application des normes de description. Elle s'acquitte en outre de certaines fonctions techniques et opérationnelles nécessaires à l'acquisition, à la conservation et à l'entreposage des documents et coordonne les activités de la division reliées aux expositions et publications de l'institution.

La *Section de l'accès aux archives gouvernementales* veille à ce que les documents d'archives conservés à la division soient communiqués aux chercheurs conformément à la *Loi sur l'accès à l'information* et à la *Loi sur la protection des renseignements personnels*. Elle répond aux particuliers qui demandent à consulter des documents dont la communication n'est pas encore autorisée et elle s'occupe de la déclassification des documents d'archives.

Notion de groupes d'archives

Les archivistes divisent les documents en groupes, eux-mêmes divisés en séries et en sous-séries de documents. Puisque la notion de groupe d'archives est fondamentale dans le fonctionnement de la division et dans l'organisation du présent guide, il est bon que l'utilisateur des fonds comprenne bien cette notion.

Lorsqu'ils organisent les archives, les archivistes s'appuient sur deux principes : d'une part, le principe de provenance, selon lequel les documents d'une même provenance ne doivent pas être mélangés à ceux d'une autre provenance et, d'autre part, le principe du respect de l'ordre primitif, en vertu duquel on doit, dans la mesure du possible, respecter ou recréer le classement ou le système de classification utilisé dans le bureau d'origine (qui peut ne pas correspondre à l'ordre de réception aux Archives). Procéder autrement, classer et organiser les documents par domaine de recherche, par lieu géographique ou par période, détruirait la valeur de témoignage que représentent les documents eux-mêmes; en effet, cela les sortirait du contexte où ils ont été créés et détruirait ainsi une part importante de l'information qu'ils contiennent. C'est pourquoi les fonds de la division sont répartis en groupes d'archives distincts afin de respecter ces deux principes.

Le terme groupe d'archives (RG) désigne généralement un ensemble de documents provenant d'un ministère, d'un organisme ou d'une direction qui a fait preuve d'une certaine continuité administrative. Traités suivant un même mode d'enregistrement, les documents sont apparentés à la fois sur le plan structural et sur le plan fonctionnel. On pourra constater que chacun des groupes d'archives est consacré à un seul ministère ou à une direction importante d'un ministère. À l'intérieur des groupes d'archives, les séries suivent généralement le même principe. Elles comprennent les documents des subdivisions administratives du ministère ou organisme qui a produit le groupe d'archives dans son ensemble. L'ordre original des documents et des systèmes est conservé au sein des séries et des sous-séries. Par exemple, trois dossiers relatifs au même sujet et portant peut-être le même titre, mais provenant de trois systèmes de classification différents au sein du même ministère, *ne seront pas réunis*, mais plutôt placés dans trois séries différentes au sein du groupe d'archives, pour refléter les trois systèmes de classification auxquels ils appartenaient à l'origine.

Dans certains cas, cependant, la formule a connu quelques variantes dues à la complexité de l'organisme et au volume de documents concernés. Il arrive souvent, par exemple, que plus d'un groupe d'archives se rapportent à une même organisation. C'est le cas du ministère des Affaires indiennes et du Nord canadien (AINC) qui, de 1966 à 1979, comptait trois grands secteurs de compétence : les populations autochtones, les parcs nationaux et lieux historiques et l'administration du Yukon et des Territoires du Nord-Ouest. D'importantes unités administratives autonomes au sein des AINC administraient ces trois secteurs, et chacune de ces unités, qui avait pu faire partie de l'un ou l'autre des quatre ou cinq organismes ayant précédé les AINC, avait son propre système d'enregistrement des dossiers. C'est

pourquoi on les retrouve dans trois groupes d'archives distincts : Affaires indiennes (RG 10), Parcs Canada (RG 84) et Affaires du Nord (RG 85). Par ailleurs, certaines parties des AINC (cabinet du sous-ministre, Division du contentieux, Services d'information, Service du génie et de la construction, etc.) chevauchaient les trois secteurs de compétence; leurs dossiers sont donc réunis dans un quatrième groupe d'archives, celui des Affaires indiennes et du Nord canadien (RG 22). Il en va de même pour Énergie, Mines et Ressources (RG 21), Environnement (RG 108), Citoyenneté et Immigration (RG 26) et Emploi et Immigration (RG 118).

D'autres groupes d'archives réunissent pour plus de commodité de petits ensembles de dossiers de même nature qui n'ont cependant ni rapport ni continuité administrative. C'est le cas du RG 33, qui regroupe les dossiers de 147 commissions royales d'enquête, et du RG 36, qui rassemble les dossiers de 37 comités, commissions et bureaux. Ce dernier ne regroupe que des organismes de courte durée ou de moindre importance; les organismes permanents et plus importants font l'objet de groupes distincts, par exemple la Commission canadienne des grains (RG 80), la Commission des champs de bataille nationaux (RG 90), le Conseil des ports nationaux (RG 66) et l'Office national de l'énergie (RG 99).

L'évolution de l'organisation gouvernementale a vu naître deux tendances. D'une part, dans la mesure où un ministère prend de l'ampleur grâce à de nouvelles directions et divisions, ses documents acquièrent une complexité croissante. Cela se fait souvent sentir lorsque ces documents parviennent à la division, qui doit alors créer de nombreux groupes d'archives. Les archives du ministère de l'Intérieur (RG 15) en sont le meilleur exemple. Les dossiers principaux, ceux du Bureau des terres fédérales, font partie du RG 15, mais ceux qui se rapportent à d'autres fonctions du ministère de l'Intérieur sont dispersés dans toutes sortes de groupes d'archives : Affaires indiennes (RG 10), Service canadien des forêts (RG 39), Commission géologique du Canada (RG 45), Observatoires du Canada (RG 48), Direction de l'immigration (RG 76), Service canadien des parcs (RG 84), Programme des affaires du Nord (RG 85), Direction des mines (RG 86), Direction des levés et de la cartographie (RG 88) et Direction des ressources hydrauliques (RG 89), pour ne citer que les plus importants. D'autre part, il arrive que des organismes indépendants soient réorganisés ou fusionnés; dans ce cas, les Archives nationales rassemblent leurs dossiers en un seul groupe. C'est pourquoi les dossiers de la Commission des transports, de la Commission maritime canadienne et de la Commis-

sion des transports aériens sont tous compris dans le RG 46, celui de la Commission canadienne des transports, organisme qui a succédé aux trois précédents et les a regroupés.

Les documents informatiques posent également de nouveaux défis dans l'application des principes archivistiques traditionnels concernant l'organisation des groupes de documents. Il peut arriver par exemple que des bases de données complexes servent deux ou plusieurs directions d'un grand ministère, ou même possèdent une fonction inter-ministérielle. On doit alors diviser en au moins deux groupes de documents l'unique fichier de données dont les deux directions peuvent au même titre revendiquer la propriété.

En résumé, la notion de groupe d'archives évolue constamment, à l'instar des organismes gouvernementaux et de leurs modes sans cesse changeants de création de documents. Les chercheurs qui consultent la présente publication doivent donc se rappeler que les sources de documentation sur un sujet donné peuvent fort bien être réparties dans de nombreux groupes d'archives et dans bien des séries ou fichiers de données qui les composent. Il est rare, en effet, qu'un ministère ou organisme ait été le seul à s'intéresser à une question, quelle qu'elle soit. Il faut donc comprendre les structures, les liens et les changements administratifs pour exploiter au maximum les possibilités de consultation des archives fédérales. Par conséquent, les chercheurs doivent toujours vérifier s'il existe des renvois et des liens organiques entre les divers groupes d'archives.

2 Services de la Division des archives gouvernementales ___

Outre le présent guide, la Division des archives gouvernementales met à la disposition des chercheurs trois autres catégories d'outils de référence :

Inventaires

L'inventaire d'un groupe d'archives donne, pour chacune des séries du groupe, un bref historique de l'unité ou une notice biographique de la personne qui a produit les documents, un aperçu général du type et de la nature des documents textuels et informatiques qui la constituent, ainsi que les dates et la mesure linéaire des documents. Les inventaires contiennent également un historique plus complet de tout l'organisme, des renvois aux instruments de recherche disponibles et une mention générale des restrictions à l'accès. Ils décrivent en outre brièvement tous les documents non encore traités, y compris ceux qui se trouvent dans les fonds de la division à Vancouver, Edmonton, Winnipeg et Halifax. Plusieurs inventaires ont été publiés (RG 2, 10, 11, 18, 20, 27, 31, 33, 39, 43, 46, 55, 64, 65, 69, 81, 84, 85, 88, 115 et 126) et ils sont disponibles sur demande à la Division des communications des Archives nationales. Le présent guide tente de résumer les renseignements les plus pertinents contenus dans chacun des inventaires de la division.

Instruments de recherche

La division indexe ou répertorie les documents textuels jusqu'au dossier individuel qui constitue l'unité de base. La panoplie des instruments de recherche va des registres contemporains de correspondance et d'index aux répertoires, catalogues topographiques, listes de dossiers, index sur fiches et index-matières informatisés pour les groupes d'archives plus vastes et plus utilisés. Quant aux documents informatiques, chaque fichier informatique fait l'objet d'un dossier documentaire qui indique la disposition des documents, décrit les rubriques et le système, fournit

des organigrammes de données, mentionne les publications connexes et les sorties d'imprimantes, etc. Les chercheurs peuvent également interroger la base de données informatisée selon le titre, l'enquêteur principal et le sujet.

Guides thématiques

La division prépare également des guides thématiques spéciaux qui regroupent les références sur un sujet donné, extraites de plusieurs ou de la totalité des groupes d'archives. Ces guides thématiques concernent les domaines les plus fréquemment étudiés. La plupart d'entre eux sont dactylographiés et ne peuvent être consultés qu'aux Archives nationales, mais certains ont été publiés et les chercheurs peuvent se les procurer sans frais. Il s'agit de : *Documents sur les parcs nationaux du Canada*; *Documents sur la Deuxième Guerre mondiale*; *Documents pour l'étude du Nord canadien*; *Dossiers de recherches en promotion de la santé; Dossiers sur l'usage de l'alcool, des drogues et du tabac*; et *Dossiers de données sur les loisirs et la récréation*. De plus, les fonds de la division font souvent l'objet d'articles signés par les archivistes dans le *Bulletin des archives ordinolingues* et dans *l'Archiviste*.

Installations de recherche

On conseille aux chercheurs de communiquer avec les Archives nationales avant de s'y rendre. Tout d'abord, les archivistes peuvent indiquer au chercheur si le nombre de documents pertinents disponibles sur le sujet justifie le déplacement. Dans certains cas, quelques documents, voire même tous, ont été microfilmés. Les microfilms peuvent être empruntés au nom du chercheur par une bibliothèque locale ou par tout autre établissement muni d'un lecteur de microfilm et qui participe au système de prêt entre institutions. Deuxièmement, si les documents ne sont pas encore à la disposition des chercheurs à cause des restrictions imposées par la *Loi sur l'accès à l'information* ou par la *Loi sur la protection des renseignements personnels*, ils devront être réexaminés par la Section de l'accès, ce qui nécessite un certain temps. Troisièmement, les chercheurs ne peuvent consulter directement les documents informatiques. Si le chercheur communique d'abord avec les Archives, celles-ci pourront retrouver les documents nécessaires et, si possible, les reproduire.

Les chercheurs qui communiquent pour la première fois avec les Archives nationales, que ce soit en personne, par courrier ou par téléphone, doivent d'abord s'adresser à la Division des services de la référence et des services aux chercheurs, Direction des programmes publics (a.s. Archives nationales du Canada, 395, rue Wellington, Ottawa (Ontario) K1A 0N3, téléphone : 1-613-995-8094). Cette division oriente les chercheurs, les inscrit, leur fournit un laissez-passer, les initie aux inventaires et aux instruments de recherche placés dans la salle de consultation, qui décrivent les fonds des divisions, et effectue les recherches nécessaires pour répondre aux questions générales ainsi qu'à toutes les questions qui touchent à la généalogie. Pour les questions spécialisées ou plus détaillées, la division s'assure aussi que les chercheurs sont orientés vers les archivistes désignés des divisions concernées. Les chercheurs orientés vers la Division des archives gouvernementales aux fins de consultation spécialisée peuvent s'adresser aux archivistes et au personnel de cette division entre 8 h 30 et 16 h 45. Les documents textuels ou microfilmés qui intéressent le chercheur peuvent être commandés pendant les mêmes heures au comptoir du prêt de la salle de recherche principale. Pour consulter les fonds conservés dans les centres régionaux de documents, il est nécessaire de communiquer d'abord avec la Division des archives gouvernementales à Ottawa pour obtenir les références exactes, ainsi qu'un guide des services offerts.

Comme la plupart des documents sont conservés à l'extérieur de l'édifice principal des Archives nationales, on recommande au chercheur de consulter le guide de localisation des documents au comptoir du prêt afin de prévoir les retards éventuels. La salle de recherche principale est ouverte vingt-quatre heures par jour, sept jours par semaine, y compris les jours fériés. Le personnel du comptoir de prêt met à la disposition des chercheurs qui veulent poursuivre leurs travaux après les heures d'ouverture, des casiers situés dans une salle adjacente où ils peuvent déposer provisoirement leurs documents. Ces documents doivent être commandés et placés dans les casiers pendant les heures d'ouverture. Outre le personnel du comptoir de prêt, un employé est affecté à plein temps à la salle de lecture des microfilms pour aider les chercheurs à localiser et à utiliser les microfilms. Les chercheurs doivent obtenir un laissez-passer valide délivré par les Archives nationales pour avoir accès à ces installations. Les manteaux et autres effets personnels, qu'il est interdit d'apporter dans les salles de recherche, peuvent être déposés en toute sécurité dans des casiers situés au rez-de-chaussée.

Par mesure d'équité pour les autres chercheurs et pour prévenir toute perte ou détérioration des documents, aucun original ne peut être sorti de l'immeuble des Archives. Toutefois, pour protéger les originaux

fragiles et pour permettre à un plus vaste public d'y avoir accès, les Archives ont mis sur pied un important programme de microfilmage de leurs fonds. Un grand nombre de séries fréquemment consultées ont déjà été microfilmées. Le présent guide mentionne l'existence de microfilms le cas échéant, pour chaque groupe d'archives. Pour plus de renseignements sur la collection de microfilms, les chercheurs peuvent s'adresser à la Division des services de la référence et des services aux chercheurs à l'adresse mentionnée plus haut.

En outre, la division offre, dans une certaine mesure, un service de reprographie. Les commandes, payées comptant, de photocopies et de copies faites à l'aide d'un lecteur-reproducteur sont exécutées le jour même dans les salles de recherche, tandis que les commandes plus importantes sont facturées et envoyées plus tard par la poste. On peut aussi commander des reproductions de microfilms et de photographies. On notera que le nombre de photocopies peut être limité et que les délais d'exécution des demandes de reprographie peuvent varier en fonction de la quantité de commandes.

À l'heure actuelle, la division n'autorise pas les chercheurs à consulter directement les documents informatiques. Elle fournit cependant, aux frais du chercheur, des copies des données sur bande magnétique ou sur disquette, ainsi qu'une copie du dossier documentaire décrit plus haut qui permet d'interpréter les données. La division offre d'autres services, comme la banalisation des renseignements personnels, qui permet la communication, autrement impossible, du fichier informatique et la création de sous-ensembles de données à partir de fichiers plus importants.

On peut obtenir plus de renseignements sur les fonds de la division, ses services et ses activités en s'adressant à la Division des archives gouvernementales, Archives nationales du Canada, Ottawa (Ontario), Canada, K1A 0N3 (téléphone : 1-613-996-8507).

Accès aux documents de l'administration fédérale

L'accès aux documents de la plupart des institutions fédérales, y compris ceux des Archives nationales du Canada, est assujetti à la *Loi sur l'accès à l'information* et à la *Loi sur la protection des renseignements personnels*. Les Archives nationales répondent aux demandes présentées en vertu de ces lois lorsqu'elles concernent les documents qui leur ont été confiés à des fins archivistiques ou historiques. En bref, la *Loi sur l'accès à l'information* donne au public un droit d'accès aux documents de l'administration fédérale, sauf aux documents expressément

exemptés, tandis que la *Loi sur la protection des renseignements person-nels* élargit le droit d'accès des individus aux renseignements personnels qui les concernent et en garantit la protection.

Les documents non encore examinés et susceptibles d'être consultés par des chercheurs doivent être évalués afin de s'assurer que les renseignements qu'ils contiennent ne tombent pas dans l'une des catégories d'exemption prévues par la *Loi sur l'accès à l'information* ou ne violent pas les droits individuels garantis par la *Loi sur la protection des renseignements personnels*.

La division a mis au point un processus informel de demande d'accès, complémentaire aux procédures officielles de demande de documents gouvernementaux en vertu des deux lois citées plus haut. Il est recommandé aux chercheurs qui veulent consulter les fonds d'archives d'utiliser cette procédure informelle. Celle-ci, qui prévoit l'examen des documents à la lumière des dispositions des deux lois mentionnées, compte pour 90 pour 100 du travail de révision accompli par la Section de l'accès des Archives nationales. Les chercheurs peuvent engager ce processus informel en remplissant le bordereau normal de demande au comptoir de prêt. Si les documents demandés ne sont pas encore ouverts à la consultation, le personnel du comptoir de prêt en informera le chercheur. Celui-ci peut aussi consulter la liste de contrôle de l'accès, disponible dans les secteurs de référence. Cette liste indique les possibilités de consultation des boîtes de documents de l'administration fédérale confiés aux Archives nationales.

Comme on l'a déjà signalé, le temps requis pour l'examen préalable à la consultation varie en fonction de l'ampleur de la demande et des retards qui peuvent avoir été accumulés dans le traitement d'autres demandes. Aussi les chercheurs doivent-ils présenter leurs demandes longtemps avant les dates d'échéance qu'ils veulent respecter et, si possible, avant leur visite à Ottawa. Pour plus de renseignements, on s'adressera à la Section de l'accès à l'adresse mentionnée à la page 14.

Quelques organismes du gouvernement fédéral ne sont assujettis ni à la *Loi sur l'accès à l'information* ni à la *Loi sur la protection des renseignements personnels*. Dans ces cas particuliers, des ententes ont été conclues entre l'organisme et les Archives nationales. Le personnel préposé à la référence se fera un plaisir d'expliquer aux chercheurs la teneur de ces ententes.

3 Fonds de la Division des archives gouvernementales —

On trouvera dans ce guide une description de chaque groupe d'archives par ordre numérique, suivie d'un index-matières, puis d'un index alphabétique des groupes d'archives. Les notices sont à jour au 30 juin 1989.

Dans cette nouvelle édition, la division s'est efforcée de prévoir l'évolution de la collectivité archivistique canadienne vers les normes de de description au niveau du fonds. Elle espère que ces notices serviront de point de départ à l'établissement de descriptions complètes des fonds des futurs groupes de documents.

Dans le corps du texte, les notices des groupes de documents se composent de quatre éléments :

1. La **mention du titre** contient le nom du ministère ou de l'organisme dont les documents sont décrits, le numéro du groupe de documents et les dates extrêmes des documents décrits.

2. La mention d'**étendue des fonds** indique, le cas échéant, le nombre de mètres de documents textuels, le nombre de fichiers informatiques, de microfilms et de microfiches. L'absence d'inscription concernant l'un ou l'autre de ces supports signifie que ce groupe de documents n'en comprend pas encore.

3. L'**historique** reconstitue le contexte dans lequel ces documents ont été créés. Il comprend un bref rappel des principales fonctions et de l'histoire administrative du ministère, de la direction ou de l'organisme. Dans la mesure où l'espace le permettait, on s'est efforcé d'établir à l'intention des chercheurs les liens essentiels entre les diverses unités administratives, celles qui les ont précédées ou leur ont succédé et les organismes dont elles relèvent (souvent avec des renvois aux numéros des groupes d'archives en question). Lorsque des documents de nature semblable, sans liens administratifs ont été réunis dans un même RG, l'historique fournit des informations générales sur le genre d'organisme qui les a créés.

4. La notice d'**organisation et** de **contenu** n'est pas une liste des titres des séries et des fichiers de données qui constituent le groupe de documents comme c'était le cas auparavant, mais une description plus globale des principaux sujets et thèmes couverts par les documents. Elle vise à donner une idée générale plutôt qu'à énumérer simplement les fonds d'archives de l'organisme. Les chercheurs ne doivent pas oublier qu'à de très rares exceptions près, les documents informatiques non traités ne sont pas inclus dans ces descriptions, et que les documents textuels non traités ne sont inclus que si les archivistes ont pu en vérifier le contenu. De même, sauf exception, les documents conservés par la division à Vancouver, Edmonton, Winnipeg et Halifax ne sont pas pris en considération.

Quant aux notices proprement dites des groupes de documents, il n'est peut-être pas inutile d'ajouter quelques précisions. Les dates extrêmes renvoient toujours aux documents mêmes et non à l'unité administrative. La Direction des terres minières et du Yukon du RG 85, par exemple, a existé de 1909 à 1922, mais ses archives vont de 1884 à 1968. Cela veut donc dire que cette direction a repris à son compte certains dossiers des organismes qui l'ont précédée et que certains de ses propres dossiers ont à leur tour été repris par ses successeurs.

L'expression « dossiers du service central » figure dans un grand nombre de notices d'**organisation et** de **contenu**. Le service central des dossiers d'un organisme gouvernemental est chargé du système de classement des dossiers de tout l'organisme — bien que, dans les plus grands ministères, il puisse y avoir plusieurs services centraux au niveau des directions et des programmes, en plus du service central concernant tout le ministère. Les dossiers du service central constituent donc généralement la série la plus complète d'un groupe de documents parce qu'ils couvrent la plupart, voire même l'ensemble, des fonctions et des attributions du ministère. En fait, ils représentent l'une des plus importantes sources d'information de tout groupe de documents. Afin de comprendre la portée des dossiers du service central, les chercheurs doivent connaître l'historique, les mandats législatifs et les principales attributions de l'organisme concerné, car ces éléments indiquent la nature des sujets qui se trouvent dans ces dossiers. L'**historique** de chaque notice fournit certes l'essentiel de ces informations, mais on trouvera plus de précisions dans les historiques complets qui figurent dans l'inventaire de chaque groupe de documents (voir **Inventaires**, p. 11), ainsi que dans l'*Annuaire du Canada, 1976-1977 : Édition spéciale* (Ottawa, 1977), *L'Administration fédérale du Canada, 1978-1979* (Ottawa, 1979), les rapports annuels des ministères et les documents eux-mêmes.

L'index-matières des groupes d'archives qui suit le texte principal n'offre évidemment qu'une catégorisation globale destinée à guider les chercheurs. Les divers regroupements utilisés ne s'excluent en aucun cas mutuellement. L'index indique cependant les corrélations entre les divers organismes représentés par les groupes d'archives et la nécessité pour les chercheurs de comprendre les liens administratifs — et par conséquent archivistiques — qui existent entre ces organismes. Aux chercheurs qui savent déjà vers quels ministères orienter leurs recherches, l'index alphabétique qui suit fournit les numéros des groupes d'archives qui les intéressent.

Notices des groupes d'archives par ordre numérique

Archives du Conseil exécutif : RG 1
1764-1867

Ce groupe d'archives est conservé à la Division des manuscrits des Archives nationales du Canada.

Archives du Bureau du Conseil privé : RG 2
1867-1986

682,8 mètres
417 microfilms

Historique : Dirigé par le greffier du Conseil privé, le Bureau du Conseil privé (BCP) fait office de secrétariat administratif du Conseil et il en assiste le président. En 1940, le Bureau a adopté des procédures analogues à celles du monde des affaires : préparation d'ordres du jour avant les réunions du Cabinet, enregistrement des décisions adoptées, notification aux ministères des mesures à prendre et création d'un système de classement central. En 1968, la structure du BCP a été modifiée par l'adjonction d'une Division des opérations chargée de fournir au Cabinet et à ses comités des services de secrétariat plus complets, d'une Division des plans qui assiste les comités de planification et d'une Division des relations fédérales-provinciales qui assure la liaison entre les ministères du gouvernement et les provinces.

Organisation et contenu : Les documents sont répartis en quatre grandes séries : les archives du Bureau du greffier du Conseil privé et du secrétaire du Cabinet (1867-1986), les archives administratives (1867-1955), les documents des organes spéciaux chargés d'enquêtes ou de mandats administratifs (1912-1984) et les autres documents (1867-1943). Les séries générales se subdivisent en plusieurs sous-séries im-

portantes qui renferment des décrets, des annexes, les documents à l'appui et les documents inactifs (1867-1986); des dépêches (1867-1911); des documents du Cabinet (1867-1958); des registres d'assermentés (1946-1966); des dossiers de référence (1867-1907), dont certains sur la question des pêches, les frontières de l'Alaska et la crise de l'abdication royale; les dossiers du service central des dossiers (1940-1958), qui traitent de sujets tels que les projets de défense du Nord-Ouest, la reconstruction de l'après-guerre, les politiques sociales, et les affaires du Cabinet; les dossiers du Conseil des commissaires des chemins de fer (1912-1936), de la Direction générale de la censure (1939-1963), du Bureau du représentant spécial du premier ministre pour l'évolution constitutionnelle dans les Territoires du Nord-Ouest (1977-1984), et de divers groupes de travail (1966-1984) et commissions (1974-1985).

Archives des Postes : RG 3
1799-1987

141,53 mètres
512 microfilms

Historique : Bien que les opérations postales au Canada remontent à 1755, le ministère fédéral des Postes n'a été créé qu'en 1867; jusqu'en 1851, l'administration des postes relevait des autorités britanniques. En 1981, les Postes sont devenues une société d'État. La Société des Postes est chargée de mettre sur pied et d'assurer la bonne marche d'un éventail complet de services postaux au pays. Ses activités se répartissent en plusieurs catégories : affaires corporatives, services opérationnels, commercialisation, finances, personnel et administration, systèmes et ingénierie.

Organisation et contenu : Les documents sont divisés en plusieurs séries constituées de dossiers administratifs et opérationnels couvrant tous les aspects des activités des Postes, comme, par exemple, l'ouverture ou la fermeture de bureaux de poste, le service postal aérien, la censure, la distribution du courrier en régions rurales, les patrouilles de l'Arctique oriental, l'équipement, les communications internationales, les contrats, le service postal ferroviaire, le service postal maritime, le personnel et diverses enquêtes. On trouve également des documents qui proviennent du Bureau du ministre des Postes (1862-1917) et du Bureau du ministre adjoint des Postes (1851-1920); du service central des dossiers (1851-1976); des inspecteurs des Postes (1838-1961); des services postaux/Direction des transports (1799-

1970); des services administratifs (1830-1960); des services financiers (1841-1952); des commissions, comités et groupes d'étude (1980-1985); ainsi que des dossiers locaux et régionaux (1807-1953).

Archives des bureaux des secrétaires civils et provinciaux : Québec, Bas-Canada et Canada-Est : RG 4
1760-1867

Ce groupe d'archives est conservé à la Division des manuscrits des Archives nationales du Canada.

Archives des bureaux des secrétaires civils et provinciaux : Haut-Canada et Canada-Ouest : RG 5
1791-1867

Ce groupe d'archives est conservé à la Division des manuscrits des Archives nationales du Canada.

Archives du Secrétariat d'État : RG 6
1848-1978

135,7 mètres
117 microfilms

Historique : Lors de sa création à l'époque de la Confédération, le Secrétariat d'État était chargé entre autres des communications entre les Canadiens et leur gouvernement et entre le gouvernement du Canada et celui de Grande-Bretagne. Il s'occupait également des affaires indiennes et des terres fédérales et assumait les fonctions de registraire général. À diverses époques, il a été chargé de la GRC, de la Commission de la fonction publique, du protocole officiel, des brevets, marques de commerce et dessins industriels, du droit d'auteur, des élections, des imprimés et des fournitures du gouvernement, du séquestre des biens ennemis, des arts et de la culture. De nos jours, le Secrétariat d'État demeure responsable de la citoyenneté et de la naturalisation, du multiculturalisme, de l'aide à l'éducation et de l'application de la *Loi sur les langues officielles*. Il fournit en outre des services de traduction aux ministères et organismes gouvernementaux.

Organisation et contenu : Ce groupe d'archives comprend une série de correspondance générale (1867-1952) qui contient des documents relatifs aux armoiries du Canada, ainsi qu'une section de documents portant sur la plupart des fonctions gouvernementales. Les archives du greffier de la Couronne à la Chancellerie (1866-1917) renferment de la

correspondance générale et des ordonnances d'élections. Les archives du Secrétariat d'État aux provinces (1867-1873) sont constituées de correspondance générale relative aux questions constitutionnelles et d'ordre pratique, à la création de la province du Manitoba et à la rébellion de Louis Riel. Les archives du protocole officiel et des événements spéciaux (1868-1973) concernent les médailles, les intronisations officielles, les visites royales et le Comité du drapeau canadien, et les documents du censeur en chef de la presse (1915-1920). On y retrouve aussi des documents de la citoyenneté relatifs à la Direction de l'enregistrement et à la Direction du multiculturalisme, coordination interministérielle (1857-1972); les archives de la guerre (1914-1951) relatives au séquestre des biens ennemis de la Première Guerre mondiale, aux opérations d'internement, aux œuvres de bienfaisance en temps de guerre, quelques dossiers-matières relatifs à la Seconde Guerre mondiale ainsi que les archives de la Direction des affaires culturelles (1950-1978) formées de registres et de dossiers-matières.

Archives du Cabinet du gouverneur général : RG 7
1774-1984

278,77 mètres
316 microfilms

Historique : Le Cabinet du gouverneur général est le résultat d'une longue évolution. Durant les régimes français et anglais en Amérique du Nord, les souverains respectifs ont eu des représentants qui siégeaient au sein de leurs gouvernements coloniaux. L'*Acte de l'Amérique du Nord britannique* de 1867 créait le poste de gouverneur général pour le Dominion du Canada et décrivait certains des pouvoirs qui lui étaient conférés. À cette époque, le gouverneur général était le chef de l'État, mais il gouvernait sur l'avis des conseillers privés du roi au Canada. Actuellement, le gouverneur général reste le chef de l'État, mais certains des pouvoirs qui lui avaient été confiés à la Confédération ont été modifiés par les circonstances et par la loi. La Conférence impériale de 1926 abolit les derniers liens qui unissaient le Cabinet du gouverneur général et le gouvernement impérial, ne laissant au gouverneur général que le rôle de représentant de la Couronne. Les lettres patentes de 1947 confiaient au Cabinet du gouverneur général certaines responsabilités qui, auparavant, incombaient à la Couronne. Le titulaire du poste est nommé par la reine sur avis du Conseil privé au Canada.

Organisation et contenu : Les documents de ce groupe d'archives antérieurs à la Confédération sont confiés à la garde de la Division des manuscrits. Les documents postérieurs à la Confédération sont répartis en dix-neuf séries selon le type de documents. Six de ces séries se

composent de dépêches échangées avec le Colonial Office à Londres (1856-1913) ou avec le ministre de Grande-Bretagne à Washington (1804-1914). Une des séries est formée de copies de dépêches adressées au Colonial Office (1867-1902). Deux séries proviennent du service des dossiers (1818-1941 et 1859-1966) et quatre autres sont constituées d'un grand nombre de lettres sur divers sujets, tels que les affaires extérieures, les nominations, la milice et la défense. Deux autres séries sont constituées des dossiers (1867-1909) de deux fonctionnaires attachés au Cabinet du gouverneur général, le secrétaire militaire (1813-1907) et le secrétaire civil (1867-1909). Quatre autres séries concernent les ordres et décorations, les visites royales, l'administration interne et Rideau Hall.

Archives militaires et navales britanniques : RG 8
1757-1903

Ce groupe d'archives est conservé à la Division des manuscrits des Archives nationales du Canada.

Archives du ministère de la Milice et de la Défense : RG 9
1776-1960

1 515,9 mètres
337 microfilms

Historique : Les lois sur la milice remontent à 1777 pour le Bas-Canada et à 1793 pour le Haut-Canada. Bien que la milice ait été organisée dans les Canadas dès la fin du dix-huitième siècle, elle n'a relevé d'un ministère autonome qu'à partir de 1868. La création, en 1916, d'un ministère des Forces militaires outre-mer devait soulager le ministère de la Milice et de la Défense de l'administration des forces d'outre-mer et permettre d'établir un ministère à Londres, en contact direct avec le gouvernement de Sa Majesté et au cœur même des opérations. En 1922, le ministère de la Milice et de la Défense fusionnait avec le ministère du Service de la marine et de la Commission de l'air pour former le ministère de la Défense nationale (RG 24).

Organisation et contenu : Ce groupe de documents comprend trois séries générales. La série pré-Confédération (1776-1869) renferme des documents qui proviennent des bureaux des adjudants généraux du Haut et du Bas-Canada et contient de la correspondance (1777-1869), des relevés (1793-1869), des ordonnances (1805-1868), des listes de paye (1812-1868) et des registres d'employés (1808-1869). Les archives postérieures à la Confédération (1847-1960) sont organisées de la façon

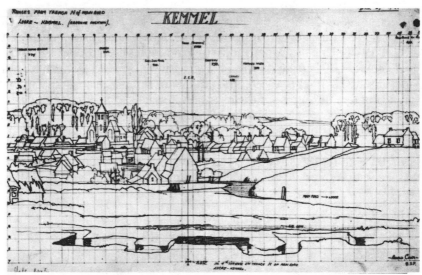

Croquis de la ville de Kemmel en Belgique, montrant les lignes d'artillerie dans les tranchées au nord du chemin Locre-Kemmel. (RG 9, III, C-3, vol. 4119, dossier 15) (C-96604)

suivante : de 1867 au 1ᵉʳ juillet 1903, la correspondance de l'administration centrale du ministère de la Milice et de la Défense était enregistrée dans la direction appropriée au sein du ministère. Par conséquent, on trouve souvent plusieurs dossiers du ministère qui traitent du même sujet. Un service central des dossiers a été mis sur pied le 1ᵉʳ juillet 1903 et est demeuré en activité en tant que service central des dossiers de l'administration centrale jusqu'en 1946. Les dossiers de l'administration centrale créés depuis 1903 puis transférés aux Archives nationales se trouvent dans RG 24. La série de documents postérieurs à la Confédération comprend des archives qui proviennent du Bureau du sous-ministre (1847-1960), du Bureau de l'adjudant général (1867-1922), du Service de renseignements (1895-1913), de la Direction des contrats (1896-1912), de la Direction du génie (1880-1903), de la Direction des comptes et de la paye (1855-1915), de la Direction des magasins (1864-1903), du quartier-maître général (1893-1898), de l'inspecteur en chef des armes et des munitions (1906-1922), de l'Artillerie royale canadienne (1871-1922), des écoles d'instruction militaire (1864-1932). Les registres de médailles font partie des documents du Bureau du sous-ministre (1847-1960). On y trouve des renseignements succincts sur les médaillés de l'incursion des Féniens de 1866, de l'expédition de la rivière Rouge, de la rébellion du Nord-Ouest et de la guerre des Boers. La dernière série est formée des archives des Forces armées outre-mer du Canada et du Corps expéditionnaire canadien (CEC) (1914-1922), qui comprennent des documents du ministère des Forces militaires

outre-mer (1914-1919) et des sections canadiennes basées aux quartiers généraux (1915-1919), des dossiers du CEC en Sibérie (1918-1919), des services administratifs (1914-1920), et du corps canadien et de ses différentes unités (1914-1922), ainsi que des dossiers du Service canadien des dossiers de guerre (1914-1920), qui renferment des journaux de guerre.

Archives du ministère des Affaires indiennes : RG 10
1677-1987

2 155,13 mètres
257 microfilms
898 microfiches
46 fichiers de données informatiques

Historique : Pendant le dix-huitième siècle et la première moitié du dix-neuvième siècle, le gouvernement impérial britannique a exercé un contrôle des relations entre les colons d'origine européenne et les peuples aborigènes d'Amérique du Nord essentiellement par l'entremise des commandants militaires, des gouverneurs généraux et des lieutenants-gouverneurs. Dans les Maritimes, les parlements coloniaux de la Nouvelle-Écosse, du Nouveau-Brunswick et de l'Île-du-Prince-Édouard réglaient les affaires indiennes en nommant des commissaires et en adoptant des lois au fur et à mesure des besoins. Dans la province du Canada, le ministère des Terres de la Couronne assuma, à partir de 1860, la responsabilité de l'administration des affaires indiennes dans le Canada-Est et dans le Canada-Ouest. Les premiers contacts de la Grande-Bretagne avec les nations indiennes des Prairies et de la Colombie-Britannique se firent par le biais des opérations de la Compagnie de la baie d'Hudson. À la Confédération, le Secrétariat d'État (RG 6) se chargea des relations du gouvernement canadien avec les Amérindiens du Canada. À partir de 1873, les Affaires indiennes relevèrent du ministère de l'Intérieur (RG 15). En 1880, la création d'un ministère des Affaires indiennes conféra le statut de ministère à ce qui n'était auparavant qu'une direction. Cet état de choses dura cinquante-six ans, après quoi les Affaires indiennes retournèrent à leur situation antérieure de direction au sein des ministères suivants : Mines et Ressources (voir RG 21 et 22) de 1936 à 1949; Citoyenneté et Immigration (RG 26) de 1949 à 1965; Nord canadien et Ressources nationales (RG 22) de 1965 à 1966; et Affaires indiennes et Nord canadien (RG 22) de 1966 à nos jours. Le Programme des affaires du Nord et ses prédécesseurs (RG 85) s'occupèrent des programmes inuit jusqu'en 1971, date à laquelle le Programme des affaires indiennes et esquimaudes (aujourd'hui Programme des affaires indiennes et inuit) (RG 10) fut mis sur pied. Ce

programme s'occupe de l'autonomie gouvernementale autochtone et d'une grande variété de revendications, de l'enregistrement des terres indiennes et de l'effectif des bandes, du financement de l'éducation, du développement économique et de l'aide sociale. Finalement, dans le cadre actuel de la politique des Affaires indiennes, les bandes amérindiennes acquièrent de plus en plus de responsabilités dans l'administration de nombreux services importants.

Organisation et contenu : Les archives administratives du gouvernement impérial (1677-1864) sont constituées de dossiers antérieurs à la Confédération, datant surtout approximativement de 1750 à 1864. Cette série se compose essentiellement de documents créés ou recueillis par le « Northern Department » du gouvernement britannique (chargé des colonies du nord-est du continent américain), ou constitués dans le Haut et le Bas-Canada (1791-1840) et dans la province du Canada (1841-1867). Les archives militaires, des gouverneurs et des surintendants des Affaires indiennes illustrent quantité d'aspects des premiers contacts entre les Britanniques et les Indiens d'Amérique du Nord. Elles traitent essentiellement de questions générales touchant les régions du sud de l'Ontario et du Québec d'aujourd'hui, mais on rencontre également quelques documents d'intérêt local créés par des fonctionnaires des Affaires indiennes en poste en Colombie-Britannique. S'y trouvent de nombreux documents relatifs aux terres et aux questions financières, certains documents de recensement et quelques procès-verbaux de conseils indiens. Les archives administratives ministérielles (1680-1980) se composent surtout de dossiers de l'administration centrale. Comme il s'agit de documents créés ou conservés à Ottawa, ils témoignent de la gestion du gouvernement fédéral et de sa responsabilité fiduciaire en matière de terres et de ressources monétaires indiennes partout au Canada, ainsi que de l'administration de divers programmes, et en particulier de ceux qui sont destinés aux Indiens inscrits. La sous-série des dossiers du service central couvre un grand nombre de sujets. En outre, d'autres sous-séries concernent des sujets précis, tels que les écoles, les questions financières et certaines commissions. Parmi les dossiers on retrouve des dossiers de cas, des formulaires de recensement et les premières archives des surintendants généraux adjoints (sous-ministres) des Affaires indiennes. On y trouve également quelques documents relatifs aux Inuit, aux Métis et aux Indiens non inscrits. Les archives des bureaux régionaux (1809-1987) sont formées de documents créés ou conservés par le personnel des Affaires indiennes en poste dans diverses agences et dans les bureaux d'inspection, surintendances ou bureaux régionaux partout au Canada. Ces documents concernent généralement les affaires de certaines bandes, d'agences ou de localités indiennes en particulier. Le groupe RG 10 contient des documents

provenant de presque toutes les agences, mais quelques-uns d'entre eux sont conservés dans d'autres dépôts d'archives. Les archives des terres indiennes (1680-1978) sont disséminées à travers ce groupe de documents, mais celles qui traitent exclusivement des transactions territoriales et de la gestion des terres ont été rassemblées dans cette série qui comprend des documents de cession, de vente et de location de terres partout au pays. Les fichiers informatiques qui figurent dans ce groupe d'archives proviennent de divers programmes gérés par le ministère. Ils contiennent des données sur l'effectif des bandes, le logement en dehors des réserves et l'éducation.

Archives du ministère des Travaux publics : RG 11
1827-1980

1 443,52 mètres
533 microfilms
2 fichiers informatiques

Historique : La Commission des travaux a été créée en 1839 pour le Bas-Canada, puis, en 1841, sa juridiction a été étendue à la province du Canada. Après une importante réorganisation en 1846, elle a été remplacée, en 1859, par le ministère des Travaux publics. Cet organisme était responsable des canaux, des ouvrages en eaux navigables, des ports, des phares, des balises et bouées, des glissoirs et estacades, des routes, des ponts et des immeubles publics. En 1867, le ministère fédéral des Travaux publics a assumé ces fonctions et a fait de même au Nouveau-Brunswick et en Nouvelle-Écosse. À la Confédération, les provinces se sont chargées du contrôle de la plupart des routes et des ponts ainsi que de certains édifices publics. L'exploitation et l'administration des ouvrages maritimes, mais non leur construction, ont été transférées, en 1868, à la Direction de la marine du nouveau ministère de la Marine et des Pêcheries (RG 42). En 1879, le ministère des Chemins de fer et Canaux (RG 43) a assumé la responsabilité de tous les chemins de fer et canaux et des ouvrages connexes. Le Service télégraphique gouvernemental, qui relevait du ministère des Travaux publics depuis 1876, a été transféré au ministère des Transports (RG 12) en 1968. De nos jours, le ministère des Travaux publics gère des biens immobiliers; s'occupe de la construction et de l'entretien des édifices publics, des quais et des jetées, des routes et des ponts, de l'aménagement des ports et des voies navigables, et de l'acquisition de terrains et de locaux pour les besoins du gouvernement fédéral.

Organisation et contenu : Les archives du ministère des Travaux publics, y compris celles de la Commission des travaux (1827-1866), sont formées de six systèmes centraux de dossiers qui couvrent les

années 1839 à 1980 comprenant de la correspondance générale, des dossiers-matières, des registres et des index servant à retrouver l'information à l'intérieur de ces systèmes qui ont été en exploitation de 1839 à 1979. Elles incluent également des dossiers des systèmes utilisés par la Direction des chemins de fer (1867-1879), et par le Service télégraphique gouvernemental (1910-1948); elles renferment des documents de divers comités et commissions, des rapports et des prévisions budgétaires. Les autres séries d'archives sont constituées des documents du Bureau de l'arbitre (1821-1887) renfermant des procès-verbaux, de la correspondance relative à des réclamations et à diverses causes, des documents du Bureau de l'ingénieur en chef (1867-1946), parmi lesquels on retrouve de la correspondance, des dossiers relatifs au projet du canal de navigation de la baie Georgienne et à la région du Pacifique, et les documents du Bureau de l'architecte en chef (1873-1920), qui consistent en correspondance, plans et devis. Les documents informatiques concernent le Répertoire immobilier central pour 1976 et 1977.

Archives du ministère des Transports : RG 12
1825-1984

1 496,3 mètres
1 287 microfilms
28 500 microfiches
27 555 jaquettes
42 fichiers informatiques

Historique : Créé en novembre 1936 par la fusion du ministère de la Marine (RG 42), du ministère des Chemins de fer et Canaux (RG 43) et de la Direction de l'aviation civile du ministère de la Défense nationale (RG 24), le ministère des Transports a essentiellement pour fonction de présider au développement et au fonctionnement d'un système national de transports sûr et efficace. Il fournit une aide financière et des programmes administratifs aux transports aériens, maritimes et de surface, élabore des politiques et contrôle l'application des lois fédérales relatives au transport. Au cours des ans, le ministère a également assumé la responsabilité de plusieurs autres domaines administratifs connexes, tels que les voyages et le tourisme (RG 20, RG 25, RG 124), le téléphone et le télégraphe, les radiocommunications, la télévision, la radiodiffusion privée et commerciale, les télécommunications (RG 41, RG 97, RG 100) et la météorologie (RG 93). Ce ministère est une entité constituée de diverses sociétés d'État plus ou moins autonomes, et de plusieurs organismes et conseils qui font rapport au Parlement par l'intermédiaire du ministre des Transports : Air Canada (RG 70), Chemins de fer nationaux du Canada (RG 30), Corporation des ports Canada (anciennement Con-

CANADA

CERTIFICAT DE NAVIGABILITÉ N°

HYDRAVION FLUVIAL utilisable en mer calme avec un poids total de 1425 KGS

(PLUS LOURDS QUE L'AIR)

En mer agitée cet hydravion peut être utilisé comme HYDRAVION MARITIME avec un poids total ne dépassant pas 1350 KGS. L'utilisation de cet hydravion en mer est limitée à des trajets ce-

PREMIÈRE PARTIE.

Nom, prénoms, adresse, nationalité des propriétaires tiers ou des tra-
ou de la société propriétaire. venées ne dépassant pas une
demi-heure.

1. Nom : COMPAGNIE AERIENNE FRANCAISE
2. Prénoms :
3. Adresse : 18 Rue de Nanterre - SURESNES
4. Nationalité : francaise

Nom du constructeur.

5. Nom : SCHRECK

Marques de nationalité et d'immatriculation.

6.

Description de l'aéronef.

7. Type Schreck   Série 17 HT 4   N° industriel 122
8. Lieu et année de fabrication de l'aéronef : Argenteuil 1929

Genre de l'aéronef....
9. Avion, hydravion ou amphibie : hydravion
10. Nombre de plans : deux
11. Nombre de moteurs : un
12. Nombre de places (équipage compris) : quatre

Classement de l'aéronef.
13. Catégorie : aéraale
14. Subdivision : transport public pour passagers

Certificat habilitant à voler délivré par l'ancienne Direction de l'aviation civile du ministère de la Défense nationale. (RG 12, vol. 58, dossier CF-AEF) (C-76361)

seil des ports nationaux, RG 66), Administration de la voie maritime du Saint-Laurent (RG 52), Bureau canadien de la sécurité aérienne (documents inclus dans RG 12), Office national des transports (anciennement Commission canadienne des transports, RG 46), Administration de pilotage du Pacifique (RG 136) et VIA Rail, pour n'en citer que quelques-uns.

Organisation et contenu : Environ 90 pour 100 des documents de ce groupe sont des dossiers par sujets du service central (1841-1984). Le service central se subdivise en trois grands domaines : transports aériens, maritimes, de surface. Les dossiers par sujets relatifs aux transports aériens traitent de l'immatriculation et de l'exploitation des aéronefs, des types d'appareils et de leurs caractéristiques, de la construction et de l'exploitation des aéroports, des opérations de navigation aérienne, de la médecine aéronautique, du contrôle de la navigation aérienne, des pilotes, des ingénieurs et des contrôleurs de la navigation aérienne. Les archives du transport maritime concernent les agences de transport et les entrepôts, les havres et les ports, les sauvetages, les aides à la navigation, la protection des eaux navigables, le pilotage maritime, l'enregistrement des équipages, les navires du gouvernement canadien, les mesures et l'arpentage, l'immatriculation des navires, l'inspection des bateaux à vapeur, les naufrages, les accidents et les sauvetages. Dans le groupe des transports de surface figurent des archives sur la sécurité des véhicules à moteur, l'élaboration de mesures correctives pour ces véhicules, les règlements relatifs à la sécurité des véhicules, les subventions aux chemins de fer, les terres réservées aux chemins de fer, les bâtiments ferroviaires, l'affrètement de trains, la construction de voies ferrées, les routes, le transport routier et les traversiers. Ce groupe d'archives contient également d'autres dossiers par sujets regroupés pour des raisons purement administratives ou par mesure de sécurité (dossiers confidentiels).

Les 10 pour 100 de documents restant dans ce groupe d'archives ont été créés et maintenus par diverses entités administratives au sein du ministère, mais ils n'ont pas été intégrés dans les systèmes centraux. Ces documents ont été répartis en cinq séries. Les archives de l'Administration du transport maritime (1825-1975) comprennent des registres de navires canadiens (1904-1965), des rapports sur les naufrages (1936-1974), des registres de certificats maritimes (1872-1971), des rapports d'enquête sur les pertes de la marine (1936-1960), des registres de naufrages (1870-1975), des dossiers de la Division des canaux (1825-1976), des dossiers du Registre central des marins (1900-1983) et les documents de l'historien de la marine (v. 1885-1975). Les archives de l'Administration des transports aériens (1939-1980) renferment des registres d'aéroport (1939-1941), et des dossiers de l'Aviation civile internationale (1945-1977) et de la Commission d'enquête sur la sécurité aérienne (1979-1980). Les archives de l'Administration des transports de surface (1866-1951) incluent l'Index des chemins de fer (1866-1936) et des copies de lettres de l'ingénieur en chef du Bureau des canaux Ontario-Saint-Laurent. Les documents administratifs (1936-1972) contiennent les contrats, les actes et les baux relatifs à tous les

aspects du travail du ministère. Les archives du Bureau du ministre (1975-1979) proviennent du bureau de l'honorable Otto Lang. Les documents informatiques renferment des données relatives aux décolages et aux atterrissages d'aéronefs dans les aéroports canadiens (1971-1975), aux campagnes nationales de détection du taux d'alcool sanguin des automobilistes canadiens (1974) et aux enquêtes sur les voyages au Canada (1978-1981), destinées à mieux comprendre les caractéristiques des voyageurs en fonction des moyens de transport qu'ils choisissent, ainsi qu'à étudier le comportement des voyageurs et des touristes.

Archives du ministère de la Justice : RG 13
1597-1976

443,6 mètres
365 microfilms
28 fichiers informatiques

Historique : La création du ministère de la Justice a été sanctionnée le 22 mai 1868 au cours de la première session du Parlement du Dominion du Canada, et ce ministère est aujourd'hui régi par la *Loi sur le ministère de la Justice*. Les attributions du ministère sont demeurées essentiellement les mêmes depuis l'adoption de la loi de 1868. Le ministère est le conseiller juridique officiel du gouvernement et du Conseil privé de la reine pour le Canada. Il s'occupe de toutes les questions relatives à l'administration de la justice au Canada qui n'entrent pas dans les attributions des gouvernements provinciaux, rédige les lois, les contrats et les autres documents juridiques et donne avis sur les lois et délibérations des corps législatifs provinciaux. Le ministre de la Justice est d'office le procureur général et, à ce titre, il donne avis aux ministères du gouvernement fédéral, il règle ou dirige la demande ou la défense des contestations formées pour ou contre le gouvernement ou un ministère public. Les fonctions juridiques du ministère sont exercées par une administration centrale à Ottawa et neuf bureaux régionaux.

Organisation et contenu : Dans ce fonds étroitement lié aux différentes fonctions du ministère se trouve d'abord une série de dossiers du service central (1859-1934) renfermant un ensemble de répertoires alphabétiques et de registres à entrées numériques. Ceux-ci servent à repérer le courrier reçu ou adressé par le ministère. Cette série contient aussi des dossiers sur les nominations et traitements des juges (1848-1958), sur des procédures d'extradition (1848-1951), sur les relations canado-américaines, de la correspondance sur des causes seigneuriales, des demandes d'amendements au code criminel, entre autres. Une deuxième série rassemble des dossiers des services juridiques, notamment ceux portant sur des causes entraînant la peine capitale (1867-

1976), sur les ordonnances de restrictions ou de détentions (1939-1941), sur l'arbitrage de comptes non réglés entre le Dominion, le Québec et l'Ontario (1867-1901), sur les contestations civiles mettant en cause le gouvernement (1863-1934), ainsi que des dossiers de la section de la législation responsable de la rédaction des bills territoriaux (1948-1949). En plus des registres de rémissions et des dossiers individuels dans la série de la Direction des pardons (1888-1962), le fonds comprend de la documentation sur la réforme du système pénal dans la série de la Direction des pénitenciers (1834-1962). Une des séries de dossiers particuliers regroupe des renseignements sur un ensemble de questions relevant du procureur général du Canada-Ouest (1832-1866). Elle regroupe aussi des dossiers sur des controverses historiques dont celles qui portaient sur la frontière du Labrador (1926), sur les pêcheries de l'Atlantique Nord et la décision du tribunal d'arbitrage de La Haye (1910), sur les annexionnistes américains (1893-1894) et sur la préparation, par le conseiller technique James White, de la défense du Dominion relativement à la frontière entre le Canada et Terre-Neuve (1597-1926). Cette série comprend de la documentation sur Louis Riel et la rébellion du Nord-Ouest (1873-1886). Ce fonds renferme par ailleurs des documents de la Direction des faillites (1932-1955) et des sections des Contestations civiles et des biens (1884-1897, 1904-1950). Il comprend en plus des fichiers informatiques sur la procédure et la disposition de causes entendues par la Cour de l'Échiquier, par la Cour fédérale et la Cour suprême (1920-1979), ainsi que copie des lois constitutionnelles.

Archives du Parlement : RG 14
1828-1984

562 mètres
666 microfilms
153 fichiers informatiques

Historique : Le Parlement du Canada a été créé en 1867 conformément aux dispositions de l'*Acte de l'Amérique du Nord britannique*. Il est composé d'une chambre haute dont les membres sont nommés, le Sénat, et d'une chambre basse dont les membres sont élus au suffrage universel, la Chambre des communes. La constitution confère au Parlement le pouvoir législatif. La plupart des documents de la Chambre des communes sont postérieurs à 1916, date à laquelle l'édifice central du Parlement a été détruit par le feu.

Organisation et contenu : Ces documents sont généralement postérieurs à la proclamation de la Confédération. La plupart des archives parlementaires antérieures à la Confédération sont conservées à

la Division des manuscrits des Archives nationales. Les documents sont organisés en fonction des sessions parlementaires. Ils comprennent les archives de la Chambre des communes (1866-1983) : documents parlementaires (1916-1983), appendices aux journaux de la Chambre (1919-1965), projets de lois et statuts (1869-1960), dossiers des comités (1874-1945), dossiers électoraux (1867-1950), débats (1867-1974), dossiers du greffier et de l'orateur et listes d'assermentation (1867-1974), copies manuscrites des procès-verbaux (1903-1968), dossiers administratifs (1828-1945), procès-verbaux (1926-1961), affaires inachevées (1896-1965), résolutions budgétaires (1909-1963) et dossiers de la Masse (1917). Les archives du Sénat (1867-1974) renferment les dossiers du gentilhomme-huissier de la verge noire (1903-1974), les documents parlementaires, des copies de lettres du Conseil législatif (1854-1870) et des dossiers du Sénat et des comités (1895-1971). Au nombre des autres documents parlementaires figurent ceux de la bibliothèque du Parlement (1858-1956) et des documents de l'Union interparlementaire (1926, 1933-1937). Les fichiers informatiques contiennent les débats de la Chambre des communes (1973-1986) et certains procès-verbaux de comités des Communes (1979-1986).

Archives du ministère de l'Intérieur : RG 15
1821-1961

654,3 mètres
169 microfilms
258 livres de cartes à fenêtre

Historique : Le ministère de l'Intérieur a été institué en 1873 pour administrer toutes les terres fédérales et les ressources naturelles des Prairies canadiennes, de la Railway Belt de la Colombie-Britannique et du Grand Nord. Héritant de fonctions auparavant exercées par le Secrétariat d'État (RG 6) et le ministère des Travaux publics (RG 11), il devait veiller à la colonisation des grandes étendues vierges du Canada et voir à ce que cette démarche s'intègre à la politique nationale de John A. Macdonald en vue de réaliser l'objectif d'une nation s'étendant d'un océan à l'autre. Quand la population s'est mise à envahir l'Ouest, il a reçu en 1892 une nouvelle responsabilité, celle de l'immigration, exercée jusque-là par le ministère de l'Agriculture (RG 17). Le développement rapide de l'Ouest et du Nord à partir du milieu des années 1890 jusqu'à la Première Guerre mondiale l'a forcé à élargir ses horizons et ses structures; bon nombre de ses directions ont été divisées, puis subdivisées, pour répondre à leurs besoins devenus beaucoup plus importants.

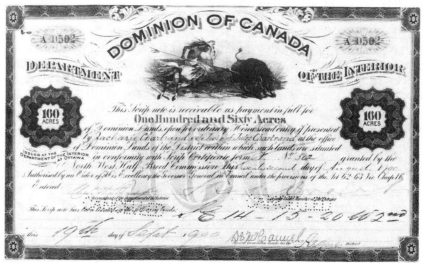

Un exemple de notes émises par le ministère de l'Intérieur. Le détenteur pouvait réclamer de l'argent ou l'échanger contre 160 acres de terres agricoles. À diverses époques, ces notes ont été délivrées aux Métis, aux premiers colons blancs de la région de la rivière Rouge et aux miliciens. (RG 15, vol. 1407, 22 août 1900) (C-89332)

En 1930, quand le processus de peuplement a été à peu près achevé, l'administration des terres publiques et des ressources naturelles des Prairies a été confiée aux gouvernements provinciaux, de sorte que le ministère de l'Intérieur n'avait pratiquement plus de raison d'être. Lorsqu'il a été aboli en 1936, une bonne partie des dossiers actifs du ministère, et plus particulièrement ceux qui traitaient de l'arpentage des terres, du bois, de l'eau et des minéraux, ont été transférés aux trois provinces des Prairies. Les autres ont été confiés au nouveau ministère des Mines et des Ressources (puis à ses nombreux successeurs; voir RG 21 et RG 22).

Les diverses directions du ministère de l'Intérieur avaient leurs propres systèmes de classification de dossiers, qui, après 1936, ont été conservés tels quels dans d'autres ministères. C'est pourquoi ces dossiers se retrouvent aujourd'hui dans différents groupes d'archives, y compris Affaires indiennes (RG 10), Gendarmerie royale du Canada (RG 18), Forêts (RG 39), Commission géologique du Canada (RG 45), Observatoires du Canada (RG 48), Immigration (RG 76), Parcs nationaux (RG 84), Programme des affaires du Nord (RG 85), Mines (RG 86), Direction des ressources minérales (RG 87), Direction des levés et de la cartographie (RG 88), Direction des ressources hydrauliques (RG 89), Commission des champs de bataille nationaux (RG 90), Gouvernement du territoire du Yukon (RG 91) et Direction de la

géographie (RG 92). La principale fonction du ministère de l'Intérieur a été la colonisation et l'administration des terres. Les documents de la Direction des terres et des sections connexes constituent donc l'essentiel du RG 15, bien qu'y soient aussi représentées dans une certaine mesure toutes les directions qui ont fait partie du ministère à un moment ou à un autre.

Organisation et contenu : On trouvera les documents administratifs et opérationnels du ministère dans la série du Cabinet du sous-ministre (1873-1958); les documents financiers dans Direction des comptes (1876-1959); et les documents juridiques dans Direction du solliciteur (1898-1928). La série de l'Administration des terres fédérales (1821-1959) contient des documents administratifs et des dossiers-matières sur l'administration et le peuplement des terres de l'Ouest, y compris le peuplement par des groupes ethniques et des compagnies de colonisation. Les archives qui concernent plus particulièrement les terres de l'Artillerie se trouvent dans Direction des terres de l'Artillerie et de l'Amirauté (1821-1947), et celles qui concernent les terres des écoles sont classées dans Direction des terres des écoles (1904-1934). Les registres des subventions aux colons désireux de s'établir et les lettres patentes sont inclus dans la série de la Direction des concessions de terrains (1835-1961). La série de la Direction du bois et des pâturages (1873-1953) contient des documents relatifs au développement des ressources naturelles par le secteur privé, en particulier la location de pâturages et les permis d'abattage du bois, d'irrigation et d'exploitation minière. Ce groupe d'archives comprend également trois autres séries de moindre envergure : la série de la Direction des territoires du Nord (1873-1883), qui comprend principalement des lettres adressées au ministre de l'Intérieur et la correspondance du lieutenant-gouverneur des Territoires du Nord-Ouest; la série de la Direction des terres de la Colombie-Britannique (1885-1957), qui renferme de la correspondance relative au Railway Belt en Colombie-Britannique; et la série de la Direction des terres de l'Artillerie, de l'Amirauté et des chemins de fer (1922-1932), qui consiste en notes d'arpentage prises sur le terrain.

Archives du ministère du Revenu national : RG 16
1787-1981

215 mètres
61 microfilms

Historique : Le ministère du Revenu national ou, comme on l'appelle de nos jours, Revenu Canada, a été créé peu après la Confédération. En effet, dès 1868, le gouvernement canadien a mis sur pied deux ministères distincts : le ministère des Douanes, chargé de percevoir les droits de

douane et les péages sur les canaux, et le ministère du Revenu intérieur, auquel on laissait le soin de prélever tous les droits d'accise, les taxes indirectes et les droits de timbre.

En 1887, les deux ministres sont devenus de simples contrôleurs qui allaient relever par la suite du ministère du Commerce de 1892 à 1897. En 1897, ils ont de nouveau été élevés au rang de ministres. En 1918, les deux ministères ainsi rétablis ont été fusionnés de nouveau pour former le ministère des Douanes et du Revenu intérieur. De 1921 à 1927, ce dernier a changé de nom pour celui de ministère des Douanes et de l'Accise. La perception de l'impôt, qui incombait au ministère des Finances depuis 1917, a été confiée, à partir de 1924, au ministère des Douanes et de l'Accise. En 1927, ce dernier prend le nom de ministère du Revenu national.

Le ministère actuel est divisé en deux composantes organiques : *Douanes et Accise* et *Impôt*.

Organisation et contenu : Les documents sont organisés en trois séries. La première regroupe les documents relatifs à la douane, à l'accise et au revenu intérieur. On y retrouve principalement la correspondance et les rapports provenant des receveurs des ports douaniers et adressés au commissaire des douanes (1790-1882). Cette correspondance est organisée par nom de port et chronologiquement. Les archives des ports (1795-1965) contiennent les registres de contrôle des navires, et des importations et exportations ainsi que des livres de comptabilité. Sous la rubrique des dossiers spéciaux (1928-1970), ont été classés les lois, proclamations, décrets du Conseil, circulaires et directives ayant trait à l'administration du ministère. Certains dossiers relatifs à l'application des tarifs (1920-1965) ont été conservés comme échantillons. Les dossiers du commissaire des douanes (1893-1963) traitent de la réglementation s'appliquant aux distilleries et aux producteurs de tabac. La seconde série est constituée de dossiers de Douanes et Accise provenant du Cabinet des sous-ministres (1925-1961), et contient, d'une part, les réponses du ministre à la Chambre des communes et, d'autre part, des documents relatifs à certaines pratiques frauduleuses au sein du ministère. La troisième série, intitulée Impôt, comprend les exemplaires de formulaires d'impôt (1917-1965), certains procès-verbaux de la Commission sur l'organisation du gouvernement (Glassco) (1962-1968), un échantillonnage des régimes de pension présentés par les sociétés émettrices de régimes de pension, certains dossiers se rapportant à la *Loi de la taxe de guerre* sur les bénéfices du commerce (1915-1921) et enfin, un échantillonnage de dossiers individuels sur les droits de sucession.

Archives du ministère de l'Agriculture : RG 17
1845-1987

1 632,40 mètres
435 microfilms
1 fichier informatique

Historique : Initialement, nombre de responsabilités assumées par le ministère fédéral de l'Agriculture n'étaient pas directement reliées à l'agriculture. Songeons par exemple, à l'immigration (RG 76, 26, 15), au recensement et aux statistiques (RG 31), aux hôpitaux pour immigrants et marins (RG 29), aux expositions internationales (RG 72), aux brevets, droit d'auteur et dessins industriels (RG 105), aux archives (RG 37), à la quarantaine et à la santé publique (RG 29). Au tournant du siècle, le système des fermes expérimentales a permis de développer considérablement la recherche agricole théorique et appliquée et d'accroître les activités agricoles du ministère. Au début du vingtième siècle, les responsabilités du ministère s'étaient étendues et incluaient tous les aspects de la recherche, de la production, de la mise en marché, du commerce et de l'aide économique agricoles. Entre 1867 et 1919, les fonctions non agricoles du ministère ont été progressivement transférées à d'autres ministères fédéraux, et le mandat du ministère de l'Agriculture a de plus en plus reflété des préoccupations purement agricoles.

Organisation et contenu : RG 17 se divise en plusieurs séries. Le premier grand système central de classification de dossiers, dossiers du ministre, du sous-ministre et du secrétaire (1852-1920), documente les activités du ministère dans le domaine de l'agriculture, de l'immigration, de la quarantaine et de la santé publique, des recensements et des statistiques, des brevets, du droit d'auteur, des marques du bois, des expositions internationales et des archives. (Des séries moins volumineuses contiennent des copies de lettres et de la correspondance relatives aux fonctions énumérées ci-dessus.) Le deuxième système de classification de dossiers du ministère, dossiers du service central et index (1918-1953), et plusieurs systèmes connexes provenant de certaines directions, illustrent abondamment les activités ministérielles entre 1920 et le début des années 50. Ces documents traitent du système des fermes expérimentales, de tous les aspects de la recherche sur les animaux, les plantes et la production agricole, de la biologie forestière, de l'administration pendant la guerre, des paris dans les hippodromes, de la commercialisation des produits agricoles, de la certification et de l'inspection des denrées alimentaires, du commerce international, des programmes d'aide et de l'administration du ministère. Créé en 1960, le troisième système de classification de dossiers, dossiers du service central (1959-1974), contient des dossiers-matières dont certains con-

cernent le milieu des années 80 et témoignent des activités des directions opérationnelles d'Agriculture Canada : Recherche, Production et Inspection des aliments, Communications, Commercialisation et Économie, Finance et Administration, et Direction générale du soutien du revenu agricole. D'autres séries de documents traitent de questions connexes, telles que les travaux de la Commission d'examen de l'alachlore (1987). Le fichier informatique contient des renseignements sur les producteurs de la Commission canadienne du lait pour l'année 1975.

Archives de la Gendarmerie royale du Canada : RG 18
1863-1982

473 mètres
416 microfilms

Historique : La Police montée du Nord-Ouest a été créée en 1873 pour administrer la justice dans les Territoires du Nord-Ouest, plus particulièrement pour pacifier les Indiens, réprimer le trafic d'alcool et percevoir les redevances douanières. À l'origine, la PMNO comptait deux centres de responsabilité : le contrôleur, établi à Ottawa, qui faisait rapport au Parlement par l'entremise du ministère responsable, et le commissaire, installé dans l'Ouest, qui relevait du contrôleur pour les opérations quotidiennes du corps policier.

Lors de la réorganisation de 1920, la PMNO a pris le nom de Gendarmerie royale du Canada (GRC), le Bureau du contrôleur a été aboli et celui du commissaire transféré à Ottawa. À cette époque, la GRC a assumé les responsabilités du maintien de la sécurité intérieure qui incombaient auparavant à la police fédérale, et elle en a récupéré le personnel.

La GRC s'occupe aujourd'hui de l'application de toutes les lois fédérales au Canada et, en vertu d'une entente, des lois pénales et provinciales dans toutes les provinces à l'exception du Québec et de l'Ontario. Depuis 1873, elle a relevé de nombreux ministères, mais elle fait rapport au Parlement par l'entremise du solliciteur général.

Organisation et contenu : Ces archives sont organisées par centres de responsabilités et débutent avec les documents du Bureau du contrôleur (1874-1919) et ceux du Bureau du commissaire (1876-1920). Ces deux séries de documents, formées de dossiers-matières classifiés selon le même système, contiennent des lettres reçues qui sont représentatives de toutes les activités du corps policier. Très souvent, les dossiers incluent aussi des copies des lettres envoyées. Ces deux séries sont complétées par des copies de lettres. Elles renferment également des documents

relatifs aux finances, aux approvisionnements, aux services de quarantaine, aux patrouilles du Nord et aux premières enquêtes criminelles. D'autres séries d'archives sont formées des dossiers des divisions et détachements (1874-1980), sorte d'échantillonnage de journaux personnels, de télégrammes, de règlements locaux et de copies de lettres de certaines divisions et de certains détachements (on trouvera plus de détails sur les opérations quotidiennes des divisions et des détachements dans les dossiers du Bureau du commissaire); des dossiers de la police fédérale (1872-1919), comprenant des copies de lettres du commissaire de police et des registres du personnel; les dossiers du Yukon (1898-1951), formés de copies de lettres, de journaux, de règlements généraux et de quelques dossiers-matières (les dossiers du Bureau du contrôleur et du Bureau du commissaire contiennent aussi des rapports de patrouille, des rapports d'enquête et des dossiers administratifs relatifs au Yukon); des dossiers de la Gendarmerie royale du Canada (1902-1982), des dossiers provenant du service central du quartier général créé après 1920; des dossiers de la Direction des enquêtes criminelles; des dossiers relatifs à la sécurité, et les dossiers du personnel (1873-1954) qui couvrent la PMNO, la PMRNO et la GRC.

Archives du ministère des Finances : RG 19
1775-1981

835 mètres
835 microfilms

Historique : Bien qu'on puisse retracer ses origines dans les fonctions exercées par le Bureau du receveur général mis sur pied au dix-huitième siècle, le ministère des Finances a été officiellement créé en 1869. À différents moments de son histoire, il s'est occupé du Conseil du Trésor (RG 55), de la Monnaie royale canadienne (RG 120), de la perception de l'impôt (RG 16), des pensions de vieillesse, du fonds de retraite et de la Commission du tarif (RG 79). Certaines de ces attributions ont été confiées à d'autres ministères et organismes au cours des années 30 de sorte qu'il a pu dès lors se consacrer à un travail central d'analyse et d'élaboration des politiques. Aujourd'hui, il est chargé principalement d'aider le gouvernement à élaborer et mettre en œuvre les politiques fiscales ou à prendre des mesures d'ordre financier et économique qui répondent le mieux à ses grands objectifs en matière de fiscalité. Les différentes tâches que cela comporte sont réparties entre les directions suivantes : politique et législation de l'impôt, relations fédérales-provinciales et politique sociale, programmes économiques et finances de

l'État, politique fiscale et analyse économique, finances et commerce international. Enfin, le ministre des Finances est responsable de l'application de plus de soixante lois du Parlement.

Organisation et contenu : Les archives du ministère des Finances ont été organisées selon six grandes séries. La première, celle des documents sur l'abolition du régime seigneurial (1853-1929), comprend la correspondance générale, les pièces justificatives des index et des registres. La série du Bureau du receveur général (1775-1879) contient les livres de comptes, les autorisations de paiement et la correspondance reçue et envoyée. La série des organismes et lois administrés par le ministère renferme les dossiers relatifs aux lois et aux agences dont il a été chargé. Les archives financières (1810-1966) servent de complément à celles du Bureau du receveur général décrites précédemment. Elles contiennent divers documents de comptabilité, tels que les grands livres généraux, les autorisations de paiement, la liste de paie. La correspondance ministérielle comprend des documents qui font état de la correspondance reçue et envoyée par le ministère de 1840 à 1957. Tout comme celles qui suivent, ces archives sont très consultées par les chercheurs. La principale caractéristique de celles-ci est de tenir compte des ministres, sous-ministres et fonctionnaires supérieurs qui ont œuvré au sein du ministère au cours de cette période. On y retrouve aussi des dossiers relatifs à divers comités. Les dossiers du registre central, à l'exception des dossiers du Bureau du ministre des Finances Donald M. Fleming, rassemblent les documents créés par les diverses directions et divisions du ministère. Ils couvrent des sujets relatifs aux programmes internationaux, aux relations économiques internationales, au tarif, aux finances internationales, à la législation, au Conseil spécial en matière d'imposition et au Comité sur la structure fiscale. En font partie aussi des dossiers traitant des relations fédérales-provinciales, de la politique sociale, des programmes sur les ressources, du développement économique et des finances de l'État. Une rubrique intitulée « sujets spéciaux » et incluant les dossiers de la Société canadienne d'hypothèques et de logement, une collection de communiqués de presse et des dossiers de la Société d'assurance-dépôt du Canada et de l'Office de développement municipal et de prêts aux municipalités complètent cette série.

Archives du ministère de l'Industrie et du Commerce : RG 20
1880-1983

1 339,9 mètres
161 microfilms
29 fichiers informatiques

Historique : Créé en 1892, le ministère du Commerce s'est vu confier les affaires commerciales qu'administrait jusqu'alors le ministère des Finances (RG 19). À différents moments de son histoire, il a été chargé des subventions aux transporteurs maritimes et aux courriers postaux, de

Un étalage de produits canadiens dans une vitrine d'un magasin de Glasgow représentant l'effort promotionnel du Canada. (RG 20, vol. 203, dossier 28804, partie 3) (C-98901)

l'immigration chinoise (RG 76), du recensement et de la statistique (RG 31), du commerce des grains, de la Commission des expositions (RG 72) et d'une foule d'autres attributions aujourd'hui exercées par d'autres ministères.

Créé en 1963, le ministère de l'Industrie avait pour mandat de favoriser l'expansion de l'industrie manufacturière canadienne; d'améliorer la balance des paiements; de favoriser la recherche et le développement et de promouvoir l'efficacité et la rentabilité industrielles. En outre, l'Agence de développement régional du ministère était chargée de concevoir et d'implanter des activités de développement économique dans certaines régions.

En 1969, le ministère du Commerce et celui de l'Industrie ont été fusionnés pour former le ministère de l'Industrie et du Commerce. Il a pour principal objectif de favoriser la croissance, la productivité, les possibilités d'emploi et la prospérité de l'économie canadienne grâce à une saine évolution des industries de fabrication et de transformation et à l'expansion du commerce et du tourisme. En 1982, les responsabilités liées au développement des industries canadiennes ont été transférées à un nouveau ministère appelé Expansion industrielle régionale, et les fonctions associées au commerce international ont été confiées aux Affaires extérieures (RG 25).

Organisation et contenu : Une grande partie des archives du RG 20 proviennent des systèmes centraux de dossiers des trois ministères concernés et elles couvrent tous les aspects de leurs activités. Le ministère du Commerce disposait de quatre systèmes; un système pour la correspondance et trois systèmes de dossiers par sujet utilisés respectivement de 1893 à 1905; de 1906 à 1961; de 1961 à 1966 et de 1966 à 1969. Le ministère de l'Industrie et le ministère de l'Industrie et du Commerce n'ont utilisé qu'un seul système de dossiers durant toute leur existence. Outre les systèmes centraux, ce groupe d'archives comprend des documents produits par certaines composantes des ministères. Ce sont : dossiers administratifs et de référence de la Direction des recherches et du développement économique (1926-1955); dossiers de la Direction des ressources (1946-1959); dossiers de la Direction de l'esthétique industrielle, devenue Design Canada, qui renferment de la correspondance, des dossiers d'employés et des documents relatifs aux distinctions (1947-1985); dossiers de la Direction des relations commerciales internationales qui traitent de sujets tels que les tarifs internationaux et le GATT (1912-1969); documents relatifs à Expo 67 provenant de la Direction des foires et des missions (1963-1971); dossiers du Service des délégués commerciaux qui consistent essentiellement en rapports de délégués (1921-1960); et dossiers de la Direction de

l'agriculture et des pêches qui traitent principalement de la production et de l'exportation des grains. On trouve également dans RG 20 des dossiers administratifs et des dossiers-matières créés par différents ministres et sous-ministres de ces ministères (1892-1977). Dossiers de la Section historique (1892-1977) compilés par l'historien du ministère. Les documents informatiques contiennent des enquêtes sur le tourisme (1971-1974), les habitudes de consommation (1977), les investissements et l'industrie (1975-1978), l'histoire de l'emploi et de la main-d'œuvre (1977-1979) et les vacances (1967-1983).

Archives du ministère de l'Énergie, des Mines et des Ressources : RG 21
1883-1985

97,2 mètres
7 fichiers informatiques

Historique : Lorsque le ministère de l'Intérieur (RG 15) a été démantelé en 1936, les responsabilités gouvernementales en matière de cartographie, d'arpentage, de mines, d'énergie et de quantité d'autres ressources ont été transférées successivement aux trois ministères suivants : Mines et Ressources (1936-1949), Mines et Relevés techniques (1949-1966) et Énergie, Mines et Ressources (1966-1979). (On trouvera d'autres renseignements sur les successeurs directs du ministère de l'Intérieur à la notice du RG 22.) RG 21 est constitué essentiellement de dossiers généraux relatifs à l'élaboration des politiques, qui proviennent des services centraux de documents des ministères concernés. Les documents opérationnels qui traitent de la mise en œuvre de ces politiques, y compris ceux qui datent de l'époque où les fonctions relevaient du ministère de l'Intérieur, sont maintenant conservés dans les groupes d'archives suivants : Commission géologique du Canada (RG 45), Observatoires du Canada (RG 48), Office fédéral du charbon (RG 81), Direction des mines (RG 86), Direction des ressources minérales (RG 87), Direction des levés et de la cartographie (RG 88), Direction des ressources hydrauliques (RG 89) et Direction de la géographie (RG 92). À la différence de chacun de ces groupes d'archives qui traitent de sujets particuliers, RG 21 documente l'ensemble de ces fonctions. Par ailleurs, certains documents du RG 21 concernent les activités d'un certain nombre d'organismes qui font rapport au Parlement par l'entremise du ministère de l'Énergie, des Mines et des Ressources, à savoir, Énergie atomique du Canada Ltée, Eldorado Nucléaire Ltée et ses filiales (RG 134), la Commission de contrôle de l'énergie atomique (RG 60), l'Office national de l'énergie (RG 99), Uranium Canada Ltée et la Commission des frontières interprovinciales.

Organisation et contenu : Ces archives sont réparties dans plusieurs séries. Les documents du Cabinet du sous-ministre (1931-1969, 1983-1984) informent sur toutes les activités du ministère et de ses prédécesseurs, ainsi que sur les comités, les conseils, les groupes consultatifs et les questions relatives à des ressources ou sources d'énergie particulières. La série des dossiers du service central (1930-1981) contient à la fois des dossiers administratifs et des dossiers opérationnels relatifs aux fonctions et aux activités du ministère et de ses diverses directions. On trouve dans cette série des dossiers traitant de l'administration, des finances, des services généraux, des propriétés, du personnel, de la gestion du matériel et des services d'information et d'un large éventail de questions opérationnelles. Ce groupe d'archives renferme en outre des séries de documents relatifs à la Direction des projets spéciaux (1939-1949), et au Comité permanent canadien des noms géographiques (1883-1973), et des dossiers sur l'Institut canadien des mines et de la métallurgie (1965-1975), la Commission de l'énergie (Commission Borden, 1958-1959) et le programme ENER-SAVE/HOMEPLAN (1966-1985). Les fichiers informatiques contiennent des données sur la répartition et la concentration des traces de métaux dans les sédiments lacustres.

Archives du ministère des Affaires indiennes et du Nord canadien : RG 22
1867-1988

219,7 mètres
2 fichiers informatiques

Historique : Après l'abolition, en 1936, du ministère de l'Intérieur (RG 15), nombre de ses responsabilités en matière de questions autochtones et de développement des ressources de l'Ouest et du Nord ont incombé successivement à quatre ministères fédéraux : Mines et Ressources (1936-1949), Ressources et Développement économique (1949-1953), Nord canadien et Ressources nationales (1953-1966) et Affaires indiennes et Nord canadien (1966). (On trouvera d'autres renseignements sur les successeurs directs du ministère de l'Intérieur à la notice du RG 21.) Les diverses responsabilités du ministère de l'Intérieur ont donc été réparties, au cours des ans, entre les nombreuses, et très éphémères, composantes administratives de ces ministères. Simultanément, ceux-ci ont été chargés d'un grand nombre de responsabilités nouvelles.

Les quatre successeurs du ministère de l'Intérieur (voir ci-dessus) ont conservé séparément les archives relatives à l'élaboration des politiques et celles qui concernent la mise en œuvre de ces politiques dans différents secteurs de programmes. Ce sont les archives relatives à

l'élaboration des politiques que l'on trouve dans RG 22. Les documents relatifs aux opérations des divers programmes administrés par un ou plusieurs de ces ministères, y compris par le ministère de l'Intérieur, sont conservés dans des groupes d'archives distincts : Affaires indiennes (RG 10), Service canadien des forêts (RG 39), Service canadien des parcs nationaux (RG 84), Direction des affaires du Nord (RG 85), Direction des mines (RG 86), Direction des ressources minérales (RG 87), Direction des levés et de la cartographie (RG 88), Direction des ressources hydrauliques (RG 89), Commission des champs de bataille nationaux (RG 90), Territoire du Yukon (RG 91) et Service canadien de la faune (RG 109).

RG 22 contient également des dossiers créés par un certain nombre de commissions et de comités mis sur pied après 1936 (tels que la Commission d'enquête sur le gazoduc de la route de l'Alaska) qui concernent les politiques des divers secteurs de programmes administrés par les successeurs du ministère de l'Intérieur. Parmi les autres documents figurent ceux des nombreux organismes qui font rapport au Parlement par l'entremise des ministres responsables de ces ministères, à savoir ceux du commissaire du Yukon, du commissaire des Territoires du Nord-Ouest et de la Commission d'énergie du Nord canadien (RG 96).

Organisation et contenu : Les documents sont regroupés en séries qui reflètent les activités des ministères qu'elles représentent, à savoir le ministère des Ressources et du Développement économique (1867-1957), le ministère des Affaires du Nord et des Ressources nationales (1944-1966), le ministère des Affaires indiennes (1937-1975), le Cabinet du sous-ministre (1953-1967), les Affaires indiennes et du Nord canadien (1922-1977) et les Affaires indiennes et du Nord canadien (1967-1988). Les archives créées par le Cabinet du sous-ministre (1922-1983), la Division de l'information et ses prédécesseurs (1920-1972), la Direction de l'ingénierie et de l'architecture et ses prédécesseurs (1913-1976) et le Programme de l'administration (1937-1977), présentent un intérêt tout particulier. On trouve également dans ce groupe d'archives des séries de documents qui concernent la Commission consultative de l'évolution du gouvernement dans les Territoires du Nord-Ouest (1965-1966), la Commission d'enquête sur le gazoduc de la route de l'Alaska (1974-1977), le coordonnateur du Comité consultatif de la mise en valeur du Nord (1953-1967), le conseiller supérieur en sciences (1968-1977), le Bureau des revendications autochtones (1976-1987) et le Bureau du groupe de travail chargé de la révision des politiques des revendications globales (1973-1986). Les fichiers informatiques con-

tiennent des enquêtes relatives à l'utilisation des canaux en 1977-1978 et renseignent sur le trafic des canaux administrés par le gouvernement fédéral.

Archives du ministère des Pêches et des Océans : RG 23
1883-1984

544,8 mètres
372 microfilms
1 fichier informatique

Historique : En 1868, le nouveau Dominion a créé le ministère de la Marine et des Pêcheries, qui était chargé de promouvoir et de protéger la pêche dans les zones côtières ct dans les eaux intérieures du Canada. Après avoir été placé sous l'autorité du ministère du Service naval en 1914, Marine et Pêcheries est redevenu un ministère autonome en 1920. En 1930, le ministère des Pêcheries est devenu autonome et ce, jusqu'en 1969, date à laquelle les programmes fédéraux de la pêche et des forêts ont été fusionnés pour former le ministère des Pêches et des Forêts (voir RG 39). Celui-ci a été aboli peu après et, en 1972, ses programmes sont devenus les principales composantes du nouveau ministère de l'Environnement. Après l'abolition, au milieu des années 70, de l'éphémère ministère des Pêches et de l'Environnement, les activités liées à la pêche ont été transférées, en 1979, au nouveau ministère des Pêches et des Océans.

Depuis la fin du dix-neuvième siècle, divers organismes du gouvernement canadien ont participé à la recherche océanographique (voir RG 42 et 139), particulièrement au cours des années 30 et 40. L'attention croissante accordée au droit maritime, pendant les années 50 et 60, tant au Canada que dans le monde entier, a incité le gouvernement fédéral à accroître ses activités océanographiques sur les côtes canadiennes et à les organiser de façon plus formelle et structurée, que leurs objectifs soient scientifiques, défensifs ou économiques. Au début des années 60, le ministère des Mines et des Relevés techniques a travaillé de façon active aux levés et à la recherchc dans les eaux côtières canadiennes, ce qui a amené la création, en 1961, d'une Division de la recherche océanographique au sein de la Direction des levés et de la cartographie, puis, un an plus tard, d'une Direction des sciences de la mer. Cette direction a hérité du Service hydrographique du Canada (RG 139), de la Division de la recherche océanographique et de la Division des navires. C'est aussi à cette époque, en 1962, qu'a été créé l'institut Bedford d'océanographie et l'Institut des sciences de la mer. La Direction des sciences de la mer a par la suite été transférée au ministère de l'Énergie, des Mines et des Ressources (RG 21) en 1966, puis, en 1972,

au ministère de l'Environnement (RG 108). Finalement, en 1979, le programme océanographique a été confié à Pêches et Océans, où se trouvent actuellement réunis les programmes du gouvernement fédéral de gestion des pêches et de sciences océanographiques.

Organisation et contenu : Les archives de Pêches et Océans sont réparties dans les séries suivantes : les dossiers administratifs (1908-1979) concernent divers conseils, comités et commissions et proviennent des cabinets de plusieurs ministres et sous-ministres; les archives du service central (1883-1915) couvrent un vaste éventail de sujets liés à la protection et à la conservation des pêcheries; les dossiers du service central (de 1915 aux années 60), où l'on trouve, outre les sujets déjà traités dans le précédent système de classification, des dossiers relatifs aux lois et règlements, aux conférences, congrès et assemblées, aux recherches sur les espèces et sur la pisciculture, aux bateaux de pêche, aux techniques d'entreposage et de capture du poisson, aux programmes de développement économique, aux accords scientifiques et économiques internationaux et à la coopération internationale; et les archives du Conseil de recherches sur les pêcheries du Canada (1953-1979), qui renferment des dossiers du service central et des transcriptions d'interviews avec des personnalités du gouvernement. Enfin, ce groupe d'archives contient des dossiers qui proviennent d'un système central de dossiers ouvert plus récemment par Pêches et Océans. Ces dossiers traitent de questions analogues à celles évoquées plus haut et s'échelonnent des années 40 aux années 70. Le fichier informatique contient des données de 1977 tirées du Système d'information sur la délivrance de permis aux bateaux de pêche étrangers.

Archives du ministère de la Défense nationale : RG 24
1870-1982

8 290,4 mètres
6 506 microfilms
870 microfiches
19 fichiers informatiques

Historique : Ce ministère a été établi en 1922 lorsqu'on a fusionné le ministère de la Milice et de la Défense (RG 9), le ministère du Service de la marine et la Commission de l'air. En 1968, la Marine royale canadienne, l'Armée canadienne et l'Aviation royale du Canada ont été fusionnées pour former les Forces armées canadiennes. Le ministère de la Défense nationale est chargé de la haute direction des Forces armées et de toutes les questions relatives à la défense nationale, y compris la construction et l'entretien des établissements et des installations de défense.

Organisation et contenu : Les archives sont divisées en huit séries générales, à savoir celles du Cabinet du ministre (1917-1920, 1947-1957), des fonctions interarmées (1942-1970), de l'état-major interarmées, de l'armée de terre (1870-1967), de la marine (1903-1970), de l'aviation (1920-1965), des Forces armées canadiennes (1940-1982) et du Conseil de recherches pour la défense (1943-1974). Chacun des corps d'armée, le Conseil de recherches pour la défense et les services relatifs au personnel disposaient de leur propre système de classification de dossiers, que les Archives ont conservé au sein de chacune des séries. Les trois corps d'armée, puis les Forces armées après la réunification, ont constitué des dossiers au service central de leurs quartiers généraux. Certains sont à caractère administratif, d'autres politique, d'autres encore opérationnel. On trouve également des dossiers sur quantité de sujets, tels que le recrutement et l'entraînement, les salaires et les avantages sociaux, les règlements, les comités, les armes, l'équipement, la recherche. Certains dossiers proviennent de la Direction de l'histoire. Les archives de l'armée de terre contiennent des documents relatifs aux corps d'armée et aux unités, des journaux de campagne, des archives des districts militaires, des dossiers de revendications et d'internement, ainsi que des documents du quartier général de l'Armée canadienne à Londres pendant la Seconde Guerre mondiale. Les archives de la marine renferment des journaux, des livres et des dossiers de bord, les documents des services de renseignements de la marine, ceux des commandements de l'Atlantique, du Pacifique et de Terre-Neuve, des divisions de la marine et de la liaison navale canadienne. Les archives de l'aviation comprennent des journaux d'unités et des comptes rendus d'opérations, des plans d'aménagement des gares aériennes et les procès-verbaux de la Commission de l'air. Quant aux archives des Forces armées canadiennes, elles concernent, d'une part, les fonctions plus protocolaires des Forces et, d'autre part, la réunification. Les archives du Conseil de recherches pour la défense se composent de dossiers administratifs et de dossiers opérationnels, des dossiers du président, des documents relatifs aux relations publiques et de coupures de journaux. Ce groupe d'archives contient aussi les dossiers de la Commission du ravitaillement, des documents parlementaires, des dossiers du Conseil d'administration des allocations familiales supplémentaires et des documents sur les transmissions. Les fichiers informatiques se composent d'un fichier de renseignements personnels relatifs à tous les aviateurs canadiens de la Première Guerre mondiale que l'on a pu retracer, ainsi que des évaluations des recrues, des dossiers relatifs aux dispositions au travail, à la qualité de la vie, à la motivation des officiers, aux évaluations, à la réaffectation et aux renvois de personnel.

Archives du ministère des Affaires extérieures : RG 25
1803-1984

1 052 mètres
154 microfilms

Historique : À sa création, en 1909, le ministère des Affaires extérieures a été chargé d'assurer les relations avec les autres pays de l'Empire britannique. En 1931, le Statut de Westminster a étendu ses responsabilités à tous les aspects des relations internationales. De nos jours, le ministère détermine et coordonne toutes les activités internationales du Canada, en ce qui a trait aux postes diplomatiques, à la représentation canadienne dans les organismes internationaux et aux négociations d'accords et de traités avec l'étranger.

Organisation et contenu : Ces documents sont classés en fonction des bureaux qui les ont créés et de leur rôle dans les activités du ministère. Ils se répartissent en plusieurs séries : administration centrale, postes à l'étranger, conférences et commissions internationales et négociations internationales. L'organisation des documents de l'administration centrale (1887-1974) suit la hiérarchie du ministère. On trouve d'abord les dossiers du secrétaire et du ministre des Affaires extérieures (1973-1984), puis les dossiers du sous-secrétaire des Affaires extérieures (1908-1952), ceux des services centraux (1909-1976), les livres d'instructions (1887-1976) et, enfin, les dossiers des divisions (1891-1963). La série des postes à l'étranger (1880-1984) est organisée selon les postes qui ont créé les dossiers. Cette série se compose essentiellement des archives du haut-commissariat canadien à Londres (1880-1976) et de celles de l'ambassade du Canada à Washington (1927-1970). Le reste de la série concerne treize autres postes diplomatiques canadiens. La série des conférences et commissions internationales (1911-1984) rassemble des dossiers de conférences ou de réunions d'une durée indéterminée. On trouve dans cette série les conférences des pays constitutifs de l'Empire britannique (1897-1933), de la Société des Nations (1922-1938), du Commonwealth (1944-1973), des Nations unies (1945-1958), de la francophonie (1960-1985) et un certain nombre d'autres conférences et réunions (1922-1984). La série des négociations internationales (1883-1965) se divise en deux sous-séries. La première contient des traités, des ententes, des lois et des protocoles signés par le Canada (1910-1985). La seconde comprend de la correspondance et des imprimés connexes à ces négociations ou à d'autres tractations (1883-1985). La série de documents divers (1803-1976) se compose essentiellement de documents créés par des organes étrangers ou internationaux auxquels le Canada s'est intéressé. Sont intégrés dans cette série les

imprimés du Foreign Office (1803-1949), les documents des services de renseignements du Royaume-Uni (1915-1919) et les documents relatifs aux crimes de guerre (1944-1948).

Archives du ministère de la Citoyenneté et de l'Immigration : RG 26
1880-1979

23,6 mètres

Historique : Jusqu'en 1917, l'immigration a relevé du ministère de l'Agriculture (RG 17), puis du ministère de l'Intérieur (RG 15). En 1917, on a créé le ministère de l'Immigration et de la Colonisation. Depuis lors, l'Immigration a été un ministère autonome, sauf de 1936 à 1949, période pendant laquelle l'immigration a été confiée au ministère des Mines et des Ressources. Le ministère de la Citoyenneté et de l'Immigration a pris la relève de 1949 à 1966, puis le ministère de la Main-d'œuvre et de l'Immigration (créé en 1966 et rebaptisé depuis 1977, ministère de l'Emploi et de l'Immigration) lui a succédé. Outre l'immigration, le ministère de la Citoyenneté et de l'Immigration s'occupait de divers programmes dont la citoyenneté (RG 6), les affaires indiennes (RG 10 et RG 22), le Musée des beaux-arts du Canada et les Archives nationales du Canada (RG 37). Les documents d'exploitation de la Direction de l'immigration, de 1893 à nos jours, constituent une série distincte et ont été conservés tels quels dans RG 76.

Organisation et contenu : La principale série de RG 26 rassemble les documents du sous-ministre (1923-1972). Ces archives contiennent des dossiers-matières qui proviennent du service des dossiers du sous-ministre, des dossiers juridiques, des ordres du jour de comités, des procès-verbaux de réunions, de la correspondance, des rapports, des tables de statistiques et divers livres d'instructions. L'essentiel des documents concerne trois des programmes du ministère : immigration, main-d'œuvre et affaires indiennes. Le reste des archives a trait à la citoyenneté, au Musée des beaux-arts du Canada, aux Archives nationales et au carillonneur du Dominion. Les dossiers-matières du sous-ministre portent sur les politiques, les lois et les règlements de l'immigration, l'organisation du ministère et divers comités parlementaires, ministériels ou interministériels sur l'immigration. Certains dossiers concernent l'administration du programme de l'Immigration. Ils témoignent de la sélection qui est faite en fonction de l'occupation des requérants, du traitement et de la documentation des demandes, des examens de santé et de sécurité, de l'établissement des immigrants, des services d'emploi et de bien-être, de l'aide à l'immigration et des services non gouvernementaux. Les dossiers juridiques contiennent des documents de référence sur des questions telles que les affaires in-

diennes, les terres et les ressources fédérales, l'immigration, la citoyenneté, la main-d'œuvre et la censure radiophonique. Viennent s'ajouter à cette série deux documents statistiques relatifs à l'immigration au Canada, de 1880 à 1964. Les archives de la Direction de la citoyenneté (1941-1961) comprennent celles de la Section de la rédaction, responsable de la recherche, de la traduction et de la correspondance occasionnées par le rapport sur les caractéristiques politiques de la presse ethnique au Canada pendant la Seconde Guerre mondiale.

Archives du ministère du Travail : RG 27
1882-1988

1 750 mètres
305 microfilms

Historique : Le ministère du Travail a été créé en vertu de la *Loi de la conciliation* de 1900. Il devait essentiellement publier la *Gazette du Travail*, résoudre les conflits de travail en vertu de la *Loi de la conciliation*, garantir des salaires équitables et de bonnes conditions de travail aux travailleurs employés par le gouvernement, et administrer les lois sur le travail des aubains. L'administration du nouveau ministère a d'abord été confiée au ministre des Postes. (Il a fallu attendre jusqu'en 1909 pour que le ministre du Travail bénéficie d'un portefeuille séparé.)

Avec les années, le ministère s'est vu confier d'autres responsabilités importantes. Après 1918, il a participé à la création d'un réseau national de bureaux de main-d'œuvre et, après 1926, il a instauré le premier système de pensions de vieillesse au Canada. Pendant la Dépression, il a été chargé de l'aide gouvernementale à l'embauche, et, de concert avec le ministère de la Défense nationale, de la gestion des camps de chômeurs célibataires. En 1940, le ministère s'est occupé de l'assurance-chômage au Canada. Pendant la Seconde Guerre mondiale, par l'entremise du Service sélectif national, le ministère du Travail a été responsable des politiques de main-d'œuvre du gouvernement fédéral. Après 1945, il a participé de plus en plus activement à l'élaboration, à la planification et à l'administration du *Code canadien du travail*.

De nos jours, Travail Canada administre nombre de lois relatives aux conditions de travail (applicables aux travailleurs du gouvernement fédéral), telles que les horaires de travail, le salaire minimum, les congés annuels, les congés payés, l'équité salariale, les congédiements injustes, les licenciements individuels ou collectifs, les indemnités de départ, la réglementation des contrats de construction, de restauration, de réparation ou de démolition signés avec le gouvernement fédéral en

vertu de la *Loi sur les justes salaires et les heures de travail*; les services gouvernementaux de médiation et de conciliation; l'indemnisation des employés et des marins marchands; la santé et la sécurité au travail; et les prestations d'adaptation aux travailleurs touchés par les licenciements.

Organisation et contenu : Les archives de Travail Canada se divisent en soixante-neuf séries. Presque tous les documents de ce groupe sont des dossiers du service central. RG 27 comprend plus de dix mètres de dossiers provenant du Bureau du ministre et près de quatre-vingt-dix mètres de dossiers du Bureau du sous-ministre. Les archives sont plus complètes pour les années postérieures à 1930 et, pour les années 1900-1914, les dossiers du sous-ministre sont peu nombreux. Les dossiers Lacelle incluent plus de vingt mètres de documents qui traitent des principales activités du Bureau du sous-ministre entre 1902 et 1945. Les séries de l'aministration et des services généraux renferment les principaux dossiers-matières et dossiers de correspondance du Bureau du sous-ministre pour les années 1930-1974, tandis que la série des comités, conférences, réunions témoigne de la participation du ministère du Travail à un grand nombre de commissions importantes et de conférences fédérales-provinciales qui ont eu lieu entre 1920 et 1966. Un aspect important du mandat primitif du ministère du Travail était de recueillir des informations relatives aux relations industrielles et de les mettre à la disposition des employeurs et des syndicats canadiens, tout en les conservant pour ses besoins internes. Dans RG 27, trois séries sont issues de cette fonction. Les dossiers sur les grèves et les lock-out renseignent sur les grèves et les lock-out qui ont eu lieu au Canada entre 1907 et 1977. Composés principalement de coupures de presse, ces dossiers ont été microfilmés. Cette série s'accompagne de la série des conventions collectives (1910-1986) et des dossiers relatifs à la conciliation et à l'arbitrage (1944-1981). Pendant de nombreuses années, le ministère a disposé d'une Division des coupures de presse qui prélevait dans les journaux canadiens des articles sur un large éventail de sujets intéressant les dirigeants du ministère (1900-1971). La bibliothèque du ministère avait constitué des dossiers de référence qui contiennent d'anciens dépliants, des feuillets et des bulletins relatifs à des questions de travail, qu'il est difficile de trouver dans d'autres collections. (La bibliothèque du ministère conserve une copie de ces dossiers sur microfiches, ainsi qu'un index pour en faciliter la consultation.) Les autres séries de ce groupe d'archives illustrent d'autres activités importantes du ministère. En 1930, le ministère a été chargé du programme gouvernemental d'allocations d'aide à l'embauche versées aux provinces et aux municipalités. Pendant la Seconde Guerre mondiale, il s'occupait des politiques fédérales de main-d'œuvre, ce dont témoigne

la série du Service national sélectif. (Les activités de la Division du Japon constituent une section des dossiers du service central.) À la fin de la Seconde Guerre mondiale, le ministère du Travail a partagé, avec le ministère de l'Immigration, les responsabilités des politiques gouvernementales en matière d'immigration au Canada. À la même époque, il supervisait également un vaste programme de main-d'œuvre agricole. Au cours des vingt dernières années, la participation de Travail Canada à l'élaboration et à l'application du *Code canadien du travail* dans les industries relevant du gouvernement fédéral n'a cessé de s'accroître. Citons au nombre des séries importantes la Direction des normes du travail (1949-1979), la Direction des relations en matière d'emploi et conditions de travail (1944-1983) et la Direction de la sécurité et de l'hygiène au travail (1919-1981). On trouve également dans ce groupe d'archives des dossiers relatifs aux politiques et à l'administration, ainsi que des dossiers sur les vérifications de conformité faites auprès de certains employeurs et quelques dossiers de plaintes.

Archives du ministère des Munitions et des Approvisionnements : RG 28
1939-1953

153,2 mètres
1 microfilm

Historique : Créé en septembre 1939, le ministère des Munitions et des Approvisionnements était chargé de répartir et de réglementer les matières premières et les services, d'adapter l'industrie à la production de guerre, de créer de nouvelles industries et de maintenir des prix équitables pour les besoins de la guerre. En 1944, le ministère de la Reconstruction a été créé pour élaborer et coordonner des programmes et des projets de reconstruction. Les deux ont fusionné en décembre 1945 pour former le ministère de la Reconstruction et des Approvisionnements, remplacé en 1951 par le ministère de la Production de défense (RG 49). Dès 1947, la fonction d'approvisionnement comme telle avait été transférée à la Corporation commerciale canadienne (RG 65).

Organisation et contenu : Ces archives sont réparties dans deux séries : Munitions et Approvisionnements (1939-1953) et Reconstruction et Approvisionnements (1942-1949). La série des Munitions et Approvisionnements contient des dossiers qui témoignent des activités du ministère pendant la guerre. Elle comprend les dossiers dits historiques, les dossiers du service central relatifs au projet canadien d'énergie atomique en temps de guerre, ceux de la Direction de l'économie et de la statistique qui s'occupait des ressources en matière d'industrie et de main-d'œuvre; les dossiers du bureau de H.R. Kotlarsky relatifs au personnel, de la Commission de contrôle des industries en temps de

guerre et enfin les dossiers des Approvisionnements de guerre Ltée et divers documents connexes. Les dossiers de la série Reconstruction et Approvisionnements portent sur la planification élaborée après la guerre. Ils comprennent une série de dossiers de référence qui proviennent du Cabinet du ministre, les dossiers du service central, les dossiers financiers et les études préparées par la Direction du développement de l'aéronautique, ceux de la Direction des recherches économiques et de la Wartime Shipbuilding Limited et des documents connexes.

Archives du ministère de la Santé nationale et du Bien-être social : RG 29
1815-1986

1 973,5 mètres
4 microfilms
56 fichiers informatiques

Historique : De 1867 à 1919, la santé publique et la quarantaine relevaient du ministère de l'Agriculture (RG 17). En 1919, une épidémie de grippe porcine a entraîné la création d'un ministère distinct de la Santé, qui a fusionné avec le ministère du Rétablissement des soldats à la vie civile (1918-1928) pour former le ministère des Pensions et de la Santé nationale en 1928. Ce dernier a été remplacé à son tour, en 1944, par les ministères des Affaires des anciens combattants (RG 38) et de la Santé nationale et du Bien-être social (RG 29). Celui-ci fournit des services de santé et de bien-être social à un grand nombre de Canadiens. Les programmes de santé comprennent les services aux Amérindiens, aux Inuit et autres habitants du Nord canadien, aux fonctionnaires fédéraux, aux immigrants et au personnel de l'aéronautique civile, la quarantaine, l'inspection des aliments et des drogues, l'inspection des instruments médicaux, l'hygiène du milieu, l'assurance-maladie et l'assurance-hospitalisation (de concert avec les provinces), la réglementation des poisons, l'aide aux aveugles et la recherche médicale. Le ministère administre toute une gamme de programmes de sécurité du revenu, tels que la sécurité de la vieillesse, le régime de pensions du Canada, les suppléments du revenu garanti, les allocations familiales, les allocations à la jeunesse et les subventions au bien-être social. Il est également responsable de la condition physique et du sport amateur, qui font rapport au Parlement par l'intermédiaire d'un ministre d'État distinct.

Organisation et contenu : Ce groupe d'archives contient un vaste éventail de documents qui comprennent des dossiers du service central de nature administrative ou opérationnelle, des dossiers-matières, des dossiers de cas individuels, des dossiers relatifs aux politiques et aux subventions de recherche, des recueils de procès-verbaux, des grands

livres (principalement sur la fréquentation des hôpitaux), des dossiers médicaux, des livres d'instructions, des publications et des dépliants, des dossiers de correspondance, des documents de travail et divers rapports. Les sujets couverts dans ces documents se rapportent aux domaines de responsabilité de Santé nationale et Bien-être social, comme, par exemple, l'administration des règlements de quarantaine; l'instauration de l'assurance-maladie et de l'assurance-hospitalisation; l'inspection des aliments, des drogues et des instruments médicaux, soit avant la mise en marché au Canada, soit à la suite de plaintes de consommateurs; l'administration de divers programmes de sécurité du revenu, tels que les allocations familiales, les allocations à la jeunesse, la sécurité de la vieillesse, le supplément du revenu garanti et le régime de pensions du Canada; l'amélioration des normes alimentaires et des habitudes des Canadiens; le traitement des problèmes de santé mentale; l'encouragement au conditionnement physique; le financement du sport amateur; et les services médicaux aux autochtones, aux habitants du Nord, aux employés de la fonction publique et aux immigrants. Ce groupe d'archives renferme également une grande quantité de documents de recherche et de statistiques sur la santé et le bien-être social. La majorité des documents remontent à la fin de la Seconde Guerre mondiale, et plus précisément de la fin des années 50 au début des années 80. Les documents informatiques contiennent essentiellement des données d'enquêtes réalisées surtout depuis les années 70 dans le cadre d'études demandées par Santé nationale et Bien-être social sur des sujets tels que l'usage de drogues dangereuses, les effets de la retraite, l'utilisation des installations récréatives, la nature et l'importance de la consommation d'alcool, l'alimentation au Canada, la consommation de tabac, les attitudes et le comportement face aux questions de santé.

Archives des Chemins de fer nationaux du Canada : RG 30
1836-1975

1 540,4 mètres
1 208 microfilms

Historique : Les Chemins de fer nationaux ont été constitués en société en 1919 dans le but de regrouper les chemins de fer, les travaux d'infrastructure et les entreprises connexes, y compris le Canadian Northern, et à les exploiter avec les chemins de fer du gouvernement canadien en un seul système national de chemins de fer. En 1923, le chemin de fer du Grand Tronc fusionnait avec le Canadien National (CN), qui a, par la suite, absorbé de nombreuses compagnies de chemins de fer, y compris les compagnies mentionnées plus haut, qui sont elles-mêmes issues de nombreuses fusions et de multiples réorganisations. Le

CN résulte de la fusion de plus de six cents composantes. C'est une société mandataire chargée d'exploiter et d'administrer un réseau national de chemins de fer et d'autres moyens de transport et de services connexes, notamment le camionnage et le transport par autocar, les télécommunications, l'hôtellerie, la radiodiffusion, l'immobilier et les services maritimes. Au cours des dernières années, le CN a abandonné un grand nombre de ces activités auxiliaires pour se concentrer presque exclusivement sur le transport ferroviaire des marchandises.

Organisation et contenu : Les documents sont répartis en cinq grandes séries correspondant à autant de « systèmes » ferroviaires : le Grand Tronc, le Central Vermont Railway System, le Canadian Northern System, les Chemins de fer du gouvernement canadien et les Chemins de fer nationaux du Canada. Les documents sont ensuite subdivisés par groupes de chemins de fer constitutifs des systèmes plus importants : Grand Tronc Pacifique, Great Western Railway System, Northern Railway Group, Midland Railway Group, Canada Atlantic System et Intercolonial Railway. Le groupe d'archives contient également un certain nombre de regroupements artificiels qui permettent d'organiser certains ensembles de documents de façon plus rationnelle à l'intérieur même des séries consacrées aux systèmes. Ce sont, par exemple, les propriétés du Grand Tronc au Québec et en Nouvelle-Angleterre, en Ontario, et aux États-Unis, le Canadian Northern Railways dans les Prairies, en Ontario, et au Québec, et les compagnies immobilières du Canadian Northern. Le gouvernement a été propriétaire de chemins de fer au Nouveau-Brunswick, en Nouvelle-Écosse et au Québec, le Newfoundland Railway, le Northern Alberta Railways, le London and Port Stanley Railway, pour n'en nommer que quelques-uns. La série des Chemins de fer nationaux du Canada a été subdivisée non seulement par filiales mais aussi par services, tels que le Bureau de l'économie, le Département de la recherche et du développement, le Département de l'exploitation et de l'entretien, le Bureau de l'ingénieur en chef, le Département de l'agriculture et de la colonisation, l'Association de la concession des terres du Canadien National, et le Service juridique. Finalement, les sociétés qui ont précédé le CN ou qui en font partie, et dont les archives ont été déposées aux Archives nationales, font chacune l'objet d'une seule série. Ces séries portent le nom de la société concernée.

Elles contiennent essentiellement des journaux, des livres de caisse, des grands livres, des livres d'actions et d'obligations, des registres de procès-verbaux, des registres relatifs au trafic et à l'équipement, des registres et des dossiers de correspondance, des dossiers-matières créés par les services d'exploitation et les cadres supérieurs, des rapports annuels, des contrats et des baux, des bilans et des états financiers, des registres de personnel, des tarifs, des documents

d'exploitation et d'ingénierie relatifs aux constructions et aux propriétés. Ce groupe d'archives renferme également une collection assez importante de documents de toutes sortes (affiches, menus, horaires, billets et titres de chemins de fer, photographies, correspondance, etc.), qui sont pour la plupart rassemblés dans la série Train-musée.

Restriction à l'accès : L'accès aux archives décrites plus haut est sujet aux exigences imposées par le donateur, que les Archives nationales sont tenues de faire respecter. Ces conditions sont expliquées dans l'inventaire. Certains documents contiennent des renseignements qui sont soumis à des conditions qui en restreignent l'accès.

Archives de Statistique Canada : RG 31
1825-1983

201,09 mètres
1 255 microfilms
53 fichiers informatiques

Historique : L'origine de Statistique Canada remonte à 1847, année où a été créée la Commission de l'enregistrement et de la statistique, qui a, en 1855, été intégrée au Bureau de l'agriculture. Au moment de la Confédération, la responsabilité du recensement et de la statistique a été confiée au ministère de l'Agriculture (RG 17). En 1918, le gouvernement a centralisé ses opérations statistiques en mettant sur pied le Bureau fédéral de la statistique (aujourd'hui Statistique Canada). L'organisme actuel est chargé principalement de compiler, d'analyser et de publier des données statistiques sur les activités commerciales, industrielles, financières et sociales des Canadiens, ainsi que sur leurs conditions de vie en général, et de procéder régulièrement au recensement de la population et au recensement agricole du Canada.

Organisation et contenu : Les archives sont formées de dossiers administratifs et de dossiers d'exploitation qui proviennent essentiellement du Bureau du statisticien en chef (1900-1975) et du Bureau du statisticien en chef adjoint (1941-1973). S'y ajoutent des documents de recensement créés par le Secteur du recensement (1825-1901) et des fichiers informatiques qui contiennent le Projet d'index du recensement de 1871 entrepris par la Société généalogique de l'Ontario.

Archives de la Commission de la fonction publique : RG 32
1868-1984

490,6 mètres
13 microfilms

Historique : C'est en 1908 que la *Loi du service civil* créait la Commission du Service civil (CSC). Par cette loi, le principe de la nomination au mérite était introduit et trouvait son expression dans la formule des concours pour les employés postés à Ottawa. La Loi de 1918 confiait à la CSC l'entière responsabilité de la fonction publique, la chargeant de son contrôle et de son organisation, notamment du recrutement, de la sélection, de la nomination, de la classification et de la rémunération. La *Loi sur le Service civil* de 1962 réaffirmait l'indépendance de la commission et la *Loi sur l'emploi dans la Fonction publique* de 1967 redéfinissait ses pouvoirs et modifiait son nom. Devenue Commission de la fonction publique, elle devenait l'organisme central de dotation en personnel qui pouvait déléguer ses pouvoirs aux ministères. Tout en étant relevée des responsabilités de la rémunération, de la classification et des conditions d'emploi, qui deviennent à ce moment la charge du Conseil du Trésor, la commission conservait la responsabilité de la procédure d'appel. La commission fait directement rapport au Parlement, et c'est le Secrétaire d'État qui est responsable de la présentation de son rapport à la Chambre des communes.

Organisation et contenu : Ce fonds d'archives comprend une série de dossiers relatifs aux concours (1921-1979) contenant de la correspondance, des listes ou registres concernant les examens administrés aux candidats et les concours de la fonction publique, ainsi que des décisions rendues lors des appels des nominations. Une série comprend des organigrammes des ministères du gouvernement (1935-1960) ainsi que certaines données sur les traitements salariaux. Une collection de dossiers du personnel (1885-1972) contient des notices biographiques pour un ensemble d'anciens cadres supérieurs de la fonction publique; des dossiers-matières (1882-1960) traitent de différentes questions, dont la démobilisation des années 1940-1946, des grèves, des politiques, des procédures, mais aussi, de l'historique de la commission. Des dossiers du service central (1918-1960) rassemblent de la correspondance, des sondages, des rapports, des procès-verbaux et des statistiques sur l'organisation et les divers programmes de la commission. Des analyses sur les opérations de divers ministères (1946-1967) forment une série; d'autres séries comportent des documents du Comité spécial sur la gestion du personnel et sur le principe du mérite (1977-1979) ainsi que des documents sur les opérations du Bureau du président de la commission (1963-1976). À ce fonds s'intègre aussi de la documentation sur la

réaffectation des cadres supérieurs en rapport au programme de perfectionnement biculturel (1966-1977), sur les nominations de groupes sous-
représentés, sur les nominations à la catégorie de la gestion, sur le
programme des langues officielles et sur les opérations régionales de la
commission.

Archives des commissions royales d'enquête : RG 33
1873-1987

916,3 mètres
176 microfilms
88 fichiers informatiques

Historique : Une commission royale d'enquête peut découler d'un
mémoire présenté au gouverneur général en conseil par un ministre
fédéral ou par le premier ministre, qui y expose le besoin de mener une
enquête publique sur un sujet donné. Une fois approuvé, ce mémoire
constitue le fondement d'un décret du conseil qui détermine le mandat
de la commission d'enquête tel que projeté. On y nomme aussi le ou les
commissaire(s) et, en règle générale, le texte réglementaire qui régit les
activités de la commission. Dans le cas d'une commission « royale », le
texte réglementaire cité dans le décret du conseil est la partie I de la *Loi
sur les enquêtes,* laquelle régit les « enquêtes publiques ». (Le premier
règlement de l'Amérique du Nord britannique relatif aux enquêtes publiques a été adopté en 1846.)

Après l'adoption du décret du conseil, les commissaires sont
nommés en vertu de pouvoirs délégués des lettres patentes sous le Grand
Sceau du Canada. La commission est le véhicule réglementaire officiel
en vertu duquel les commissaires sont habilités à mener leur enquête.
Toujours en vertu des pouvoirs délégués, lesquels s'apparentent au
décret du conseil, on définit alors le mandat de la commission et
l'autorisation statutaire de l'enquête. Les commissions instituées en
vertu du Grand Sceau du Canada sont qualifiées de « royales »
puisqu'elles découlent de directives émises par la Couronne. En réalité,
les commissions sont constituées par le gouverneur général sur recommandation du gouverneur général en conseil (Cabinet).

La plupart des documents de ce groupe proviennent des commissions royales. Les autres sont soit des « enquêtes ministérielles »
instituées en vertu de la partie II de la *Loi sur les enquêtes*, soit des
enquêtes mises sur pied en vertu de la *Loi sur les enquêtes* mais dont on
ignore en vertu de quelle partie de la loi elles ont été mises sur pied, ou
encore des enquêtes dont on ne sait pas en vertu de quelle loi elles ont
été instituées.

Organisation et contenu : Ces archives sont formées de pièces à conviction, de mémoires, de comptes rendus d'audiences, de correspondance, de documents de travail, de rapports, de procès-verbaux de réunions, de travaux de recherche et d'études. Elles sont organisées en séries, qui contiennent chacune les dossiers d'une seule commission (par ex. RG 33/1, RG 33/2). On trouvera ci-après une liste des 147 commissions par série, mentionnant le sujet, le nom du ou des commissaire(s) et les dates extrêmes des documents. Certaines séries contiennent des documents informatiques.

1. Chemin de fer Canadien Pacifique, 1873. Commissaire :
    C. D. Day.

2. Pénitencier de Stony Mountain (Manitoba), 1897. Commissaire :
    F.C. Wade.

3. Voies de transport des produits canadiens par les ports canadiens, 1903-1905. Commissaire : J. Bertram.

4. Assurances sur la vie, 1891-1907. Commissaire :
    D.B. MacTavish.

5. Commerce des grains, 1906-1908. Commissaire : J. Miller.

6. Pont de Québec, 1897-1910. Commissaire : H. Holgate.

7. Avantages commerciaux découlant de la construction du canal de la baie Verte (Canada), 1875. Commissaire : J. Young.

8. Construction de hangars d'exercice dans la province de l'Ontario, 1915. Commissaire : R.A. Pringle.

9. Ministère de la Main d'œuvre et de l'Immigration à Montréal, 1959-1976. Commissaire : Mme C. L'Heureux-Dubé.

10. Les transactions financières d'Air Canada, 1968-1975. Commissaire : W.Z. Estey.

11. État des archives fédérales du Canada, 1912-1914. Commissaire : J. Pope.

12. Chemins de fer et transports au Canada, 1905-1920. Commissaire : A.H. Smith.

13. Bois à pâte, 1923-1925. Commissaire : J. Picard.

14. Radiodiffusion, 1923-1939. Commissaire : J. Aird.

15. Services techniques et professionnels du service public, 1928-1931. Commissaire : E.W. Beatty.

16. Chemins de fer et transports au Canada, 1917-1932. Commissaire : L.P. Duff.

17. La banque et la monnaie au Canada, 1928-1934. Commissaire : H.P. Macmillan.

18. Écarts des prix, 1921-1935. Commissaire : H.H. Stevens.

19. Accords financiers entre le Dominion et les provinces maritimes, 1863-1935. Commissaire : W. T. White.

20. Industrie textile, 1871-1938. Commissaire : W.F.A. Turgeon.

21. Charbon anthracite, 1936-1937. Commissaire : H.M. Tory.

22. Grains, 1907-1938. Commissaire : W.F.A. Turgeon.

23. Relations entre le Dominion et les provinces, 1936-1940. Commissaires : N.W. Rowell et J. Sirois.

24. Taxation des rentes viagères et des corporations de famille, 1943-1945. Commissaire : W.C. Ives.

25. Coopératives, 1937-1945. Commissaire : E.M.W. McDougall.

26. Classification administrative, 1940-1946. Commissaire : W.L. Gordon.

27. Transports, 1877-1951. Commissaire : W.F.A. Turgeon.

28. Avancement des arts, lettres et sciences au Canada, 1946-1951. Commissaire : V. Massey.

29. Location de lots dans les parcs nationaux de Banff et de Jasper, 1950. Commissaire : H.O. Patriquin.

30. Exploration pétrolière dans les Territoires du Nord-Ouest et au Yukon, 1951. Commissaire : K.J. Christie.

31. Exploitation des mines de quartz et de placer du Yukon, 1954. Commissaire : G.E. Cole.

32. Brevets, droit d'auteur, marques de commerce et dessins industriels, 1954-1955. Commissaire : J.L. Ilsley.

33. Pertes causées par l'inondation de la vallée de la rivière Humber et des terres avoisinantes en Ontario, 1954. Commissaire : J.B. Carswell.

34. Cabotage, 1931, 1945-1958. Commissaire : W.F. Spence.

35. Perspectives économiques du Canada, 1951-1960. Commissaire : W.L. Gordon.

36. Radio et télévision, 1950-1957. Commissaire : R.M. Fowler.

37. Emploi de chauffeurs sur les locomotives diesel du chemin de fer Canadien Pacifique, 1903-1958. Commissaire : R.L. Kellock.

38. Finances de Terre-Neuve, 1947-1958. Commissaire : J.B. McNair.

39. Énergie, 1950-1960. Commissaire : H. Borden.

40. Écarts de prix des denrées alimentaires, 1948-1960. Commissaire : A. Stewart.

41. Chemin de fer du Grand lac des Esclaves, 1954-1961. Commissaire : M.E. Manning.

42. Houille, 1954-1960. Commissaire : I.C. Rand.

43. Accusations d'ingérence politique portées contre Edmond Louis Paradis, 1960. Commissaire : J.V. Tremblay.

44. Plaintes portées contre la station de télévision CHEK, Victoria (Colombie-Britannique), 1960. Commissaire : A. Stewart.

45. Industrie automobile, 1950-1961. Commissaire : V.W. Bladen.

46. Organisation du gouvernement, 1951-1963. Commissaire : J.G. Glassco.

47. Publications, 1949-1963. Commissaire : M.G. O'Leary.

48. *Loi sur l'assurance-chômage*, 1961-1963. Commissaire : E.C. Gill.

49. Transports, 1899-1963. Commissaire : M.A. MacPherson.

50. Ressources naturelles de la Saskatchewan, 1900-1935. Commissaire : A.K. Dysart.

51. Ressources naturelles de l'Alberta, 1870-1935. Commissaire : A.K. Dysart.

52. Ressources naturelles du Manitoba, 1868-1929. Commissaire : W.F.A. Turgeon.

53. Vente, prix et approvisionnement du papier journal fabriqué au Canada, 1916-1921. Commissaire : R.A. Pringle.

54. Transactions conclues par les commissaires du port de Toronto, 1926-1927. Commissaire : J.H. Denton.

55. Courses de chevaux et paris au Canada, 1919-1920. Commissaire : J.G. Rutherford.

56. Événements de juillet 1941 à Arvida (Québec), 1941. Commissaires : S. Létourneau et W.L. Bond.

57. Désordres survenus à Halifax les 7 et 8 mai 1945, 1939-1945. Commissaire : R.L. Kellock.

58. Prix, 1948-1949. Commissaire : C.A. Curtis.

59. L'incident du *Northland*, 1919. Commissaire : F.E. Hodgins.

60. Activités de la société japonaise « Black Dragon » en Colombie-Britannique, 1939 et 1942. Commissaire : J.C.A. Cameron.

61. Contrats du Comité des obus, 1915-1916. Commissaires : W.R. Meredith et L.P. Duff.

62. Espionnage au sein du gouvernement (l'Affaire Gouzenko), 1942-1946. Commissaires : R. Taschereau et R.L. Kellock.

63. Charbon, 1930-1947. Commissaire : W.F. Carroll.

64. Système bancaire et financier, 1945-1964. Commissaire : D.H. Porter.

65. Fiscalité, 1950-1967. Commissaire : K.L.M. Carter.

66. Contrat relatif à la mitrailleuse Bren, 1929-1938. Commissaire : H.H. Davis.

67. Achat de terrains situés dans le canton de Sandwich West (Ontario), acquis en vertu de la *Loi sur les terres destinées aux anciens combattants*, 1945. Commissaire : D.M. Brodie.

68. Qualifications des anciens combattants, 1939-1946. Commissaire : W. Bovey.

69. Plaintes de citoyens canadiens d'origine japonaise (Colombie-Britannique), 1935-1950. Commissaire : H.I. Bird.

70. Distribution des wagons couverts, 1951-1958. Commissaire : J. Bracken.

71. Plaintes du public, discipline interne et procédures de règlement des griefs au sein de la GRC, 1974-1975. Commissaire : R.J. Marin.

72. La mise en marché du bœuf, 1974-1976. Commissaire : M.W. Mackenzie.

73. Réclamations des provinces Maritimes, 1926. Commissaire : A.R. Duncan.

74. Application de la *Loi des pensions*, 1932-1933. Commissaire : T. Rinfret.

75. Congédiement de George Walker de l'Administration de l'assistance à l'agriculture des Prairies, 1960-1964. Commissaire : H.W. Pope.

76. Accusations de malversation contre des fonctionnaires du Yukon, 1898. Commissaire : W. Ogilvie.

77. Application de la *Loi du service civil* et des lois connexes, 1907. Commissaire : J.M. Courtney.

78. Services de santé, 1961-1965. Commissaire : E.M. Hall.

79. Problèmes de commercialisation de l'industrie du poisson d'eau douce, 1965-1967. Commissaire : G.H. McIvor.

80. Bilinguisme et biculturalisme, 1963-1971. Commissaires : A.D. Dunton et A. Laurendeau.

81. Industrie du poisson salé de l'Atlantique, 1964-1965. Commissaire : D.B. Finn.

82. Détournement de fonds de Martineau et autres questions, 1903. Commissaire : J.M. Courtney.

83. Service public, 1911. Commissaire : A.B. Morine.

84. Écrasement de l'aéronef DC –8F de Trans-Canada Airlines à Sainte-Thérèse-de-Blainville (Québec), 1963-1965. Commissaire : G. Challies.

85. Plaintes de Walter H. Kirchner relatives aux services de pension aux anciens combattants, 1948. Commissaire : J.J. McCann.

86. Partisanerie politique au ministère du Rétablissement des soldats à la vie civile, 1927. Commissaire : A.T. Hunter.

87. Avenir de la base de révision de Trans-Canada Airlines à l'aéroport international de Winnipeg, 1965. Commissaire : D.A. Thompson.

88. Ministère des Douanes et de l'Accise, 1926-1927. Commissaires : F. Lemieux et J.I. Brown.

89. Situation de la femme au Canada, 1969-1971. Commissaire : Mme F.B. Bird.

90. Conditions de travail au ministère des Postes, 1965. Commissaire : A. Montpetit.

91. Machines agricoles, 1966. Commissaire : C.L. Barber.

92. Tractations de l'honorable juge Léo A. Landreville avec la Northern Ontario Gas Limited, 1958-1966. Commissaire : I.C. Rand.

93. Extradition de Lucien Rivard, 1965. Commissaire : F. Dorion.

94. Pilotage, 1962. Commissaire : Y. Bernier.

95. Relations industrielles, 1919. Commissaire : T.G. Mathers.

96. Enquête sur l'Affaire Gerda Munsinger, 1966. Commissaire : W.F. Spence.

97. Salaires dans les mines de charbon de la Colombie-Britannique et de l'Alberta, 1943-1944. Commissaire : G.B. O'Connor.

98. Imprimerie et dépôt de papeterie du gouvernement, 1920. Commissaire : G.C. Snyder.

99. Immigration d'ouvriers italiens à Montréal, 1903-1905. Commissaire : J. Winchester.

100. Naturalisation, 1931. Commissaire : J.G. Wallace.

101. Usage non médical des drogues, 1969-1974. Commissaire : G. LeDain.

102. Profits de l'acier, 1974. Commissaire : W.Z. Estey.

103. Commission d'enquête sur les aéroports, 1973-1974. Commissaire : H.F. Gibson.

104. Terres indiennes et affaires indiennes dans la province de la Colombie-Britannique (McKenna-McBride), 1913. Commissaire : N.W. White.

105. Potentiel de l'industrie du renne et du bœuf musqué dans l'Arctique, 1919. Commissaire : J.G. Rutherford.

106. Écrasement d'un aéronef Panarctic Electra à Rea Point dans les Territoires du Nord-Ouest, le 30 octobre 1974, 1974-1976. Commissaire : W.A. Stevenson.

107. Revendications relatives à la chasse pélagique du phoque, 1913-1915. Commissaire : L.A. Audette.

108. Témoignages des sages de tribus, 1977. Commissaire : L. Barber.

109. Rétrocession de terres à la Colombie-Britannique, 1927. Commissaire : W.M. Martin.

110. Concessions minières de Treadgold et autres au Yukon, 1903-1904. Commissaires : B.M. Britton et J.E. Hardman.

111. Manutention et transport du grain, 1975-1977. Commissaire : E. Hall.

112. Locaux parlementaires, 1974-1976. Commissaire : D.C. Abbott.

113. Groupements de sociétés, 1975. Commissaire : R.B. Bryce.

114. Fonctionnement de la Division des lois de la Chambre des communes, 1912. Commissaires : W.D. Hogg et A. Shortt.

115. Revendications des Indiens, 1966-1977. Commissaire : L. Barber.

116. Ports pétroliers de la côte Ouest, 1977-1978. Commissaire : A.R. Thompson.

117. Industrie canadienne de l'automobile, 1973-1978. Commissaire : S.S. Reisman.

118. Groupe de travail sur l'unité canadienne, 1976-1979. Commissaires : J.-L. Pepin et J.P. Robarts.

119. Transports de Terre-Neuve, 1949-1979. Commissaire : A.M. Sullivan.

120. Organisation, autorisation et envoi du corps expéditionnaire canadien à la colonie impériale de Hong Kong, 1942. Commissaire : L.P. Duff.

121. Bilinguisme dans les services de contrôle de la circulation aérienne au Québec, 1976-1979. Commissaires : W.R. Sinclair, J.H. Chouinard et D.V. Heald.

122. Gestion financière et imputabilité, 1976-1979. Commissaire : A.T. Lambert.

123. Conflit de travail à l'usine de Windsor de la société Chrysler du Canada, 1941. Commissaire : W.H. Furlong.

124. Coût du transport ferroviaire du grain, 1952-1978. Commissaire : C.M. Snavely.

125. Accident ferroviaire de Mississauga, 1979-1981. Commissaire : S.G.M. Grange.

126. Journaux, 1980-1982. Commissaire : T.W. Kent.

127. Transactions de la Commission canadienne du lait, 1966-1981. Commissaire : H.F. Gibson.

128. Certaines activités de la GRC, 1967-1981. Commissaire : D.C. McDonald.

129. Situation dans le service extérieur, 1980-1981. Commissaire : Mme P.A. McDougall.

130. L'aliénation mentale comme défense dans les causes criminelles, 1952-1956. Commissaire : J.C. McRuer.

131. Le droit pénal et les psychopathes sexuels, 1948-1958. Commissaire : J.C. McRuer.

132. Politique des pêcheries du Pacifique, 1976-1982. Commissaire : P. Pearse.

133. Équité en matière d'emploi, 1982-1985. Commissaire : Mme R.S. Abella.

134. Commercialisation de la pomme de terre dans l'Est du Canada, 1984. Commissaire : F.G. Carter.

135. Industrie pharmaceutique, 1984-1985. Commissaire : H. Eastman.

136. Tragédie de la plate-forme de forage *Ocean Ranger*, 1982-1985. Commissaire : T.A. Hickman.

137. Union économique et perspectives de développement du Canada, 1983-1986. Commissaire : D.S. Macdonald.

138. Les phoques et la chasse au phoque au Canada, 1984-1986. Commissaire : A. Malouf.

139. Assurance-chômage, 1985-1987. Commissaire : C. Forget.

140. Faillite de la Banque commerciale du Canada et de la Northland Bank, 1985-1986. Commissaire : W.Z. Estey.

141. Revendications étrangères, 1945-1987. Commissaire : T.D. MacDonald.

142. Détermination de la peine, 1984-1987. Commissaire : J.R.O. Archambault.

143. Collision ferroviaire de Hinton, 1986-1987. Commissaire : R.P. Foisy.

144. Criminels de guerre, 1986. Commissaire : J. Deschênes.

145. Immigration chinoise et japonaise en Colombie-Britannique, 1900-1902. Commissaire : R.C. Clute.

146. Fraudes et commerce de l'opium imputables aux Chinois de la côte du Pacifique, 1910-1911. Commissaire : D. Murphy.

147. Bande indienne de Westbank, 1986-1987. Commissaire : J.E. Hall.

Archives de la Commission de la capitale nationale : RG 34
1883-1985

188,15 mètres
23 microfilms

Historique : Successeur en droite ligne de la Commission d'aménagement de la ville d'Ottawa (CAO) (1899-1927) et de la Commission du district fédéral (CDF) (1927-1959), la Commission de la capitale nationale est chargée d'aménager la région de la capitale pour lui donner un aspect digne de son importance nationale en tant que siège du gouvernement canadien. La commission acquiert, aménage et entretient les terrains fédéraux dans la région de la capitale nationale, entreprend des projets d'urbanisme, accorde un appui financier aux municipalités de la région et conseille le ministère des Travaux publics sur l'emplacement et l'apparence de tous les immeubles fédéraux de la région.

Organisation et contenu : Les archives sont réparties en dix séries générales, dont deux seulement concernent exclusivement les prédécesseurs de la CCN. Elles contiennent des copies de lettres du secrétaire (1899-1911) et de l'ingénieur (1900-1905) de la CAO. Les autres documents relatifs à la CAO et à la CDF sont conservés dans trois séries qui ont été continuées par la CCN : les dossiers du service central (1883-1958), les registres de procès-verbaux du Comité exécutif (1899-1985) et les rapports annuels (1901-1981). Ces trois séries, qui couvrent tous les aspects des fonctions et responsabilités de la commission depuis sa création, comprennent des dossiers administratifs et d'exploitation. Les archives de la Division de l'information rassemblent les documents du commissaire de la CDF relatifs à la publicité et au personnel (1948-1966). Les documents relatifs aux transactions immobilières se trouvent dans les dossiers de la Division des biens immobiliers (1929-1981). La série des contrats et accords (1958-1975) renferme les contrats et spécifications techniques d'un certain nombre de réalisations de la CCN, tandis que la série des registres du patrimoine, dossiers individuels (1930-1976) renseigne sur les propriétés qui font partie du patrimoine de la région de la capitale nationale. Les documents du Bureau du président (1978-1984) contiennent de la correspondance, des transcriptions et des copies de discours de C.M. Drury.

Archives des comités interministériels : RG 35
1897-1966

10,2 mètres

Historique : Ce groupe d'archives rassemble les documents de sept comités interministériels. D'autres archives de ces comités peuvent se trouver avec les archives des ministères qui les ont créés.

Organisation et contenu : Ces archives se composent de procès-verbaux, de correspondance, de mémoires, d'études et de rapports.

1. Commission ministérielle des archives fédérales, 1897.

2. Comité d'enquête sur les imprimés et les fournitures, 1933.

3. Commission de la statistique, 1912.

4. Comité interministériel du logement, 1942-1946.

5. Comité interministériel du Livre du Souvenir, 1931-1942.

6. Comité interministériel des affaires des anciens combattants, 1945-1946.

7. Comité des archives fédérales, 1909-1966 (créé en 1945).

Archives des comités, commissions et bureaux : RG 36
1896-1972

189,3 mètres

Historique : Ce fonds comprend des documents émanant de toutes sortes de comités, de commissions et de bureaux non permanents, dont certains sont des commissions d'enquête instituées en vertu de la partie II de la *Loi sur les enquêtes*. (On trouve également certaines commissions ministérielles dans les archives des commissions royales, RG 33.) Ce groupe d'archives est fermé, c'est-à-dire qu'on n'y ajoute plus de documents. Les documents des commissions ministérielles se trouvent maintenant soit avec les archives du ministère responsable soit avec celles du ministère qui présente le rapport de la commission.

Organisation et contenu : Ces archives se composent d'ordres du jour, de correspondance, de textes de délibérations, de témoignages, de documents de travail, d'études, de rapports et de coupures de presse. Ce groupe d'archives rassemble les documents de trente-sept commissions.

1. Commissaires du chemin de fer Transcontinental, 1904-1921.

2. Commission de la rivière Saint-Jean, 1909-1916.

3. Commission canadienne de la marine marchande, 1939-1946.

4. Conseil national du travail en temps de guerre, 1941-1947.

5. Commission des manuscrits historiques, 1907-1915.

6. Commission du commerce, 1918-1921.

7. Bureau du commissaire spécial chargé des projets de défense dans le Nord-Ouest du Canada, 1943-1947.

8. Commission du tarif, 1896-1897, 1920.

9. Comité de la conservation des forêts dans la région Est des Rocheuses, 1947-1955.

10. Ministère du Travail, conseils d'arbitrage (chemin de fer), 1949-1962.

11. Conseil consultatif du tarif et de l'impôt, 1926-1930.

12. Commission du commerce et de l'industrie, 1935-1949.

13. Commission consultative de l'évolution du gouvernement dans les Territoires du Nord-Ouest, 1965-1966.

14. Comité de lutte contre les insectes forestiers nuisibles, 1945-1953.

15. Commission canadienne de l'alimentation, 1917-1919.

16. Commission des produits spéciaux, 1941-1949.

17. Commission du tarif, Fielding, 1898-1906.

18. Commission des allocations familiales, 1942-1955.

19. Commission industrielle de la défense, 1948-1951.

20. Commissaire général aux visites d'État, 1966-1967.

21. Conseil de l'aide mutuelle, 1940-1947.

22. Comité des dépenses d'élection, 1965-1966.

23. Comité consultatif de la radiodiffusion, 1964-1965.

24. Comité canadien des corrections, 1965-1969.

25. Comité mixte des ingénieurs, fleuve Saint-Laurent, 1952-1963.

26. Commission des études marémotrices dc l'Atlantique, 1966-1970.

27. Commission de sécurité de la Colombie-Britannique, 1942-1948.

28. Comité préliminaire des négociations collectives dans la fonction publique, 1960-1967.

29. Commission d'étude industrielle du transport sur les Grands Lacs et le fleuve Saint-Laurent, 1962-1963.

30. Commission des prix et des revenus, 1969-1972.

31. Commission de l'information en temps de guerre, 1939-1946.

32. Comité d'étude sur l'organisation et le fonctionnement de la Commission canadienne des pensions, 1965-1968.

33. Comité de la délinquance juvénile, 1961-1963.

34. Comité de planification correctionnelle, 1958-1960.

35. Conseil d'arbitrage, chemin de fer Grand Tronc, 1920.

36. Conseil d'arbitrage, chemins de fer Intercolonial et Grand Tronc, 1904-1905.

37. Conseil d'arbitrage, chemin de fer Canadian Northern, 1917.

Archives des Archives nationales du Canada : RG 37
1871-1985

111,41 mètres
2 fichiers informatiques

Historique : Les Archives nationales du Canada (Archives publiques du Canada jusqu'en 1987) ont été créées en 1872 pour recueillir, conserver et mettre à la disposition des chercheurs les documents utiles à la compréhension de l'histoire du Canada. Outre les archives fédérales et les documents privés, elles acquièrent des cartes, des peintures, des photographies, des bandes sonores, des films et des documents informatiques dignes d'être préservés. Il leur appartient également de promouvoir l'efficacité et l'économie dans la gestion des documents du gouvernement fédéral. Jusqu'en 1903, les Archives étaient une direction du ministère de l'Agriculture (RG 17). Par la suite, elles ont fait rapport par l'entremise du Secrétaire d'État (RG 6) et, depuis 1981, par l'entremise du ministre des Communications (RG 97).

Organisation et contenu : Ce groupe d'archives renferme divers types de documents, tels que de la correspondance, des inventaires et des dossiers administratifs ou opérationnels provenant du service central, relatifs aux acquisitions, aux locaux, aux politiques, aux différents services et aux expositions. Les anciens dossiers-matières et dossiers de correspondance des archivistes nationaux présentent un intérêt tout particulier. Au nombre des autres sujets abordés dans ce fonds, mentionnons l'inventaire des archives de guerre, les trophées de guerre et le manuscrit de la publications *The Canadian Directory of Parliament*. Les ordres du

jour et les procès-verbaux de la Commission canadienne des noms géographiques et de la Commission des lieux et monuments historiques (dont certains documents connexes se trouvent dans RG 84) figurent dans ce groupe de documents. On y rencontre aussi des dossiers du Bureau des Archives nationales à Londres. Les fichiers informatiques comprennent la version électronique du *Guide des archives photographiques canadiennes* et un catalogue collectif des collections de photographies des archives canadiennes.

Archives des Affaires des anciens combattants : RG 38
1896-1985

67,7 mètres
51 microfilms
21 fichiers informatiques

Historique : L'origine des Affaires des anciens combattants remonte à la création de la Commission des hôpitaux militaires en 1915. En février 1918, la commission est démantelée et remplacée par le ministère du Rétablissement des soldats à la vie civile. En 1928, celui-ci fusionne avec le ministère de la Santé pour former le ministère des Pensions et de la Santé nationale. En 1944, un ministère des Affaires des anciens combattants est constitué. Le Bureau de services juridiques des pensions, la Commission canadienne des pensions, le Conseil de révision des pensions et la Commission des allocations aux anciens combattants font rapport au Parlement par l'entremise du ministère des Affaires des anciens combattants.

Organisation et contenu : Les documents comprennent des états de service, des demandes d'allocation de terres et quelques dossiers de pensions d'anciens combattants de la guerre des Boers (1899-1902); des procès-verbaux, des circulaires et des dossiers-matières de la Commission des hôpitaux militaires (1915-1918). Les documents d'archives du ministère des Pensions et de la Santé nationale incluent des dossiers relatifs à l'hôpital Westminster (1933-1944), aux services neuro-psychiatriques du ministère et quelques dossiers-matières. Les archives des Affaires des anciens combattants se composent d'instructions et de dispositions ministérielles, de dossiers de recherche médicale, de quelques demandes de pensions, de coupures de presse et de communiqués et de quelques dossiers-matières. Les dossiers de l'Administration des terres des anciens combattants comprennent quelques dossiers individuels (provenant de l'administration centrale et du bureau de district de Toronto), des fiches de revendications d'anciens combattants, des états financiers et une série de rapports de recherche historique sur divers aspects de la colonisation. Ce groupe d'archives renferme

aussi certains dossiers de l'Agence canadienne de la Commission impériale des sépultures de guerre, des fac-similés des Livres du Souvenir et des états de service du Royal Newfoundland Regiment (1914-1919). Les fichiers informatiques concernent les responsabilités générales du ministère en matière de gestion des programmes spéciaux destinés aux anciens combattants.

Archives du Service canadien des forêts : RG 39
1874-1979

246 mètres

Historique : En 1884, une Commission des forêts a été créée au sein du ministère de l'Intérieur (RG 15) pour enquêter sur l'état des forêts canadiennes. En 1898, la Direction du bois et des forêts a été chargée de l'exploitation active et de la conservation des forêts. Un service de protection contre les incendies a été inauguré en 1900 et, en 1904, une pépinière forestière a été ouverte. En 1906, plus de vingt réserves forestières dans les quatre provinces de l'Ouest ont été confiées au surintendant des forêts. De 1908 à 1911, la direction a aussi contrôlé les parcs nationaux (RG 84) et, de 1908 à 1912, l'irrigation (RG 89). Après le démantèlement du ministère de l'Intérieur en 1936, le secteur forestier a relevé successivement, de 1936 à 1960, de trois ministères distincts (voir RG 22). En 1960, un nouveau ministère des Forêts a été formé par la fusion de l'ancien Service canadien des forêts du ministère des Affaires du Nord et de la Division de la biologie forestière de la Direction de la recherche du ministère de l'Agriculture (RG 17). En 1966, il devenait le ministère des Forêts et du Développement rural (RG 124), puis, en 1969, le ministère des Pêches et des Forêts (RG 23). L'appellation Service canadien des forêts est devenue le nom officiel de la composante forestière du nouveau ministère qui a formé à son tour le noyau du ministère de l'Environnement créé en 1971 (RG 108). En 1985, le service est devenu un ministère d'État relevant d'Agriculture Canada, et, en 1988, il a été élevé au rang de ministère sous le nom de Forêts Canada.

Organisation et contenu : Les archives sont regroupées en séries correspondant aux services administratifs constitutifs du Service canadien des forêts (SCF): dossiers du service central (1894-1973), Laboratoire des produits forestiers de l'Est (1911-1974), dossiers des bureaux régionaux (1919), Bureau du garde forestier en chef de la Commission de la conservation (1909-1922) et Institut d'aménagement forestier (1963-1973). Ces dossiers sont organisés selon un système de classification ou, dans certains cas, par genre de documents : dossiers cadastraux, enquêtes ou projets spéciaux. Ces archives renseignent sur

les activités du SCF en tant que principal agent du gouvernement dans le domaine de la foresterie et des produits forestiers. Elles traitent des débuts de l'administration de l'inspection du bois et de l'abattage, du développement de la sylviculture, de la gestion et de la protection des ressources forestières. Elles comprennent des rapports d'enquête sur les forêts et des études économiques sur la forêt canadienne. Le groupe d'archives contient également des transcriptions d'entrevues avec d'anciens employés, précieuses pour l'histoire du service, et il renseigne sur le fonctionnement des Laboratoires des produits forestiers de l'Est et de l'Ouest avant leur privatisation sous le nom de Forintek en 1979.

Bureau du surintendant des institutions financières : RG 40
1839-1982

9,9 mètres

Historique : Auparavant connu sous le nom de Département des assurances, ce groupe d'archives porte dorénavant le titre de Bureau du surintendant des institutions financières et remplit, depuis 1987, les fonctions autrefois assumées par le Département des assurances (créé en 1875) et de l'Inspecteur général des banques. Ainsi, le surintendant a pour tâche de protéger le public contre les pertes financières pouvant résulter des opérations des compagnies d'assurance et des organismes financiers enregistrés ou munis d'un permis en vertu d'une loi fédérale, d'assurer la solvabilité des régimes de pension et de fournir des services d'actuariat aux ministères et aux organismes de l'État.

Organisation et contenu : La première série comprend tous les documents se rapportant à l'ancien Département des assurances. Elle contient les comptes rendus annuels de compagnies d'assurance canadiennes, britanniques et autres (1872-1934), les dossiers du service central (1930-1961), certains dossiers relatifs à la préparation de la *Loi sur l'assurance-chômage* (1934-1955) ainsi que les dossiers des liquidation de compagnies d'assurance (1839-1904). La deuxième série se rapporte à l'ancien Bureau de l'inspecteur général des banques. Elle se compose des dossiers du registre central (1921-1982), parmi lesquels on retrouve les rapports d'inspection des différentes banques et des dossiers créés par le Bureau de l'inspecteur général (1870-1964).

Archives de la Société Radio-Canada : RG 41
1923-1982

283,3 mètres
11 microfilms

Historique : Radio-Canada est une société d'État mise sur pied en 1936 pour remplacer la Commission canadienne de la radiodiffusion créée en 1932. Chargée d'assurer un service national de radiodiffusion, elle diffuse des émissions de radio et de télévision dans les deux langues officielles et administre Radio-Canada international et le service de radiodiffusion du Nord. La Société est responsable devant le Parlement par l'entremise du ministre des Communications (RG 97).

Organisation et contenu : Les archives du siège social de la Société Radio-Canada (1923-1982) constituent l'essentiel de ce fonds. On y trouve des procès-verbaux, des ordres du jour, des rapports, des mémoires, des coupures de presse, des dossiers-matières et de la correspondance provenant du Bureau du président ou des cadres supérieurs, de la Commission canadienne de la radiodiffusion et du Service des affaires générales. Les archives de la Section des archives historiques de Radio-Canada (1923-1979), qui traitent de toutes les activités de l'organisme au siège social à Ottawa, à la Division des services anglais à Toronto et à la Division des services français à Montréal, sont particulièrement intéressantes. Mentionnons également l'intérêt des dossiers-matières et des dossiers de programmes du Bureau du service central (1933-1967). Ce groupe de documents contient en outre les dossiers de la Division des services anglais (1948-1976), les dossiers des administrateurs et des transcriptions de programmes spéciaux, ainsi que les documents du Service de radio-télédiffusion régionale (1948-1967) créés par le Service du Nord et le Service aux Forces armées de la Division des services anglais.

Archives de la Direction de la marine : RG 42
1762-1967

178,6 mètres
119 microfilms

Historique : En 1868, une direction a été créée au sein du ministère de la Marine et des Pêcheries pour administrer les services maritimes nationaux et s'occuper de toutes les questions relatives à la navigation dans les eaux territoriales : aides à la navigation, pilotes et pilotage, havres et ports, classification et enregistrement des navires, examen et certification des capitaines et des matelots, inspection des bateaux à vapeur, enquêtes sur les naufrages, commissaires et agents maritimes,

hôpitaux de la marine, services de sauvetage, gestion des navires du gouvernement canadien. Au cours de son existence, la direction a été élevée à deux reprises (1884-1892; 1930-1936) au rang de ministère et, en 1936, elle a même été fusionnée avec le ministère des Chemins de fer et Canaux (RG 43) et la Direction de l'aviation civile du ministère de la Défense nationale (RG 24) pour former le ministère des Transports (RG 12). Outre ses activités strictement reliées à la marine et à la navigation, la direction s'est occupée de diverses questions dont certaines touchaient aux domaines médical, scientifique et technologique, y compris à la radiodiffusion et à la radiotélégraphie (RG 12, RG 41, RG 97), à l'hydrographie (RG 139) et à l'exploration du Nord (RG 85).

Organisation et contenu : Ces archives sont réparties en cinq séries générales subdivisées par sujet, par fonction administrative ou par type de documents. Les archives des administrations précédentes (1762-1866) sont constituées de documents provenant des bureaux qui ont été intégrés à la Direction de la marine après la Confédération. Elles comprennent des certificats de pilotage sur le fleuve Saint-Laurent délivrés à Québec (1762-1840), ou à Trinity House à Montréal (1832, 1866) et des documents relatifs à la station de quarantaine de Grosse Île (1833-1839). Les dossiers de l'administration centrale de la direction sont divisés en deux séries, qui correspondent approximativement aux deux systèmes centraux de dossiers qui se sont succédé vers 1923. Les archives du service central pour les années 1868-1923 contiennent une grande quantité de dossiers du service central (1887-1923) qui traitent de tous les aspects des activités de la Direction de la marine, des documents relatifs à l'expédition canadienne dans l'Arctique (1913-1918), aux enquêtes sur l'*Empress of Ireland* (1914) et sur le *Princess Sophia* (1918-1919). On y trouve aussi des copies de rapports adressés par la Direction de la marine au Conseil privé (1868-1910), des dossiers de pilotage (1913-1918), des documents du Service de la radiotélégraphie du gouvernement canadien (1912-1923) et diverses séries de documents comprenant des journaux de bord (1909-1914) et des examens destinés aux ingénieurs de la marine (1871-1909). De même, les dossiers de l'administration centrale jusqu'en 1936 sont constitués de dossiers du service central ou de divers bureaux et de documents divers : dossiers du commissaire fédéral des naufrages (1901-1936), dossiers de l'expédition dans le détroit d'Hudson (1927-1928), journal de la Direction de la radio (1927-1936) et certificats de la marine (1872-1936). La quatrième série générale contient essentiellement des documents locaux créés ou recueillis par les agents de l'immatriculation maritime des ports de Québec (1850-1945), Toronto (1886-1958), Parrsboro (1916-1951), Pictou (1872-1907), Port Rowan (1882-1925) et Ottawa (1881-1965). Elle renferme aussi divers journaux

de bord de navires, des contrats (1895-1938) et des registres des combats navals (1887). La dernière série se compose de registres maritimes compilés dans divers ports canadiens, qu'il s'agisse des tout premiers registres ou de ceux des transactions suivantes (1787-1966).

Archives du ministère des Chemins de fer et Canaux : RG 43
1791-1964

336,25 mètres
267 microfilms

Historique : L'origine du ministère des Chemins de fer et Canaux, créé en 1879, remonte à la Direction des chemins de fer du ministère des Travaux publics (RG 11) à laquelle a été confiée l'administration des canaux qui relevait auparavant du Bureau de l'ingénieur en chef. Ainsi est né le nouveau ministère composé de deux directions (la Direction des chemins de fer et la Direction des canaux). La Direction des chemins de fer doit construire, exploiter et entretenir les réseaux ferroviaires de l'État, ainsi qu'administrer un programme d'aide financière aux compagnies de chemin de fer (allocations de terres, subventions, etc.) destiné à encourager la construction de nouvelles lignes. La Direction des canaux assume des responsabilités similaires pour le réseau de canaux canadiens et s'occupe du creusement des nouveaux canaux. En 1936, le ministère des Chemins de fer et Canaux fusionne avec le ministère de la Marine (RG 42) et la Direction de l'aviation civile du ministère de la Défense nationale (RG 24) pour former le ministère des Transports (RG 12). En 1959, l'administration des canaux de Welland, Cornwall, Lachine et Sault-Sainte-Marie a été transférée du ministère des Transports à l'Administration de la voie maritime du Saint-Laurent (RG 52) et, en 1972, Parcs Canada (RG 84) se voit confier la responsabilité des canaux Rideau et Trent, Sainte-Anne-de-Bellevue, Murray, Carillon, Saint-Ours, Chambly, Beauharnois, Saint-Pierre, Chignectou et Grenville.

Organisation et contenu : Les documents sont divisés en quatre grandes séries : archives de la Direction des chemins de fer (1867-1936), archives de la Direction des canaux (1838-1955), archives sur les canaux (1819-1964) et archives juridiques (1791-1957). Chacune de ces séries générales comporte un certain nombre de subdivisions. La Direction des chemins de fer et la Direction des canaux disposaient chacune de leur propre système de dossiers, qui, à l'origine, était des registres de correspondance (1879-1901). Après 1901, elles ont utilisé des systèmes de classification numérique de dossiers-matières (jusqu'en 1936) qui renseignent sur toutes les facettes de leurs activités respectives. Les divers services administratifs alimentaient le système central et conservaient en

outre des documents d'exploitation, des dossiers de correspondance, des contrats, des estimations, des rapports, des registres et des répertoires. Au sein de la Direction des chemins de fer, le Bureau de l'ingénieur en chef possédait des documents relatifs aux chemins de fer qui relevaient directement du gouvernement fédéral, comme, par exemple, certains tronçons du Canadien Pacifique (1875-1892), les Cape Breton Railway (1886-1892), Oxford and New Glasgow Railway (1887-1897), Annapolis and Digby Railway (1889-1892) et Intercolonial and Prince Edward Island Railways (1877-1906), ainsi que des documents généraux relatifs à la construction de divers chemins de fer au Canada. De même, le Bureau de l'ingénieur en chef des canaux conservait des dossiers de correspondance, des dossiers-matières (1868-1907, 1912-1936) et des copies de lettres (1873-1896), bien que les archives postérieures à 1892 remontent à une époque où la Direction des chemins de fer et la Direction des canaux avaient déjà été regroupées sous la responsabilité d'un seul ingénieur en chef. Comme tous les canaux étaient placés sous contrôle fédéral, le ministère a établi une série de bureaux chargés des activités quotidiennes d'exploitation, d'entretien et d'administration de chacun des canaux. Ces bureaux faisaient rapport à l'ingénieur en chef à Ottawa par l'intermédiaire d'un surintendant. Leurs archives comprennent des copies de lettres et des registres de correspondance, des dossiers-matières, des rapports d'inspection, des journaux de maîtres-éclusiers, des dossiers de trésoriers, des livres de comptes, des grands livres, etc., qui se rapportent principalement aux canaux Rideau (1834-1942) et Welland (1824-1959), mais aussi aux canaux Trent (1837-1959), Lachine (1819-1842), Saint-Pierre (1885-1929) et aux canaux du Saint-Laurent (1833-1950, Beauharnois, Cornwall, Farran's Point, Rapide Plat et Galops). La série des archives juridiques (1791-1957) rassemble des contrats, des actes, des baux et de la correspondance relative aux canaux et aux chemins de fer, ainsi que différents dossiers de travaux publics antérieurs à 1879 (routes, prisons, palais de justice, quais, phares, etc.).

Archives des Services nationaux de guerre : RG 44
1939-1949

17,43 mètres

Historique : Le ministère des Services nationaux de guerre a été créé en 1940 pour coordonner les activités des organismes de guerre bénévoles en vue d'éviter tout double emploi dans leurs services. En 1941, une Division de la récupération nationale a été mise sur pied et le ministère a accordé une attention croissante à l'organisation des services bénévoles féminins à caractère communautaire. En 1942, quand le

78

gouvernement fédéral a décidé de financer tous les services auxiliaires fournis par des organismes nationaux, les responsabilités du ministère ont augmenté considérablement. Ce dernier a été chargé de l'administration de la *Loi des secours de guerre* et une Division du contrôle des économies dans les bureaux du gouvernement canadien a été établie. En 1947, les principales fonctions qui restaient au ministère ont été transférées au ministère de la Santé nationale et du Bien-être social.

Organisation et contenu : Ces archives se composent de dossiers-matières et de dossiers de correspondance relatifs aux principales fonctions du ministère. Seul un petit nombre de ces dossiers faisait partie du système central du ministère. La principale série comprend des dossiers qui proviennent des cabinets du ministre et du ministre adjoint, de la Régie des économies dans les bureaux du gouvernement et des divisions chargées des organismes de charité et du secours bénévole en temps de guerre.

Archives de la Commission géologique du Canada : RG 45
1842-1966

53,3 mètres
42 microfilms

Historique : La Commission géologique du Canada a été créée en 1842 pour effectuer des recherches scientifiques et des études sur le terrain dans le but de mesurer l'étendue des ressources naturelles du Canada, notamment de ses ressources énergétiques et minérales non renouvelables. Elle s'acquitte de son mandat en réalisant des enquêtes géologiques sur le terrain complétées par des études en laboratoire. Organisme scientifique autonome, la commission a fait rapport au Parlement par l'entremise successive de nombreux ministères, en particulier : Secrétaires civils et provinciaux, 1842-1867 (RG 4 et RG 5); Secrétariat d'État, 1867-1873 (RG 6); Intérieur, 1873-1890 (RG 15); Mines, 1907-1936 (RG 86); Mines et Ressources, 1936-1949 (RG 21); Mines et Relevés techniques, 1949-1966 (RG 21); et Énergie, Mines et Ressources, 1966-1980 (RG 21). De 1890 à 1907, elle constituait un ministère indépendant. Enfin, elle a été chargée des musées nationaux (RG 132) pendant de nombreuses années et s'est occupée de recueillir des statistiques minérales (RG 87).

Organisation et contenu : La correspondance de la Commission géologique du Canada et de ses chercheurs est répartie dans plusieurs séries : registres des lettres reçues (1869-1881, 1869-1919 et 1914-1921); copies de lettres de R.W. Ells (1884-1910); copies de lettres du

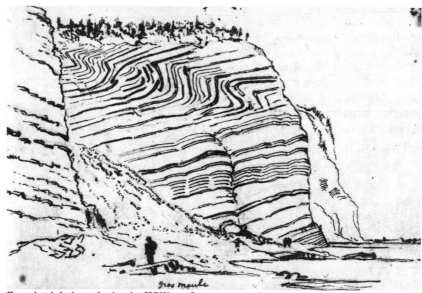

Croquis tiré du calepin de William Logan, premier directeur de la Commission géologique du Canada, 1844-1845. (RG 45, vol. 158) (C-102974)

directeur (1865-1908); dossiers du service central (1863-1966); et correspondance diverse (1866-1897). Les dossiers relatifs au travail sur le terrain accompli par le personnel scientifique de la commission se trouvent dans les carnets de note d'arpentage de Robert Bell (1860-1907), les carnets de note d'arpentage de George Mercer Dawson (1875-1900), les carnets de notes d'arpentage (1842-1925) et le registre de l'équipement utilisé (1872-1876). La série de la Division des statistiques minérales et des mines (1858-1887) renferme des brouillons de rapports statistiques préparés par Eugène Coste sur la production minérale au Canada. La série du Bureau du géologue en chef (1934-1956) comprend un vaste éventail de documents sur des sujets très divers, tels que l'emploi de certaines personnes, les publications, le travail sur le terrain et les relations avec les associations professionnelles. Les rapports du personnel de la commission relatifs à la qualité de la nappe phréatique sont conservés dans les dossiers relatifs aux eaux de source (1943-1947) et les rapports sur les ressources en eaux souterraines, provinces des Prairies (1936-1954).

Archives de la Commission canadienne des transports : RG 46
1857-1979

298,7 mètres
7 microfilms

Historique : Le Bureau des commissaires des chemins de fer du Canada-Uni a été créé en 1857 pour établir des normes de construction et d'exploitation de chemins de fer et les faire appliquer. À l'époque de la Confédération, ses responsabilités ont été confiées au Comité des chemins de fer du Conseil privé. En 1888, les pouvoirs du comité ont été étendus de façon à lui permettre de trancher les différends entre compagnies de chemins de fer. Mise sur pied en 1904, la Commission des chemins de fer devait assumer les fonctions du comité et approuver les tarifs. En 1908 et 1910, les commissaires ont été chargés de réglementer l'industrie du télégraphe et du téléphone, puis l'industrie des câbles sous-marins. En 1933, ils devaient ratifier tous les abandons de voies ferrées. En 1938, la commission a été rebaptisée Commission des transports, et ses responsabilités ont été étendues à la réglementation des services aériens et de la navigation intérieure sur les voies d'eau. Les services aériens ont été transférés, en 1944, à la Commission des transports aériens, et, en 1948, la Commission maritime canadienne a été établie pour contrôler et développer l'industrie canadienne de la navigation. En 1967, la Commission canadienne des transports a été créée par le regroupement de la Commission des transports, de la Commission des transports aériens et de la Commission maritime canadienne. En vertu de la *Loi nationale sur les transports* de 1967, la Commission canadienne des transports a été remplacée par l'Office national des transports.

Organisation et contenu : Les archives du RG 46 consistent essentiellement en comptes rendus de travaux de chacun des organismes constitutifs de la commission, en dossiers de correspondance et dossiers-matières provenant de leurs systèmes centraux de dossiers. Les délibérations comprennent les procès-verbaux du Bureau des commissaires des chemins de fer (1857-1864) et du Comité des chemins de fer du Conseil privé (1869-1904); de la Commission des chemins de fer et de la Commission des transports (1918-1956); de la Commission des transports aériens (1944-1960) et de la Commission maritime canadienne (1948-1967). On trouve également des transcriptions des audiences (1904-1955, 1959-1979) accompagnées de pièces justificatives et d'index, ainsi que les ordonnances qui ont découlé des audiences. Ce groupe d'archives renferme aussi de la correspondance et des journaux et registres d'accompagnement qui proviennent du service central du Comité des chemins de fer du Conseil privé (1867-1903). Les dos-

siers-matières ont été créés par les commissaires des chemins de fer et du transport (1904-1967), la Commission des transports aériens (1945-1967) et la Commission maritime canadienne (1918-1967). On y trouve également les rapports annuels des compagnies de chemin de fer et des compagnies de messageries (1878-1949); les dossiers de la Direction des subventions de la Commission maritime canadienne (1892-1973), qui comprennent des documents provenant du ministère du Commerce (1892-1967); et des documents de la Park Steamship Company (1942-1966).

Archives des conférences fédérales-provinciales : RG 47
1927-1971

10,2 mètres

Historique : Le Bureau des conférences fédérales-provinciales est de création récente (1975). Les fonctions en revenaient auparavant à une division du Bureau du Conseil privé.

Organisation et contenu : Les documents qui composent ce groupe d'archives proviennent du Secrétariat des conférences fédérales-provinciales. Ils se composent normalement de copies de mémoires, de présentations faites par les premiers ministres, de propositions et d'énoncés de principes. Nous énumérons ci-après les conférences pour lesquelles nous possédons des documents, et ce, de façon fragmentaire.

1. Conférence sur les ressources et notre avenir (23 au 28 octobre 1961), 1959-1962.

2. Conférence fédérale-provinciale (3 au 10 novembre 1927), 1927.

3. Conférence fédérale-provinciale (10 au 13 décembre 1935), 1935-1937.

4. Conférence fédérale-provinciale sur le transport routier, 1933.

5. Conférence fédérale-provinciale (janvier 1934), 1933-1934.

6. Conférence fédérale-provinciale sur la reconstruction, 1946.

7. Comité national des finances (créé par la conférence fédérale-provinciale de 1935), 1936.

8. Conférence fédérale-provinciale, 1941.

9. Conférence fédérale-provinciale sur la dette en souffrance (31 mars 1944), 1944.

10. Conférence fédérale-provinciale, 1945.

11. Conférence fédérale-provinciale sur la réforme correctionnelle, 1968.

12. Secrétariat fédéral-provincial, conférence constitutionnelle (Ottawa, février et décembre 1969 et septembre 1970, Victoria, juin 1971), 1968-1971.

Archives des Observatoires du Canada : RG 48
1842-1980

39 mètres

Historique : Au dix-neuvième siècle, l'arpentage se faisait essentiellement à partir de données magnétiques et astronomiques. Aussi, quand le premier astronome en chef a été nommé en 1890, il a été rattaché à la Direction des levés topographiques (RG 88) du ministère de l'Intérieur (RG 15). La construction d'un nouvel observatoire à Ottawa a amené la création, en 1903, d'une Direction de l'astronomie distincte, la première de plusieurs qui allaient successivement voir le jour au sein du ministère. L'observatoire fédéral d'astrophysique de Victoria, terminé en 1917, a considérablement augmenté le travail de la direction. Lorsque le ministère de l'Intérieur a été aboli, en 1936, la direction est demeurée une unité administrative distincte, relevant tour à tour de divers ministères (voir RG 21). En 1970, les attributions de la Direction des observatoires relatives à l'astronomie ont été transférées au Conseil national de recherches (RG 77), tandis que ses activités relatives à la géophysique étaient regroupées à la Direction de la physique du globe au ministère de l'Énergie, des Mines et des Ressources (RG 21).

Organisation et contenu : Ce groupe d'archives se compose des séries suivantes : observatoire fédéral d'astrophysique (1842-1930), qui comprend des documents de l'observatoire royal de Greenwich (Angleterre) portant sur la délimitation de la frontière internationale (1842-1848), et les dossiers du capitaine D.R. Cameron, commissaire de la frontière internationale (1872-1876); dossiers du Cabinet de l'astronome fédéral (1945-1947); documents de la Division du géomagnétisme (1948-1969); et dossiers relatifs au projet de construction du télescope reine Élisabeth II (1959-1972). Ces archives comprennent également de nombreux dossiers du service central, la correspondance du directeur, des rapports techniques et des données de recherche qui proviennent de l'observatoire fédéral d'astrophysique de Victoria (Colombie-Britannique) (1909-1980).

Archives du ministère de la Production de défense : RG 49
1942-1968

172,5 mètres

Historique : Créé en avril 1951 en vertu de la *Loi sur la production de défense*, ce ministère a succédé aux ministères des Munitions et des Approvisionnements et de la Reconstruction et des Approvisionnements (RG 28). Il était chargé des approvisionnements nécessaires à la défense, ainsi que de la mobilisation, de la préservation et de la coordination des moyens économiques et industriels en temps de guerre. À partir de 1966, ce ministère a centralisé les fonctions d'achat et d'approvisionnement du gouvernement fédéral. Le ministère a été réorganisé en 1969 et est devenu le ministère des Approvisionnements et Services (RG 98).

Organisation et contenu : La plus importante série de documents de ce groupe d'archives est constituée de dossiers du service central (1942-1968) qui touchent à tous les aspects des fonctions d'administration et d'exploitation confiées au ministère. Le RG 49 contient également un petit nombre de dossiers qui proviennent du Cabinet du ministre (1963-1968), du Cabinet du sous-ministre (1951-1966) et de la Direction du programme international (1961-1969).

Archives de la Commission d'assurance-chômage : RG 50
1900-1982

498,26 mètres

Historique : La Commission de l'assurance-chômage a été instituée en 1940 pour administrer la *Loi sur l'assurance-chômage*. Cette loi conférait au gouvernement fédéral le pouvoir de promouvoir la sécurité sociale et économique des Canadiens en les protégeant des aléas de l'emploi par le versement de primes ou de contributions destinées à les aider en cas de chômage. La Commission d'assurance-chômage est une personne morale qui fonctionne par l'intermédiaire du réseau des centres d'emploi du Canada. En 1977, la commission fusionnait avec le ministère de la Main-d'œuvre et de l'Immigration pour former le ministère de l'Emploi et de l'Immigration (voir RG 118).

Organisation et contenu : Ces archives comprennent des dossiers d'exploitation et des dossiers-matières du service central, ainsi que de nombreux dossiers de cas créés par la Commission d'assurance-chômage. Les dossiers du service central contiennent de la correspondance, des procès-verbaux de comités de la haute direction, des manuels de politiques, des rapports statistiques et des coupures de presse qui renseignent sur l'évolution de ses politiques et de ses activités. La

plupart des documents datent des années 60 et 70, mais certains volumes couvrent des sujets tels que les amendements à l'*Acte de l'Amérique du Nord britannique*, la création et l'organisation de la commission, les principes d'admissibilité à l'assurance-chômage et les changements au programme législatif. Ce groupe d'archives renferme également de nombreux dossiers d'appels relatifs à l'assurance-chômage (surarbitrage, commission arbitrale, et ministériel), des réclamations de prestations, des rentes et des dossiers personnels de plaintes et de demandes de renseignements.

Archives de la Commission mixte internationale : RG 51
1909-1978

3,2 mètres

Historique : La Commission mixte internationale a été créée, en 1909, par un traité conclu entre la Grande-Bretagne et les États-Unis et ratifié par le gouvernement canadien en 1911. La commission est formée de six membres (trois de chaque pays) et exerce un droit de regard sur l'utilisation, l'obstruction ou la dérivation des eaux limitrophes (c'est-à-dire les eaux traversées par la frontière internationale). On lui soumet également toutes sortes de problèmes posés par l'existence de la frontière internationale. C'est elle aussi qui coordonne les activités entreprises sous l'autorité de l'accord canado-américain relatif à la qualité de l'eau dans les Grands Lacs. Enfin, un certain nombre de bureaux internationaux ont été mis sur pied sous ses auspices pour enquêter sur les problèmes écologiques communs aux deux pays.

Organisation et contenu : Pour mener ses enquêtes, la commission fait appel à des spécialistes et des techniciens d'autres organismes et ministères du gouvernement. C'est pourquoi bon nombre de ses dossiers se trouvent intégrés à ceux d'autres ministères. Les documents conservés dans ce groupe consistent en un manuel résumant les problèmes de navigation et de mise en valeur des eaux communes aux États-Unis et au Canada. Ils comprennent aussi une collection de 112 rapports compilés par le bureau de la commission à Windsor sur les divers aspects de la qualité de l'eau dans les Grands Lacs.

Archives de l'Administration de la voie maritime du Saint-Laurent : RG 52
1868-1982

145,7 mètres

Historique : L'Administration de la voie maritime du Saint-Laurent est une corporation de propriétaire mise sur pied en 1954 pour acquérir les terrains et construire, entretenir et exploiter, de concert avec l'autorité compétente des États-Unis, tous les ouvrages nécessaires aux transports sur la voie maritime du Saint-Laurent. Elle fait rapport au Parlement par l'entremise du ministre des Transports.

Organisation et contenu : Les documents sont organisés en six grandes séries incluant les dossiers du service central (1868-1982), des coupures de presse (1955-1973) et des informations sur les niveaux des eaux (1912-1959). On y retrouve également un grand nombre de références sur le projet du canal Welland (1964-1967). La Division des archives cartographiques et architecturales possède une cinquantaine de plans se rapportant au tronçon international de la voie maritime du Saint-Laurent (1919-1936). Finalement, signalons l'existence de dossiers et de photos concernant les directeurs de la voie maritime du Saint-Laurent (1954-1970).

Archives de l'Office national du film : RG 53
1939-1969

1,5 mètre
2 microfilms

Historique : L'Office national du film (ONF) a été créé en 1939 pour étudier les activités cinématographiques du gouvernement. En 1941, il absorbe le Bureau cinématographique canadien, qui fait alors partie du ministère du Commerce (RG 20) depuis 1921. En 1950, la *Loi nationale sur le film* abroge la législation antérieure et redéfinit les fonctions et les objectifs de l'ONF, qui a maintenant l'autorisation d'entreprendre et de favoriser la production et la distribution en anglais et en français de films propres à servir l'intérêt national en faisant connaître et comprendre le Canada aux Canadiens et aux citoyens des autres pays.

Organisation et contenu : Les archives de l'ONF comportent deux séries : les procès-verbaux et prévisions budgétaires (1939-1943) sont des copies de procès-verbaux des réunions de cet organisme et de ses prévisions budgétaires. La série de l'étude de l'université McGill sur l'Exposition universelle de 1967 (1967-1969) rassemble des copies de rapports et des documents de travail réalisés dans le cadre d'un projet de

recherche, entrepris par l'université McGill pour le compte de l'ONF, visant à étudier et à évaluer les aspects audio-visuels et multi-médias de certains pavillons nationaux et thématiques de l'Expo 67.

Archives du Bureau du contrôleur du Trésor : RG 54
1930-1969

31,2 mètres

Historique : Le Bureau du contrôleur du Trésor a été établi en 1931 et placé sous l'égide du ministère des Finances. Le contrôleur était chargé par le vérificateur général (RG 58) de contrôler les sorties de deniers publics et de vérifier les dépenses gouvernementales avant qu'elles ne soient engagées. Des agents du Trésor étaient détachés auprès de tous les ministères pour y assurer un service de comptabilité et d'émission de chèques. Les fonctions du Bureau du contrôleur ont été absorbées par le ministère des Approvisionnements et Services (RG 98) en 1969.

Organisation et contenu : Ces archives comprennent une série de dossiers du service central (1930-1969), ainsi qu'une série séparée de dossiers de comptabilité et de journaux du contrôleur. Elles renferment en outre trois séries qui reflètent les activités des agents du Trésor dans deux ministères : Santé nationale et Bien-être social (1946-1967) et Défense nationale (1946), ainsi que de l'agent du Trésor canadien d'outre-mer (1939-1941). Ce groupe de documents contient également les dossiers de la Conférence des agents du Trésor, qui s'est tenue à Ottawa, en 1965.

Archives du Conseil du Trésor : RG 55
1868-1988

599,65 mètres
416 microfilms
20 823 microfiches
1 fichier informatique

Historique : Le Conseil du Trésor a été créé le 2 juillet 1867 à titre de Comité du Conseil privé chargé d'approuver les dépenses du gouvernement fédéral. Les responsabilités administratives et autres fonctions du Conseil du Trésor ont relevé du ministère des Finances jusqu'en 1966, date à laquelle un ministère distinct a été établi en vertu de la *Loi sur l'organisation du gouvernement* (1966). C'est à cette époque que le poste de président du Conseil du Trésor a été créé. Avant cette date, ces responsabilités incombaient d'office au ministre des Finances. En plus de contrôler les dépenses, le Conseil du Trésor est responsable des

politiques sur les langues officielles et de la coordination des politiques relatives au personnel et à l'administration dans la fonction publique fédérale.

Organisation et contenu : Les archives de ce groupe sont réparties dans quatorze séries représentatives des attributions et des activités du Conseil du Trésor. Les registres de décisions et la documentation afférente (1868-1984) constituent la plus importante série de ce groupe. On appelle « décision », toute question soumise à l'évaluation du Conseil du Trésor ou Comité du Conseil privé. Cette série contient donc les décisions, ainsi que les répertoires et les registres qui permettent d'en comprendre l'organisation. Les dossiers du service central (1916-1967) constituent le système central de classement du secrétariat du Conseil du Trésor. Ils traitent de sujets tels que les pensions, la classification des emplois, les opérations bancaires et les travaux publics. La série des comités spéciaux se compose de documents provenant de comités mis sur pied pour étudier les réclamations et conseiller le gouvernement sur des questions relevant du Conseil du Trésor (1872-1963). La série de la politique et gestion du personnel (1886-1982) renferme des documents relatifs aux examens, aux conventions collectives, aux avantages sociaux et à la recherche rémunérée. La série des budgets et prévisions budgétaires (1920-1967) renseigne sur les budgets et les prévisions budgétaires du gouvernement fédéral. Les dossiers de la Direction de la politique administrative (1959-1980) traitent de la préparation des normes administratives, de l'étude des marchés, des politiques relatives aux biens immobiliers et des systèmes d'information. Certains dossiers concernent la participation du gouvernement fédéral à la planification des Jeux olympiques de 1976. Le fonds comprend aussi des dossiers du Cabinet du secrétaire du Conseil du Trésor (1968-1973) et des dossiers de la Direction des langues officielles (1962-1980) qui témoignent du développement des politiques linguistiques et contiennent des rapports, des études et des questions connexes. La série de la Direction de la politique concernant le personnel (1954-1976) renferme des documents relatifs aux problèmes de personnel portés devant le gouvernement, y compris les échelles salariales, les règlements, les griefs et les conditions d'emploi. Les archives de la Direction de la planification (1962-1979) concernent à la fois la planification et l'analyse des programmes. Cette série contient également des documents sur l'organisation des ministères du gouvernement. Les dossiers du Cabinet du président (1963-1988) proviennent du Cabinet du ministre responsable du Conseil du Trésor. Les documents de la Direction des programmes (1960-1980) concernent l'étude des prévisions budgétaires des ministères et le contrôle général des programmes du gouvernement; les dossiers de la Direction des ressources humaines (1955-1975) se composent de documents relatifs à

la formation professionnelle et au perfectionnement et à l'utilisation des ressources humaines dans la fonction publique. On retrouve aussi dans ce groupe d'archives une série de documents divers (1951-1972). Enfin, les archives relatives au Conseil du Trésor contiennent également des documents informatiques relatifs à une enquête sur les habitudes de voyage (1975-1976).

Archives de la Société canadienne d'hypothèques et de logement : RG 56
1935-1985

306 mètres

Historique : La *Loi sur l'habitation* de 1935 (remplacée en 1938 par la *Loi nationale sur l'habitation*), qui avait permis de libérer des fonds pour les hypothèques domiciliaires, était administrée par le ministère des Finances (RG 19). En 1945, la Société centrale d'hypothèques et de logement (SCHL) a été créée pour assurer à son tour l'application de la Loi ainsi que d'autres mesures du temps de la guerre en matière de logement, et pour préparer l'essor du logement prévu pour l'après-guerre. En plus de l'assurance des prêts hypothécaires, la SCHL s'est occupée de divers programmes, dont ceux de l'aménagement de terrains, de l'aide au logement locatif à prix modéré, ainsi que de la vérification des matériaux de construction en collaboration avec le Conseil national de recherches (RG 77). La SCHL a également participé à l'aide au logement autochtone, au logement coopératif et au logement public, et à l'aide pour l'accession à la propriété. De 1971 à 1979, la SCHL a fait rapport par l'entremise du ministre d'État aux Affaires urbaines (RG 127). En 1979, elle a été rebaptisée Société canadienne d'hypothèques et de logement et elle a relevé successivement des ministres de l'Expansion économique régionale (RG 124), des Travaux publics (RG 11), du Travail (RG 27), à nouveau des Travaux publics (RG 11) et, plus récemment, du ministère d'État au Logement.

Organisation et contenu : Ces archives sont réparties en un certain nombre de séries, dont les dossiers du service central (1950-1964) (exploitation et administration) créés au siège social et dans les bureaux régionaux, qui comprennent les dossiers de la Banque centrale d'hypothèques, Originaux (1938-1945), du projet d'aménagement Ajax (1943-1967), des prêts hypothécaires mixtes (1935-1969) et des décrets (1935-1968). Les autres séries sont formées de dossiers administratifs (1942-1954) concernant la conférence sur la planification communautaire et les prêts d'agrandissement domiciliaires, et des documents relatifs au logement rural des Maritimes, Logement d'urgence (1944-1953), qui traitent des activités de l'Administration des besoins

urgents de logement (1944-1946). Ces archives contiennent également une série consacrée au projet de recherche de la SCHL sur les solutions de rechange au système hypothécaire actuel. En outre, ce groupe d'archives contient des documents relatifs au prix Vincent Massey (1971-1975), des dossiers de prêts et des dossiers du Cabinet du président (correspondance et dossiers reflétant les relations fédérales-provinciales dans le secteur du logement).

Archives de l'Organisation des mesures d'urgence : RG 57
1948-1976

52 mètres

Historique : L'Organisation des mesures d'urgence (OMU) a été créée le 1er juin 1957 au sein du Conseil privé, pour planifier l'exercice de l'autorité, les services gouvernementaux essentiels et la gestion des ressources en cas de guerre nucléaire. En 1959, l'OMU a été chargée de coordonner la planification de la défense civile confiée aux ministères et aux organismes gouvernementaux, ainsi que d'assurer la liaison avec divers organismes provinciaux, avec l'OTAN et avec d'autres pays. En 1974, l'OMU devenait le Centre national de planification des mesures d'urgence du ministère de la Défense nationale, puis, par la suite, Planification d'urgence Canada. Ses responsabilités ont alors été étendues à la planification des mesures civiles d'urgence.

Organisation et contenu : Les archives de Planification d'urgence Canada et de ses prédécesseurs consistent en une série de dossiers du service central (1952-1976), qui traitent de tous les aspects de la réinstallation du gouvernement, de la planification d'urgence et de la liaison avec divers organismes (1949-1976); une série de dossiers du service central de la Division de la coordination des opérations d'urgence (1950-1970); des livres qui précisent les domaines de responsabilité pour le rétablissement du gouvernement, de la situation économique et des opérations de routine en cas de catastrophe nationale (1948-1958); des transcriptions de la Division de la planification économique qui traitent en détail de toute une gamme de conditions économiques; ainsi que les dossiers du Comité de planification d'urgence de l'OTAN (1958-1967).

Archives du Bureau du vérificateur général : RG 58
1827-1982

714,6 mètres

Historique : Le Bureau du vérificateur général a été établi en 1878 afin de vérifier les comptes publics du gouvernement. Malgré quelques changements apportés en 1931 en vertu des amendements à la *Loi sur le revenu consolidé et la vérification*, le Bureau du vérificateur général est resté relativement inchangé jusqu'à ce que son mandat soit redéfini et élargi par l'adoption de la *Loi sur le vérificateur général* (1976-1977). Le vérificateur général doit vérifier les comptes des ministères, organismes gouvernementaux et sociétés d'État, ainsi que les comptes publics du Canada et faire rapport à la Chambre des communes. Les vérificateurs peuvent réaliser trois types de vérification selon les fonctions à examiner : les vérifications d'attestation, qui doivent être faites chaque année, les vérifications intégrées, qui n'ont lieu que tous les quatre ans, et les vérifications spéciales, qui portent sur certaines fonctions particulières.

Organisation et contenu : Ces archives comportent plusieurs séries qui témoignent des activités des nombreux organismes qui ont précédé le Bureau du vérificateur général et dont celui-ci a assumé les responsabilités en totalité ou en partie. Elles contiennent les dossiers du vérificateur général des comptes publics, Bas-Canada (1827-1840), de l'inspecteur général des comptes publics, Haut-Canada (1832-1840), de la Commission de vérification (1855-1867), du Bureau de vérification (1855-1882) et du contrôleur des *Free Banks* (1854-1870). Les dossiers du Cabinet du vérificateur général (1899-1982) consistent essentiellement en dossiers-matières sur la vérification.

Archives du Bureau du Commissaire à la représentation : RG 59
1964-1976

5,4 mètres

Historique : C'est en vertu de la *Loi sur le Commissaire à la représentation* que la tâche de réviser les frontières des circonscriptions électorales a été confiée, en 1963, au Bureau du Commissaire à la représentation. Le Commissaire a ainsi la responsabilité de faire préparer les cartes indiquant, à la suite d'un recensement décennal, la répartition de la population et de proposer à la lumière de celles-ci diverses positions concernant les circonscriptions électorales de chaque province et des Territoires du Nord-Ouest. Il doit fournir la carte appropriée à chacune des onze commissions de délimitation des circonscriptions constituées pour les provinces et les Territoires. Il exerce

également une fonction d'analyse en rapport aux méthodes d'inscription des électeurs et il doit faire rapport des recommandations qui découlent de cette analyse. La *Loi sur l'organisation du gouvernement* ayant aboli la fonction de Commissaire, en 1979, ses fonctions ont été confiées au directeur général des élections.

Organisation et contenu : Ce fonds contient les rapports des commissions de délimitation des circonscriptions électorales pour les années 1964-1965 et 1972-1976. S'y trouvent également les procès-verbaux des réunions des diverses commissions ainsi que les comptes rendus de leurs audiences publiques en différentes localités des provinces. Le fonds rassemble aussi des présentations faites par des particuliers durant des audiences publiques, des avis publics sur les audiences, de la correspondance entre les commissaires, avec la presse ou le grand public.

Archives de la Commission de contrôle de l'énergie atomique : RG 60
1947-1982

9,3 mètres

Historique : Créée en 1946 à titre d'établissement public, la Commission de contrôle de l'énergie atomique (CCEA) assume deux fonctions connexes. D'une part, par souci de la sécurité nationale, elle collabore avec les ministères du Commerce (RG 20) et du Revenu national (RG 16) à l'établissement d'un régime complet de licences et de permis visant à contrôler le mouvement du matériel et des substances radioactives. D'autre part, de concert avec les autorités fédérales et provinciales de la santé, elle réglemente et inspecte l'exploitation et la construction de réacteurs nucléaires et d'accélérateurs de particules, ainsi que la manipulation des substances radioactives et joue un rôle consultatif en ces domaines. Les archives de l'Eldorado Nucléaire Limitée (RG 134), qui, jusqu'en 1958, était chargée de la vente de l'uranium et de ses concentrés produits au Canada, sont étroitement liées à celles de la CCEA.

Organisation et contenu : Ce groupe d'archives contient les documents généraux de la Commission de contrôle de l'énergie atomique (1947-1955, 1980-1981), créés par le groupe de travail sur la récupération de Cosmos 954, satellite soviétique qui s'est écrasé dans les Territoires du Nord-Ouest en 1978 (1978-1982), les procès-verbaux des réunions du Comité consultatif sur les minéraux radioactifs (1948-1951), et des renseignements sur l'aide de la CCEA aux universités (1950-1977).

Archives de la Société des approvisionnements de guerre des Alliés : RG 61
1940-1946

1,5 mètre

Historique : Créée en juin 1940 pour les besoins de la guerre, la Société des approvisionnements de guerre des Alliés était chargée de contrôler, d'administrer et de diriger la construction et l'exploitation de toutes les usines de produits chimiques, d'explosifs et de munitions de l'État. Elle a été démantelée en 1948.

Organisation et contenu : Ces archives contiennent un historique de la société préparé par John Leslie en 1945, des dossiers sommaires de tous les projets administrés, entre 1940 et 1946, par la Société des approvisionnements de guerre des Alliés et des dossiers-matières qui traitent de la production de nitrate d'ammonium-ammoniaque.

Archives de Loto Canada/Société canadienne des paris sportifs : RG 62
1966-1985

140,62 mètres

Historique : Établie comme société d'État en juin 1976, Loto Canada a commencé ses opérations à la suite de la disparition de la Loterie olympique en septembre 1976. Elle a contribué au financement des jeux du Commonwealth de 1978 à Edmonton. En 1979, suite à un accord entre Ottawa et les provinces qui cédait les loteries aux provinces, Loto Canada a cessé la vente des billets et a fermé ses bureaux régionaux. De 1980 à 1984, le personnel de Loto Canada à Ottawa a mis sur pied un système de paris adapté aux compétitions de sport professionnel, ce qui a donné naissance, en 1983, à la Société canadienne des paris sportifs. Les autorités provinciales ont soutenu que le nouveau système violait l'accord de 1979 et, en 1985, une loi votée par le Parlement a amené la dissolution de Loto Canada et de la Société canadienne des paris sportifs.

Organisation et contenu : Ces archives se composent de dossiers de l'administration centrale et de documents généraux (procès-verbaux de la direction, statuts, etc.) de Loto Canada et de la Société canadienne des paris sportifs. Elles comprennent aussi les dossiers des bureaux régionaux de London, Toronto, Ottawa et Vancouver pour la Société canadienne des paris sportifs uniquement. Les dossiers du service central couvrent toutes les activités importantes des deux organismes.

Archives du Conseil des Arts du Canada : RG 63
1956-1989

595,69 mètres

Historique : Le Conseil des Arts est une société d'État créée en 1957 par la *Loi sur le Conseil des Arts du Canada* pour encourager les arts, les humanités et les sciences sociales. Un amendement apporté en avril 1978 a eu pour effet de transférer au Conseil de recherches en sciences humaines les attributions touchant les humanités et les sciences sociales. Le Conseil des Arts favorise l'étude, la jouissance des arts et la production d'œuvres d'art. Il est partiellement responsable des relations culturelles du Canada avec l'étranger et il administre un important programme de bourses, de récompenses et de subventions.

Organisation et contenu : Les archives sont divisées en deux séries générales : les dossiers d'exploitation et les dossiers de subventions. Les dossiers d'exploitation (1956-1975) contiennent des renseignements sur les enquêtes menées entre 1958 et 1962 sur les ballets, les orchestres symphoniques et les orchestres en général. Cette série renferme également des documents sur Stanley House, les donations, les politiques du Conseil des Arts en matière de bourses d'études, et des documents sur les relations fédérales-provinciales dans le domaine des politiques relatives aux arts. Les dossiers de subventions (1958-1973) consistent en demandes de subventions et en dossiers de prix approuvés par le Conseil des Arts. Ils sont classés par catégories selon la division ou le programme qui les a produits. Au nombre de ces catégories, citons la Division des arts, la Division des sciences sociales et humaines, le programme Explorations et le Programme d'échanges culturels.

Archives de la Commission des prix et du commerce en temps de guerre : RG 64
1939-1951

180 mètres

Historique : Mise sur pied en septembre 1939, la Commission des prix et du commerce en temps de guerre devait protéger le public contre les hausses injustes des prix des aliments, du combustible et des autres produits de première nécessité, et assurer un approvisionnement suffisant et une distribution adéquate de ces produits pendant la guerre. Elle était aussi habilitée à enquêter sur les coûts, les prix et les profits. Installée à Ottawa, la commission comprenait un certain nombre de services chargés d'un secteur donné de produits ou d'activités commerciales et agissait par l'intermédiaire d'organismes régionaux et locaux établis partout au Canada. Pour réaliser son mandat, la commission dut

aussi créer plusieurs sociétés : la Corporation de stabilisation des prix des produits de base, la Corporation des denrées en temps de guerre, la Commission canadienne de la laine et la Corporation canadienne de stabilisation des prix du sucre. La Commission des prix et du commerce en temps de guerre a été démantelée en 1951.

Organisation et contenu : Les archives de la commission sont formées des dossiers du service central, qui portent sur l'exploitation et l'administration de la commission (1939-1951) et qui incluent les dossiers créés par les bureaux du président et du secrétaire de la commission. Le classement des dossiers du service central témoignent des activités des secteurs suivants : produits alimentaires; produits laitiers; thé, café et épices; cacao, chocolat et confiserie; huiles et graisses; produits en bois et en métal; crédit à la consommation; mise en œuvre des décisions; distribution et commerce; biens d'équipement; magasins d'approvisionnement des navires; recherche et statistiques; pâtes et papiers; métaux non ferreux; machines de bureau et équipement hospitalier; Comité consultatif Stove. Les sous-séries comprennent les documents de la Division de la simplification des méthodes, de la Division des prix à Ottawa, du Contrôle des importations d'urgence, de la Direction des consommateurs et du Comité interministériel sur les études industrielles. Ce même système central contient les archives de sociétés créées pour les besoins de la guerre : Corporation de stabilisation des prix des produits de base (1941-1951), Corporation des denrées en temps de guerre (1941-1951), Commission canadienne de la laine (1942-1947), Wartime Salvage Limited (1942-1943) et Corporation canadienne de stabilisation des prix du sucre (1940-1950).

Archives de la Corporation commerciale canadienne : RG 65
1944-1972

9,6 mètres

Historique : Créée en 1946 par la *Loi sur la Corporation commerciale canadienne*, la corporation se voyait confier les fonctions de la Commission canadienne d'exportation en matière d'achat de biens et de services au Canada pour le compte des Nations unies et de certains gouvernements étrangers. En 1947, elle a été chargée des approvisionnements de la Défense nationale jusqu'à la création du ministère de la Production de défense (RG 49) en 1951. En 1963, elle a été incorporée à ce dernier, devenu aujourd'hui le ministère des Approvisionnements et Services (RG 98). À partir de 1976, elle s'employa davantage à faciliter les exportations en collaborant plus étroitement avec le secteur privé, se dotant même, en 1978, d'une administration centrale indépendante du ministère des Approvisionnements et Services et dirigée par un conseil

composé en majorité de représentants du secteur privé. La CCC a pour principales fonctions de contribuer à l'expansion des exportations et d'aider les Canadiens à se procurer des biens et des services à l'étranger.

Organisation et contenu : Ces archives se composent de dossiers-matières qui incluent les procès-verbaux du conseil d'administration (1946-1952) et du Comité des prix (1944-1947), les ententes conclues avec la Ming Sung Industrial Company pour l'exportation de biens et d'approvisionnements en Chine (1946-1950), de dossiers généraux relatifs à l'exploitation et à l'administration de la corporation (1944-1952) et une série spéciale relative à l'opération Pinetree, dispositif canado-américain de défense aérienne, renfermant essentiellement des contrats d'approvisionnements militaires (1950-1951).

Archives du Conseil des ports nationaux : RG 66
1886-1981

59,3 mètres

Historique : « Corporation de mandataire » créée en 1936, le Conseil des ports nationaux a juridiction sur divers ports et élévateurs à grain, dont les ports de Saint-Jean (Terre-Neuve); Halifax (Nouvelle-Écosse); Saint-Jean et Belledune (Nouveau-Brunswick); Chicoutimi, Baie-des-Ha! Ha!, Québec, Sept-Îles, Trois-Rivières et Montréal (Québec); Churchill (Manitoba); Prince-Rupert et Vancouver (Colombie-Britannique); et les élévateurs à grain de Prescott et de Port Colborne (Ontario). Avant la création du conseil, une commission locale administrait chaque port national. Le conseil fait rapport au Parlement par l'entremise du ministre des Transports.

Organisation et contenu : La grande majorité des documents se regroupe à l'intérieur du système des dossiers du service central (1936-1981). On retrouve aussi des manuels de procédures (1954-1959), pour l'usage des bureaux du Conseil, un dossier de référence du remorqueur d'inspection du port de Montréal (1910-1968), de même que des dossiers financiers (1962-1965) et de la documentation sur les conventions collectives (1943-1967).

Archives de la Société pour l'expansion des exportations : RG 67
1944-1976

24,1 mètres

Historique : La Société pour l'expansion des exportations a succédé en 1969 à la Société pour l'assurance des crédits à l'exportation, société d'État créée en 1944 pour favoriser le commerce en assurant les exportateurs canadiens contre le non-paiement par les acheteurs étrangers. Elle a été autorisée en 1959 à accorder une aide financière pour l'achat de biens au Canada.

Organisation et contenu : En plus des dossiers du service central (1944-1970), signalons l'Union de Berne (1946-1976) et les études de cas (1954-1974), incluant les dossiers sur les enquêtes et les politiques (1945-1974).

Archives du Registraire général : RG 68
1760-1988

93,07 mètres
650 microfilms

Historique : Le registraire général consigne tous les instruments d'assignation tels que proclamations, commissions, lettres patentes et autres documents émis sous le Grand Sceau et le sceau privé du gouverneur général. Avant la Confédération, cette fonction était exercée par le secrétaire provincial de chaque province. En 1867, c'est le Secrétariat d'État (RG 6) qui en a été chargé. En 1966, on a mis sur pied un ministère distinct du registraire général, mais, dès 1967, toutes ces fonctions et attributions étaient confiées au nouveau ministère de la Consommation et des Corporations (RG 103).

Organisation et contenu : Ces documents comprennent essentiellement des registres classés par ordre chronologique contenant des copies de documents émis sous les divers sceaux du Canada. Ils renferment des documents tels que proclamations, commissions, mandats d'arrêt et lettres de grâce, obligations, lettres patentes, chartes d'incorporation, documents fonciers, permis, ordonnances, ampliations. S'y trouvent également quelques originaux de proclamations, copies de lettres, reçus, correspondance et autorisations d'utiliser le Grand Sceau.

Archives de la Commission du centenaire : RG 69
1960-1970

197,1 mètres

Historique : Les préparatifs du centenaire de la Confédération canadienne ont commencé dès 1959. Société d'État, la commission a été mise sur pied en 1963 pour intéresser le public à cet événement historique et pour organiser et mettre en œuvre des programmes et des projets connexes. Pour réaliser ses objectifs, la commission s'est dotée de comités dont les directeurs étaient chargés de la planification, des relations publiques et de l'information, ainsi que des bureaux régionaux. La commission faisait rapport au Parlement par l'entremise du Secrétaire d'État.

Organisation et contenu : L'organisation de ces archives reflète la structure administrative et le système de comités mis en place par la commission. Les documents du Bureau des commissaires et du secrétariat (1960-1970) et des administrateurs supérieurs de la commission comprennent les dossiers du Cabinet du ministre, du commissaire et président de la commission, du directeur adjoint, du Bureau de l'adjoint aux commissaires et au secrétaire de la Commission du centenaire. Les dossiers de la Direction de la planification (1963-1968) renferment les archives du Bureau du directeur à la planification, de la Division des trains et des caravanes, de la Division culturelle, de la Division des arts d'interprétation, de la Division de l'athlétisme, de la Division historique, de la Division du défilé des coureurs de bois et de la Division du cérémonial. Les dossiers de la Direction des relations publiques et de l'information (1963-1968) rassemblent les archives produites par les bureaux du directeur et du directeur adjoint, du coordonnateur de la promotion à l'étranger, de la Division de la publicité, de la Division de l'information, de la bibliothèque et du centre d'information, du Bureau des conférenciers, de la Division de la promotion et de la Division des publications. Les documents des bureaux régionaux (1963-1968) comprennent les dossiers des bureaux des directeurs et des représentants dans les provinces. Ce groupe d'archives contient également une série de dossiers du service central.

Archives d'Air Canada : RG 70
1936-1980

97,9 mètres
8 microfilms

Historique : Filiale à part entière des Chemins de fer nationaux du Canada, la Société Air Canada a été constituée en 1937 sous le nom de Lignes aériennes Trans-Canada, en vue d'assurer le transport aérien de passagers, de courrier et de marchandises au Canada et hors du pays. Depuis sa constitution en société, ses services et ses activités ont connu une expansion considérable. Elle est devenue la propriété du gouvernement fédéral en 1978 et fait rapport au Parlement par l'entremise du ministre des Transports. Air Canada n'a adopté sa désignation actuelle qu'en 1964. Société mandataire, les actions d'Air Canada sont disponibles au public depuis 1988.

Organisation et contenu : Le classement de la plupart des archives contenues dans RG 70 reflète l'organisation de la compagnie aérienne. Les dossiers du Bureau du président (1936-1968) témoignent de l'administration des deux premiers présidents, H.J. Symington et G.R. McGregor. Les dossiers du Bureau du secrétaire (1937-1978) traitent de finances et d'immobilier. Les documents d'exploitation comprennent les dossiers de la Direction des opérations et de la Division de la planification des opérations, de la Division des opérations de vol et de la Division du génie (1937-1970). Les archives de la Direction des achats et magasins (1937-1970) couvrent tous les aspects de l'acquisition d'installations et d'équipement, tandis que celles des Services de commercialisation (1960-1975) concernent les enquêtes, les ententes relatives à la réalisation d'études de mise en marché, les plans et les programmes de commercialisation. Ce groupe d'archives renferme également des dossiers des services administratifs et généraux (1945-1979) qui traitent essentiellement de questions internes. D'autres documents illustrent les activités de la société au Congo, en Guyane et à Expo 67. Des publications de la société, des documents publicitaires, des rapports et études mensuels et annuels, des horaires, des tarifs et des études d'itinéraires figurent également dans ce groupe de documents.

Archives de la Compagnie canadienne de l'exposition universelle (Expo 67) : RG 71
1962-1969

469,2 mètres

Historique : Constituée en 1962, cette compagnie devait planifier, organiser et administrer l'exposition universelle de 1967 qui a eu lieu à Montréal du 28 avril au 27 octobre.

Organisation et contenu : Les archives couvrent tous les aspects des activités de la société. Elles se composent de dossiers d'exploitation et de dossiers administratifs provenant du conseil d'administration et du comité directeur (1963-1969), du secrétariat (1963-1967), des Finances et de l'Administration (1963-1967), du Service des installations (1963-1967), du Service des expositions (1963-1967), de la Direction des visiteurs (1963-1967) et du Service des relations publiques (1963-1967).

Archives de la Commission des expositions du gouvernement canadien : RG 72
1875-1978

91 mètres

Historique : La Commission des expositions du gouvernement canadien est chargée de la représentation du Canada aux foires et aux expositions internationales. Administrée par le ministère de l'Agriculture (RG 17) jusqu'en 1918, par le ministère de l'Immigration et de la Colonisation jusqu'en 1927, par le ministère de l'Industrie et du Commerce (RG 20) jusqu'en 1970, puis par Information Canada (RG 94) jusqu'au démantèlement de ce ministère en 1976, la Commission des expositions relève aujourd'hui du ministère des Approvisionnements et Services (RG 98).

Organisation et contenu : Ces archives, classées par exposition, consistent en correspondance générale numérotée ou non numérotée, en copies de lettres, livres des visiteurs de marque, livres-souvenirs, plans et dessins, études préliminaires, brochures publicitaires, affiches, coupures de presse, listes de récompenses et de participants.

Archives du solliciteur général : RG 73
1834-1986

428,07 mètres
97 microfilms
1 fichier informatique

Historique : Le solliciteur général, dont le poste a été créé en 1887 par une loi du Parlement (il a fallu attendre en 1892 pour que la loi soit adoptée), était à l'origine un adjoint du ministre de la Justice. En 1966, on lui a confié un ministère distinct et plusieurs des responsabilités qui incombaient auparavant au ministère de la Justice (RG 13) : maisons de correction, prisons et pénitenciers fédéraux; libérations conditionnelles et remises de peine; et application des lois par la Gendarmerie royale du Canada (RG 18).

Organisation et contenu : Ces archives sont réparties dans quatre séries : Cabinet du ministre (1960-1980), Secrétariat (1962-1978), Direction des pénitenciers (1874-1970) et Commission nationale des libérations conditionnelles (1903-1970). Elles comprennent de la correspondance provenant du Cabinet du ministre (1967-1980) et du Secrétariat (1962-1978); les dossiers des groupes de travail sur la justice pour les victimes d'actes criminels (1982-1986), sur le rôle du secteur privé dans la justice criminelle (1972-1979) et sur le rôle du gouvernement fédéral dans l'application de la loi (1973-1981); les dossiers du président de la Commission nationale des libérations conditionnelles (1903-1970); des dossiers de détenus (1886-1972) et de libérations conditionnelles (1932-1973); les archives de divers pénitenciers : Stony Mountain (1871-1984), Colombie-Britannique (1878-1975), Dorchester (1932-1982) et Kingston (1934-1974); enfin, les dossiers d'exploitation de l'administration centrale (1874-1981) et des bureaux régionaux (1960-1973) sur les activités de divers établissements correctionnels. Le fichier informatique contient une base de données sur les détenus pour l'année 1978.

Archives de l'Agence canadienne de développement international : RG 74
1950-1977

317,4 mètres

Historique : L'Agence canadienne de développement international (ACDI) est issue de la Direction de l'assistance économique et technique du ministère du Commerce (RG 20), dont les fonctions ont été transférées au Bureau de l'aide extérieure en 1960. Devenu ministère en 1968, le bureau a été rebaptisé ACDI.

L'ACDI conseille le gouvernement canadien en matière de politiques d'aide internationale, de crédits consentis, de fonctionnement et d'administration du programme en Asie, en Afrique francophone et anglophone, dans les Caraïbes membres du Commonwealth et en Amérique latine. Le ministère a institué plusieurs directions chargées des politiques, de l'administration, du contrôle financier, ainsi que d'aspects particuliers du programme d'aide et de ses applications dans les principaux pays.

Organisation et contenu : Les archives de ce groupe se composent des dossiers du service central de la Direction de l'aide économique et technique (1950-1968), de dossiers classés par pays qui traitent de programmes régionaux particuliers (1965-1976), de dossiers relatifs à l'aide alimentaire bilatérale, incluant le programme international d'aide alimentaire (1974-1977), de dossiers de projets subventionnés présentés par des particuliers (1962-1976), de dossiers de bourses d'études et de perfectionnement du Commonwealth (1955-1971), de dossiers de la Corporation commerciale canadienne (1974-1977), de documents sur la fourniture de machines et d'équipement léger nécessaires à la réalisation des programmes d'aide alimentaire, et des dossiers du projet Warsack (1955-1958) et du Comité d'aide au développement (1959-1970).

Archives du Conseil économique du Canada : RG 75
1960-1984

113 mètres

Historique : Corporation départementale établie en 1963 par la *Loi sur le conseil économique*, cet organisme est chargé de faire des recommandations sur la façon dont le Canada peut atteindre les plus hauts niveaux d'emploi et de production pour assurer un taux élevé et régulier de croissance économique. Il est composé de représentants de l'entreprise privée, des organisations de travailleurs, des agriculteurs, de l'industrie, du commerce et du grand public. Il fait rapport au Parlement par l'entremise du premier ministre, il rédige un rapport annuel et effectue diverses études sur les perspectives économiques du Canada.

Organisation et contenu : Parmi les principales séries de dossiers, citons les dossiers du service central (1963-1984) et ceux du Conseil de la productivité nationale (1960-1963). Une bonne partie des documents du service central sont disponibles dans les deux langues officielles. Également, la série du Conseil économique du Canada (1963-1973) renseigne à la fois sur la transition du Conseil de la productivité nationale vers le Conseil économique du Canada et sur d'autres activités de ce dernier.

Archives de la Direction de l'immigration : RG 76
1865-1988

944,37 mètres
740 microfilms
16 tiroirs de fiches (index)
20 fichiers informatiques

Historique : De 1868 à 1892, l'immigration et la quarantaine ont relevé du ministère de l'Agriculture (RG 17). En 1892, les attributions en matière d'immigration ont été réunies à celles du peuplement au ministère de l'Intérieur (RG 15). Les archives relatives au peuplement de l'Ouest se trouvent dans RG 15. Une Direction de l'immigration distincte a été établie en 1893. En 1917, le ministère de l'Immigration et de la Colonisation a reçu du ministère de l'Intérieur les responsabilités liées à l'immigration. L'Immigration a bénéficié de son statut autonome jusqu'en 1936, date à laquelle elle est redevenue une direction de façon définitive, cette fois-ci au ministère des Mines et des Ressources (voir RG 21 et 22). L'afflux d'immigrants qui a suivi la Seconde Guerre mondiale a amené la création, en 1950, du ministère de la Citoyenneté et de l'Immigration, qui résultait de l'union de la Direction de l'immigration, de la Direction des affaires indiennes du ministère des Mines et des Ressources et de la Direction de la citoyenneté et de la Direction de l'enregistrement de la citoyenneté du Secrétariat d'État (RG 6). Le ministère de la Citoyenneté et de l'Immigration a été aboli en 1966, et l'immigration a été confiée au nouveau ministère de la Main-d'œuvre et de l'Immigration (RG 118). Celui-ci a fusionné avec l'ancienne Commission d'assurance-chômage en 1977 pour former la Commission canadienne de l'emploi et de l'immigration, principale composante opérationnelle du ministère de l'Emploi et de l'Immigration. La Direction de l'immigration administre le recrutement, la sélection et l'établissement des immigrants.

Organisation et contenu : Ce groupe d'archives contient divers types de documents, tels que dossiers du service central, dossiers de cas, grands livres, registres, copies de lettres, dossiers-matières, livres d'instructions, pétitions, manuels d'immigration, circulaires, instructions et formulaires. Le noyau de ce groupe d'archives est constitué de quatre séries de dossiers du service central des quartiers généraux, qui remontent à 1892. Ces séries concernent généralement l'administration et les politiques, mais elles renferment également quelques dossiers-matières sur des cas de nature exceptionnelle, des enquêtes ou des renseignements sur des sujets particuliers. Ces archives documentent maints aspects de l'immigration au Canada, comme, par exemple, l'élaboration et la mise en œuvre des politiques fédérales d'immigration,

Pères de famille... Épreuve d'une annonce publicitaire de 1925 publiée dans un journal de langue française en Nouvelle-Angleterre afin de promouvoir le rapatriement des Canadiens français au Canada. (RG 76, vol. 239, dossier 146011, bobine C-7388) (C-221058)

les activités de divers agents ou agences d'immigration/émigration et l'ouverture de l'Ouest canadien à l'immigration. On trouve également des dossiers intéressants sur l'immigration de divers groupes ethniques ou professionnels. Au nombre des séries importantes, mentionnons aussi les registres des passagers de navires (1865-1918), qui renseignent sur l'arrivée des immigrants dans les ports canadiens comme Halifax, Québec, Montréal, Saint-Jean, Vancouver et Victoria. Ce groupe d'archives contient aussi des listes de contrôle aux points d'entrée (1908-1918), des dossiers, datant des années 60 et 70, d'immigrants qui ont bénéficié d'une aide financière pour venir au Canada, des dossiers de l'étude canadienne sur l'immigration et la population (1969-1976) et des dossiers des bureaux régionaux de l'immigration postérieurs aux années 70, y compris ceux des postes du ministère des Affaires extérieures outre-mer qui assument d'importantes fonctions de sélection. Les documents informatiques comprennent soixante fichiers du Système de données sur les immigrants ayant obtenu le droit d'établissement (SDIODE), qui couvrent les années 1927-1986. Ce système d'information contient des données de base annuelles sur chaque immigrant entré au Canada pendant une année donnée.

Archives du Conseil national de recherches : RG 77
1919-1987

242,3 mètres
5 microfilms

Historique : Le Conseil national de recherches du Canada (CNRC) a essentiellement pour mandat de réaliser des recherches scientifiques et techniques, de les favoriser et de leur apporter un appui financier et technique. Créé en 1916, le Conseil national de recherches émanait du sous-comité du Conseil privé sur la recherche scientifique et industrielle. Le conseil ne disposa de son propre laboratoire qu'en 1925 et, dès 1929, il avait mis sur pied ses quatre premières divisions de recherche scientifique : chimie, physique (qui a été divisée en 1935 en physique et génie mécanique), biologie et agriculture, et recherche et information.

Le CNRC a connu une expansion considérable pendant la Seconde Guerre mondiale. Intensifiant ses recherches dans des domaines tels que le radar, la télémétrie acoustique et autres secteurs des communications, les viseurs et la balistique, la guerre biologique et l'aérodynamique, ainsi que la recherche nucléaire, le CNRC a dû augmenter son personnel, qui est passé de 300 à 3 000 personnes. La participation du Canada à la guerre a amené de nouvelles responsabilités de recherche au CNRC, une fois la paix revenue. Après la guerre, le CNRC a créé plusieurs nouvelles divisions scientifiques de grande importance : Énergie atomique (1946),

Division de la recherche en construction (1947), Laboratoire de recherches des Prairies (1948) et la Division de la recherche médicale (1948). En 1946-1947, le CNRC a également été chargé de l'administration de la toute nouvelle Commission de contrôle de l'énergie atomique de Chalk River (RG 60). Par la suite, le CNRC a mis sur pied le Laboratoire de recherches de l'Atlantique (1952), l'Établissement aéronautique national (1958), la Direction des installations de recherche spatiale (dans les années 60) et l'institut Herzberg d'astrophysique (1975).

Organisation et contenu : Ce groupe de documents est formé des archives de plusieurs des divisions scientifiques nommées ci-dessus, ainsi que de celles d'autres composantes du conseil. La plupart de ces archives font partie de l'une des cinq grandes séries suivantes : correspondance de l'organisme (1920-1973) formée de plusieurs ensembles de dossiers administratifs et opérationnels de diverses divisions, qui proviennent d'un service central créé par le CNRC dans les années 40; les carnets de notes de laboratoire (1933-1973), qui traitent de diverses expériences réalisées dans les laboratoires du CNRC et le Laboratoire de recherches des Prairies; les brevets (1924-1968) rassemblés dans un seul groupe de dossiers témoignent des inventions du personnel du CNRC; les dossiers des administrateurs (1939-1967), qui regroupent des dossiers provenant des bureaux de A.G.L. McNaughton, C.J. Mackenzie, F.T. Rossner; les dossiers de l'institut Herzberg d'astrophysique (1965-1988), qui contiennent des rapports sur les ovnis, classés chronologiquement.

Archives de la Northern Ontario Pipeline (Société d'État) : RG 78
1954-1967

5,1 mètres

Historique : Fondée en juin 1956, cette société était chargée de superviser la construction de la section nord-ontarienne du pipe-line pancanadien de gaz naturel. Cette section a par la suite été louée, avec option d'achat, à la Trans-Canada Pipeline Limited. En 1963, celle-ci s'est prévalue de son droit et a acheté la section nord-ontarienne du pipe-line. La Northern Ontario Pipeline a été dissoute quatre ans plus tard.

Organisation et contenu : Ce groupe d'archives comporte cinq séries qui renseignent sur de nombreuses activités de la société, depuis sa conception et sa planification jusqu'à son transfert au secteur privé. Ces archives comprennent des dossiers de Construction de défense Limitée (RG 83), (1954-1967).

Archives de la Commission du tarif : RG 79
1933-1985

95,8 mètres

Historique : Créée en 1931, cette commission exerçait les pouvoirs qui lui étaient dévolus par la *Loi sur la Commission du tarif*, la *Loi sur les douanes*, la *Loi sur la taxe d'accise* et la *Loi antidumping*. Elle a remplacé la Commission des douanes qui existait depuis 1903. D'après sa loi constitutive, la Commission du tarif enquêtait et faisait rapport sur tout ce qui avait trait aux importations, au Canada, de marchandises assujetties aux droits de douane ou aux taxes d'accise ou qui en étaient exemptes. D'après la *Loi sur les douanes*, la *Loi sur la taxe d'accise* et la *Loi antidumping*, elle agissait à titre de tribunal pour entendre les appels contre les décisions du ministère du Revenu national, Douanes et Accise, en ce qui concerne les taxes d'accise, la classification tarifaire, l'évaluation des droits, le *drawback* des droits de douane et la détermination de la valeur normale ou du prix d'exportation dans les affaires de dumping. Ses rapports sont déposés à la Chambre des communes par le ministre des Finances (RG 19). En 1989, la Commission du tarif a fusionné avec le Tribunal canadien des importations et la Commission du textile et du vêtement pour former le Tribunal canadien du commerce extérieur.

Organisation et contenu : Ces archives se répartissent en quatre séries : les rapports d'enquête et les recommandations relatives aux tarifs et aux échanges commerciaux se trouvent dans la série des renvois à la commission (nᵒˢ 1-163), tandis que la série des appels (nᵒˢ 1-2540) regroupe les transcriptions de dépositions. La correspondance générale et les rapports sur les tarifs et leurs répercussions sur les relations commerciales du Canada avec les autres pays se trouvent dans les dossiers nationaux (1910-1959) et les dossiers administratifs (1933-1977).

Archives de la Commission canadienne des grains : RG 80
1912-1973

8,4 mètres

Historique : Créée en 1912, la Commission des grains du Canada assurait une surveillance générale de la manutention du grain des Prairies en délivrant des permis aux exploitants d'élévateurs, en procédant à l'inspection, au classement et à la pesée du grain aux élévateurs terminus et en exploitant elle-même les élévateurs du gouvernement canadien. Installée à Winnipeg, cette commission a relevé suc-

cessivement du ministère du Commerce (RG 20), de 1912 à 1960, puis d'Agriculture Canada (RG 17). En 1971, elle devenait la Commission canadienne des grains.

Organisation et contenu : Ces archives se composent de dossiers du service central, de rapports publiés et de cartes. Dans ce groupe de documents, la série la plus complète renferme des dossiers-matières (1912-1962) qui renseignent sur l'inspection, le pesage et l'entreposage des grains, ainsi que sur l'entretien des élévateurs.

Archives de l'Office fédéral du charbon : RG 81
1917-1971

30 mètres

Historique : La création, en 1947, de l'Office fédéral du charbon a mis un terme à la longue liste d'organismes gouvernementaux qui ont été chargés de superviser l'industrie houillère canadienne. En tête de cette liste, on retrouve le Bureau du contrôleur du combustible fondé en 1917 pour pallier les pénuries de charbon pendant la Première Guerre mondiale. En 1922, l'Office fédéral du combustible a été créé pour étudier l'autosuffisance en matière énergétique. Pour éviter le dédoublement des services, la plupart de ses fonctions ont été transmises, en 1941, à l'administrateur du charbon de la Commission des prix et du commerce en temps de guerre (RG 64). Peu après la guerre, l'Office fédéral du charbon a été mis sur pied non seulement pour favoriser l'exploitation et la commercialisation du charbon canadien, mais aussi pour améliorer les conditions de travail dans les houillères. L'office a été dissous en 1970 et le reste de ses attributions ont été transférées au ministère de l'Énergie, des Mines et des Ressources. Au cours de son histoire, l'office et ses prédécesseurs ont relevé tour à tour des ministères suivants : Mines, 1922-1936 (RG 86), Mines et Ressources, 1936-1941 (RG 21), Travail, 1941-1943 (RG 27), Munitions et Approvisionnements, 1943-1948 (RG 28), Commerce, 1948-1951 (RG 20), Mines et Relevés techniques, 1951-1966 (RG 21) et Énergie, Mines et Ressources, 1966-1970 (RG 21).

Organisation et contenu : Ce groupe d'archives comporte deux séries. Les dossiers du service central des dossiers (1917-1971) et les dossiers de référence (1927-1970) témoignent du rôle joué par l'office et ses prédécesseurs dans la production, la commercialisation et l'utilisation du charbon au Canada.

Archives de la Commission d'appel de l'immigration : RG 82
1956-1988

265,7 mètres

Historique : Instituée en 1967, la Commission d'appel de l'immigration a succédé à la Commission générale des appels de l'immigration du ministère de la Citoyenneté et de l'Immigration (RG 26). Entièrement indépendante de tout autre ministère et faisant rapport au Parlement par l'entremise du ministre de l'Emploi et de l'Immigration, la commission fournissait un recours aux personnes frappées d'une ordonnance d'expulsion ou aux répondants canadiens dont la demande d'admission de parents avait été refusée. Avant 1967, les ordonnances d'expulsion étaient exécutées par la Direction de l'immigration (RG 76). En janvier 1989, la Commission d'appel de l'immigration a été remplacée par la Commission de l'immigration et du statut de réfugié.

Organisation et contenu : Ce groupe d'archives se compose de dossiers personnels relatifs à des cas d'appel présentés à la Commission d'appel de l'immigration (1956-1967 et 1967-1988), sur lesquels la commission a statué. Les dossiers contiennent des ordonnances de déportation, des avis d'appel, des avis d'audience, des procès-verbaux d'enquêtes, des sommaires d'agents enquêteurs, des décisions de la Commission d'appel, des rapports confidentiels du président de la commission au ministre et des avis envoyés par la commission à l'appelant pour lui faire part de sa décision. Certains dossiers contiennent aussi des évaluations psychologiques faites par des médecins de famille ou des organismes de services sociaux, ainsi que de la correspondance sur le statut des individus et l'éventuelle issue de leur cas.

Archives de Construction de défense Limitée : RG 83
1941-1972

23,1 mètres

Historique : Construction de défense Limitée a été créée en 1950 à titre de société d'État pour adjuger les contrats des grands travaux de construction militaire et d'entretien requis par le ministère de la Défense nationale. En 1951, Construction de défense (1951) Limitée a été constituée en vertu de la *Loi sur la production de défense* pour assumer les responsabilités de la société précédente. À l'origine, Construction de défense faisait rapport au Parlement par l'entremise du ministre de la Production de défense, mais, de 1963 à 1965, c'était par le ministre de l'Industrie. À partir d'avril 1965, elle a fait rapport au Parlement par l'entremise du ministre de la Défense nationale. La société est chargée de la construction des systèmes de défense, ce qui inclut aussi bien

l'adjudication des contrats de construction que la supervision de travaux précis. Outre sa participation aux projets de construction de la Défense nationale au Canada, la société prend part aux travaux de construction de la Défense nationale en Europe dans le cadre des accords de l'OTAN. Par ailleurs, elle aide et conseille les autres ministères et organismes gouvernementaux en matière de construction.

Organisation et contenu : Ces archives sont surtout constituées de dossiers du service central relatifs au dispositif d'alerte avancé du Canada central (1951-1969). On trouve également des documents sur l'approvisionnement en acier pour les projets de défense (1951-1952), sur le dispositif d'alerte Pinetree (1951-1959) et sur le Projet d'établissement d'expérimentation des transmissions de l'armée (1959-1960). Ce groupe d'archives contient aussi des accords et des grands livres généraux de revenus et de dépenses (1950-1962), certains dossiers de la société Wartime Housing Limited (1941-1951), qui était chargée de fournir des logements aux personnes travaillant à la fabrication de munitions ou à la réalisation de projets de défense.

Archives du Service canadien des parcs : RG 84
1873-1986

498,2 mètres
45 microfilms
988 microfiches
113 fichiers informatiques

Historique : Depuis que le gouvernement canadien a acquis les sources chaudes d'eau minérale de Banff, en 1885, le Service canadien des parcs n'a cessé de se développer. Il s'occupe maintenant de plus de trente parcs nationaux, de plus de soixante-dix parcs et lieux historiques nationaux et de dix réseaux de canaux d'importance historique. Le Service canadien des parcs planifie, développe et administre les parcs nationaux et les parcs et lieux historiques. D'abord assurée par la Direction des terres fédérales du ministère de l'Intérieur (RG 15), par l'entremise du surin-tendant du parc des montagnes Rocheuses, l'administration des parcs est devenue en 1908 une unité de la Direction des forêts (RG 39), puis, en 1911, une entité distincte connue sous le nom de Direction des parcs fédéraux (plus tard, nationaux). De 1918 à 1966, le Service canadien de la faune (RG 109) a fait partie de cette direction qui, en 1973, s'est vu confier l'administration des canaux historiques, assurée jusque-là par les ministères des Travaux publics, 1841-1879 (RG 11), puis des Chemins de fer et Canaux, 1879-1936 (RG 43), et enfin des Transports, 1936-1973 (RG 12). Le Programme de conservation ou Parcs Canada et ses prédécesseurs ont tous gardé leur identité distincte dans les divers

ministères dont ils ont relevé (voir la notice du RG 22). De 1922 à 1964, le parc national de Wood Buffalo a été administré par le Programme des affaires du Nord et ses prédécesseurs (RG 85). En 1979, Parcs Canada (comme on l'appelait alors) était intégré au ministère de l'Environnement (RG 108) et, depuis 1988, il s'appelle le Service canadien des parcs.

Organisation et contenu : Ce groupe d'archives comprend cinq séries générales de documents textuels de l'administration centrale, reflétant les divers systèmes de classification de dossiers utilisés au cours des ans, et une série de dossiers généraux du service central. Les archives de la Direction du secrétariat (1873-1928) témoignent de l'expansion des parcs nationaux au Canada, et plus particulièrement des parcs de Banff, Waterton, Yoho et autres parcs de l'Ouest, ainsi que du parc de la Pointe Pelée. La série la plus considérable de dossiers du service central provient de la Direction des parcs nationaux (v. 1886-1969); ces archives traitent de toutes les activités de l'administration des parcs nationaux et historiques, de 1911 au milieu des années 60, telles que la concession de terres, la faune, le tourisme, les camps de travail pendant la guerre, la prévention des feux de forêt et les services d'interprétation. On trouve également des dossiers de la Commission des lieux et monuments historiques (voir aussi RG 37). Les dossiers du service central du Programme de conservation de la Direction des parcs nationaux et historiques (1917-1985), réorganisée au milieu des années 60, couvrent tous les aspects du développement des parcs nationaux et historiques, à l'exception de la faune, le Service canadien de la faune (RG 109) ayant été détaché de Parcs Canada en 1966 pour devenir une direction à part entière. Les documents du Programme de Parcs Canada (1963-1981) renseignent sur toutes les activités traditionnelles des parcs et sur des activités plus récentes, telles que les audiences publiques, les réserves naturelles, les conférences fédérales-provinciales sur les parcs. Ces dernières années, le rôle joué par le Service canadien des parcs a suscité de nombreuses enquêtes socio-économiques qui sont disponibles sous forme informatisée. Ces enquêtes concernent l'utilisation des parcs, les loisirs de plein air et le tourisme.

Archives du Programme des affaires du Nord : RG 85
1867-1974

393,1 mètres

Historique : Bien qu'il ait fallu attendre 1921 pour que soit créé le premier organisme fédéral chargé de l'administration du Nord canadien, l'intervention du gouvernement fédéral dans les affaires du Nord remonte à la fin du dix-neuvième siècle. En 1898, la ruée vers l'or du

Klondike force le fédéral à établir, par le biais de diverses unités du ministère de l'Intérieur, des services gouvernementaux locaux au Yukon et l'oblige à étendre la juridiction de l'administration des terres et des mines aux régions nordiques. À la fin de la Première Guerre mondiale, la conservation de la faune et la souveraineté de l'Arctique viennent s'ajouter aux responsabilités du ministère. L'élargissement du mandat du ministère de l'Intérieur amène la création, en 1921, de la Direction des Territoires du Nord-Ouest (qui devient la Direction des Territoires du Nord-Ouest et du Yukon en 1922).

Au début des années 50, le gouvernement fédéral intervient de façon plus active dans l'administration du Nord. Cette évolution résulte des découvertes minérales dans les Territoires du Nord-Ouest au cours des années 30, de la prospérité créée par les grands travaux du temps de la guerre, tels que la route de l'Alaska et le pipe-line Canol, du rôle joué par le Nord dans la guerre froide entre les superpuissances et du besoin croissant du Nord en services sociaux ou autres. L'ampleur des services offerts par la Direction de l'administration du Nord et des terres, créée en 1950, témoigne de cette évolution dans les années qui ont suivi la Seconde Guerre mondiale. En 1973, le fédéral regroupe les services pour le Nord dans le nouveau Programme des affaires du Nord. Bien que le ministère de l'Intérieur ait été aboli en 1936, le Programme des affaires du Nord et ses prédécesseurs ont conservé leur identité distincte dans les divers ministères dont ils ont relevé (voir RG 22).

Organisation et contenu : Les archives sont organisées en séries qui reflètent les systèmes de classification de dossiers utilisés par les entités administratives qui les ont créées. Les dossiers de la Direction des terres minières et du Yukon (1884-1968) traitent du développement des mines et des ressources dans le Nord. Les archives de la Direction des Territoires du Nord-Ouest et du Yukon (1894-1954) fournissent des détails sur tous les aspects de l'intervention du fédéral dans le Nord, de la fin des années 10 au début des années 50. La série des dossiers du service central de la Direction de l'administration du Nord et des terres (1892-1973) témoigne de la participation croissante du fédéral au développement du Nord au cours des années 50 et 60. Enfin, la série de dossiers du service central du Programme des affaires du Nord (1947-1987) renseigne sur les activités du ministère des Affaires indiennes et du Nord canadien.

Archives de la Direction des mines : RG 86
1911-1968

16,7 mètres

Historique : Le Bureau du surintendant des mines, ancêtre de la Direction des mines, a été créé en 1884, à la suite de l'intensification de l'activité minière dans les montagnes Rocheuses. Cet essor a amené le ministère de l'Intérieur à nommer sur place un fonctionnaire chargé d'inspecter les opérations minières, de recueillir des statistiques et de favoriser l'activité minière sur les terres fédérales. En 1903, la Direction des mines a été établie au sein du ministère de l'Intérieur (RG 15). En 1907, cette direction a fusionné avec la Commission géologique du Canada (RG 45) pour former le ministère des Mines. La direction a continué de colliger et d'étudier les statistiques minières et de ramasser des spécimens intéressants pour les expériences en laboratoire et les expositions. Lorsque le ministère de l'Intérieur a été aboli en 1936, le secteur des Mines est devenu une simple composante de la Direction de la géologie et des mines du ministère des Mines et des Ressources. Au cours des quarante dernières années, les Mines ont formé une direction au sein de divers ministères importants (voir RG 21). En 1974-1975, la Direction des mines a été restructurée et est connue sous le nom de Centre canadien de la technologie des minéraux et de l'énergie (CANMET) du ministère de l'Énergie, des Mines et des Ressources. Ses laboratoires de recherche se spécialisent dans l'énergie, les mines, la minéralogie et la métallurgie.

Organisation et contenu : Ces archives sont réparties en cinq petites séries : Bureau du directeur (1911-1968), Division des routes minières (1936-1940), Section des combustibles et de l'énergie (1953-1966), Office fédéral de l'énergie (1918-1922), et Bureau des mines (1920-1960).

Archives de la Direction des ressources minérales : RG 87
1885-1961

37 mètres

Historique : La Division des statistiques minérales et des mines a été établie en 1886 au sein de la Direction de la Commission et du Musée d'histoire géologique et naturelle du ministère de l'Intérieur (RG 15). Recueillir des statistiques minières, publier des renseignements sur les ressources minérales et des analyses des facteurs affectant l'industrie minière, mettre sur pied des programmes de formation professionnelle et administrer les lois fédérales relatives aux mines constituent les principales fonctions de cette division. En 1907, la Commission

géologique du Canada a fusionné avec la Direction des mines (RG 86) pour former le ministère des Mines. La Division des ressources et des statistiques minérales du ministère a continué le travail de collecte et de publication des statistiques relatives à la production minérale et aux industries métallurgiques au Canada. En 1920, les fonctions relatives à la collecte des statistiques ont été transférées au Bureau fédéral de la statistique (RG 31), mais la division a continué d'analyser et d'interpréter ces informations pour le gouvernement et l'industrie. Après l'abolition du ministère de l'Intérieur en 1936, la Division des ressources minérales a été intégrée à un certain nombre de ministères plus importants (voir RG 21). En 1968, la division est devenue une direction au sein du ministère de l'Énergie, des Mines et des Ressources avant d'être dissoute lors de la réorganisation de 1973 du secteur de la politique minérale de ce ministère.

Organisation et contenu : Ces archives comprennent trois séries. Les dossiers de la Division des ressources et des statistiques minérales (1885-1920) traitent de la collecte, de la compilation et de la publication des statistiques de production minérale et métallurgique jusqu'en 1920. Les dossiers de la Division des ressources minérales (1894-1961) concernent les affaires minières internationales, les règlements relatifs à l'exploitation minière, les rapports de travail sur le terrain et les audiences de l'Office national de l'énergie (RG 99). Les dossiers du Bureau de l'agent des projets miniers spéciaux (1939-1947) se rapportent essentiellement à l'aide que le gouvernement a fourni, pendant la Seconde Guerre mondiale, aux compagnies engagées dans l'exploration des minéraux stratégiques.

Archives de la Direction des levés et de la cartographie : RG 88
1857-1971

65,6 mètres

Historique : La Direction des levés et de la cartographie a été principalement chargée de mettre en place l'infrastructure nécessaire à la cartographie exacte, complète et coordonnée de tout le territoire canadien. Les cartes et plans qu'elle produisait ont permis l'exploration, la mise en valeur et l'administration des ressources au Canada; ils étaient également considérés comme indispensables aux besoins de défense du Canada et ils jouaient un rôle important dans les domaines de l'éducation et des activités de loisir. Selon les époques, la direction et ses prédécesseurs se sont aussi occupés d'astronomie, de météorologie, d'irrigation, d'énergie hydraulique, de levés de frontières internationales et interprovinciales et de toponymie.

Quand la Terre de Rupert a été cédée au Canada en 1869, le ministère des Travaux publics a été chargé d'en faire les levés (RG 11). En 1871, un arpenteur général des terres fédérales a été nommé au Secrétariat d'État (RG 6). Transféré au ministère de l'Intérieur (RG 15) en 1873, son service a pris de l'expansion sous diverses désignations et en est venu à jouer un rôle de premier plan dans le développement de l'Ouest, d'autant plus que l'arpenteur général a parfois bénéficié du statut de sous-ministre. Après le démantèlement du ministère de l'Intérieur en 1936, la Direction des levés et de la cartographie a gardé son identité distincte au sein du ministère des Mines et des Ressources et de ses successeurs (pour plus de renseignements sur ces organismes tutélaires, voir RG 21).

Organisation et contenu : Ces archives sont organisées en fonction des trois composantes de la direction : Cabinet de l'arpenteur général (1875-1969), Direction des levés topographiques (1917-1932) et Direction des levés et de la cartographie (1857-1971). Dans les séries numérotées de dossiers (1880-1969) du Cabinet de l'arpenteur général, les documents touchent à de nombreux aspects de l'arpentage. La série des copies de lettres (1881-1915) contient des copies de lettres envoyées par l'arpenteur général. Les dossiers d'arpentage divers (1883-1923) renferment des documents sur les systèmes d'arpentage et les levés de réserves autochtones et de frontières. Les journaux et carnets de notes des arpenteurs sont conservés dans la série des carnets des arpenteurs des terres fédérales (1881-1930). Les nominations des arpenteurs généraux J.S. Dennis et E. Deville se trouvent dans les mandats de nominations (1875-1885). La série de l'administration (1917-1931) contient des rapports sur des opérations d'arpentage en Colombie-Britannique et au Yukon. L'expérimentation des instruments de levé figure dans la série du Laboratoire des expériences physiques (1917-1931). La série de la Commission des levés et des cartes topographiques (1920-1925) comprend des procès-verbaux de réunions et de délibérations relatives à la normalisation cartographique. La série du Comité interministériel des levés aériens (1924-1972) témoigne des travaux du comité. Dans la série de la Direction des levés et de la cartographie, les dossiers de l'administration comprennent les dossiers du service central, ainsi que des documents relatifs à la normalisation cartographique. La série de la Division des levés officiels (1918-1959) contient des carnets de notes sur les levés de réserves autochtones et des dossiers sur le transfert aux provinces des documents de levés fédéraux. La série du Service géodésique du Canada (1921-1943) renferme des documents sur les opérations géodésiques à Terre-Neuve dans les années 40 et la réorganisation des Levés topographiques dans les années 20. Enfin, les

dossiers qui concernent la nomination des arpenteurs des terres fédérales se trouvent dans la série de la Commission d'examinateurs des arpenteurs fédéraux (1857-1965).

Archives de la Direction des ressources hydrauliques : RG 89
1887-1982

190 mètres
2 fichiers informatiques

Historique : La Direction des ressources hydrauliques a été établie en 1955. Depuis la fin du dix-neuvième et le début du vingtième siècle, les organismes fédéraux qui l'ont précédée ont été chargés de plusieurs aspects de la gestion des ressources hydrauliques nationales : irrigation, amendement des terres, mise en valeur des ressources hydrauliques, hydrométrie et autres activités de recherche. L'adoption, en 1894, de la *Loi sur les Territoires du Nord-Ouest* conférait à la Couronne tous les droits relatifs à l'eau dans les Territoires du Nord-Ouest (Saskatchewan et Alberta) et l'habilitait à les céder à bail à des sociétés privées pour des projets d'irrigation. Au cours des trente années qui ont suivi, les fonctions du gouvernement fédéral reliées à l'irrigation et à l'énergie hydraulique et, plus tard, le service de l'amendement des terres ont été transférés successivement à diverses directions, généralement nouvelles, du ministère de l'Intérieur.

Après le démantèlement du ministère de l'Intérieur en 1936, les responsabilités liées aux ressources hydrauliques ont incombé au ministère des Mines et des Ressources jusqu'en 1949, puis aux divers ministères qui lui ont succédé, dont Ressources et Développement, 1949-1953, et Nord canadien et Ressources nationales, 1953-1966 (voir RG 31, 22 et 85). En 1966, la Direction des ressources hydrauliques a fusionné avec la Direction des sciences de la mer du ministère des Mines et des Relevés techniques (voir RG 21 et 88) pour former le Groupe ou Secteur des eaux au ministère de l'Énergie, des Mines et des Ressources. Après l'abolition du ministère des Pêches et des Forêts au début des années 70, l'essentiel de son programme, y compris les fonctions liées à la gestion des eaux, a été repris par le ministère de l'Environnement. La plupart de ces attributions incombent maintenant à la Direction générale des eaux de ce ministère.

Organisation et contenu : Ces archives comprennent cinq séries : rapports et divers dossiers du service central provenant du Service fédéral de l'énergie hydraulique et de l'amendement des terres (1894-1953), documents de référence de la Direction de l'ingénierie et des ressources hydrauliques (1950-1952), dossier et rapports de la Direction

des ressources hydrauliques (1920-1968), dossiers du service central de la Direction des eaux intérieures (1881-1948), et dossiers de la Direction des politiques et de la planification (Secteur des eaux) du ministère de l'Énergie, des Mines et des Ressources (1950-1971). Enfin, ces archives comprennent également d'autres dossiers du service central provenant de la Direction générale des eaux, de la Direction des eaux intérieures et de la Direction des ressources hydrauliques. Ce groupe d'archives comprend aussi des données informatiques de la base de données NA-QUADAT du ministère de l'Environnement (1960-1979).

Archives de la Commission des champs de bataille nationaux : RG 90
1907-1985

0,91 mètre
1 microfilm

Historique : La Commission du tricentenaire de Québec a été instituée par le maire de Québec pour conseiller la ville en matière de préservation de ses bâtiments et lieux historiques. Publié en 1907, le rapport de cette commission a contribué à élever les Plaines d'Abraham au rang de champ de bataille national. À la suite de la publication du rapport et à l'occasion du tricentenaire de Québec en 1908, la Commission des champs de bataille nationaux a été chargée d'acquérir, de restaurer et d'entretenir ce site historique qui allait commémorer de façon permanente le tricentenaire de Québec. Pendant ses premières années d'existence, les seules sources de financement de la commission ont été les campagnes de souscription auprès du public et les dons privés, servant à acheter les terrains historiques nécessaires à la réalisation du projet de parc. En 1939, les terrains avaient été acquis, les immeubles démolis, le parc aménagé, les tours Martello et autres structures restaurées, plusieurs monuments avaient été érigés et de nombreuses plaques historiques apposées. Plus tard, la commission a reçu du Parlement une subvention annuelle et elle a relevé du ministre des Affaires indiennes et du Nord canadien, qui, par le biais de Parcs Canada, était responsable d'autres sites historiques nationaux (voir RG 22). Depuis 1979, Parcs Canada (maintenant Service canadien des parcs) relève du ministère de l'Environnement (RG 108).

Organisation et contenu : Ces archives contiennent des rapports de la Commission des champs de bataille nationaux, des procès-verbaux de délibérations sur microfilm (y compris les points saillants des discussions), les dossiers du trésorier relatifs aux premières souscriptions, une liste des plaques commémoratives avec leur localisation dans la ville de Québec, des dossiers sur l'aménagement paysager et une liste des com-

missaires et des membres de la commission jusqu'à 1969. Le RG 90 renferme aussi une copie microfilmée du rapport de 1907 de la Commission du tricentenaire de Québec.

Archives du territoire du Yukon : RG 91
1894-1951

214 microfilms

Historique : La *Loi sur le Yukon* (1898) détachait le district du Yukon des anciens Territoires du Nord-Ouest et en faisait une entité politique et administrative distincte ayant ses propres institutions administratives, judiciaires et législatives. L'administration du district était confiée à un commissaire assisté d'un conseil nommé (plus tard, élu). Le commissaire relevait du sous-ministre de l'Intérieur. Il détenait des pouvoirs législatifs analogues à ceux des gouvernements provinciaux, mais il n'avait de contrôle ni sur les ressources naturelles ni sur la gestion des terres fédérales. Ottawa lui imposait en outre certaines restrictions financières et autres par le biais du ministère des Affaires indiennes et du Nord canadien et ses prédécesseurs (RG 15, 22 et 85). Après la Seconde Guerre mondiale, le gouvernement territorial a exercé un contrôle de plus en plus important sur les questions de juridiction locale.

Organisation et contenu : Les archives du territoire du Yukon sont divisées en quatre séries suivant le classement original : dossiers numérotés, dossiers-matières, copies de lettres, et registres et répertoires. Ce groupe d'archives contient des copies de lettres du Cabinet du commissaire (1899-1902), des copies de lettres du Bureau du commissaire de l'or (1899-1924) et des copies de lettres du Bureau du contrôleur (1899-1902). Tous ces documents illustrent de nombreux aspects de l'histoire du Yukon et des sujets tels que le service postal, les affaires indiennes, le système d'aqueduc de Dawson, la construction de la route territoriale, la vente de terrains, les demandes de lots, les demandes de permis de débit de boissons et les dispenses de bans de mariage.

Archives de la Direction de la géographie : RG 92
1945-1968

11,6 mètres

Historique : Un géographe en chef a été nommé en 1890 au ministère de l'Intérieur (RG 15) pour s'occuper de la nomenclature géographique canadienne, ainsi que de la production des cartes et des renseignements généraux sur les explorations et la géographie. En 1909, il a été placé à

la tête d'une direction distincte, qui a fusionné en 1923 avec le Bureau de renseignements sur les ressources naturelles. De 1933 à 1947, c'est la Direction des levés et de la cartographie (RG 88) qui a été chargée de la collecte des données géographiques et de la toponymie. En 1947, un Bureau de la géographie (qui deviendra une direction en 1949) a de nouveau été mis sur pied; il a relevé successivement de trois ministères (voir la notice du RG 21). La Direction de la géographie a été dissoute en 1968 quand ses fonctions ont de nouveau été confiées à la Direction des levés et de la cartographie.

Organisation et contenu : Les archives de ce groupe portent sur les dernières années de la direction et ont été organisées en une seule série, les dossiers du service central (1945-1968). Ces documents traitent d'un vaste éventail de sujets : géographie urbaine, études sur l'utilisation des terres, études économiques régionales, hydrologie et projets relevant de la *Loi sur l'aménagement rural et le développement agricole*. Ils renferment également des dossiers généraux sur l'administration de la direction et diverses publications de la direction.

Archives du Service de l'environnement atmosphérique : RG 93
1870-1984

166,2 mètres
5 microfilms

Historique : C'est en 1839 que la première observation météorologique officielle a été faite au Canada à partir de l'observatoire que le gouvernement britannique venait de faire construire à Toronto. Le Canada a repris l'observatoire en 1853. À l'époque de la Confédération, le service météorologique relevait du ministère de la Marine et des Pêcheries (RG 42). En 1874, ce ministère a décidé de créer le Bureau météorologique canadien. En 1936, ce dernier a été transféré au ministère des Transports (RG 12) nouvellement formé. Enfin, en 1971, sous le nom de Service météorologique canadien, il est passé au ministère de l'Environnement (RG 108) où il a pris le nom de Service de l'environnement atmosphérique. Ce service fournit aux divers ministères, principalement aux ministères des Transports et de la Défense nationale, des informations sur les conditions atmosphériques passées, actuelles et futures et fait rapport sur l'état de la mer et les glaces dans l'ensemble du pays et les eaux avoisinantes. C'est lui également qui donne au grand public les prévisions météorologiques.

Organisation et contenu : Les archives sont réparties dans les séries suivantes : registres de la correspondance (1874-1933), correspondance numérotée (1884-1913), dossiers numérotés (1901-1933), correspon-

dance de l'observatoire du Québec (1840-1947), correspondance du directeur (1880-1955), grand livre des instruments (1900-1906) et registre des comptes (1885-1921). Ce groupe de documents contient aussi des registres d'observations météorologiques quotidiennes réalisées en divers endroits de l'Ontario, du Québec et des Maritimes entre 1870 et 1914. Il renferme également un grand nombre de dossiers des systèmes centraux des ministères des Transports et de l'Environnement, qui vont des années 1900 aux années 80. Les dossiers de correspondance des séries mentionnées ci-dessus concernent des réunions, des congrès et des colloques ministériels, interministériels, nationaux et internationaux; l'établissement, l'exploitation et l'automatisation de stations météorologiques partout au Canada; la recherche scientifique sur divers phénomènes météorologiques et problèmes environnementaux; et la mise au point de technologies de contrôle, d'observation et de collecte de données météorologiques.

Archives d'Information Canada : RG 94
1969-1976

78,3 mètres

Historique : Information Canada a été créé le 1ᵉʳ avril 1970 (C.P. 1970-559 du 26 mars 1970) sur recommandation du Groupe de travail sur l'information gouvernementale. Organisme central d'information publique sur les politiques, les programmes et les services du gouvernement fédéral, Information Canada était aussi chargé de coordonner les programmes d'information fédérale impliquant plus d'un ministère et de mettre sur pied des programmes spéciaux répondant à un besoin évident du public, mais ne relevant d'aucun ministère particulier. Information Canada fournissait en outre des services d'experts aux autres organismes et ministères du gouvernement visant à améliorer la qualité et l'efficacité de leur information, à commercialiser et à diffuser les publications fédérales. Information Canada a été démantelé le 31 mars 1976.

Organisation et contenu : Les documents forment plusieurs séries constituées de dossiers administratifs et opérationnels, de discours, d'études et de procès-verbaux de réunions. Ces documents proviennent des dossiers du service central (1969-1976), du Bureau du directeur général (1972-1974), de la Direction des communications (1971-1975), de la Direction des opérations régionales (1971-1975), de la Direction des recherches et de l'évaluation (1971-1975) et de la région de l'Atlantique (1973-1976).

Archives de la Direction des corporations : RG 95
1967-1973

72 mètres

Historique : Cette direction du Bureau des corporations au ministère de la Consommation et des Corporations (RG 103) est chargée de l'administration de la *Loi sur les corporations canadiennes* et des lois qui l'ont précédée. Elle s'occupe de la constitution juridique des firmes commerciales, du classement des états financiers et des rapports annuels et de la tenue d'un registre des hypothèques. C'est le Secrétariat d'État (RG 6) qui était auparavant chargé de cette tâche, confiée depuis 1967 au ministère de la Consommation et des Corporations. En vertu de ces lois, la Direction des corporations favorise l'expansion des établissements commerciaux fédéraux par le biais de la constitution juridique et protège les investisseurs et les créanciers sur le marché financier.

Organisation et contenu : Ce groupe d'archives se compose de dossiers relatifs à des sociétés qui ont volontairement abandonné leur charte lors de la liquidation de leurs affaires (1967-1972) et des dossiers relatifs à des sociétés dissoutes (1968-1973).

Archives de la Commission d'énergie du Nord canadien : RG 96
1898-1970

0,9 mètre

Historique : Créée en 1948, la Commission d'énergie des Territoires du Nord-Ouest était chargée de superviser la construction et l'exploitation des centrales électriques et des services publics des Territoires. En 1950, son mandat a été étendu au territoire du Yukon et son nom, changé en Commission d'énergie du Nord canadien. En vertu d'ententes conclues avec les gouvernements territoriaux, le gouvernement fédéral a transféré les responsabilités de la commission aux gouvernements du Yukon et des Territoires du Nord-Ouest, en 1987 et 1988 respectivement, avant de dissoudre la commission.

Organisation et contenu : Ces archives proviennent essentiellement de diverses sociétés reprises en 1966 par la Commission d'énergie du Nord canadien (1898-1970). Au nombre de ces sociétés figurent la Northern Light, Power and Coal Limited (1909-1912), Dawson Electric Light and Power Company Limited (1898-1966), Dawson City Water and Power Company Limited (1900-1966) et Yukon Telephone Syndicate Limited (1900-1966).

Archives du ministère des Communications : RG 97
1902-1982

188,5 mètres
48 fichiers informatiques

Historique : Ce ministère a été créé en 1969 pour s'assurer du bon fonctionnement et de l'expansion ordonnée des communications au Canada en recommandant des politiques et des programmes d'envergure nationale, en favorisant la croissance et le rendement optimal des systèmes en place et en aidant à l'exploitation de nouvelles ressources et à l'aménagement de nouvelles installations de communications. Il est aussi chargé de l'application des règlements régissant l'utilisation du spectre des fréquences au Canada, de la protection des intérêts du Canada dans les affaires internationales et de la coordination des services de télécommunications des ministères et organismes du gouvernement fédéral. Avant 1969, nombre de ces fonctions relevaient de la Direction de la marine (RG 42) et du ministère des Transports (RG 12). Enfin, en 1981, les arts et la culture ont été transférés du Secrétariat d'État (RG 6) au ministère des Communications.

Organisation et contenu : Ces archives sont réparties dans sept grandes séries. Les dossiers du service central de 1969 (1904-1982) comprennent des dossiers relatifs aux politiques, à l'administration et à l'exploitation, venant pour la plupart des organismes qui ont précédé le ministère. Les dossiers du système de classement fonctionnel de 1982 (1936-1982) concernent également les politiques, l'administration et l'exploitation. Ils ont été créés par la Direction de la politique culturelle et des programmes, la Direction des relations fédérales-provinciales, la Direction des relations internationales et le Bureau du sous-ministre adjoint principal. Les dossiers du Cabinet du ministre (1968-1975) et les dossiers du Cabinet du sous-ministre (1968-1978) renferment des dossiers relatifs aux politiques, des dossiers-matières et des journaux. Les dossiers du Centre de recherche sur les communications (1962-1974) consistent en imprimés d'ordinateur porteurs de données transmises par les satellites Alouette I et II. Les dossiers des commissions et des comités (1928-1982) incluent des mémoires, de la correspondance classée chronologiquement, des horaires d'audiences, des coupures de presse et des documents de travail. On notera aussi que ce groupe d'archives contient les dossiers du Comité d'étude de la politique culturelle fédérale (1979-1982), plus connu sous le nom de Comité Applebaum-Hébert. La dernière série est formée de dossiers divers (1902-1959) qui n'étaient intégrés à aucun système central et qui traitent de divers sujets. Les

documents informatiques contiennent des données provenant du programme des communications par satellite du Centre de recherche sur les communications.

Archives du ministère des Approvisionnements et Services : RG 98
1935-1981

332,3 mètres

Historique : Ce ministère a été créé en avril 1969 par la fusion du ministère de la Production de défense (RG 49), du Département des impressions et de la Papeterie publiques détaché du Secrétariat d'État (RG 6) et de la Direction de la construction navale détachée du ministère des Transports (RG 12), du Bureau central de traitement des données du Conseil du Trésor (RG 55) et du Bureau des services de consultation en gestion de la Commission de la fonction publique (RG 32).

Pourvoyeur, fournisseur, imprimeur et intendant de l'État, le ministère des Approvisionnements et Services assure d'importants services communs dans le domaine de l'approvisionnement, de l'entreposage, de la distribution et de l'imprimerie, de la comptabilité et des paiements, de la vérification financière et de la consultation en gestion. En 1985, dans un effort d'intégration des opérations, le ministère a fusionné l'administration des Approvisionnements et celle des Services.

Organisation et contenu : Les dossiers sont divisés en six séries. La première se compose des dossiers du sous-ministre du secteur des Services (1960-1975) et renferme les documents de l'ancien contrôleur du Trésor, H.R. Balls, alors qu'il était sous-ministre des Services. La seconde comprend les dossiers du service central (1951-1974) et couvre les dossiers des nombreuses directions du ministère : construction navale (1965-1974), centre des produits industriels et navals (1951-1972), Direction des services administratifs et du personnel (1970-1973), Direction de l'aérospatiale et de l'armement (1957-1975), Direction de recherche sur les achats (1966-1970), Bureau des services de vérification (1961-1969), Direction de la comptabilité et de la gestion bancaire, dans laquelle on peut trouver les grands livres de comptabilité centrale du gouvernement (1961-1976). La troisième série se rapporte aux Services d'imprimerie du gouvernement canadien (1965-1971), et contient des dossiers du service central. Les dossiers d'Information Canada (1961-1970) forment la quatrième série. Quant à la cinquième, elle se compose de documents provenant de la Corporation commerciale canadienne (1965-1970). Enfin, la sixième série est constituée de documents relatifs à la société Polymer (1942-1970).

Archives de l'Office national de l'énergie : RG 99
1901-1983

99,2 mètres

Historique : L'Office national de l'énergie a été créé en 1959 par la *Loi sur l'Office national de l'énergie* pour garantir la meilleure utilisation possible des ressources énergétiques du Canada. En tant que cour d'archives, il détient tous les pouvoirs conférés à une cour supérieure d'archives. L'office régit également la construction et l'exploitation des oléoducs et des gazoducs, l'exportation et l'importation du pétrole et du gaz naturel et l'exportation de l'électricité. Il s'acquitte de ses fonctions par le biais d'audiences publiques et d'enquêtes et par l'émission d'ordonnances et de certificats. Après l'adoption de la *Loi sur l'administration du pétrole* de 1975, l'office a assumé la responsabilité d'administrer le régime des redevances d'exportation de pétrole brut et le barème des prix du gaz naturel sur les marchés interprovinciaux et internationaux. L'Office national de l'énergie relève du ministre de l'Énergie, des Mines et des Ressources (RG 21).

Organisation et contenu : Les archives sont réparties en plusieurs séries. La série du Bureau du président (1901-1979) contient les soumissions que les compagnies pétrolières ont adressées à l'office, des rapports et des mémoires sur les politiques énergétiques. La série des dossiers du service central (1930-1983) renseigne sur la législation, les relations entre les compagnies, les ministères, les gouvernements et l'office, et la participation de l'office à divers comités; et elle renferme divers dossiers administratifs. Ce groupe d'archives comprend aussi des contrats et des accords relatifs au gaz, qui ont été annulés, les dossiers des audiences, les dépositions faites devant la Commission royale sur l'énergie (Commission Borden, 1957-1958) et des pièces présentées à l'office par des compagnies d'exploitation des ressources, des oléoducs et des gazoducs.

Archives du Conseil de la radiodiffusion et des télécommunications canadiennes : RG 100
1910-1981

7,5 mètres
232 microfilms
229 microfiches
8 fichiers informatiques

Historique : Créé en 1968 aux termes de la *Loi sur la radiodiffusion*, le Conseil de la radiodiffusion et des télécommunications canadiennes (CRTC), qui a remplacé le Bureau des gouverneurs de la radiodiffusion

mis sur pied en 1958, réglemente et surveille tous les aspects du système canadien de radio-télévision. En avril 1976, il a été investi des pouvoirs exercés jusque-là par la Commission canadienne des transports (RG 46), soit la juridiction en matière d'entreprises de télécommunications relevant du fédéral. Le CRTC est habilité à délivrer, à renouveler ou à suspendre les permis de radiodiffusion. Il fait rapport au Parlement par l'entremise du ministre des Communications (RG 97).

Organisation et contenu : Ce groupe d'archives est formé de quatre séries générales. Les dossiers du Bureau du président (1971-1973) consistent essentiellement en rapports relatifs aux audiences publiques. Les dossiers du Bureau du secrétaire général (1947-1981) renferment des circulaires, des communiqués de presse et les transcriptions des audiences publiques tenues par la commission. Les dossiers du Bureau du directeur exécutif principal aux opérations (1970-1979) portent sur les fonctions administratives et d'exploitation et incluent des registres des émissions de stations de radio et de télévision. La série de la documentation (1925-1974) se compose de documents relatifs à la radiodiffusion au Canada, réunis par T.J. Allard, ancien directeur général de l'Association canadienne des radiodiffuseurs. Les fichiers informatiques concernent la réglementation des radiodiffuseurs publics et privés. Ces documents contiennent des registres de programmes et des données relatives à leur audience.

Archives de la Corporation de disposition des biens de la Couronne : RG 101
1943-1980

71,6 mètres

Historique : Cette société a été constituée en 1943 sous le nom de Corporation des biens de guerre ltée. Elle est devenue Corporation des biens de guerre en 1944. Elle avait pour fonction essentielle d'éliminer les biens de la Couronne devenus excédentaires à la fin de la guerre. Cinq ans plus tard, la société a pris le nom de Corporation de disposition des biens de la Couronne et assure des services spécialisés de vente des biens excédentaires de l'État en lançant des appels d'offres, en ouvrant des enchères ou en les écoulant au détail. Elle tire ses pouvoirs de la *Loi sur les biens de surplus de la Couronne* et fait rapport au Parlement par l'entremise du ministre des Approvisionnements et Services.

Organisation et contenu : Ce groupe d'archives contient des dossiers du service central qui témoignent des activités administratives et opérationnelles de la corporation. Il comprend également des dossiers-

matières, tels que les documents du bureau principal des bases américaines de Prince Rupert, Port Edward et l'île Watson, ainsi que des dossiers relatifs aux contrats et aux ventes.

Archives du ministère d'État, Sciences et Technologie : RG 102
1959-1983

28,7 mètres

Historique : Ce ministère d'État, créé en 1971, a pour principal objectif de préparer et d'élaborer des politiques concernant l'activité du gouvernement canadien dans le domaine de l'avancement et de l'application des sciences et de la technologie. Depuis 1972, le ministère a connu de nombreuses réorganisations et modifications de mandat. La dernière en date (1988), qui n'a pas encore reçu l'approbation officielle du Conseil privé, prévoit l'intégration du ministère au nouveau ministère de l'Industrie, des Sciences et de la Technologie.

Organisation et contenu : Ces archives comprennent une série de copies de lettres classées par ordre chronologique, qui proviennent du Bureau du secrétaire du ministère (1978-1983), des ordres du jour, des procès-verbaux, des lettres, des mémoires et autres documents soumis au Comité d'administration du ministère (1976-1980), et de la correspondance générale du Cabinet du ministre (1978-1983). La plupart des autres documents de ce groupe font partie du service central des dossiers de Sciences et Technologie (1964-1978). Ils traitent de la participation à des organismes scientifiques internationaux, des relations avec la communauté scientifique nationale et internationale, de l'organisation du ministère et de sa participation aux associations, comités et sociétés.

Archives du ministère de la Consommation et des Corporations : RG 103
1914-1980

78,9 mètres
13 fichiers informatiques

Historique : Créé en 1967 à la suite du transfert de toutes les responsabilités de l'ancien ministère du Registraire général au ministère de la Consommation et des Corporations, ce dernier s'occupe de la consommation, des sociétés et de leurs titres, des coalitions, des fusions, des monopoles et de la restriction du commerce (RG 110), des faillites et de l'insolvabilité (RG 104), des brevets, du droit d'auteur, des mar-

ques de commerce et des dessins industriels (RG 105). Le ministre de la Consommation et des Corporations assume les fonctions de registraire général (RG 68).

Organisation et contenu : Ces archives sont divisées en cinq grandes séries : Cabinet du ministre (1973-1974), Bureau de la propriété intellectuelle (1934-1972), Bureau de la consommation (1968-1970), Direction générale des normes (1914-1971) et Groupe de travail sur les prix (1970-1975). S'y trouvent correspondance, rapports, documents de travail sur les intérêts et les plaintes des consommateurs, normes relatives aux produits, brevets et droit d'auteur, études sur les prix et les revenus. Ce groupe d'archives contient aussi des documents informatiques sur les prix des produits pharmaceutiques (1976), sur toutes les sociétés qui se sont constituées au Canada (1971-1975), sur les salaires et la main-d'œuvre, et sur les salaires et l'inflation des prix (1947-1971).

Archives de la Direction des faillites : RG 104
1943-1976

63,8 mètres

Historique : Cette direction relève du ministère de la Consommation et des Corporations (RG 103) et est chargée d'exécuter les dispositions des lois fédérales en matière de faillite. Avant 1969, c'était le ministère de la Justice (RG 13) qui assurait l'application de la *Loi sur la faillite*.

Organisation et contenu : Ces archives sont formées de dossiers de cas relatifs à des faillites personnelles et commerciales de toutes les provinces et des territoires.

Archives des Brevets, marques de commerce, droit d'auteur et dessins industriels : RG 105
1861-1985

106,9 mètres
140 microfilms

Historique : Le Bureau de la propriété intellectuelle du ministère de la Consommation et des Corporations (RG 103) est chargé d'assurer l'application des lois relatives aux brevets, aux marques de commerce, au droit d'auteur et aux dessins industriels. Auparavant assurée par les secrétaires respectifs du Haut et du Bas-Canada, l'application des lois en matière de brevets a été confiée en 1852 au ministre de l'Agriculture (RG 17). Jusqu'en 1918, c'est le ministère de l'Agriculture qui s'est occupé des marques de commerce, du droit d'auteur, des dessins in-

dustriels et de l'enregistrement des brevets, après quoi ces fonctions ont été assumées par le ministère du Commerce (RG 20) jusqu'à leur transfert au Secrétariat d'État en 1927. Finalement, la responsabilité administrative en ce qui concerne la propriété intellectuelle a été confiée au ministère de la Consommation et des Corporations en 1967.

Organisation et contenu : Classées par ordre chronologique, ces archives comprennent des enregistrements de dessins industriels; des enregistrements de droit d'auteur et leurs répertoires; des demandes d'enregistrement de marques de commerce et leurs répertoires; des exemples de brevets d'inventions et des copies de brevets canadiens et américains de radiodiffusion; des registres de correspondance et des copies de lettres sur le droit d'auteur, les marques de commerce et les dessins industriels.

Archives du Bureau de la coordonnatrice, Situation de la femme (Condition féminine Canada) : RG 106
1965-1976

6,1 mètres

Historique : Le Bureau de la coordonnatrice a été établi en 1971 à la suite d'une recommandation de la Commission royale d'enquête sur la situation de la femme (Commission Bird, 1967-1971, RG 33/89). D'abord rattaché au Bureau du Conseil privé (1971-1976), le bureau s'est transformé en un organisme indépendant le 1er avril 1976 et est aujourd'hui connu sous le nom de Condition féminine Canada. Ses principales responsabilités sont d'analyser et d'élaborer des politiques concernant les femmes, de coordonner les demandes des groupes féminins tout en leur diffusant des renseignements sur les programmes du gouvernement fédéral qui ont trait à la condition de la femme. Son mandat l'oblige à s'assurer que le gouvernement fédéral respecte son engagement à l'égard de la promotion de l'égalité entre les hommes et les femmes dans tous les secteurs de la société canadienne.

Organisation et contenu : Des documents de travail, des procès-verbaux de réunions, des rapports, ainsi que des délibérations et de la documentation sur les projets de différents programmes pour l'Année internationale de la femme (1975), font partie de ce fonds d'archives. D'autres genres de documents, tels de la correspondance, des articles, des études portant notamment sur la question des garderies se trouvent aussi dans ce fonds.

Archives du Bureau de l'administrateur, *Loi anti-inflation* : RG 107
1975-1984

41,7 mètres

Historique : Le Bureau de l'administrateur, Loi anti-inflation, a été établi en décembre 1975. Il faisait partie des trois organismes chargés d'administrer le programme de limitation des prix et des revenus. Le Bureau de l'administrateur devait faire appliquer les dispositions de la *Loi anti-inflation* et rendre des décisions exécutoires en cas de violation de la Loi. Le bureau était aussi autorisé à examiner tous les aspects des différends suscités par la Loi et à émettre des décrets ayant force de loi qui fixaient un taux d'augmentation maximum pour les prix et les salaires. Le Bureau de l'administrateur n'existe plus depuis 1980.

Organisation et contenu : Ces archives sont constituées de dossiers de cas, de dossiers d'adhésion volontaire, de dossiers généraux, de copies de décrets et de correspondance administrative.

Archives du ministère de l'Environnement : RG 108
1899-1983

366,4 mètres
113 fichiers informatiques

Historique : Le ministère de l'Environnement a été créé en 1971 pour regrouper sous l'autorité d'un seul ministre les principales activités du gouvernement en matière de qualité de l'environnement en général et de pollution en particulier. À ce nouveau ministère, qui émanait du ministère des Pêches et Forêts (RG 23 et RG 39), sont venus s'ajouter le Service canadien de la faune (RG 109) du ministère des Affaires indiennes et du Nord canadien (RG 22), le secteur des eaux (RG 89) du ministère de l'Énergie, des Mines et des Ressources (RG 21), la Division de la prévention de la pollution atmosphérique et la Division du génie sanitaire du ministère de la Santé nationale et du Bien-être social (RG 29), le Service météorologique canadien (RG 93) du ministère des Transports (RG 12) et l'Inventaire des terres du Canada du ministère de l'Expansion économique régionale (RG 124). Depuis 1971, l'organisation du ministère a fait l'objet de nombreuses réorganisations. En 1974, les services chargés des pêches ont relevé d'un ministre d'État indépendant et ont formé avec les services chargés des ressources vivantes des océans et des eaux intérieures, le ministère des Pêches et des Océans (la Direction générale des eaux intérieures demeura à Environnement Canada). En 1979, Parcs Canada (RG 84) est passé du ministère

des Affaires indiennes et du Nord canadien au ministère de l'Environnement, et le Service canadien des forêts a été transféré au ministère de l'Agriculture (RG 17) en 1985.

Organisation et contenu : Les archives de ce groupe comprennent des dossiers administratifs et opérationnels du service central qui traitent de la pollution, de diverses lois et règlements, tels que la *Loi sur les ressources en eau du Canada*, des activités de recherche et des groupes de travail sur différents problèmes écologiques. Les problèmes reliés à l'environnement dépassant souvent les frontières officielles, quantité de ces documents témoignent du travail du ministère avec les gouvernements provinciaux et étrangers, les organismes privés et les associations internationales, telles que l'Organisation météorologique mondiale. Ce groupe d'archives contient bon nombre de documents, qui proviennent des cabinets du ministre et du sous-ministre, et qui concernent les politiques ministérielles des années 1965 à 1979. Les documents informatiques fournissent les résultats d'enquêtes réalisées dans les années 60 et 70 sur la qualité de l'eau, les usines de distribution d'eau et les systèmes de gestion des eaux usées dans les municipalités, les ressources forestières des parcs, les arbres (1918-1930) et la météorologie forestière (1931-1966).

Archives du Service canadien de la faune : RG 109
1905-1978

126,37 mètres

Historique : Après la signature, en 1916, du traité canado-américain sur la protection internationale des oiseaux migrateurs et l'adoption consécutive, en 1917, de la *Loi sur la convention concernant les oiseaux migrateurs*, un ornithologue fédéral a été nommé en 1918 à la Direction des parcs fédéraux (RG 84 et RG 22). On l'a appelé surveillant de la protection de la faune après lui avoir confié la responsabilité supplémentaire de la protection de la faune du Nord (RG 85) et des parcs nationaux. Ses attributions se sont accrues encore en 1930, lorsqu'a été adoptée la nouvelle *Loi sur les parcs nationaux*, qui faisait des parcs nationaux du Canada des réserves absolues de gibier et qui transformait les réserves fédérales en sanctuaires d'oiseaux. En 1947, cette composante de la Direction des parcs nationaux est devenue le Service fédéral de la faune (puis, en 1950, le Service canadien de la faune) avant de devenir, en 1966, une direction indépendante au sein du ministère des Affaires indiennes et du Nord canadien (RG 22). En 1971, le Service canadien de la faune se joignait au nouveau ministère de l'Environnement (RG 108). Principalement chargé de l'application des

130

règlements sur les oiseaux migrateurs, il fournit aussi des conseils aux provinces et aux parcs nationaux sur la gestion de la faune et les espèces menacées d'extinction.

Organisation et contenu : Bien qu'il ait toujours fait partie d'une direction ou d'un ministère dont il a utilisé le système de classification de dossiers, le Service canadien de la faune a toutefois eu recours à un système à part pour ses dossiers opérationnels. Les dossiers du service central (1909-1970) constituent, et de loin, la majeure partie de ce fonds. Ils renseignent sur les activités administratives et l'exploitation du service, et abordent un grand nombre de sujets, tels que l'application des lois relatives à la faune, l'ornithologie, les mammifères, les poissons, les reptiles et la gestion de la faune. D'autres documents, qui proviennent de bureaux régionaux, concernent le Projet relatif au renne canadien (1929-1973). Ils traitent, au jour le jour, de la gestion des troupeaux de rennes dans la région du delta du Mackenzie. Un petit nombre de dossiers portent sur le baguage des oiseaux au vingtième siècle partout en Amérique du Nord. Ce groupe d'archives contient également la correspondance du directeur des Oiseaux migrateurs des provinces des Prairies (1920-1954), ainsi qu'une bibliographie des études et rapports inédits du Service canadien de la faune (1978).

Archives de la Direction des enquêtes sur les coalitions : RG 110
1910-1965

24 mètres

Historique : La Direction des enquêtes sur les coalitions a été instituée en 1910 au sein du ministère du Travail. En vertu de la *Loi relative aux enquêtes sur les coalitions*, adoptée en 1910, elle était chargée de faire enquête sur les coalitions présumées et d'intenter contre elles les poursuites prévues. Sa compétence légale a été étendue en 1923 par l'adoption d'une nouvelle *Loi sur les coalitions*. En 1947, la direction a été transférée au ministère de la Justice, où elle est demeurée jusqu'à son remplacement, en 1967, par le Bureau de la politique de concurrence du nouveau ministère de la Consommation et des Corporations (RG 103).

Organisation et contenu : Ce groupe d'archives comprend une seule série, les dossiers d'enquêtes, qui renferme la documentation recueillie lors de poursuites judiciaires en vertu de la *Loi relative aux enquêtes sur les coalitions*. Sont également inclus un certain nombre de mémoires adressés au ministre de la Justice (1945-1958).

Archives de la Commission des relations de travail dans la fonction publique : RG 111
1958-1986

33,7 mètres
37 fichiers informatiques

Historique : La Commission des relations de travail dans la fonction publique, créée en 1967 par la *Loi sur les relations de travail dans la fonction publique,* représente l'intérêt public dans les conflits de travail entre la fonction publique et l'employeur. Elle est également responsable du Bureau de recherches sur les traitements, qui, pour faciliter les négociations collectives, est chargé d'étudier les échelles de traitement et les avantages sociaux offerts à la fonction publique et ailleurs.

Organisation et contenu : Ce groupe d'archives comprend six séries, qui reflètent la structure administrative de la commission et de son prédécesseur, le Bureau de recherches sur les traitements. La série de dossiers du Bureau de recherches sur les traitements (1958-1973) contient des mémoires et des études sur le salaire de divers groupes professionnels. Les archives du Comité préparatoire des négociations collectives (1963-1967) sont formées de dossiers administratifs généraux, de correspondance et de procès-verbaux de comités, qui traitent des négociations collectives dans la fonction publique. Les dossiers du service central (1968-1986) concernent des syndicats ou des associations de personnel et leurs revendications aux négociations collectives. Les dossiers du Service du contentieux (1970-1975) ont été créés par le Comité Bryden pour son étude de la *Loi sur les relations de travail dans la fonction publique.* Les dossiers du Bureau du président (1962-1975) proviennent du bureau de M. Finkelman, premier président de la commission. Ils renferment des documents généraux sur la négociation collective à la fonction publique. La série du Service de médiation (1968-1980) est constituée de dossiers de cas particuliers, qui contiennent une demande de conciliateur, un récépissé, la réponse du Conseil du Trésor, l'avis de nomination et le rapport du conciliateur. Les documents informatiques (1973-1982) fournissent des données de recherche sur les traitements de certains groupes professionnels, tels que les agents du service extérieur, la police et le personnel hospitalier.

Archives du Conseil consultatif des districts bilingues : RG 112
1970-1975

4,5 mètres
1 fichier informatique

Historique : Afin que soient offerts des services aux minorités anglophones ou francophones par tous les pouvoirs publics intéressés, la Commission royale sur le bilinguisme et le biculturalisme (1963-1971) proposait la création de districts bilingues fédéraux. C'est pourquoi en 1969, la création de tels districts a été intégrée à la *Loi sur les langues officielles*, une telle délimitation devant être assurée, selon la Loi, par un Conseil consultatif des districts bilingues. À cet effet, un conseil consultatif composé de cinq à dix commissaires devait être créé pour représenter les habitants des diverses provinces ou principales régions du pays. Le gouvernement n'ayant pas jugé les recommandations proposées par les deux conseils (celui de 1970 et celui de 1972) compatibles avec sa politique sur les langues officielles, la décision a été prise de ne pas créer de districts bilingues.

Organisation et contenu : Ce fonds contient des procès-verbaux des réunions des premier et deuxième conseils, des rapports, des recommandations, des notes d'information et de la correspondance avec divers ministères du gouvernement fédéral. Il rassemble aussi des comptes rendus des audiences publiques dans les diverses régions du pays, des données statistiques des ententes de collaboration avec divers ministères fédéraux et des mémoires ou des présentations par des particuliers. Le fichier informatique contient les résultats d'une enquête de 1972 sur un district bilingue.

Archives du Bureau du directeur général des élections (Élections Canada) : RG 113
1867-1980

6 mètres
994 microfilms
6 fichiers informatiques

Historique : Ce sont les dispositions de la *Loi sur les élections fédérales* de 1920 qui créaient ce bureau. Auparavant, la tenue des élections dépendait des lois provinciales et était décalée, de 1867 à 1884, d'une circonscription à l'autre, le droit de voter ou de se faire élire étant réservé à une minorité de propriétaires masculins. La *Loi des élections du Dominion* de 1874 établissait le scrutin secret et la tenue de l'élection générale le même jour dans toutes les circonscriptions du pays. À compter de 1920, la responsabilité du processus électoral est confiée au

Bureau du directeur général des élections. Ce bureau est depuis 1952 désigné comme ministère faisant rapport directement au Parlement et ayant comme son porte-parole le président du Conseil privé. Aujourd'hui connu sous le nom Élections Canada, ce bureau continue à assurer la direction et la conduite administrative générale des élections fédérales y compris des élections des membres des Conseils du Yukon et des Territoires du Nord-Ouest.

Organisation et contenu : Ce fonds d'archives contient de la correspondance, des rapports (1867-1980) et de la documentation relative à la nomination du directeur général des élections et des scrutateurs ainsi que de la documentation sur l'administration opérationnelle du bureau. Il contient en outre des séries de microfilms où se trouvent des avis d'élections (1945-1979) décrivant les limites géographiques des circonscriptions dans chacune des provinces et présentant la liste des candidats et des électeurs s'étant portés leurs garants. D'autres séries de microfilms contiennent d'une part, les listes préliminaires des électeurs (1935-1979) pour les élections générales et partielles dans les provinces et pour les élections aux Conseils des Territoires du Nord-Ouest (1951-1975), et d'autre part, des données statistiques et comparatives sur les résultats d'élections (1867-1980), ainsi que les rapports statutaires du directeur général des élections. Les fichiers informatiques fournissent les résultats des élections depuis 1972 et comprennent des données sur certaines circonscriptions électorales, les candidats, le nombre de voix qu'ils ont recueillies et les dépenses électorales.

Archives de la Commission de surveillance du prix des produits alimentaires : RG 115
1973-1976

21,5 mètres
10 fichiers informatiques

Historique : Créée en mai 1973 (CP 1973-1239) pour effectuer des recherches et préparer des publications sur les mouvements des prix des produits alimentaires, la Commission de surveillance du prix des produits alimentaires s'est aussi livrée à des enquêtes et s'est occupée de surveiller les prix et de recommander des lignes de conduite. Elle a été démantelée en octobre 1975 pour faire place à la Commission de lutte contre l'inflation.

Organisation et contenu : La majorité des documents se retrouvent dans les dossiers du service central faisant partie du Bureau du secrétaire (1973-1975). Ils décrivent essentiellement les activités administratives et opérationnelles de la commission, de même que son rôle, ses

responsabilités et ses fonctions. Ce groupe d'archives renferme également une grande quantité d'articles de journaux (1973-1975), donnant une idée de ce que la presse écrite pensait du rôle de la commission. À signaler que ce groupe d'archives contient aussi dix fichiers informatiques qui, pour la plupart, concernent des sondages effectués durant les années 70 sur le prix des aliments dans certaines grandes villes canadiennes.

Archives de la Compagnie des jeunes Canadiens : RG 116
1965-1976

39,4 mètres

Historique : Société contrôlée par l'État, la Compagnie des jeunes Canadiens avait été créée en 1966 pour orienter les énergies et les talents des jeunes Canadiens vers des activités utiles au développement économique et social. La *Loi sur la Compagnie des jeunes Canadiens* permettait à celle-ci d'encourager les programmes bénévoles de développement social, économique et communautaire au Canada et à l'étranger. La compagnie relevait du Secrétariat d'État (RG 6) et était habilitée, dans la poursuite de ses objectifs, à entretenir des relations avec les autorités fédérales, provinciales ou autres. Elle a été dissoute au début de 1976.

Organisation et contenu : Ce fonds se compose principalement de dossiers d'exploitation et de dossiers-matières du service central. On y trouve de la correspondance, des études internes, des rapports d'experts, des brouillards, des feuillets d'information sur des projets et autres documents divers qui renseignent sur les activités, les fonctions, les projets et la dissolution finale de la compagnie. La majeure partie de ces documents datent des années 1970-1976 et traitent de sujets tels que l'organisation de la compagnie, les relations de travail, les programmes, la planification sociale et le développement domiciliaire.

Archives du Bureau du séquestre des biens ennemis : RG 117
1903-1975

97,57 mètres
183 microfilms

Historique : Le Bureau du séquestre des biens ennemis a été créé en 1916 en vertu de la *Loi des mesures de guerre* de 1914. Il était chargé d'appliquer les règlements relatifs au commerce avec l'ennemi, ce qui incluait la saisie et la liquidation des biens ennemis. De 1919 à 1939, il s'est occupé de l'administration des réclamations et des réparations de

guerre. Lors de la déclaration de la Seconde Guerre mondiale, le bureau s'est de nouveau vu confier les règlements relatifs au commerce avec l'ennemi. En 1942, son rôle a été étendu à l'administration des biens saisis aux Japonais du Canada.

Organisation et contenu : Les archives de ce groupe sont réparties en quatre grandes séries selon les services du Bureau du séquestre et leurs fonctions. La série des dossiers du service central (1903-1975) contient des dossiers qui couvrent toute la gamme des activités du bureau tout en portant surtout sur les fonctions relatives aux réclamations et aux réparations de guerre. Les dossiers du bureau central (1920-1939) proviennent du Bureau du séquestre à Londres qui devait travailler avec son équivalent britannique à l'administration des réclamations et des réparations de guerre. Les documents du bureau de Vancouver (1904-1958) contiennent des renseignements sur la saisie de biens appartenant à des particuliers d'origine ennemie et sur l'évacuation des Canadiens japonais des régions côtières de la Colombie-Britannique. Les dossiers de la Direction des réclamations de guerre (1950-1969) renferment des documents relatifs aux demandes de dédommagement déposées par des Canadiens pour des pertes humaines, des pertes de biens ou des blessures personnelles dues à la Seconde Guerre mondiale.

Archives du ministère de l'Emploi et de l'Immigration : RG 118
1918-1985

1084,26 mètres
86 microfilms
19 fichiers informatiques

Historique : Le ministère de la Main d'œuvre et de l'Immigration a été créé en 1966 pour favoriser au maximum le développement et l'utilisation des ressources humaines. Le ministère réunissait sous une même administration la Direction de l'immigration de l'ancien ministère de la Citoyenneté et de l'Immigration (RG 26 et RG 76) et un certain nombre de services qui relevaient auparavant du ministère du Travail (RG 27). En 1977, en vertu de la *Loi régissant l'emploi et l'immigration*, la Commission d'assurance-chômage (RG 50) a fusionné avec le ministère de la Main-d'œuvre et de l'Immigration pour former Emploi et Immigration Canada. Ce nouveau ministère, formé de la Commission canadienne de l'emploi et de l'immigration et du ministère de l'Emploi et de l'Immigration, devait assumer la responsabilité de tous les programmes d'emploi, de lutte contre le chômage et d'immigration au Canada.

Organisation et contenu : Ce groupe d'archives est formé de dossiers opérationnels provenant du service central et de nombreuses séries de dossiers de cas produits par Emploi et Immigration Canada et les organismes qui l'ont précédé. Les dossiers du service central contiennent des documents relatifs aux politiques, des études, des rapports de planification et d'évaluation, des dossiers administratifs et des dossiers de projets qui donnent quantité de détails sur les programmes et les services du ministère. Les dossiers relatifs aux politiques et à l'exploitation renseignent sur les programmes, les services et les activités de recherche d'Emploi et Immigration Canada dans le domaine de l'emploi, du chômage et de l'immigration. Ce fonds renferme également des documents informatiques qui contiennent des données sur les programmes de création d'emploi, tels que le Programme de formation de la main d'œuvre, Canada au travail, Perspectives-Jeunesse et le Programme d'initiatives locales.

Archives du Secrétariat canadien de la conférence Habitat : RG 119
1966-1979

58,2 mètres

Historique : Habitat, conférence des Nations unies sur les établissements humains, s'est déroulée à Vancouver du 31 mai au 11 juin 1976. Hôte et participant, le Canada s'est doté d'un secrétariat chargé de formuler ses politiques et de coordonner ses activités à cette conférence. Le Secrétariat canadien de la conférence Habitat est un organisme distinct qui fait rapport au ministre d'État chargé des Affaires urbaines (voir RG 127).

Organisation et contenu : Ces archives sont constituées des documents administratifs et des discours du secrétaire général de la délégation canadienne à Habitat et des dossiers du commissaire général responsable de la conférence. Les dossiers sur l'historique d'Habitat (1975-1976) renferment des coupures de presse, des rapports de la conférence Habitat et des publications. On trouve également dans ce groupe de documents les dossiers du service central (1973-1976) du Secrétariat de la conférence Habitat, ainsi que les dossiers créés individuellement par les employés du secrétariat. Ce fonds comprend en outre des dossiers de l'Association canadienne de service aux organisations pour les établissements humains (ACSOEH) (1972-1979), qui s'est occupée de l'organisation d'Habitat Forum, nom collectif de toutes les activités non gouvernementales liées à la conférence.

Archives de la Monnaie royale canadienne : RG 120
1899-1974

14 mètres

Historique : La Monnaie royale canadienne existe depuis 1908. D'abord simple succursale d'Ottawa de la Monnaie royale de Londres, elle est devenue en 1931 une entreprise canadienne à part entière, rattachée au ministère des Finances (RG 19). En 1969, elle a été constituée en société d'État faisant rapport au Parlement par l'entremise du ministre des Approvisionnements et Services (RG 98). Cette société s'occupe de la fabrication de pièces de monnaie du Canada et de pays étrangers, de la fonte, de l'essai et de l'affinage de l'or et d'autres métaux, de l'achat et de la vente de ces métaux, de la fabrication de matrices pour la frappe de monnaies, de médailles et de sceaux officiels, et de l'administration de divers règlements émanant de la *Loi sur la monnaie*, en plus de l'Hôtel des monnaies et du fonds des changes.

Organisation et contenu : Ce fonds contient les archives comptables (1907-1973), parmi lesquels on peut trouver des registres de salaires (1908-1931) et des registres relatifs à la réserve métallique (1907-1973). Viennent ensuite certains documents du premier sous-directeur de la Monnaie, James Bonar (1899-1907), ainsi que des dossiers provenant du Cabinet du directeur de la Monnaie.

Archives de la Société canadienne des brevets et d'exploitation Limitée : RG 121
1919-1981

43 mètres

Historique : Société d'État créée en 1947, la Société canadienne des brevets et d'exploitation Limitée est une filiale à part entière du Conseil national de recherches du Canada (CNRC) (RG 77). D'abord chargée de s'occuper des inventions brevetables mises au point au CNRC ou grâce à d'autres recherches financées par le gouvernement, elle est devenue en 1954, par l'adoption de la *Loi sur les inventions des fonctionnaires*, la première autorité habilitée à accorder des brevets et des licences pour les inventions des fonctionnaires; celles-ci appartiennent au gouvernement fédéral.

Organisation et contenu : La majorité de la documentation consiste en des dossiers de cas (1926-1981) sur des inventions, de même qu'en documents se rapportant aux délibérations du Comité des brevets (1949-1971), ou encore à la Commission des inventions du Conseil national de recherches (1939-1947).

Archives du Commissaire aux langues officielles : RG 122
1970-1984

7,5 mètres
1 fichier informatique

Historique : Le Bureau du Commissaire aux langues officielles a été créé (1969) à la suite d'une recommandation de la Commission royale d'enquête sur le bilinguisme et le biculturalisme (1963-1971). En vertu de la première *Loi sur les langues officielles* (1969), recommandée par cette commission, le commissaire est un mandataire indépendant, directement responsable devant le Parlement. Il doit voir à la protection des droits linguistiques de tous les Canadiens; de s'assurer que les ministères et organismes fédéraux se conforment aux exigences de la Loi; et d'encourager, par ses efforts, l'égalité des langues officielles.

Organisation et contenu : Ce fonds d'archives contient de la correspondance, des rapports, des opinions qui ont trait à la *Loi sur les langues officielles* et qui ont été présentés par des étudiants, par des fonctionnaires ou par des particuliers. Il comprend également des commentaires reçus de certains enfants qui ont utilisé la trousse *Oh! Canada*. D'autres documents portent sur les responsabilités du commissaire mentionnées ci-dessus. Nous retrouvons des dossiers de plaintes et de suivi; des politiques et procédures ministérielles; des comptes rendus de réunions, conférences, colloques et symposiums; ainsi que de la correspondance sur le contentieux linguistique et les vérifications ministérielles. Le fonds rassemble également de la documentation sur les politiques et programmes de liaison et du matériel publicitaire utilisé dans la protection des droits des groupes linguistiques minoritaires. Le fichier informatique fournit les résultats d'une enquête, menée en 1976, sur la seconde langue officielle utilisée par les diplômés de la fonction publique.

Archives de la Société de développement de l'industrie cinématographique canadienne (Téléfilm Canada) : RG 123
1961-1976

1,2 mètre

Historique : Connue depuis 1983 sous le nom de Téléfilm Canada, la Société de développement de l'industrie cinématographique canadienne a été établie en 1967. Elle a pour objet de favoriser et d'encourager le développement d'une industrie du long métrage au Canada en effectuant des placements financiers dans des productions, en consentant des prêts aux producteurs, en accordant des récompenses et en fournissant aide et

conseils dans les affaires de distribution et d'administration. Elle fait rapport au Parlement par l'entremise du ministre des Communications (RG 97).

Organisation et contenu : Ces archives sont formées de dossiers du service central (1961-1976). Il s'agit surtout de dossiers relatifs à l'exploitation qui témoignent des diverses activités de la société.

Archives du ministère de l'Expansion économique régionale : RG 124
1949-1982

338,6 mètres
3 fichiers informatiques

Historique : Le ministère de l'Expansion économique régionale a été créé en 1969 pour réunir les services fédéraux travaillant à la réduction des inégalités économiques régionales. Il devait favoriser la croissance économique et la création d'emplois dans les régions défavorisées. Le noyau du nouvel organisme a été la Direction du développement rural du ministère des Forêts et du Développement rural (RG 39), qui administrait la *Loi sur l'aménagement rural et le développement agricole* (ARDA), la *Loi sur le Fonds de développement économique rural* (FODER) et la *Loi sur l'utilisation des terrains marécageux des provinces Maritimes* (UTMM). À ce noyau sont venus s'ajouter l'Agence de développement régional du ministère de l'Industrie, le Conseil de développement de la région de l'Atlantique, la Direction des projets expérimentaux (Programme de relance du Canada) du ministère de la Main-d'œuvre et de l'Immigration (RG 118 et 27) et la *Loi sur le rétablissement agricole des Prairies* du ministère de l'Agriculture (RG 17). Parmi les nouveaux programmes figurent le programme ARDA spécial, mis sur pied en 1972 pour aider les régions à fort peuplement autochtone, ainsi que les accords de développement général et les accords sur les régions spéciales signés avec les provinces et les territoires. En 1983, le ministère de l'Expansion économique régionale a fusionné avec certaines composantes du ministère de l'Industrie et du Commerce (RG 20) pour former le ministère de l'Expansion industrielle régionale.

Organisation et contenu : Les dossiers de l'administration centrale (1949-1979) produits par le ministère renferment des dossiers provenant du Bureau du sous-ministre (1968-1977) relatifs à la création et à la réorganisation du ministère, aux comités et aux réunions, et aux relations avec d'autres ministères, avec les provinces et avec le secteur privé. Les autres dossiers de l'administration centrale sont constitués de dossiers administratifs (1963-1972) et de dossiers de l'ARDA produits par le ministère de l'Agriculture (1963-1972), qui couvrent les activités de

l'ARDA considérées d'un point de vue général ou appliquées à des cas particuliers. On trouve d'autres documents relatifs à l'ARDA dans les dossiers régionaux (1975-1977) créés dans la région de l'Ouest. Les archives du Conseil de développement de la région de l'Atlantique comprennent des dossiers produits par la Division de la planification (1962-1972) et d'autres documents relatifs à la Conférence sur la pauvreté et les possibilités d'emploi (1965). Les dossiers du Conseil canadien de l'aménagement rural (1965-1979) traitent de questions administratives ainsi que des recherches et des activités du conseil. Ils incluent, par ailleurs, des rapports et des études. Les documents informatiques contiennent des enquêtes sur la qualité de la vie, réalisées au Nouveau-Brunswick, pour la période 1971-1973, dans le cadre du programme de relance.

Archives de la Cour suprême du Canada : RG 125
1875-1987

99,35 mètres
492 microfiches

Historique : Constituée d'un juge en chef et de huit juges puînés, la Cour suprême du Canada a été créée en 1875 par la *Loi de la Cour suprême et de la Cour de l'Échiquier*. Depuis 1949, date à laquelle la Section judiciaire du Conseil privé a perdu son statut de cour d'appel, la Cour suprême est devenue le plus haut tribunal habilité à juger les questions juridiques de compétence fédérale et provinciale. Elle détient la juridiction finale d'appel au Canada en matières civile et criminelle et peut être saisie de questions d'interprétation de la Constitution, de la Charte des droits et libertés, de l'*Acte de l'Amérique du Nord britannique* et de questions de compétence fédérale et provinciale.

Organisation et contenu : La majorité de ces documents sont des dossiers de cas individuels organisés de façon numérique, qui traitent d'appels entendus par la Cour suprême de 1876 à 1922 et peuvent être retrouvés au moyen des registres de jugements et des index. Ce fonds comprend en outre des listes du barreau, des dossiers administratifs, des registres de jugements et des rapports sur les projets de loi classés par ordre alphabétique.

Archives de l'Enquête sur le pipe-line de la vallée du Mackenzie : RG 126
1970-1977

15,8 mètres

Historique : Effectuée sous la direction de son commissaire, le juge Thomas R. Berger, l'enquête a permis d'étudier les conditions dans lesquelles un pipe-line pourrait être construit dans la vallée du Mackenzie. Les enquêteurs ont accordé une attention particulière aux incidences sociales, économiques et écologiques d'un tel projet sur la vallée fluviale ainsi qu'aux revendications territoriales autochtones. Mise sur pied en 1974, la commission a déposé son rapport en 1977.

Organisation et contenu : Les archives se répartissent en plusieurs séries de transcriptions d'audiences, de pièces diverses et de dossiers administratifs. Cette enquête ayant tenu de nombreuses audiences sur un territoire très vaste, ces archives reflètent tous les aspects de la vie dans le Nord.

Archives du ministère des Affaires urbaines : RG 127
1969-1979

317,81 mètres
1 fichier informatique

Historique : Créé en 1971, le département d'État chargé des Affaires urbaines a élaboré des politiques fédérales visant à améliorer les effets de l'urbanisation croissante, à intégrer ces politiques à d'autres politiques et programmes fédéraux et à coordonner l'aménagement urbain en collaboration avec les provinces et les municipalités. Il s'est particulièrement distingué en 1976 lors de la tenue à Vancouver de la conférence des Nations unies sur les établissements humains, plus communément appelée Habitat (RG 119). Il a été dissous en 1979 et ses projets inachevés ont été confiés à la Société canadienne d'hypothèques et de logement (RG 56), au ministère des Transports (RG 12) et au ministère des Travaux publics (RG 11).

Organisation et contenu : Ces archives contiennent des dossiers-matières qui proviennent du Bureau du secrétaire (1972-1978), et des dossiers du service central (1969-1979). De nature administrative et opérationnelle, ces derniers sont constitués de dossiers-matières et de dossiers de projets qui traitent de développement urbain, de transport, de relations intergouvernementales, des projets du ministère et des politiques fédérales de gestion territoriale. On trouve également dans cette série les procès-verbaux du comité de direction des Affaires urbaines et de la conférence Habitat tenue à Vancouver. Trois séries plus modestes

renferment des rapports et des études du ministère, des exemplaires du bulletin *Urbanite* et des dossiers-matières portant sur différentes questions relatives aux fonctions législatives du ministère. Une autre série contient des dossiers relatifs à la participation du ministère au colloque tenu à Ottawa en 1977 de la Commission économique des Nations unies pour l'Europe sur l'importance de l'énergie sur les établissements humains. Les documents informatiques fournissent des données sur la perception que les Montréalais avaient de leur voisinage en 1973-1974.

Archives du Conseil de recherches médicales : RG 128
1954-1983

193,2 mètres

Historique : De 1960 à 1969, le Conseil de recherches médicales était un organisme autonome au sein du Conseil national de recherches (RG 77) avant de devenir une corporation départementale au sens où l'entend la *Loi sur l'administration financière*. Le conseil est essentiellement chargé de promouvoir et de subventionner les recherches dans le domaine des sciences de la santé au Canada. Pour ce faire, il accorde des bourses aux chercheurs et aux stagiaires en recherche, il subventionne des programmes de recherches dans les universités canadiennes, les hôpitaux et instituts affiliés et il encourage toute nouvelle activité importante en matière de recherches. Il gère également le Fonds canadien de recherches de la Reine Elizabeth II. Le conseil se compose de 21 membres nommés par le gouverneur en conseil et il fait rapport au Parlement par l'entremise du ministre de la Santé nationale et du Bien-être social (RG 29).

Organisation et contenu : Ces archives se composent de dossiers du service central qui concernent principalement les fonctions de liaison du conseil, de dossiers administratifs et de dossiers-matières, de procès-verbaux de comités, de dossiers de recherche, de rapports opérationnels et de dossiers de récompenses accordées par le Comité des subventions. Ce fonds comprend aussi un grand nombre de dossiers de subventions qui incluent les demandes de subventions, les rapports sur les résultats de la recherche, les évaluations et les demandes de prolongation. Une autre importante série contient de la correspondance, des discours, des rapports et des documents de recherche préparés par le docteur G. Malcolm Brown, premier président du conseil à plein temps, de 1965 à 1977. Les dossiers du Comité des subventions renseignent sur les activités de cinq comités de subventions : métabolisme clinique, endocrinologie et néphrologie, biologie moléculaire, microbiologie et pathologie, métabolisme et endocrinologie, et psychologie. Ce fonds contient aussi

des dossiers relatifs aux relations du conseil avec d'autres organismes et ministères, tels que la Défense nationale, l'Organisation mondiale de la santé et le ministère de la Santé de l'Ontario.

Archives du Conseil des sciences du Canada : RG 129
1947-1978

70,1 mètres
3 fichiers informatiques

Historique : Créé en 1966, le Conseil des sciences du Canada évalue les ressources, les besoins et les possibilités du Canada sur le plan scientifique et technologique. Il est également chargé de rendre le public plus conscient des problèmes et possibilités scientifiques et technologiques, ainsi que de l'interdépendance de la population, des pouvoirs publics, des industries et des universités dans le développement et les applications des sciences et de la technologie. Pour ce faire, le conseil met sur pied des groupes de recherche temporaires chargés de faire des études et de mener des enquêtes spécialisées, dont les résultats peuvent être communiqués au public.

Organisation et contenu : Ces archives sont constituées de documentation et de dossiers de réunions créés ou rassemblés lors de la préparation d'études en informatique, géodésie, psychologie, climatologie et démographie; énergie, mathématiques, sciences de la santé, politiques et poisons, développement du Nord, information, politiques générales et énergétiques; objectifs de la recherche fondamentale, recherche industrielle et répercussions écologiques. Les documents informatiques traitent de l'ajustement nécessaire aux diplômés canadiens en physique pour s'adapter au marché du travail, depuis la fin des années 50 jusque dans les années 60. Ils contiennent en outre un inventaire des diplômés en mathématiques en 1975.

Archives de la Commission du pipe-line du Nord : RG 130
1977-1978

4 mètres

Historique : Après la découverte, en 1968, de pétrole et de gaz naturel à Prudhoe Bay (Alaska), le Canada et les États-Unis ont entrepris des négociations en vue de déterminer le meilleur moyen d'amener ces ressources vers les marchés du sud. La Commission du pipe-line du Nord a été créée en 1978 pour mettre en œuvre l'entente de construction d'un pipe-line transcanadien signée en 1977 entre les deux pays. Ayant été investie des pouvoirs fédéraux exercés auparavant par les Affaires

indiennes et du Nord canadien (RG 22), Énergie, Mines et Ressources (RG 21) et l'Office national de l'énergie (RG 99), la commission est devenue l'organisme central de réglementation chargé de surveiller les répercussions du point de vue social, économique et environnemental du pipe-line.

Organisation et contenu : Ces archives ne comprennent qu'une seule série, les dossiers du service central et du Bureau de la Commission du pipe-line du Nord (1977-1978). Les dossiers renseignent sur la participation du gouvernement fédéral à la construction du pipe-line en 1977-1978.

Archives du ministère d'État chargé du Développement social : RG 131
1978-1982

10,2 mètres

Historique : Le ministère d'État chargé du Développement social a été créé en juin 1980 en vertu de la *Loi sur les départements et ministres d'État*. Il était chargé de formuler et de coordonner les nouvelles politiques générales de tous les ministères et organismes fédéraux dont les activités touchaient le bien-être social des individus, des familles et des collectivités. En tant que « super ministère », il devait apporter son soutien au ministre d'État chargé du Développement social, qui, par l'entremise du Comité du Cabinet sur le développement social, était responsable de la planification et de la coordination des politiques sociales et des priorités connexes du fédéral. Ce ministère a été démantelé en 1984 lors de la réorganisation du gouvernement fédéral.

Organisation et contenu : Ce groupe d'archives contient, d'une part, des dossiers d'exploitation et des dossiers-matières du service central du Groupe consultatif sur les Métis et les Indiens non inscrits, et, d'autre part, des dossiers de l'adjoint du ministre. Les dossiers du premier groupe concernent les discussions sur le développement économique entre le gouvernement provincial et les associations autochtones. Ceux du second groupe se composent principalement de rapports et d'études sur différents organismes canadiens de développement social, tels que le Conseil des autochtones du Canada, la Commission de réforme de la Constitution, l'Union des étudiants acadiens et diverses universités canadiennes.

Archives des Musées nationaux du Canada : RG 132
1881-1983

18,6 mètres
3 fichiers informatiques

Historique : Créés en 1968 à titre de société d'État par la *Loi sur les musées nationaux*, les Musées nationaux du Canada regroupaient sous une seule administration sept composantes organisationnelles : le Musée des beaux-arts du Canada; le Musée national de l'homme et le Musée canadien de la guerre; le Musée national des sciences naturelles; le Musée national des sciences et de la technologie et le Musée national de l'aviation; la Direction des programmes nationaux; la Direction de la gestion centrale; et la Direction des services à la corporation. Les Musées nationaux faisaient rapport au Parlement par l'entremise du ministre des Communications (RG 97). Ils avaient pour mission de présenter les produits de la nature et les œuvres des hommes et des femmes ayant trait plus particulièrement, mais non pas exclusivement, au Canada, de façon à susciter un intérêt à leur égard et à en propager la connaissance. Les Musées nationaux ont été dissous en 1987 et leurs responsabilités ont été transférées à chacune de leurs composantes et au ministère des Communications.

Organisation et contenu : À l'heure actuelle, ce fonds ne comprend que les archives du Musée national des sciences naturelles. Une des séries renferme les notes prises sur le terrain par les premiers botanistes, tandis que l'autre rassemble les notes de célèbres paléontologistes des vertébrés. Ce groupe de documents contient aussi des dossiers opérationnels du musée (1964-1983) qui traitent de divers sujets, tels que les relations du musée avec les musées provinciaux, les ministères du gouvernement fédéral et divers groupes et associations, et son rôle dans un certain nombre de comités (comme le Comité international sur les musées). Les fichiers informatiques contiennent un inventaire des saules d'Amérique du Nord (1966-1977) et un fichier des espèces (1968-1979).

Archives du Conseil de recherches en sciences humaines du Canada : RG 133
1978, 1981

2 fichiers informatiques

Historique : Le Conseil de recherches en sciences humaines du Canada a été créé en 1977. En 1978, il recevait la responsabilité des programmes auparavant administrés par la Division des sciences sociales et des humanités du Conseil des Arts du Canada (RG 63). Le conseil administre

les fonds fédéraux destinés à la recherche universitaire et à d'autres activités de haut savoir. Organisme subventionnaire, le conseil est chargé de promouvoir et d'aider la recherche et l'érudition en sciences humaines et de conseiller le ministre sur les questions relatives à la recherche qui sont soumises à l'attention du conseil.

Organisation et contenu : Les archives de ce groupe se présentent sous forme informatisée. Elles contiennent un inventaire des dépôts d'archives au Canada pour 1978 et un inventaire des professeurs canadiens de droit pour 1981.

Archives de l'Eldorado Nucléaire Limitée : RG 134
1932-1982

63 mètres

Historique : Eldorado Gold Mines a jalonné son premier terrain minier au Grand Lac de l'Ours dans les Territoires du Nord-Ouest en 1930. En 1933, la compagnie avait commencé à extraire de la pechblende à Port Radium et à transporter le minerai brut à la raffinerie de radium de Port Hope (Ontario). La mine, la raffinerie et la Northern Transportation Company Limited, filiale qui assurait le transport du minerai, ont été étatisées par le gouvernement canadien en 1944.

Le premier puits de mine de la compagnie, creusé à Beaverlodge (Saskatchewan), a été terminé en 1952, un an avant que lui soit accordée sa seconde filiale, Eldorado Aviation Limitée. Au cours des années 50, la compagnie a fait rapport au Parlement par l'entremise des ministres des Munitions et des Approvisionnements, de Production de défense, et du Commerce. Après la création, en 1966, du ministère de l'Énergie, des Mines et des Ressources, Eldorado a relevé de ce ministre. Elle a été privatisée en 1985. Les archives de l'Eldorado Nucléaire Limitée sont étroitement liées à celles de la Commission de contrôle de l'énergie atomique (RG 60), qui s'occupe de la sécurité nationale et des aspects des substances nucléaires liés à la santé et à la sécurité.

Organisation et contenu : Les archives d'Eldorado Nucléaire Limitée sont réparties dans trois séries. Les documents généraux (1932-1975) touchent à tous les aspects des activités de la compagnie. Les dossiers des différents membres de la haute administration se trouvent dans la série réservée à l'administration (1937-1981). Les cadres supérieurs disposaient d'un système de dossiers particulier, et ces archives viennent enrichir la documentation historique relative aux activités de la compagnie. En 1976, Eldorado a mis sur pied un projet de recherche historique visant à localiser et à examiner les sources d'information sur l'histoire de la compagnie. Tous les aspects de cet historique se retrouvent dans les

dossiers. On remarquera la présence de dossiers créés en 1945, après que J. Grant Glassco eut été nommé par le ministre des Munitions et des Approvisionnements pour enquêter sur toutes les activités de l'Eldorado. Les autres documents renseignent sur l'exploitation de la mine d'uranium de la compagnie à Beaverlodge (1953-1982).

Archives de la Commission canadienne du blé : RG 135
1948-1974

0,9 mètre
92 fichiers informatiques

Historique : La Commission canadienne des grains (mise sur pied en 1917) et la première Commission canadienne du blé (créée en 1919) ont été les premiers organismes fédéraux de mise en marché du blé des Prairies. Toutes deux ont été dissoutes en 1920. Pendant la crise économique des années 30, le gouvernement fédéral s'est de nouveau préoccupé de la commercialisation du blé des Prairies et a rétabli la Commission canadienne du blé en 1935. Depuis 1949, le mandat de la commission englobe l'avoine et l'orge.

Organisation et contenu : Les fichiers informatiques de ce groupe d'archives contiennent des renseignements, pour les années 1952 à 1983, sur la superficie de l'ensemencement en blé et la production, le transport ferroviaire, l'entreposage et les producteurs de blé. Ce groupe d'archives contient une série de documents textuels produits par le Bureau du secrétaire entre 1948 et 1974. Ces documents textuels sont conservés au Centre fédéral de documents de Winnipeg. Les chercheurs désireux de les consulter doivent communiquer avec la Division des archives gouvernementales à Ottawa pour obtenir les références exactes et les directives de consultation.

Archives de l'Administration de pilotage du Pacifique : RG 136
1904-1970

0,3 mètre

Historique : La New Westminster Pilotage Authority a été créée en 1879. Le président et les commissaires étaient nommés par décret sur recommandation du ministre de la Marine (plus tard, du ministre des Transports). Elle était chargée de fournir des services de pilotage dans le port de New Westminster (Colombie-Britannique) et la région côtière environnante. En 1970, elle a été intégrée à une société d'État, l'Administration de pilotage de la Colombie-Britannique (aujourd'hui Administration de pilotage du Pacifique).

Organisation et contenu : Ces archives se composent de trois livres de procès-verbaux et d'un dossier sur l'évolution des limites de pilotage dans le port de New Westminster. Ces documents sont conservés au Centre fédéral de documents de Vancouver. Les chercheurs désireux de les consulter doivent d'abord communiquer avec la Division des archives gouvernementales à Ottawa pour obtenir les références exactes et les directives de consultation.

Archives du Centre d'information sur l'unité canadienne : RG 137
1977-1985

44,5 mètres
41 fichiers informatiques

Historique : Le Centre d'information sur l'unité canadienne a été créé en 1977 et placé sous l'égide du secrétaire d'État (à partir de 1978, il a relevé du ministre de la Justice). Ce centre d'information était chargé de contrer la « propagande subversive » du gouvernement québécois pendant les années qui ont précédé le référendum de 1980 au Québec. Le centre devait rassembler, générer et diffuser de l'information sur le fédéralisme canadien, les programmes et les services fédéraux, afin de guider et de conseiller les groupes du secteur privé, les ministères et les organismes fédéraux dans la coordination de leurs programmes d'information sur l'unité nationale. Peu après son élection à l'automne 1984, le gouvernement conservateur a mis un terme aux activités du centre d'information, le 31 mars 1985.

Organisation et contenu : Ces archives renferment de la correspondance, des documents de recherche, des sondages d'opinion publique et des enquêtes, des données, des rapports et des documents relatifs à des congrès, des comités et à la couverture médiatique. Elles traitent d'une grande quantité de sujets, tels que les problèmes constitutionnels, le référendum au Québec, la position des Canadiens de l'Ouest, la position des francophones hors Québec et d'autres questions affectant l'unité canadienne. Ce groupe d'archives contient aussi des documents sur les programmes et les services fédéraux, l'utilisation des symboles nationaux, les enquêtes réalisées par les médias, les expositions, les manifestations spéciales et l'histoire du centre d'information. La plupart des sondages d'opinion et des enquêtes sont disponibles sous forme informatisée.

149

Archives de la Bibliothèque nationale du Canada : RG 138
1947-1981

42,9 mètres

Historique : La Bibliothèque nationale du Canada (BNC) a vu le jour sous le nom de Centre bibliographique canadien, en mai 1950. Les recommandations de la Commission royale d'enquête sur l'avancement des arts, des sciences et des lettres au Canada (Commission Massey) ont amené la création officielle de la BNC le 1er janvier 1953. La BNC fonctionne actuellement en vertu de la Loi de 1969 sur la Bibliothèque nationale et fait rapport au Parlement par l'entremise du ministre des Communications (RG 97). La Bibliothèque nationale a pour mission d'assurer la conservation du patrimoine publié du Canada et de le mettre à la disposition de tous les Canadiens. Elle acquiert et fait connaître le patrimoine littéraire canadien en cataloguant les publications pour en faciliter le repérage et la consultation; en fournissant des services de référence et d'orientation; en coordonnant et en participant aux activités et programmes nationaux et internationaux dans le domaine des bibliothèques.

Organisation et contenu : Les archives comprennent des dossiers du service central et d'autres dossiers produits par la Direction des services au public, ainsi que des dossiers du service central créés par les bureaux du directeur et du directeur adjoint de cette direction. Ces documents témoignent de l'expansion des services au public depuis les années 50, expansion qui s'est accentuée avec l'informatisation de la Bibliothèque. Ce groupe d'archives contient également des dossiers opérationnels du Bureau du directeur général de la Bibliothèque (1966-1980), de la Direction du catalogage (1968), de la Direction des services au public (1970-1978), de la Direction du développement des collections (1970-1979), et du directeur général (1962-1981), et des documents de l'administration générale (1973-1974) et de la Canadian Library Association (1947-1970).

Archives du Service hydrographique du Canada : RG 139
1948-1979

4 mètres

Historique : Créé en 1883, le Service hydrographique du Canada (SHC) était chargé d'effectuer des relevés hydrographiques et de publier, de tenir à jour et de distribuer les cartes de navigation, instructions nautiques et tables de marées dont on a besoin pour naviguer efficacement et en toute sûreté dans les eaux canadiennes navigables. Depuis sa création, le service a relevé d'un certain nombre de ministères sans jamais perdre

son identité propre. Lors de sa création, le service a relevé du ministre de la Marine et des Pêcheries (RG 23) et ce, jusqu'en 1910, puis il a relevé du ministre du Service naval (RG 24). Le ministre de la Marine assume de nouveau la responsabilité du SHC en 1923. Lorsque le ministère des Mines et des Ressources a été établi en 1936, il a hérité du Service hydrographique (et l'a transmis à ses nombreux successeurs; voir RG 21). En 1971, le service a relevé du ministre de l'Environnement (RG 108), puis, en 1979, du ministre des Pêches et des Océans (RG 23).

Organisation et contenu : Ce groupe d'archives est constitué de trois séries : journaux de bord (1905-1967), notes d'études sur le terrain (1883-1909) et dossiers du service central (1938-1965), ainsi que de deux groupes de documents qui proviennent de diverses composantes du Service hydrographique. La Section des données sur l'Arctique (1948-1962) comprend essentiellement des publications (cartes, rapports, articles, etc.) qui traitent d'un vaste éventail de sujets relatifs au Nord. La série de la Direction des sciences de la mer (1962-1979) renferme des rapports, provenant de la série des manuscrits du service, sur des questions de description, de théorie et de méthodologie de l'océanographie, de l'hydrographie et de la limnologie.

Archives de l'Office canadien des provendes : RG 140
1962-1973

3,3 mètres

Historique : Société d'État, l'Office canadien des provendes fait rapport au Parlement par l'entremise du ministre de l'Agriculture (RG 17). Il a été créé par la *Loi sur l'aide à l'alimentation des animaux de ferme* de 1967. Son mandat consiste essentiellement à assurer l'approvisionnement en provendes dans l'Est du Canada et en Colombie-Britannique, à veiller à la disponibilité d'entrepôts convenables dans l'Est du Canada et à garantir la stabilité et l'équité des prix dans l'Est du Canada, en Colombie-Britannique, au Yukon et dans les Territoires du Nord-Ouest. L'office subventionne le transport des provendes dans le cadre du Programme de compensation pour le transport des provendes. Il étudie également les demandes de provendes et informe le ministre de la disponibilité des entrepôts et de toutes les questions relatives au prix des provendes. Il publie les données relatives aux prix, au transport et aux marchés de ces denrées. Les fonctions de l'office sont étroitement liées à celles de la Fédération canadienne de l'agriculture, du Conseil canadien des céréales, de la Commission canadienne des grains (RG 80) et de la Commission canadienne du blé (RG 135).

Organisation et contenu : Les archives de l'Office canadien des provendes sont formées de dossiers du service central. Les dossiers de 1962 à 1966 concernent la Winnipeg Grain Exchange et l'attribution, au gouvernement fédéral, des responsabilités en matière d'administration des provendes. Les dossiers produits entre 1967 et 1973 portent sur des réunions du comité consultatif de l'office ainsi que sur des conflits de travail qui ont affecté la manutention des céréales.

Archives du Conseil canadien des normes : RG 141
1970-1984

17,4 mètres

Historique : La *Loi sur le Conseil canadien des normes* a été adoptée en 1970 pour encourager et promouvoir la normalisation volontaire dans le domaine de la construction, de la fabrication, de la qualité, du rendement et de la sécurité des bâtiments, des structures, des produits manufacturés et d'autres biens. Bien que non expressément prévue par la Loi, cette normalisation contribue à faire progresser l'économie nationale, à favoriser la santé, la sécurité et le bien-être du public, à aider et protéger les consommateurs, à faciliter le commerce intérieur et international et à développer la coopération internationale dans le domaine des normes. Entre 1970 et 1984, bien que non mandaté par le gouvernement fédéral, le Conseil canadien des normes recevait des subsides gouvernementaux. Il est devenu une société d'État en 1984.

Organisation et contenu : Ces archives se composent, d'une part, de dossiers du service central qui renferment des procès-verbaux du comité exécutif, des comités consultatifs et des comités spécialisés, et, d'autre part, de dossiers généraux d'exploitation.

Archives de la Commission de réforme du droit du Canada : RG 143
1973-1975

2 fichiers informatiques

Historique : Organisme indépendant créé le 1ᵉʳ juin 1971, la commission a pour mandat d'étudier et de réviser, d'une façon continuelle et systématique, les lois et autres règles de droit qui constituent le droit du Canada, en vue de proposer des rectifications, des améliorations et des réformes. Celles-ci visent notamment à éliminer les anachronismes et anomalies du droit; à refléter dans le droit les concepts et les institutions distinctes des deux systèmes juridiques du Canada, le droit coutumier et le droit civil; à concilier les différences et les oppositions qui existent entre la formulation de la loi et son application; à abolir les règles de droit

tombées en désuétude; et à amener l'adoption de méthodes et de notions nouvelles répondant à l'évolution des besoins de la société canadienne moderne et des individus qui la composent.

Organisations et contenu : Ce fonds contient deux fichiers informatiques comprenant chacun une série de questionnaires adressés à des procureurs de la Couronne d'une part et à des avocats de défense à travers le pays d'autre part. Ces consultations au moyen d'enquêtes ont conduit, entre autres, à des recommandations favorisant l'abolition de l'enquête préliminaire et l'adoption d'un système formel de règles et de procédures de communication de la preuve.

Index-matières des groupes d'archives

Archives de la culture et des communications

RG 3	Postes
RG 37	Archives nationales du Canada
RG 41	Société Radio-Canada
RG 53	Office national du film
RG 63	Conseil des Arts du Canada
RG 69	Commission du centenaire
RG 71	Expo 67
RG 72	Commission des expositions du gouvernement canadien
RG 94	Information Canada
RG 97	Communications
RG 100	Conseil de la radiodiffusion et des télécommunications canadiennes
RG 123	Société de développement de l'industrie cinématographique canadienne
RG 132	Musées nationaux du Canada
RG 133	Conseil de recherches en sciences humaines du Canada
RG 137	Centre d'information sur l'unité canadienne
RG 138	Bibliothèque nationale du Canada

Archives des affaires extérieures

RG 7	Cabinet du gouverneur général
RG 25	Affaires extérieures
RG 51	Commission mixte internationale
RG 74	Agence canadienne de développement international

Archives financières

RG 16   Revenu national
RG 19   Finances
RG 54   Contrôleur du Trésor
RG 55   Conseil du Trésor
RG 58   Vérificateur général
RG 75   Conseil économique du Canada
RG 120   Monnaie royale canadienne

Archives économiques et des travaux publics

RG 11   Travaux publics
RG 20   Industrie et Commerce
RG 31   Statistique Canada
RG 34   Commission de la capitale nationale
RG 40   Bureau du surintendant des institutions financières
RG 62   Loto Canada/Société canadienne des paris sportifs
RG 64   Commission des prix et du commerce en temps de guerre
RG 65   Corporation commerciale canadienne
RG 67   Société pour l'expansion des exportations
RG 79   Commission du tarif
RG 95   Direction des corporations
RG 103   Consommation et Corporations
RG 104   Direction des faillites
RG 105   Brevets, marques de commerce, droit d'auteur et dessins industriels
RG 107   Bureau de l'administrateur, Loi anti-inflation
RG 110   Direction des enquêtes sur les coalitions
RG 115   Commission de surveillance du prix des produits alimentaires
RG 121   Société canadienne des brevets et d'exploitation Limitée
RG 124   Expansion économique régionale
RG 141   Conseil canadien des normes

Administration de la justice

RG 13   Justice
RG 18   Gendarmerie royale du Canada
RG 73   Solliciteur général
RG 125   Cour suprême du Canada
RG 143   Commission de réforme du droit du Canada

Archives militaires

RG 8   Archives militaires et navales britanniques
RG 9   Milice et Défense

RG 24   Défense nationale
RG 28   Munitions et Approvisionnements
RG 38   Affaires des anciens combattants
RG 44   Services nationaux de guerre
RG 49   Production de défense
RG 57   Organisation des mesures d'urgence
RG 61   Société des approvisionnements de guerre des Alliés
RG 83   Construction de défense Limitée
RG 117 Bureau du séquestre des biens ennemis

Archives des ressources minérales et énergétiques
RG 21   Énergie, Mines et Ressources
RG 60   Commission de contrôle de l'énergie atomique
RG 81   Office fédéral du charbon
RG 86   Direction des mines
RG 87   Direction des ressources minérales
RG 99   Office national de l'énergie
RG 134 Eldorado Nucléaire Limitée

Archives des ressources naturelles et de la recherche scientifique
RG 15   Intérieur
RG 17   Agriculture
RG 23   Pêches et Océans
RG 39   Service canadien des forêts
RG 77   Conseil national de recherches
RG 80   Commission canadienne des grains
RG 84   Service canadien des parcs
RG 89   Direction des ressources hydrauliques
RG 90   Commission des champs de bataille nationaux
RG 92   Direction de la géographie
RG 93   Service de l'environnement atmosphérique
RG 102 Sciences et Technologie
RG 108 Environnement
RG 109 Service canadien de la faune
RG 128 Conseil de recherches médicales
RG 129 Conseil des sciences du Canada
RG 135 Commission canadienne du blé
RG 140 Office canadien des provendes

Archives du Nord
RG 22   Affaires indiennes et Nord canadien
RG 78   Northern Ontario Pipeline — Société d'État

RG 85   Programme des affaires du Nord
RG 91   Archives du territoire du Yukon
RG 96   Commission d'énergie du Nord canadien
RG 126   Enquête sur le pipe-line de la vallée du Mackenzie
RG 130   Administration du pipe-line du Nord

Archives parlementaires et d'État
RG 1   Conseil exécutif
RG 2   Bureau du Conseil privé
RG 4   Bureaux des secrétaires civils et provinciaux : Québec,
         Bas-Canada et Canada-Est
RG 5   Bureaux des secrétaires civils et provinciaux : Haut-Canada et
         Canada-Ouest
RG 6   Secrétariat d'État
RG 14   Parlement
RG 32   Commission de la fonction publique
RG 33   Commissions royales d'enquête
RG 35   Comités interministériels
RG 36   Comités, commissions et bureaux
RG 47   Conférences fédérales-provinciales
RG 58   Vérificateur général
RG 59   Bureau du Commissaire à la représentation
RG 68   Registraire général
RG 98   Approvisionnements et Services
RG 101   Corporation de disposition des biens de la Couronne
RG 111   Commission des relations de travail dans la fonction publique
RG 112   Conseil consultatif des districts bilingues
RG 113   Bureau du directeur général des élections
RG 122   Commissaire aux langues officielles

Archives du développement social et de la citoyenneté
RG 10   Affaires indiennes
RG 22   Affaires indiennes et Nord canadien
RG 26   Citoyenneté et Immigration
RG 27   Travail
RG 29   Santé nationale et Bien-être social
RG 50   Commission d'assurance-chômage
RG 56   Société canadienne d'hypothèques et de logement
RG 76   Direction de l'immigration
RG 82   Commission d'appel de l'immigration
RG 106   Bureau de la coordonnatrice, situation de la femme
RG 116   Compagnie des jeunes Canadiens

RG 118   Emploi et Immigration
RG 119   Secrétariat canadien de la conférence Habitat
RG 127   Affaires urbaines
RG 131   Ministère d'État chargé du Développement social
RG 145   Conseil canadien des relations du travail*

Archives d'arpentage
RG 45   Commission géologique du Canada
RG 48   Observatoires du Canada
RG 88   Direction des levés et de la cartographie
RG 89   Direction des ressources hydrauliques
RG 139   Service hydrographique du Canada

Archives des transports
RG 12   Transports
RG 30   Chemins de fer nationaux du Canada
RG 42   Direction de la marine
RG 43   Chemins de fer et Canaux
RG 46   Commission canadienne des transports
RG 52   Administration de la voie maritime du Saint-Laurent
RG 66   Conseil des ports nationaux
RG 70   Air Canada
RG 136   Administration de pilotage du Pacifique
* La description de ce groupe d'archives nouvellement créé n'est pas encore disponible.

Index alphabétique des groupes d'archives

Annexe ──────────

La Division des archives gouvernementales et ses prédécesseurs, la Division des archives fédérales et la Division des archives ordinolingues, ont participé à la préparation des publications suivantes. Certaines d'entre elles sont épuisées, d'autres sont encore disponibles. Pour de plus amples renseignements à ce sujet, veuillez contacter la Division des communications, Archives nationales du Canada, 344, rue Wellington, Pièce 136, Ottawa (Ontario), Canada, K1A 0N3.

RG 10   *Archives ayant trait aux Affaires indiennes.* Ottawa, 1975.
RG 20   *Archives du ministère du Commerce.* Ottawa, 1977.
RG 27   *Archives de Travail Canada.* Ottawa, 1988.
RG 31   *Archives de Statistique Canada.* Ottawa, 1977.
RG 33   *Archives des commissions royales d'enquête, vol. 1 : séries 33/1 à 33/75.* Ottawa, 1989.
RG 39   *Archives du Service canadien des forêts.* Ottawa, 1982.
RG 43   *Archives du ministère des Chemins de fer et Canaux.* Ottawa, 1986.
RG 46   *Archives de la Commission canadienne des transports.* Ottawa, 1984.
RG 55   *Archives du Conseil du Trésor.* Ottawa, 1977.
RG 69   *Archives de la Commission du centenaire du Canada.* Ottawa, 1979.
RG 81   *Archives de l'Office fédéral du charbon.* Ottawa, 1981.
RG 84   *Archives de Parcs Canada.* Ottawa, 1985.
RG 88   *Archives de la Direction des levés et de la cartographie.* Ottawa, 1979.
RG 115   *Archives de la Commission de surveillance du prix des produits alimentaires.* Ottawa, 1979.
RG 126   *Archives relatives à l'enquête sur le pipe-line de la vallée du Mackenzie.* Ottawa, 1980.

Acquisitions principales, 1974/1975. Ottawa, 1975.
Acquisitions principales, 1975/1976. Ottawa, 1977.
Acquisitions principales, 1976/1977. Ottawa, 1977.
Acquisitions principales, 1977/1978. Ottawa, 1978.
Acquisitions, 1979/1980. Ottawa, 1979.
Acquisitions, 1979/1980. Ottawa, 1980.
Acquisitions, 1980/1981. Ottawa, 1981.

Acquisitions, 1981/1982. Ottawa, 1982.
Acquisitions, 1982/1983. Ottawa, 1983.
Acquisitions, 1983/1984. Ottawa, 1984.
Acquisitions, 1984/1985. Ottawa, 1985.
Acquisitions, 1985/1986. Microfiche. Ottawa, 1986.
Acquisitions, 1986/1987. Microfiche. Ottawa, 1987.

Archives ordinolingues : *Catalogue des fonds.* Ottawa, 1981.

Archives ordinolingues : *Dossiers de données sur les loisirs et la récréation.* Ottawa, 1983.

Archives ordinolingues : *Dossiers sur l'usage de l'alcool, des drogues et du tabac.* Ottawa, 1982.

Bulletin des archives ordinolingues. Ottawa, 1983.

Collection de guides généraux : Division des archives gouvernementales, Ottawa, 1991.

Collection de guides généraux : Division des archives ordinolingues. Ottawa, 1984.

Documentation relative à l'histoire ouvrière de la Colombie-Britannique dans le Groupe d'archives fédérales (RG) 27, Canada, Ministère du Travail. Ottawa, 1975.

Documents sur la Deuxième Guerre mondiale. Ottawa, 1979.

Documents sur les parcs nationaux du Canada. Ottawa, 1979.

Documents pour l'étude du Nord canadien. Ottawa, 1980.

On peut se procurer la publication suivante en écrivant au Centre d'édition du gouvernement du Canada, Approvisionnements et Services Canada, Ottawa (Ontario), Canada, K1A 0S9.

Catalogue de recensements sur microfilm, 1666-1891. Canada : 10 $; autres pays : 12 $.